Editor
DIANA SCHUTZ

Designer
CARY GRAZZINI

Publisher
MIKE RICHARDSON

This volume collects issues 61-68
of the Dark Horse comic book series *Usagi Yojimbo Volume Three*.

Visit the Usagi Dojo web site
www.usagiyojimbo.com

Published by
Dark Horse Books
A division of Dark Horse Comics, Inc.
10956 SE Main Street
Milwaukie, Oregon 97222

First edition: June 2004
ISBN 1-59307-220-1

Limited hardcover edition: June 2004
ISBN 1-59307-221-X

1 3 5 7 9 10 8 6 4 2
Printed in Canada

USAGI YOJIMBO™

— Travels With Jotaro —

Created, Written, and Illustrated by
STAN SAKAI

Introduction by
PETER LAIRD

DARK HORSE BOOKS™

Usagi Yojimbo

Introduction

Back in November of 2003, Stan Sakai came to visit us here at Mirage Studios in Massachusetts, on his way to an appearance in Connecticut. Part of Stan's reason to visit was to take part in some videotaped interview segments which would appear in the DVD release sometime next year of the episodes of the new *Teenage Mutant Ninja Turtles* animated TV series in which his characters Usagi Yojimbo and Gen appear, in a four-part story we're calling "The Big Brawl."

During the part of the interview where both Stan and I were in front of the cameras, Stan mentioned in passing that both *TMNT* and *Usagi* were having their twentieth anniversary years in 2004. I hadn't previously made that connection, and it got me thinking about those last twenty years, and specifically how *Usagi* had come into my life. I realized pretty quickly that while some things from the last twenty years are crystal clear, others are a little fuzzy.

One of those fuzzy things is where and when I first became aware of Usagi. I'm pretty sure it was in the pages of Steve Gallacci's *Albedo* comic, which featured a variety of anthropomorphic characters, including a nicely drawn *samurai* rabbit named Usagi Yojimbo. After that, I started picking up the regular issues of Stan's *Usagi* comic published by Fantagraphics, and I was hooked. Part of it was my interest in martial arts and Japanese culture, but I was also fascinated that this guy Sakai was able to create one of the most formidable fighting characters

in comics history using a rabbit. I mean — a bunny! How much more cute and cuddly and soft and unthreatening a critter can you get? In less talented, more unimaginative hands, Usagi would probably have been eight feet tall, hugely and veinily muscled, with big gnashy teeth and glowering eyes. He'd probably wear armor and carry a gun of some kind, along with all kinds of hidden weapons. And he'd likely cross his arms and pose a lot.

But Stan's Usagi is the antithesis of all that. Miyamoto Usagi is somewhat slightly built, not very tall, and usually carries only two weapons — the *samurai*'s two swords, the *katana* and *wakizashi*. His demeanor is nearly always calm and centered, even in battle. In fact, in Stan's *Usagi* comics, very often Usagi's adversaries come to bad ends because they arrogantly misinterpret Usagi's calm manner to mean he is weak or unwilling — or unable — to fight. Hah! The fools ...

I'm pretty sure the first time I ever met Stan was at the first San Diego Comic-Con that I attended, back in (if memory serves) 1985 or 1986. That was my first trip to California as well, and it was all pretty overwhelming. I wish I had a more clear memory of our first meeting, but in all honesty all I can remember is coming home with the impression that Stan seemed quite a lot like Jack Kirby had seemed, the first time I'd met him — an incredibly talented yet simultaneously really nice, humble guy. (The perfect combination of qualities, if you ask me.)

I know that a lot of people have already commented on just what a great guy Stan is, so I won't go on too much about it. But it really is true. If you spend enough time in this industry, you come to realize that some of the smallest talents come with the biggest egos. It definitely makes you appreciate people like Stan.

Over the last twenty years, I've had the great pleasure of maintaining both a friendship and a good business relationship with Stan. I wish we could see each other more often, for the sake of the friendship ... but unless Stan suddenly moves to the east coast or I start flying again, that's not going to happen. I'll just have to be satisfied with those times — like Stan's visit to Northampton this past year — when our paths cross and it feels like almost no time has passed since we saw each other last.

Business-wise, I think that anyone would be hard-pressed to find a better person to work with. My dealings with Stan, mostly through my company Mirage Studios, have included publishing *Usagi* (and Stan's spin-off *Space Usagi*) for a time, doing a few "crossover" comic book stories where Usagi meets one or more of the Turtles, co-developing a *Space Usagi* licensing proposal, getting an Usagi action figure into the original *TMNT* toy line as well as a couple of appearances of Usagi in the first *TMNT* animated series, and now incorporating Usagi into four episodes of the new animated series and into the new toy line as an action figure (which I must, happily, note will look *much* closer to the "real" Usagi of the comics than the old toy). And in all of that, Stan has shown what I think is perhaps the most valuable — but, sadly, least prevalent, in my opinion — trait in someone with whom one would want to do business: Stan is *reasonable*. He is no demanding prima donna, but he's no pushover, either. And it's refreshing to deal with someone like that.

Many people have noted the recent publication of the 300th and final issue of Dave Sim's *Cerebus* comic as a significant event in the history of comics, and it certainly is — anyone who has ever tried to do *one* issue of a comic, let alone three hundred, can grasp at least part of that significance. But I think it could be argued — even though, given the *very* different natures of the two comics, it is sort of like comparing apples to oranges — that Stan's accomplishment with *Usagi* over the last twenty years and into the future is perhaps even *more* significant. And Stan has — except for the efforts of his cover colorists and publishers, which, while not inconsequential, are surely in the final analysis relatively small — done it all himself. He has — by himself, no background artist or co-writer, etc. — written, pencilled, inked, and lettered all 130-plus issues of *Usagi* to date. That simply boggles my mind.

And even more mind-boggling is that through all of that time and all those issues, Stan has maintained the high level of quality both in art and writing. Actually, it's probably more accurate to say that Stan has maintained a steady *increase* in the level of quality in his *Usagi* comics as he becomes ever more adept and skilled, and his research into and knowledge of Japanese history and culture even more comprehensive. I have seen this in the last couple of years of reading *Usagi*, specifically in Stan's inking; always solid and appropriate, Stan's line work lately (at least to my eyes) has become deliciously lyrical, with wonderful gestures even in the simplest of lines.

I feel honored to have been asked to write the introduction to this *Travels With Jotaro* collection. I wonder if Stan thought of asking me to do it because when we saw each other last, I expressed to him my great delight with the fantastical elements of some key parts of this volume. As much as I like Stan's work on *Usagi* in general, I *really* like it when he lets loose with some more fantastic concepts and characters, as he does it so well. I think the last three or four chapters of *Travels With Jotaro* are probably my favorite Usagi tales of all.

Usagi Yojimbo is a character who is always growing, changing, developing. As good as he is right now, he knows he can get better. He still makes mistakes (not many), and learns from them. This wandering *samurai* knows that there is a long road ahead of him, filled with new and old friends and foes, wonders, and adventures. His journey is far from over.

For the last twenty years, I've been fortunate to watch this journey of the rabbit *ronin*, shepherded by the capable hands of his creator, Stan Sakai. And I hope to be around to see the rest of it.

Peter Laird
Northampton, MA
March 19, 2004

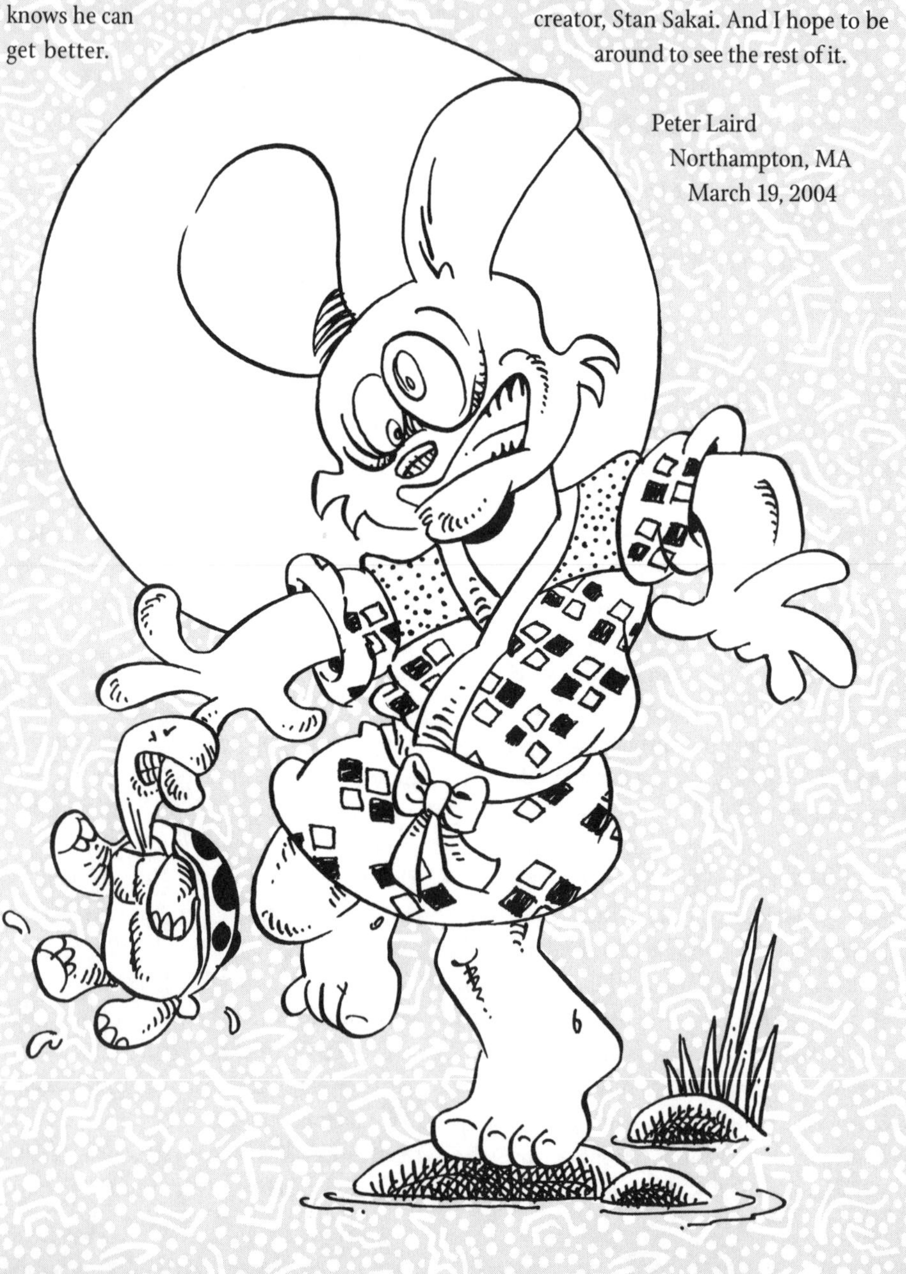

Contents

To my Auntie Ruth,
and the memory of Uncle James Emoto.

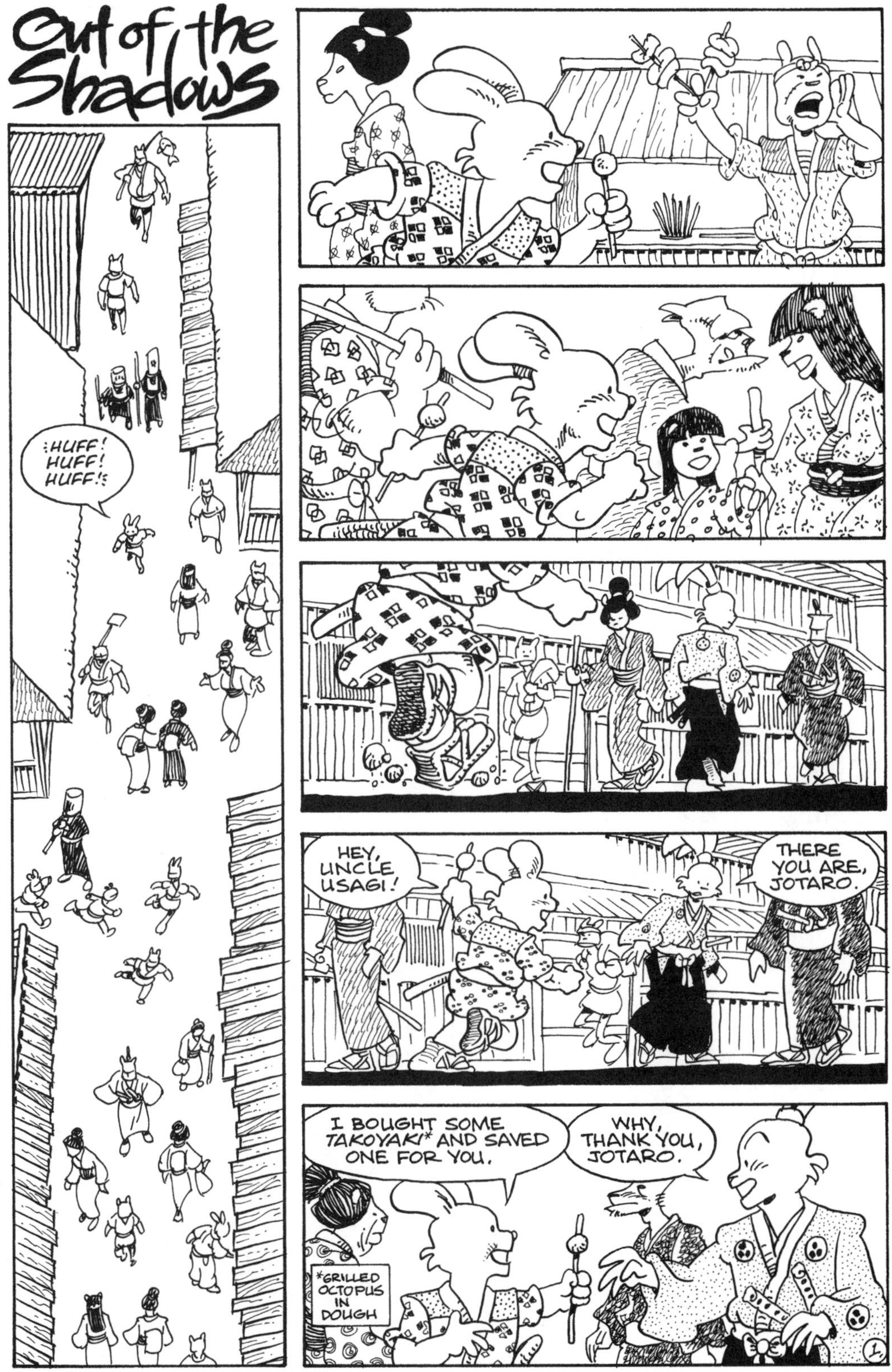
Out of the Shadows
HUFF! HUFF! HUFF!
HEY, UNCLE USAGI!
THERE YOU ARE, JOTARO.
I BOUGHT SOME TAKOYAKI* AND SAVED ONE FOR YOU.
WHY, THANK YOU, JOTARO.
*GRILLED OCTOPUS IN DOUGH
1.

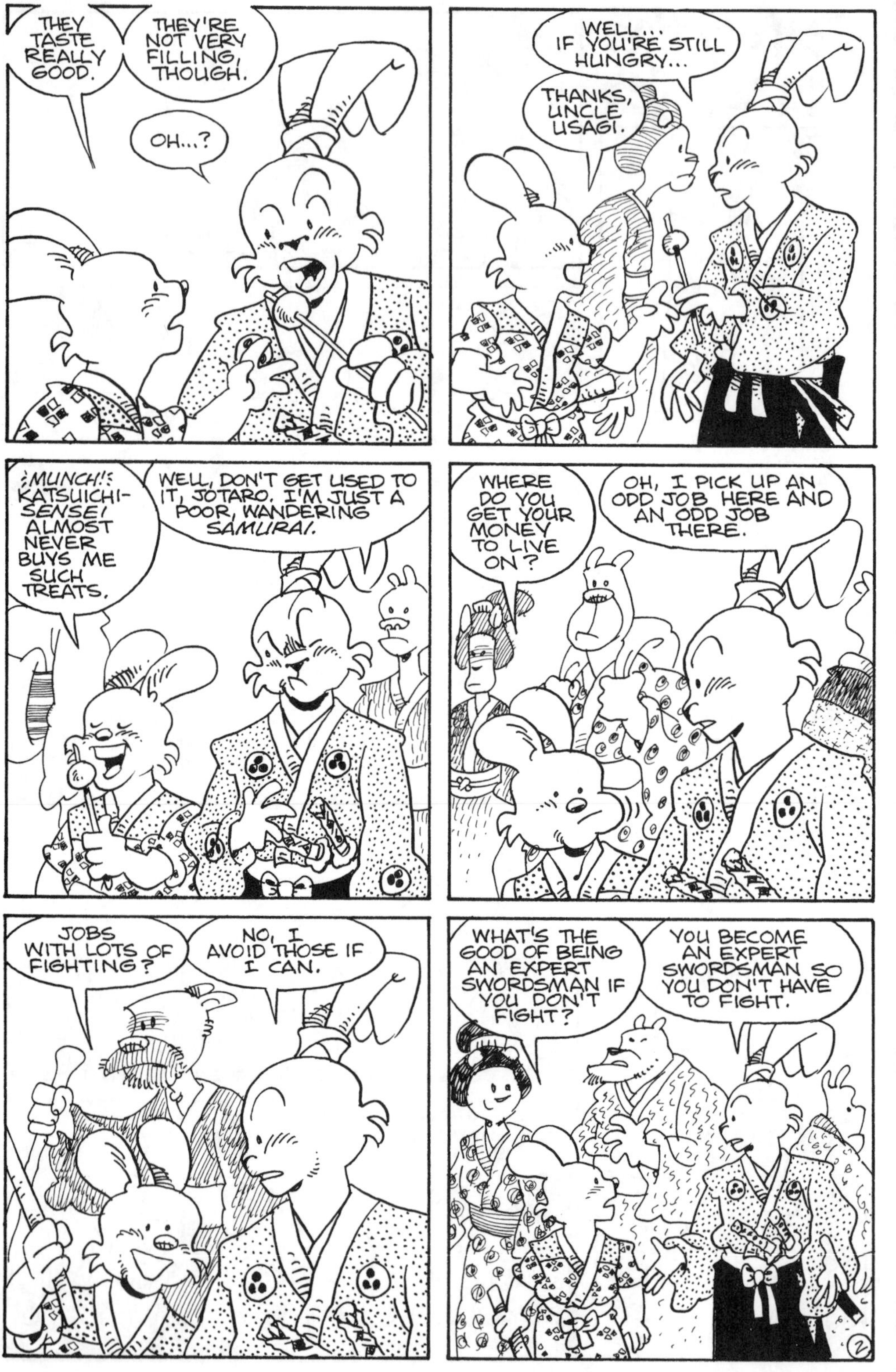
THEY TASTE REALLY GOOD.
THEY'RE NOT VERY FILLING, THOUGH.
OH...?
WELL... IF YOU'RE STILL HUNGRY...
THANKS, UNCLE USAGI.
MUNCH! KATSUICHI-SENSEI ALMOST NEVER BUYS ME SUCH TREATS.
WELL, DON'T GET USED TO IT, JOTARO. I'M JUST A POOR, WANDERING SAMURAI.
WHERE DO YOU GET YOUR MONEY TO LIVE ON?
OH, I PICK UP AN ODD JOB HERE AND AN ODD JOB THERE.
JOBS WITH LOTS OF FIGHTING?
NO, I AVOID THOSE IF I CAN.
WHAT'S THE GOOD OF BEING AN EXPERT SWORDSMAN IF YOU DON'T FIGHT?
YOU BECOME AN EXPERT SWORDSMAN SO YOU DON'T HAVE TO FIGHT.
2

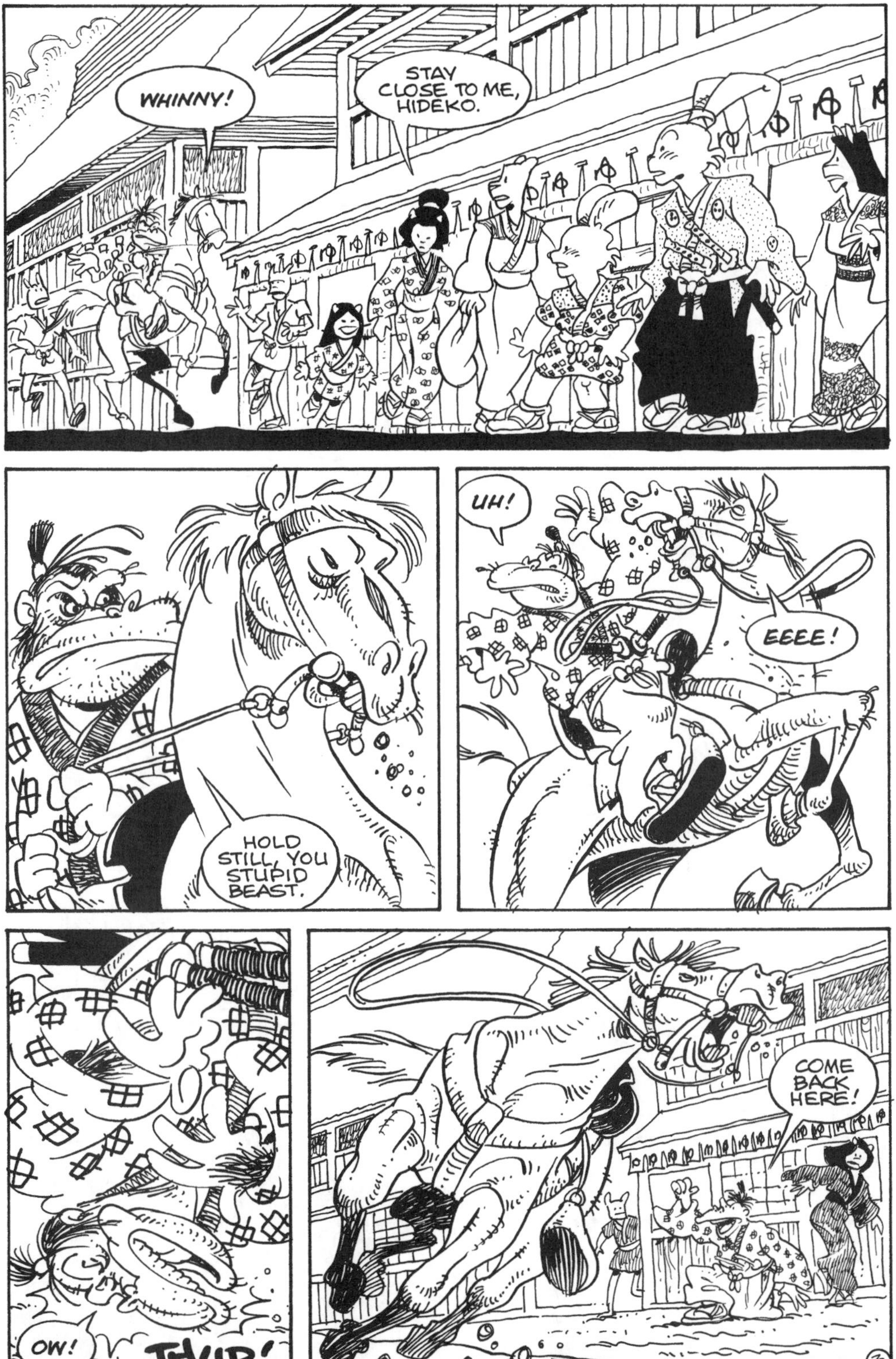
WHINNY!
STAY CLOSE TO ME, HIDEKO.
HOLD STILL, YOU STUPID BEAST.
UH!
EEEE!
OW!
THUD!
COME BACK HERE!
3.

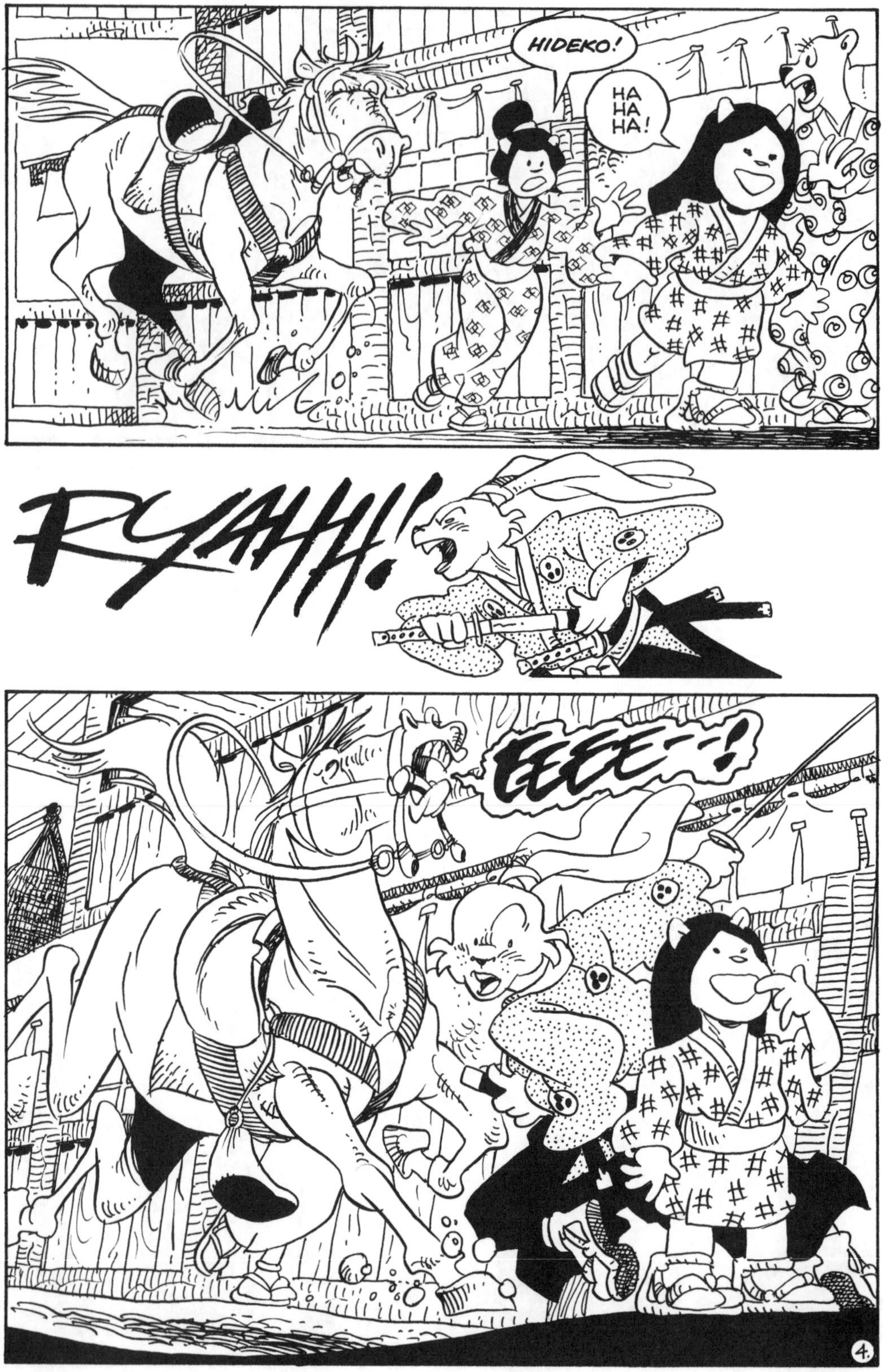
HIDEKO!
HA HA HA!
RYAHH!
EEEE--!
4.

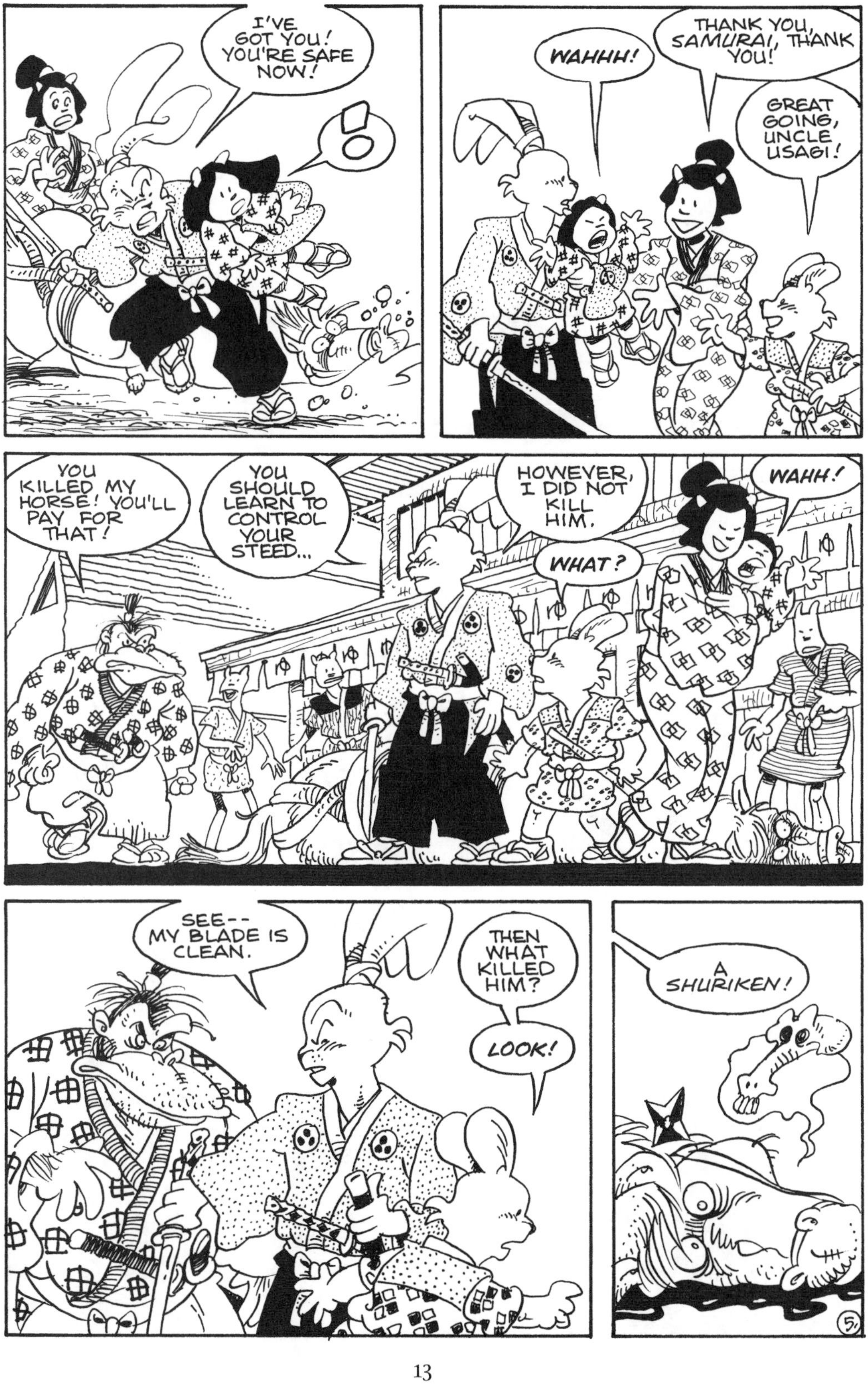
I'VE GOT YOU! YOU'RE SAFE NOW!
!
WAHHH!
THANK YOU, SAMURAI, THANK YOU!
GREAT GOING, UNCLE USAGI!
YOU KILLED MY HORSE! YOU'LL PAY FOR THAT!
YOU SHOULD LEARN TO CONTROL YOUR STEED...
HOWEVER, I DID NOT KILL HIM.
WHAT?
WAHH!
SEE-- MY BLADE IS CLEAN.
THEN WHAT KILLED HIM?
LOOK!
A SHURIKEN!
51

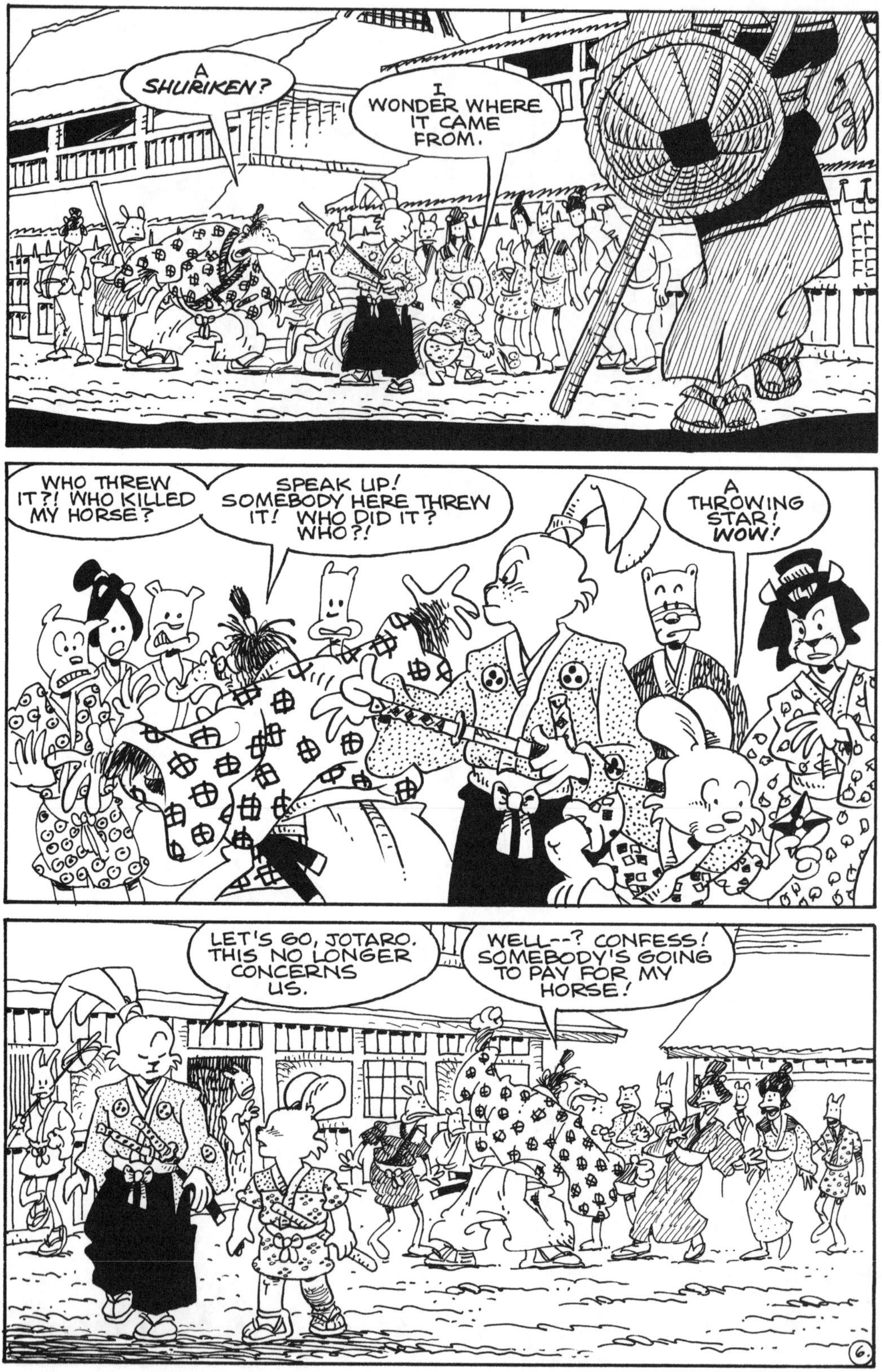
A SHURIKEN?
I WONDER WHERE IT CAME FROM.
WHO THREW IT?! WHO KILLED MY HORSE?
SPEAK UP! SOMEBODY HERE THREW IT! WHO DID IT? WHO?!
A THROWING STAR! WOW!
LET'S GO, JOTARO. THIS NO LONGER CONCERNS US.
WELL--? CONFESS! SOMEBODY'S GOING TO PAY FOR MY HORSE!
6.

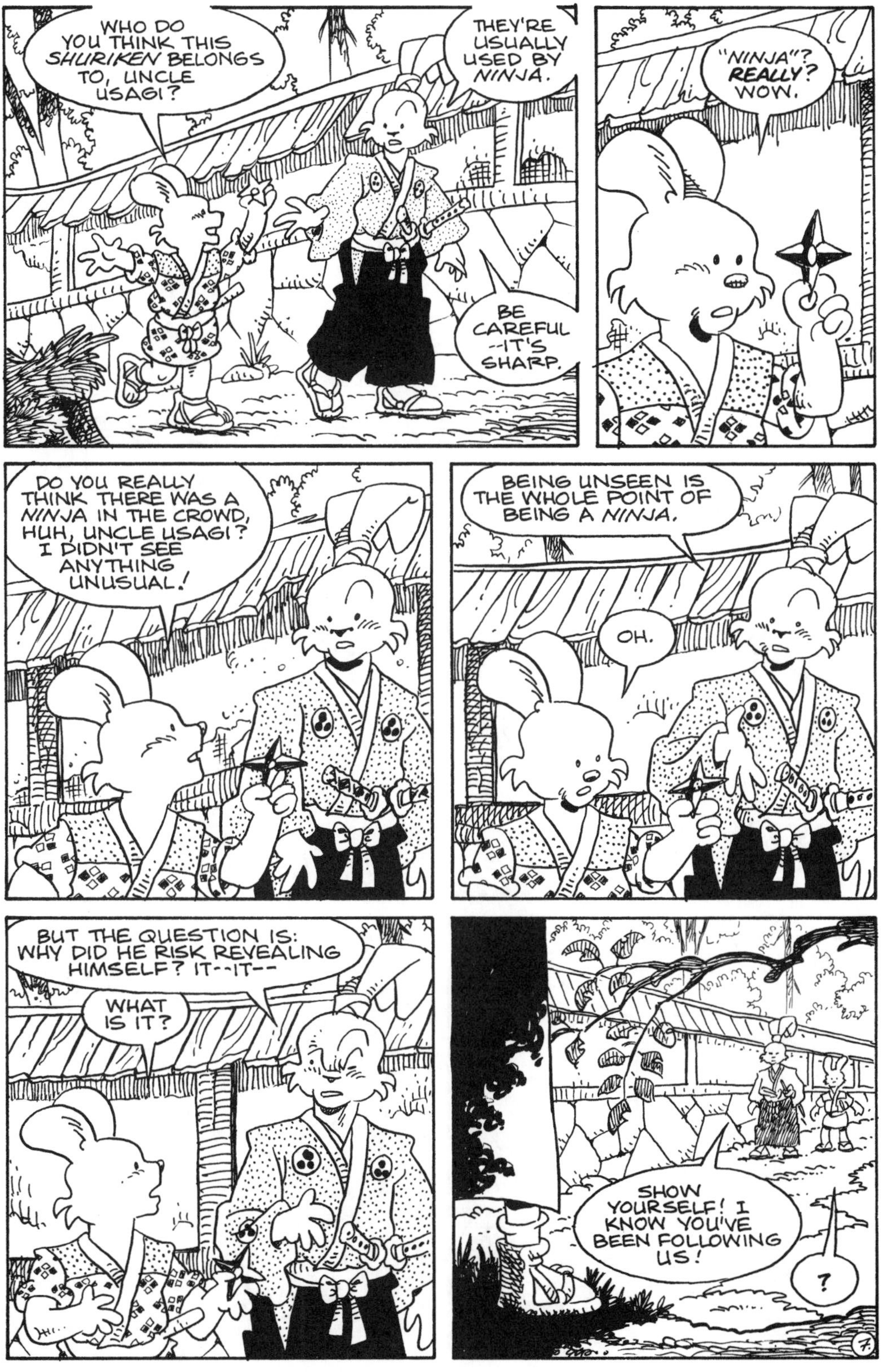
WHO DO YOU THINK THIS *SHURIKEN* BELONGS TO, UNCLE USAGI?
THEY'RE USUALLY USED BY *NINJA*.
BE CAREFUL --IT'S SHARP.
"*NINJA*"? ***REALLY***? WOW.
DO YOU REALLY THINK THERE WAS A *NINJA* IN THE CROWD, HUH, UNCLE USAGI? I DIDN'T SEE ANYTHING UNUSUAL!
BEING UNSEEN IS THE WHOLE POINT OF BEING A *NINJA*.
OH.
BUT THE QUESTION IS: WHY DID HE RISK REVEALING HIMSELF? IT--IT--
WHAT IS IT?
SHOW YOURSELF! I KNOW YOU'VE BEEN FOLLOWING US!
?
7.

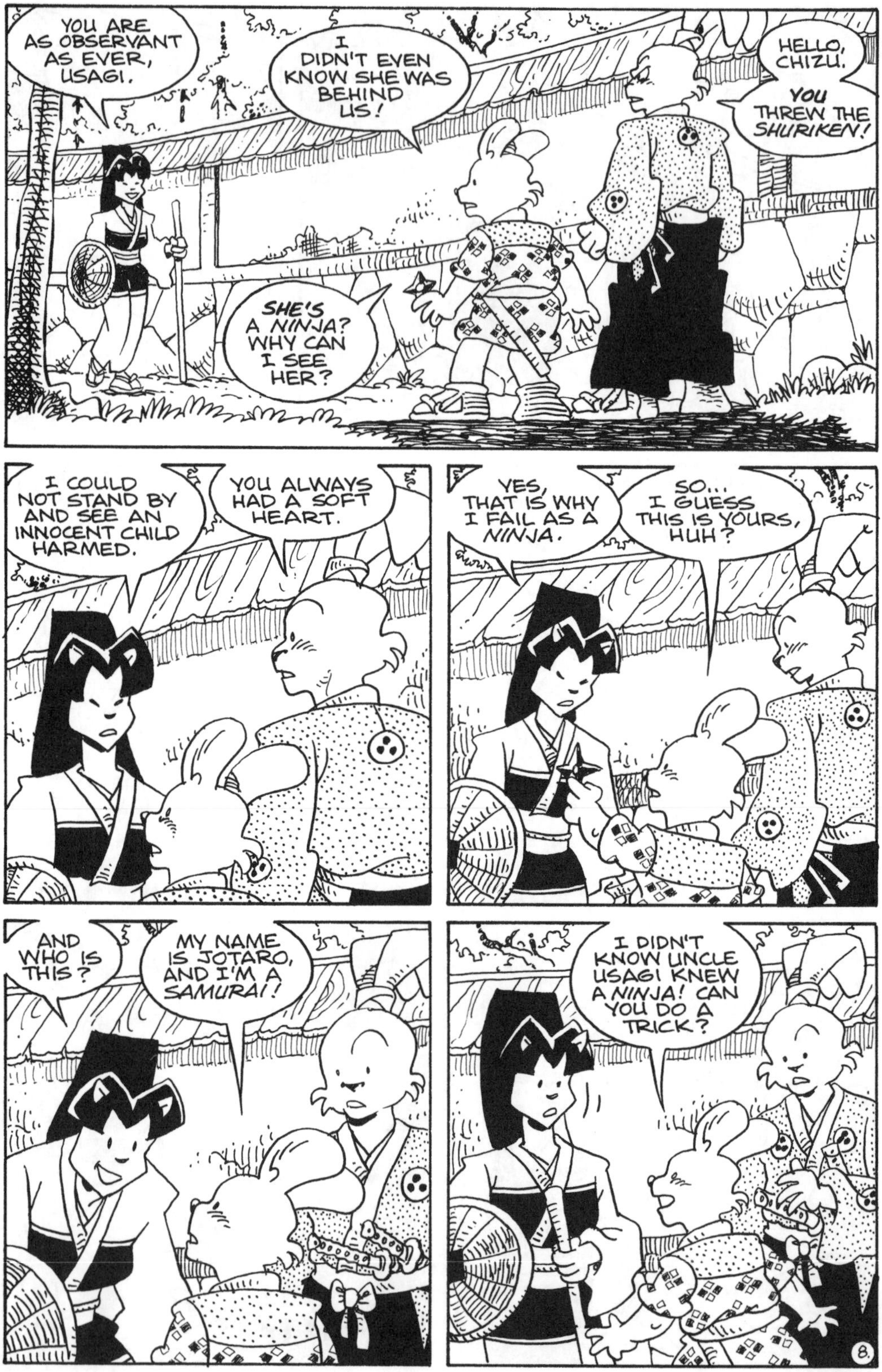
YOU ARE AS OBSERVANT AS EVER, USAGI.
I DIDN'T EVEN KNOW SHE WAS BEHIND US!
HELLO, CHIZU.
YOU THREW THE SHURIKEN!
SHE'S A NINJA? WHY CAN I SEE HER?
I COULD NOT STAND BY AND SEE AN INNOCENT CHILD HARMED.
YOU ALWAYS HAD A SOFT HEART.
YES, THAT IS WHY I FAIL AS A NINJA.
SO... I GUESS THIS IS YOURS, HUH?
AND WHO IS THIS?
MY NAME IS JOTARO, AND I'M A SAMURAI!
I DIDN'T KNOW UNCLE USAGI KNEW A NINJA! CAN YOU DO A TRICK?
8.

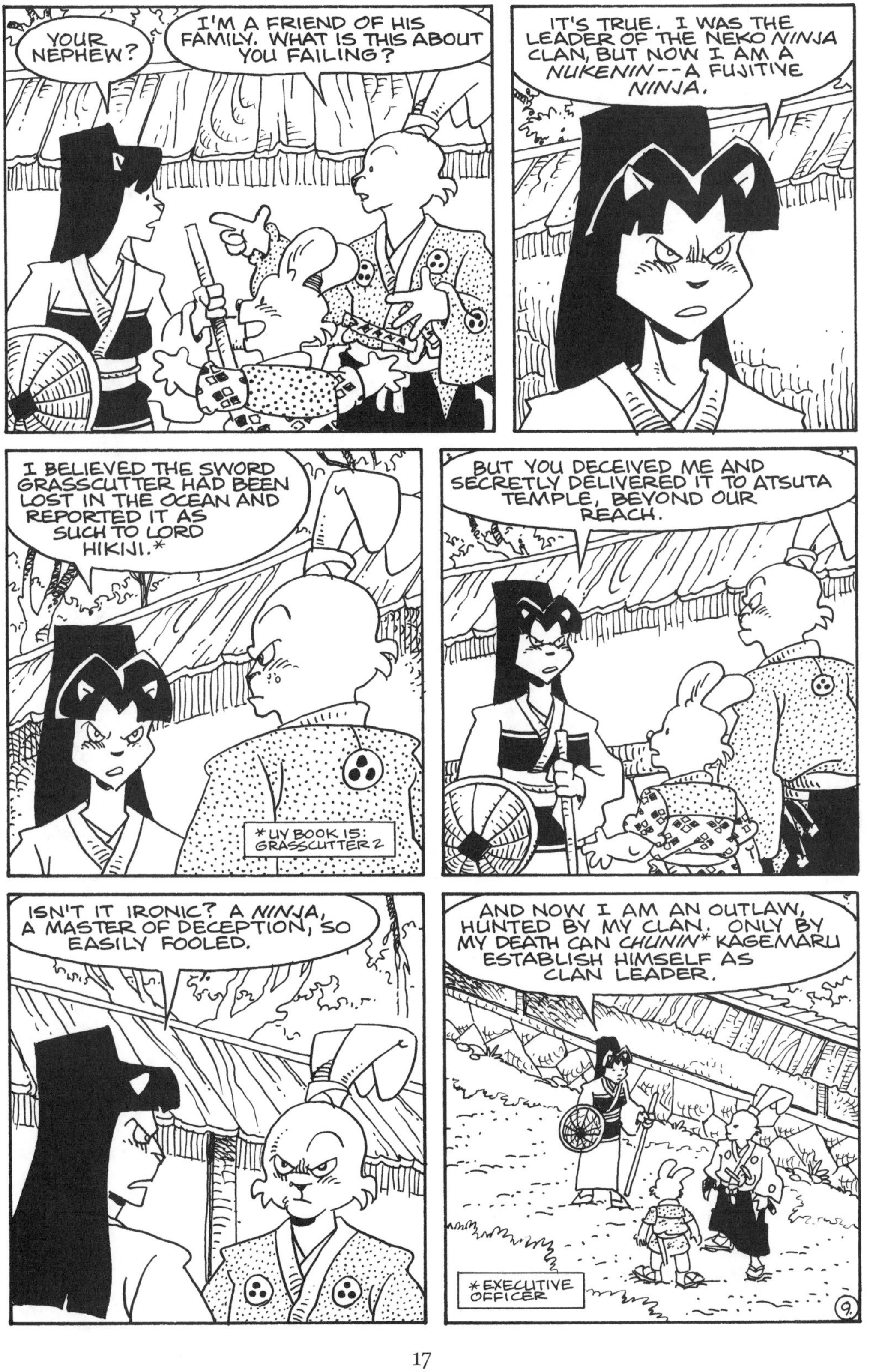
YOUR NEPHEW?
I'M A FRIEND OF HIS FAMILY. WHAT IS THIS ABOUT YOU FAILING?
IT'S TRUE. I WAS THE LEADER OF THE NEKO NINJA CLAN, BUT NOW I AM A NUKENIN--A FUJITIVE NINJA.
I BELIEVED THE SWORD GRASSCUTTER HAD BEEN LOST IN THE OCEAN AND REPORTED IT AS SUCH TO LORD HIKIJI.*
*UY BOOK 15: GRASSCUTTER 2
BUT YOU DECEIVED ME AND SECRETLY DELIVERED IT TO ATSUTA TEMPLE, BEYOND OUR REACH.
ISN'T IT IRONIC? A NINJA, A MASTER OF DECEPTION, SO EASILY FOOLED.
AND NOW I AM AN OUTLAW, HUNTED BY MY CLAN. ONLY BY MY DEATH CAN CHUNIN* KAGEMARU ESTABLISH HIMSELF AS CLAN LEADER.
*EXECUTIVE OFFICER
9.

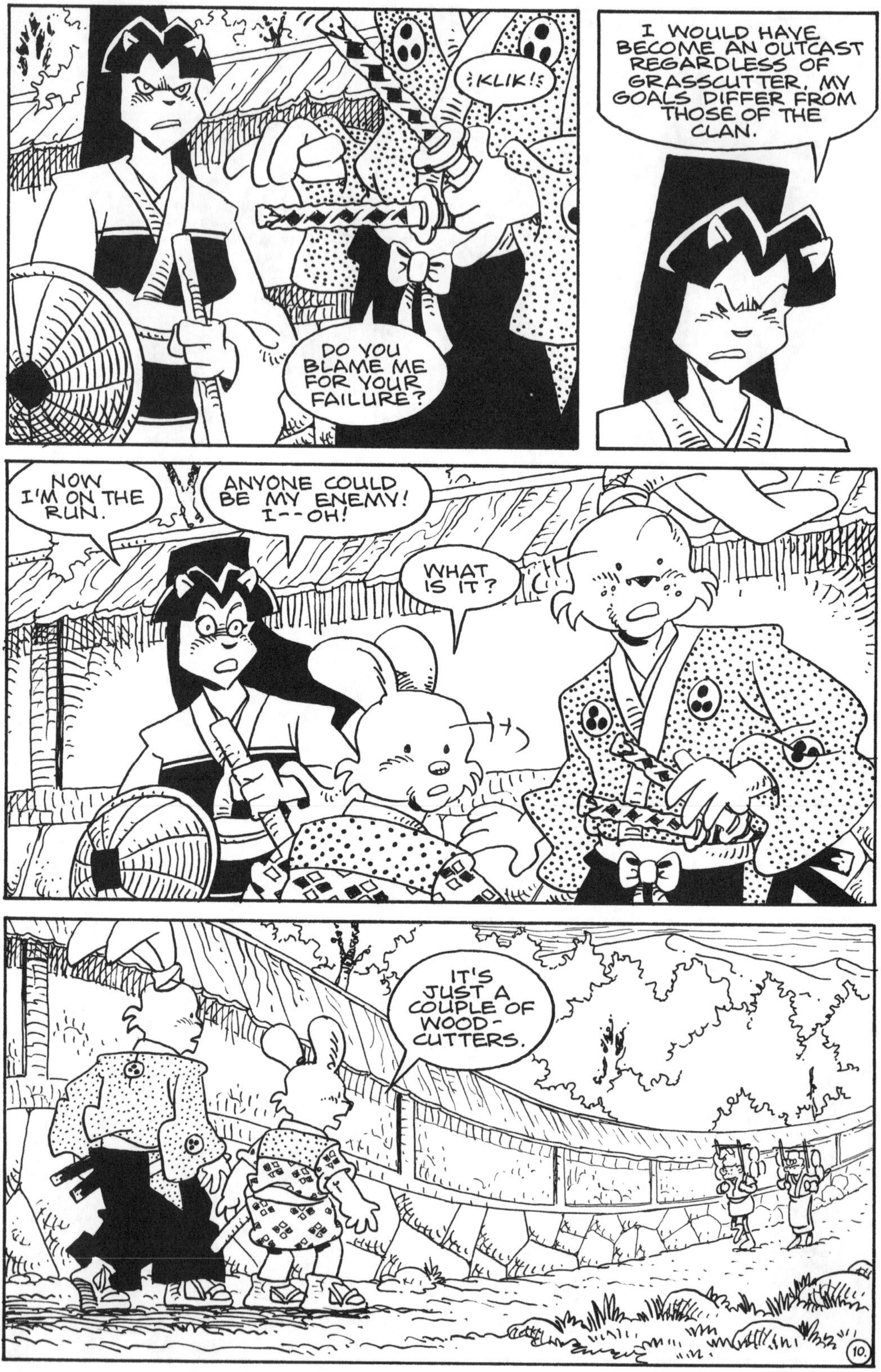
KLIK!
DO YOU BLAME ME FOR YOUR FAILURE?
I WOULD HAVE BECOME AN OUTCAST REGARDLESS OF GRASSCUTTER. MY GOALS DIFFER FROM THOSE OF THE CLAN.
NOW I'M ON THE RUN.
ANYONE COULD BE MY ENEMY! I--OH!
WHAT IS IT?
IT'S JUST A COUPLE OF WOOD-CUTTERS.
10.

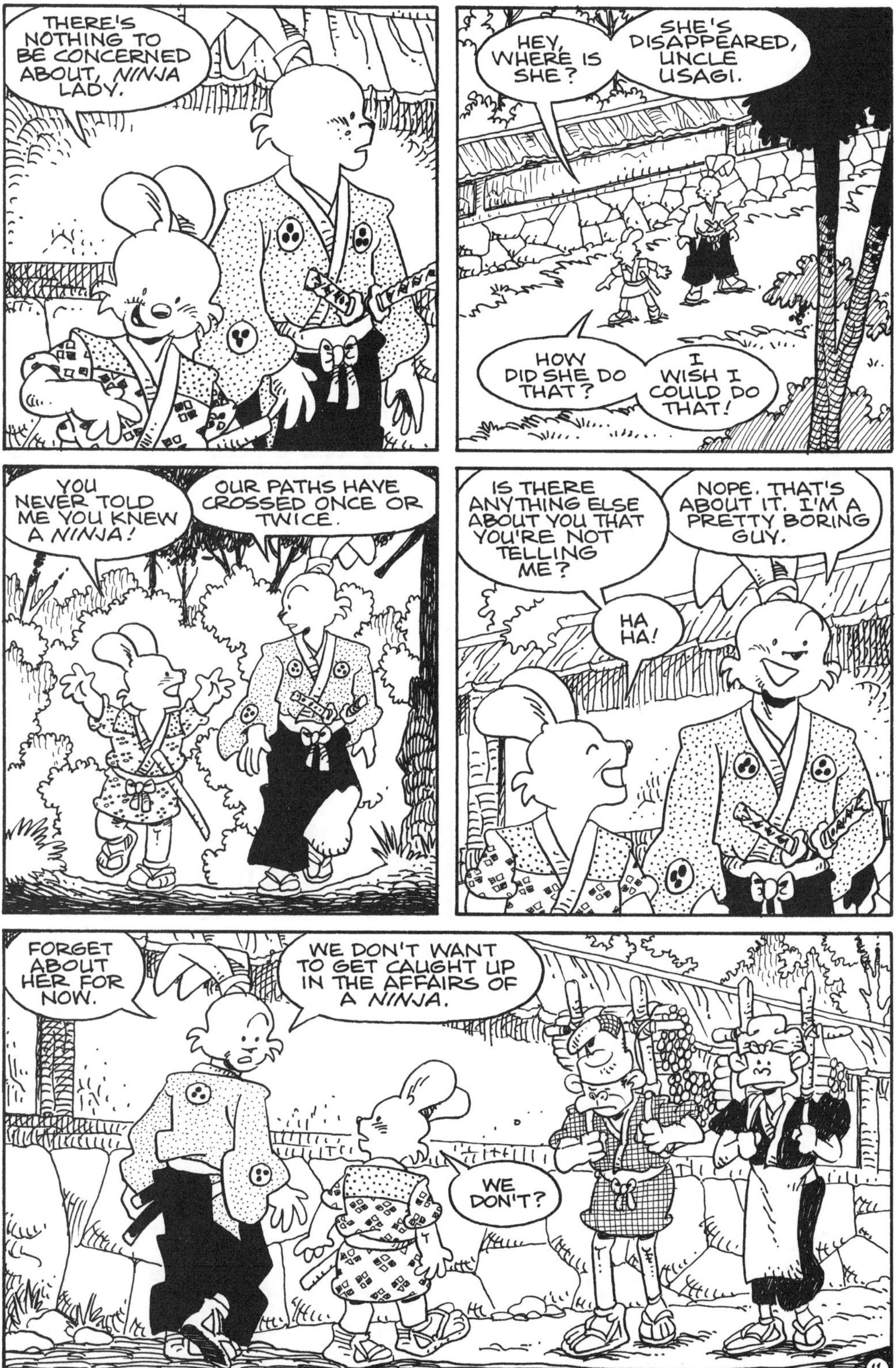
THERE'S NOTHING TO BE CONCERNED ABOUT, *NINJA* LADY.
HEY, WHERE IS SHE?
SHE'S DISAPPEARED, UNCLE USAGI.
HOW DID SHE DO THAT?
I WISH I COULD DO THAT!
YOU NEVER TOLD ME YOU KNEW A *NINJA*!
OUR PATHS HAVE CROSSED ONCE OR TWICE.
IS THERE ANYTHING ELSE ABOUT YOU THAT YOU'RE NOT TELLING ME?
NOPE. THAT'S ABOUT IT. I'M A PRETTY BORING GUY.
HA HA!
FORGET ABOUT HER FOR NOW.
WE DON'T WANT TO GET CAUGHT UP IN THE AFFAIRS OF A *NINJA*.
WE DON'T?
11.

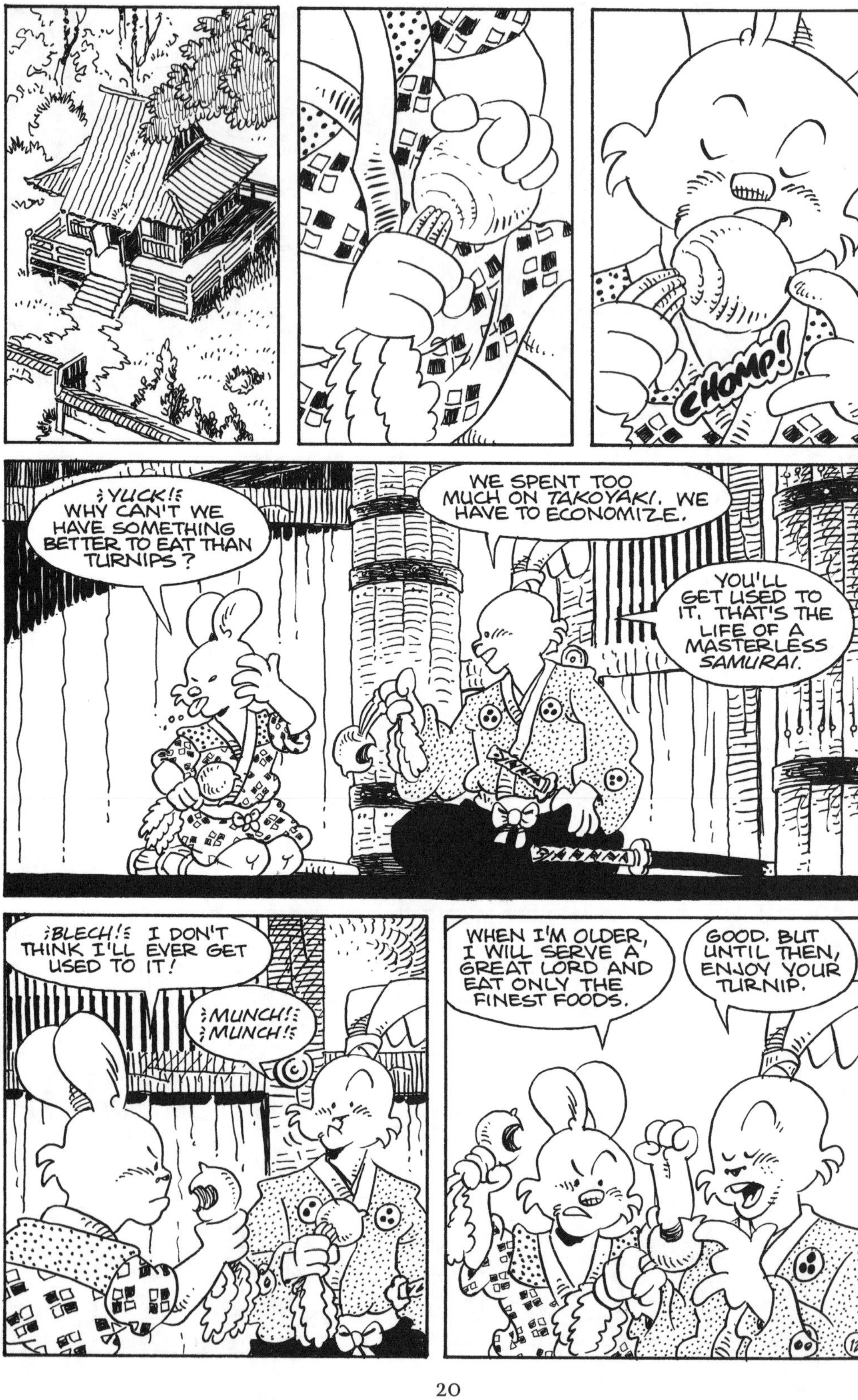
CHOMP!
¡YUCK!¡
WHY CAN'T WE HAVE SOMETHING BETTER TO EAT THAN TURNIPS?
WE SPENT TOO MUCH ON TAKOYAKI. WE HAVE TO ECONOMIZE.
YOU'LL GET USED TO IT. THAT'S THE LIFE OF A MASTERLESS SAMURAI.
¡BLECH!¡ I DON'T THINK I'LL EVER GET USED TO IT!
¡MUNCH!¡ ¡MUNCH!¡
WHEN I'M OLDER, I WILL SERVE A GREAT LORD AND EAT ONLY THE FINEST FOODS.
GOOD. BUT UNTIL THEN, ENJOY YOUR TURNIP.
12.

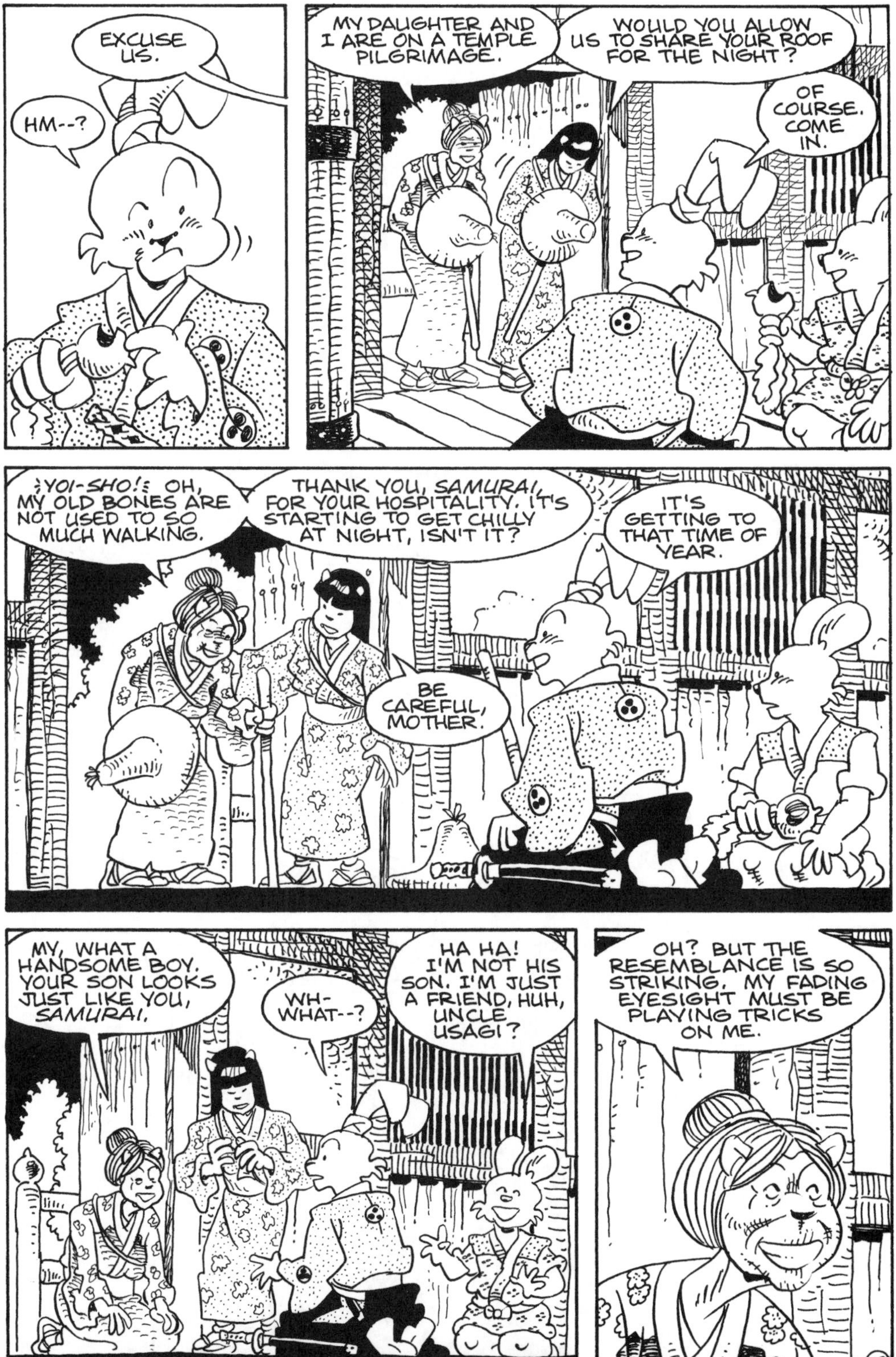
EXCUSE US.
HM--?
MY DAUGHTER AND I ARE ON A TEMPLE PILGRIMAGE.
WOULD YOU ALLOW US TO SHARE YOUR ROOF FOR THE NIGHT?
OF COURSE. COME IN.
¡YOI-SHO!¡ OH, MY OLD BONES ARE NOT USED TO SO MUCH WALKING.
THANK YOU, SAMURAI, FOR YOUR HOSPITALITY. IT'S STARTING TO GET CHILLY AT NIGHT, ISN'T IT?
IT'S GETTING TO THAT TIME OF YEAR.
BE CAREFUL, MOTHER.
MY, WHAT A HANDSOME BOY. YOUR SON LOOKS JUST LIKE YOU, SAMURAI.
WH-WHAT--?
HA HA! I'M NOT HIS SON. I'M JUST A FRIEND, HUH, UNCLE USAGI?
OH? BUT THE RESEMBLANCE IS SO STRIKING. MY FADING EYESIGHT MUST BE PLAYING TRICKS ON ME.
13

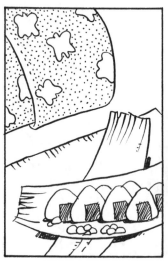

OH, EXCUSE US--WOULD YOU SHARE OUR MEAL WITH US?

SURE!

JOTARO--! DON'T BE SO RUDE!

HA HA HA! THAT'S ALL RIGHT, SAMURAI. AFTER ALL, YOU'RE SHARING YOUR ROOF WITH US, NEH?

SEE, UNCLE USAGI? IT'S OKAY.

BESIDES, WE HAVE MUCH MORE THAN WE TWO CAN EAT, AND IT WON'T TASTE AS GOOD TOMORROW.

GEE, THANKS, LADY.

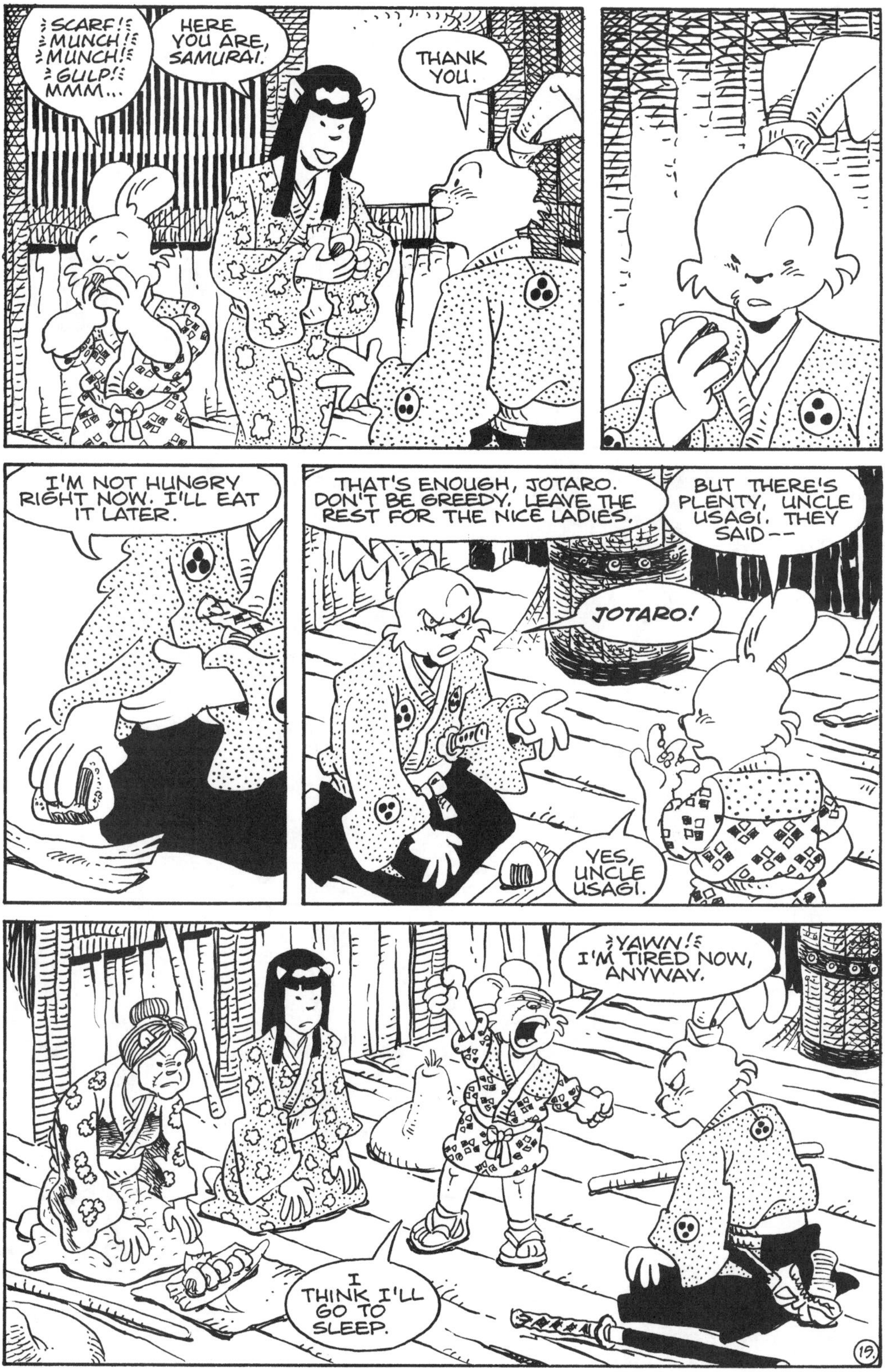

SCARF! MUNCH! MUNCH! GULP! MMM...
HERE YOU ARE, SAMURAI.
THANK YOU.
I'M NOT HUNGRY RIGHT NOW. I'LL EAT IT LATER.
THAT'S ENOUGH, JOTARO. DON'T BE GREEDY. LEAVE THE REST FOR THE NICE LADIES.
BUT THERE'S PLENTY, UNCLE USAGI. THEY SAID--
JOTARO!
YES, UNCLE USAGI.
YAWN! I'M TIRED NOW, ANYWAY.
I THINK I'LL GO TO SLEEP.
15.

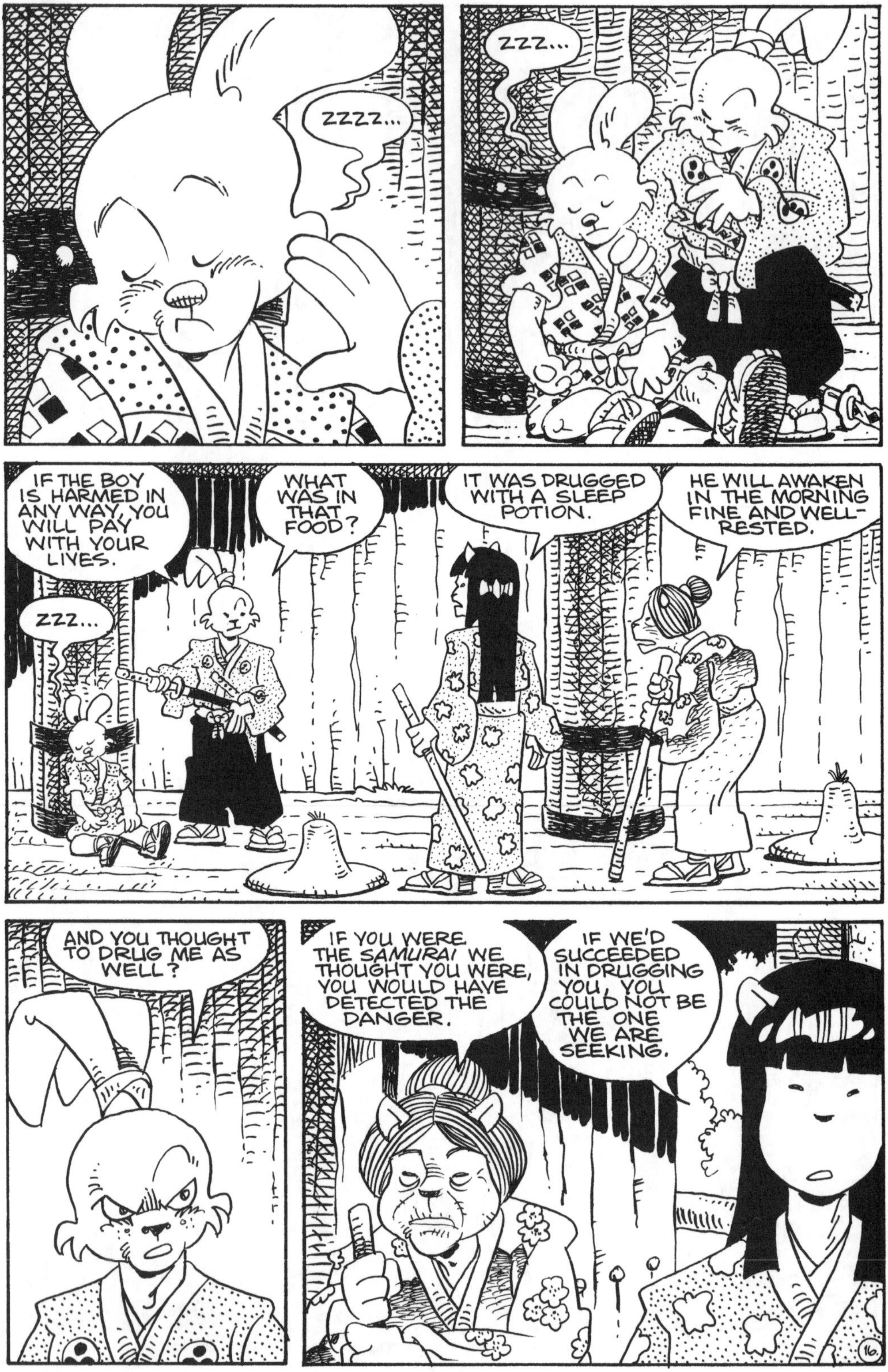
ZZZZ...
ZZZ...
IF THE BOY IS HARMED IN ANY WAY, YOU WILL PAY WITH YOUR LIVES.
WHAT WAS IN THAT FOOD?
IT WAS DRUGGED WITH A SLEEP POTION.
HE WILL AWAKEN IN THE MORNING FINE AND WELL-RESTED.
ZZZ...
AND YOU THOUGHT TO DRUG ME AS WELL?
IF YOU WERE THE SAMURAI WE THOUGHT YOU WERE, YOU WOULD HAVE DETECTED THE DANGER.
IF WE'D SUCCEEDED IN DRUGGING YOU, YOU COULD NOT BE THE ONE WE ARE SEEKING.
16.

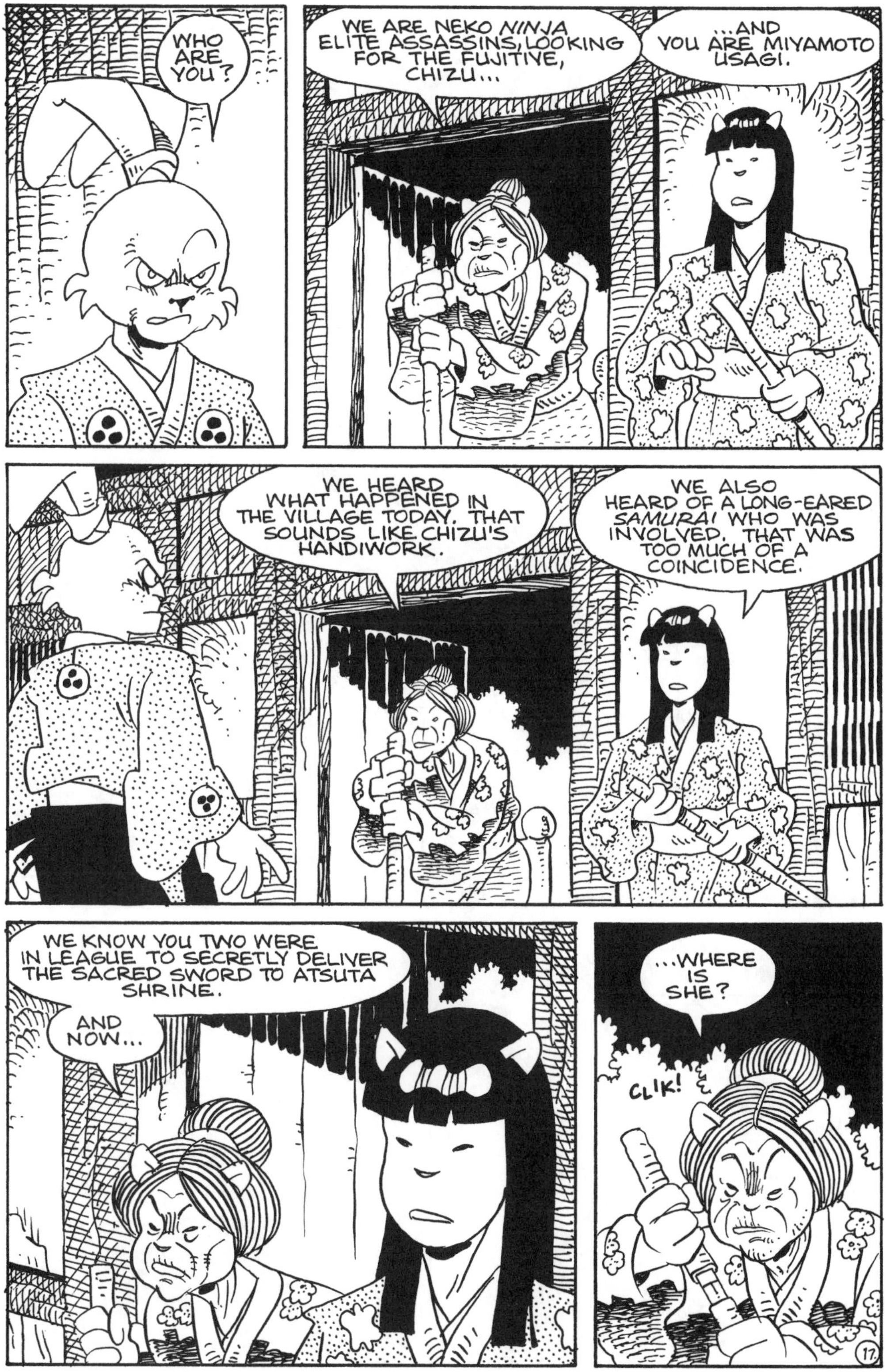
WHO ARE YOU?
WE ARE NEKO *NINJA* ELITE ASSASSINS, LOOKING FOR THE FUJITIVE, CHIZU...
...AND YOU ARE MIYAMOTO USAGI.
WE HEARD WHAT HAPPENED IN THE VILLAGE TODAY. THAT SOUNDS LIKE CHIZU'S HANDIWORK.
WE ALSO HEARD OF A LONG-EARED *SAMURAI* WHO WAS INVOLVED. THAT WAS TOO MUCH OF A COINCIDENCE.
WE KNOW YOU TWO WERE IN LEAGUE TO SECRETLY DELIVER THE SACRED SWORD TO ATSUTA SHRINE.
AND NOW...
...WHERE IS SHE?
CLIK!
17

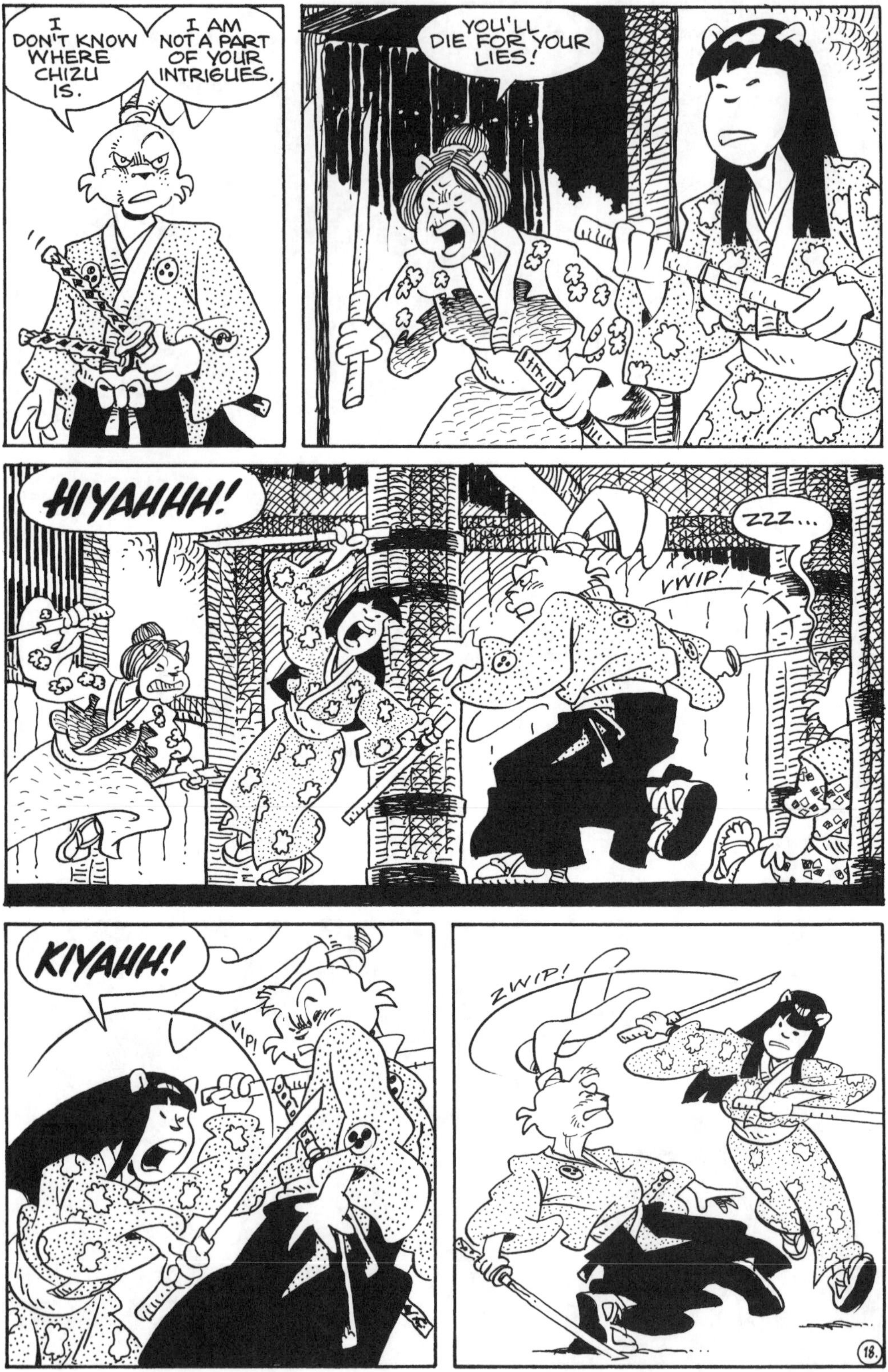
I DON'T KNOW WHERE CHIZU IS.
I AM NOT A PART OF YOUR INTRIGUES.
YOU'LL DIE FOR YOUR LIES!
HIYAHHH!
ZZZ...
VWIP!
KIYAHH!
VIP!
ZWIP!
18.

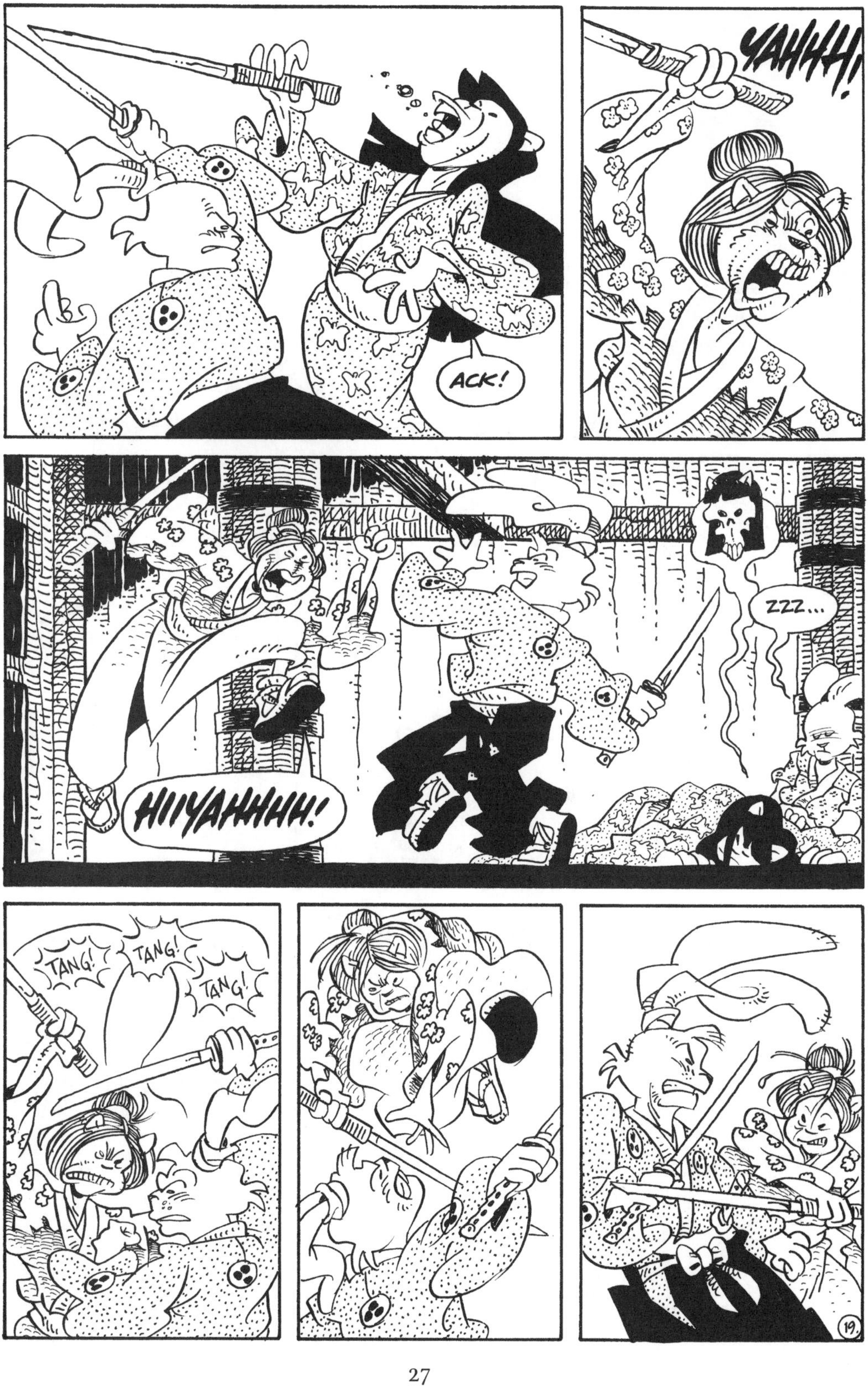
ACK!
YAHHH!
HIIYAHHHH!
ZZZ...
TANG!
TANG!
TANG!
19

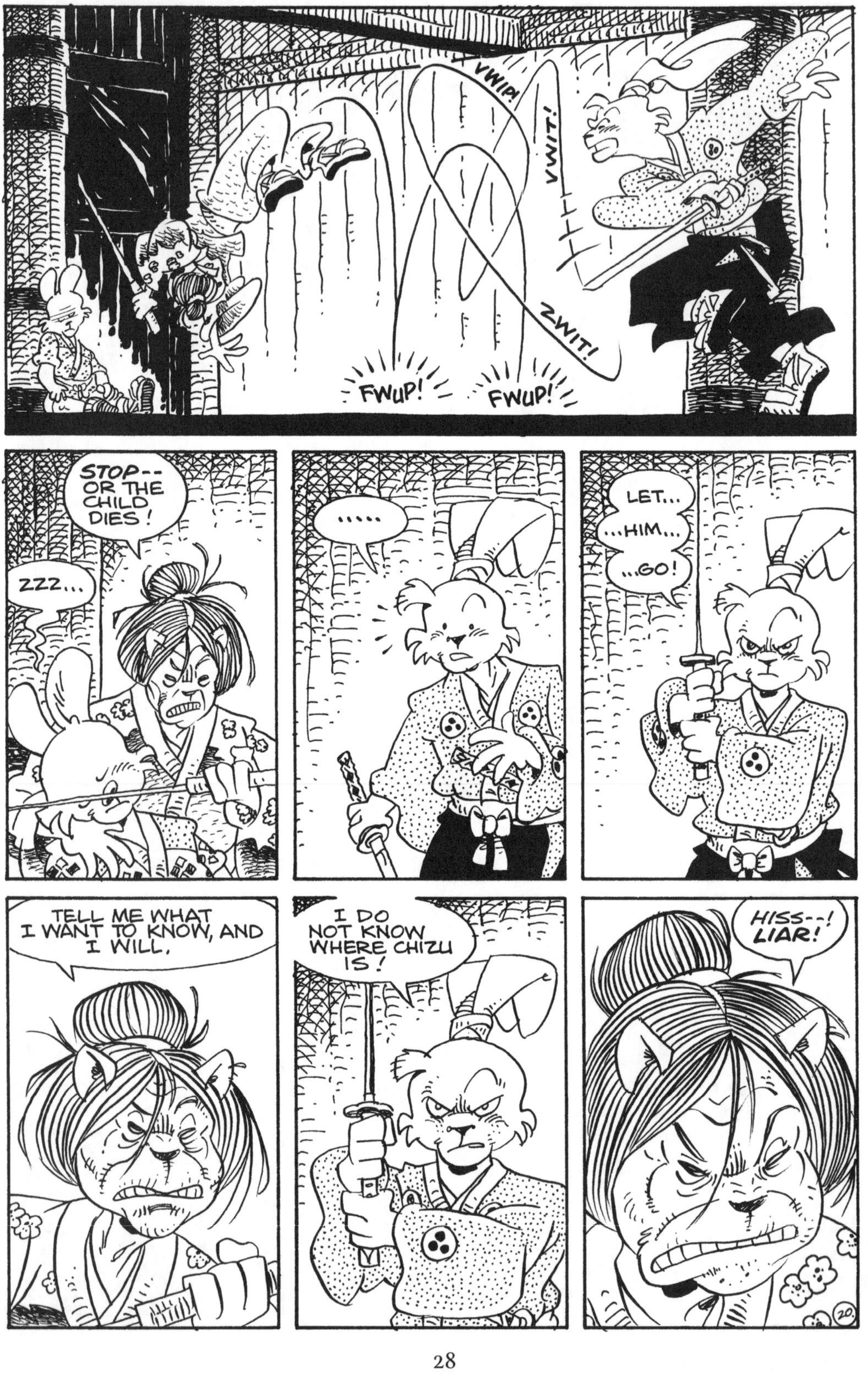
VWIP!
VWIT!
ZWIT!
FWUP!
FWUP!
STOP-- OR THE CHILD DIES!
ZZZ...
.....
LET...
...HIM...
...GO!
TELL ME WHAT I WANT TO KNOW, AND I WILL.
I DO NOT KNOW WHERE CHIZU IS!
HISS--! LIAR!
20.

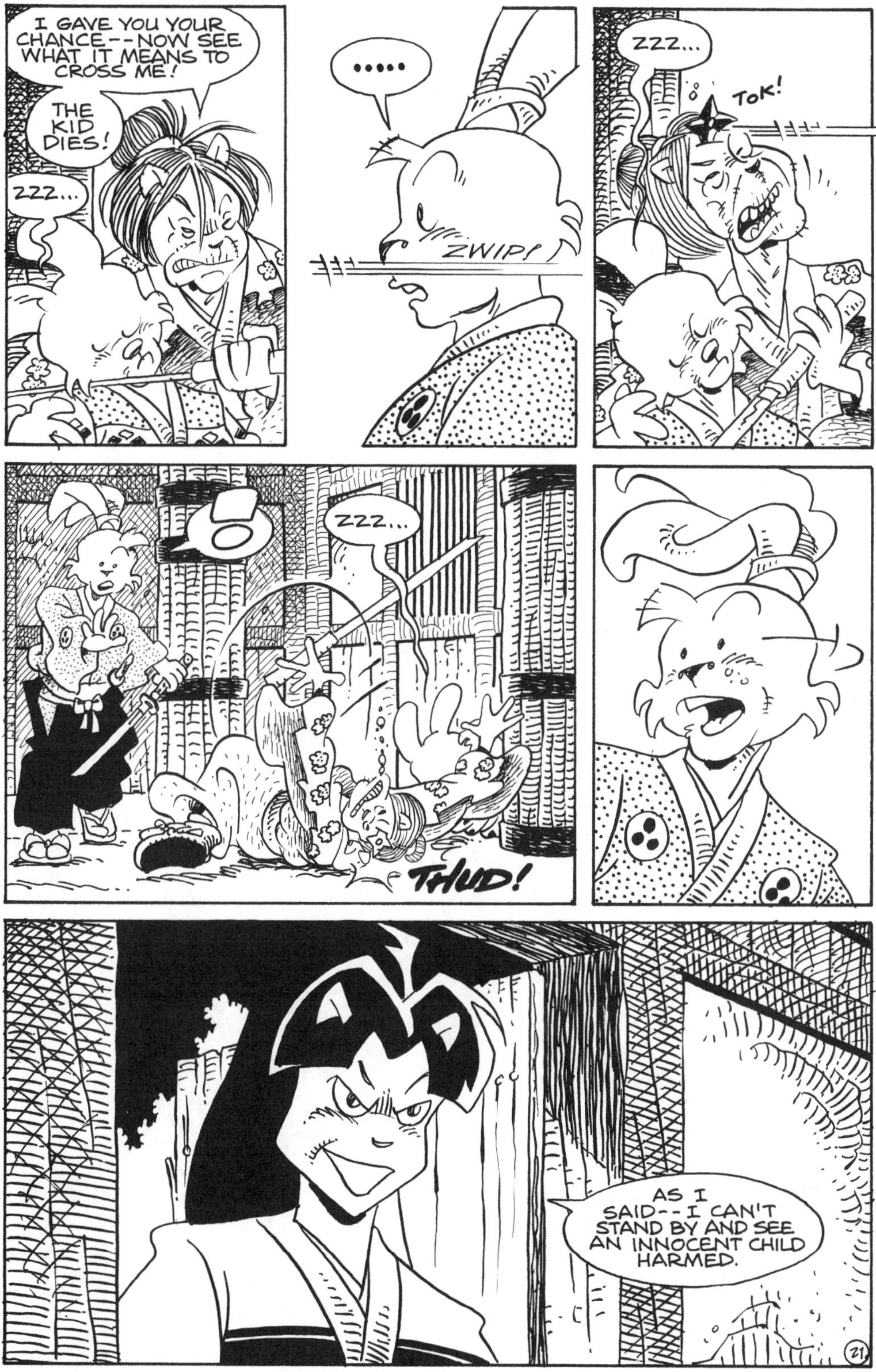
I GAVE YOU YOUR CHANCE--NOW SEE WHAT IT MEANS TO CROSS ME!
THE KID DIES!
ZZZ...
.....
ZWIP!
ZZZ...
TOK!
ZZZ...
THUD!
AS I SAID--I CAN'T STAND BY AND SEE AN INNOCENT CHILD HARMED.
21

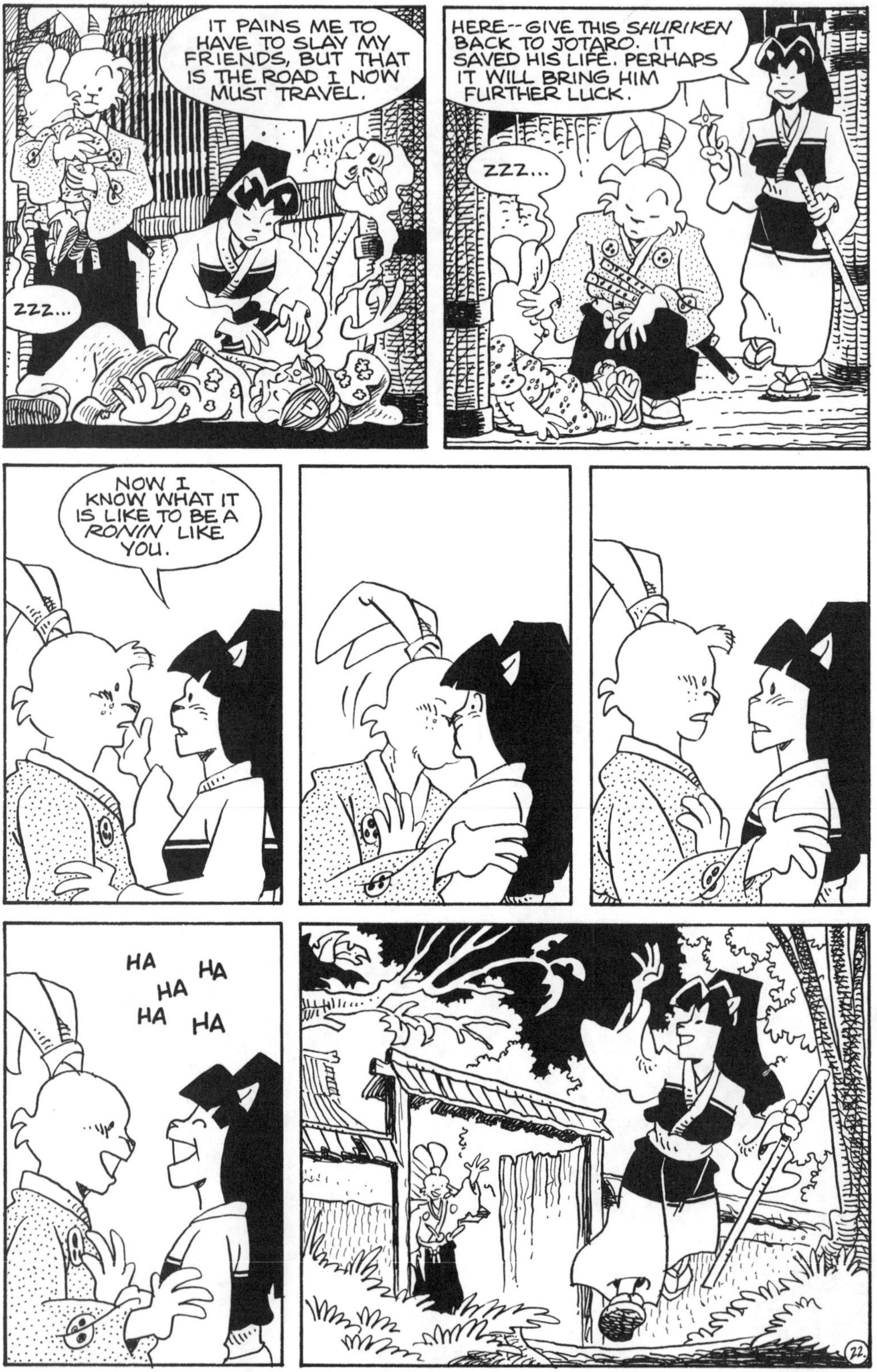
IT PAINS ME TO HAVE TO SLAY MY FRIENDS, BUT THAT IS THE ROAD I NOW MUST TRAVEL.
ZZZ...
HERE--GIVE THIS *SHURIKEN* BACK TO JOTARO. IT SAVED HIS LIFE. PERHAPS IT WILL BRING HIM FURTHER LUCK.
ZZZ...
NOW I KNOW WHAT IT IS LIKE TO BE A *RONIN* LIKE YOU.
HA HA HA HA HA
22.

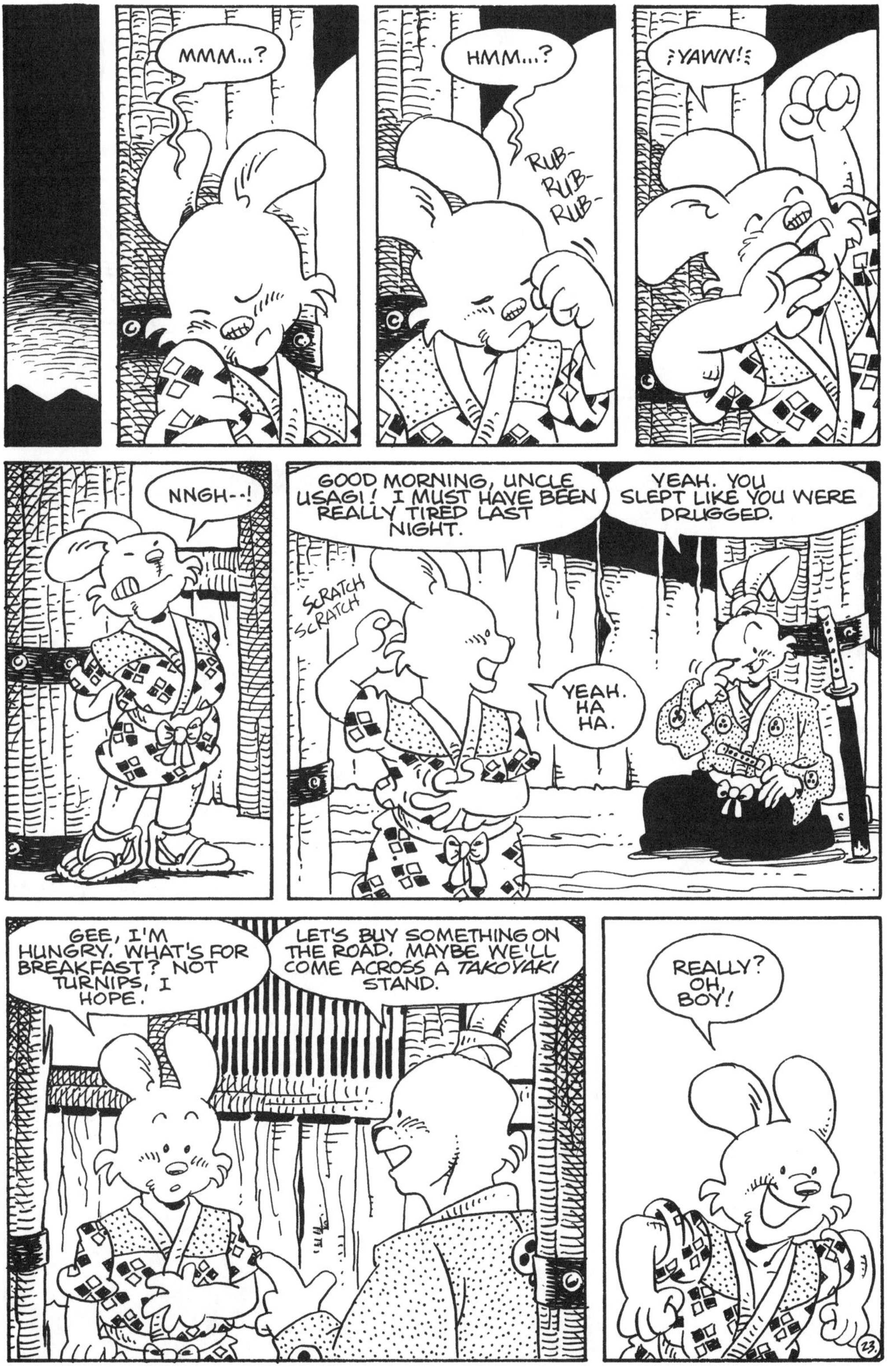
MMM...?
HMM...?
RUB-RUB-RUB-
¡YAWN!¡
NNGH--!
GOOD MORNING, UNCLE USAGI! I MUST HAVE BEEN REALLY TIRED LAST NIGHT.
SCRATCH SCRATCH
YEAH. YOU SLEPT LIKE YOU WERE DRUGGED.
YEAH. HA HA.
GEE, I'M HUNGRY. WHAT'S FOR BREAKFAST? NOT TURNIPS, I HOPE.
LET'S BUY SOMETHING ON THE ROAD. MAYBE WE'LL COME ACROSS A *TAKOYAKI* STAND.
REALLY? OH, BOY!
23.

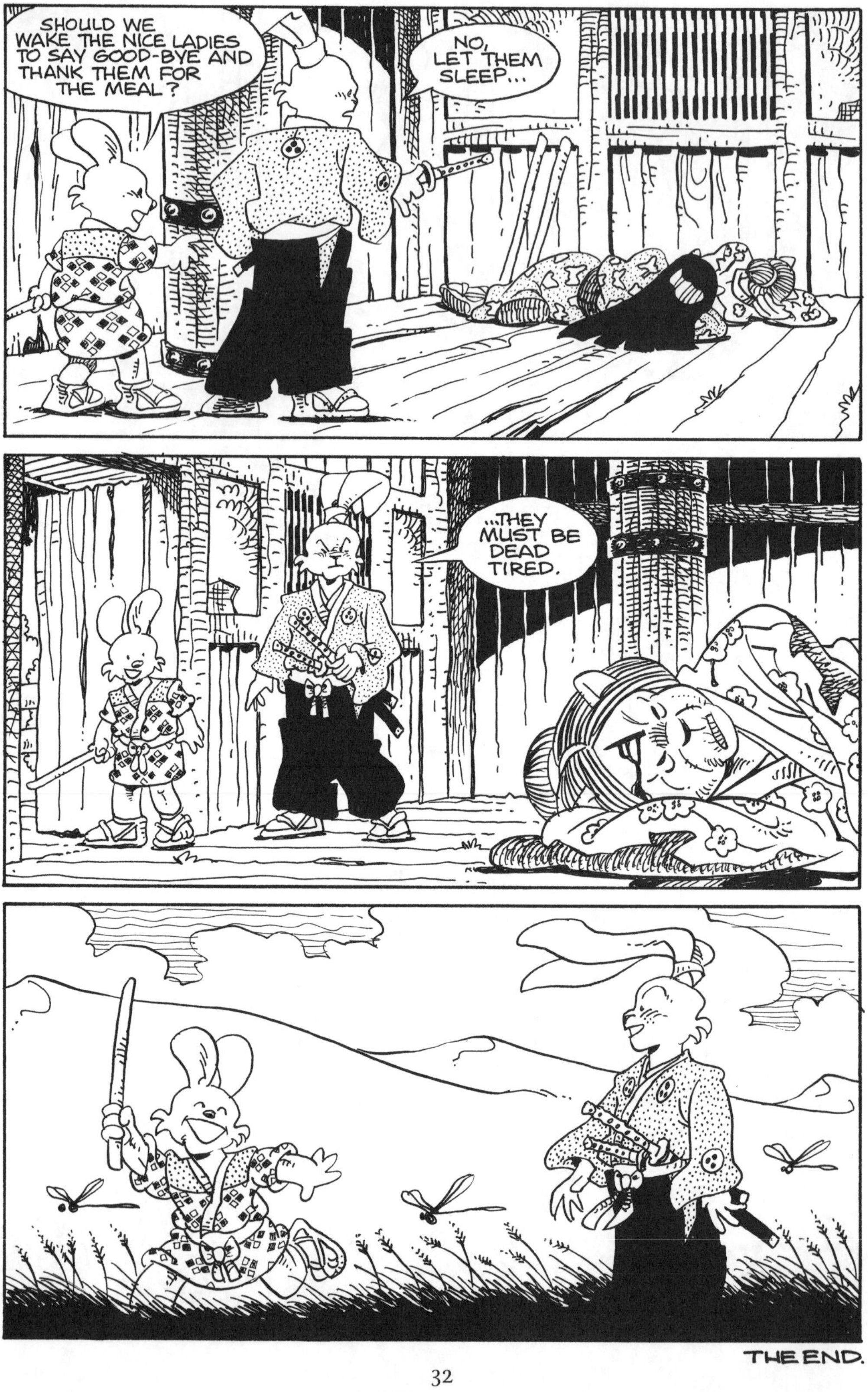

SHOULD WE WAKE THE NICE LADIES TO SAY GOOD-BYE AND THANK THEM FOR THE MEAL?
NO, LET THEM SLEEP...
...THEY MUST BE DEAD TIRED.
THE END.

GHOST WARRIORS

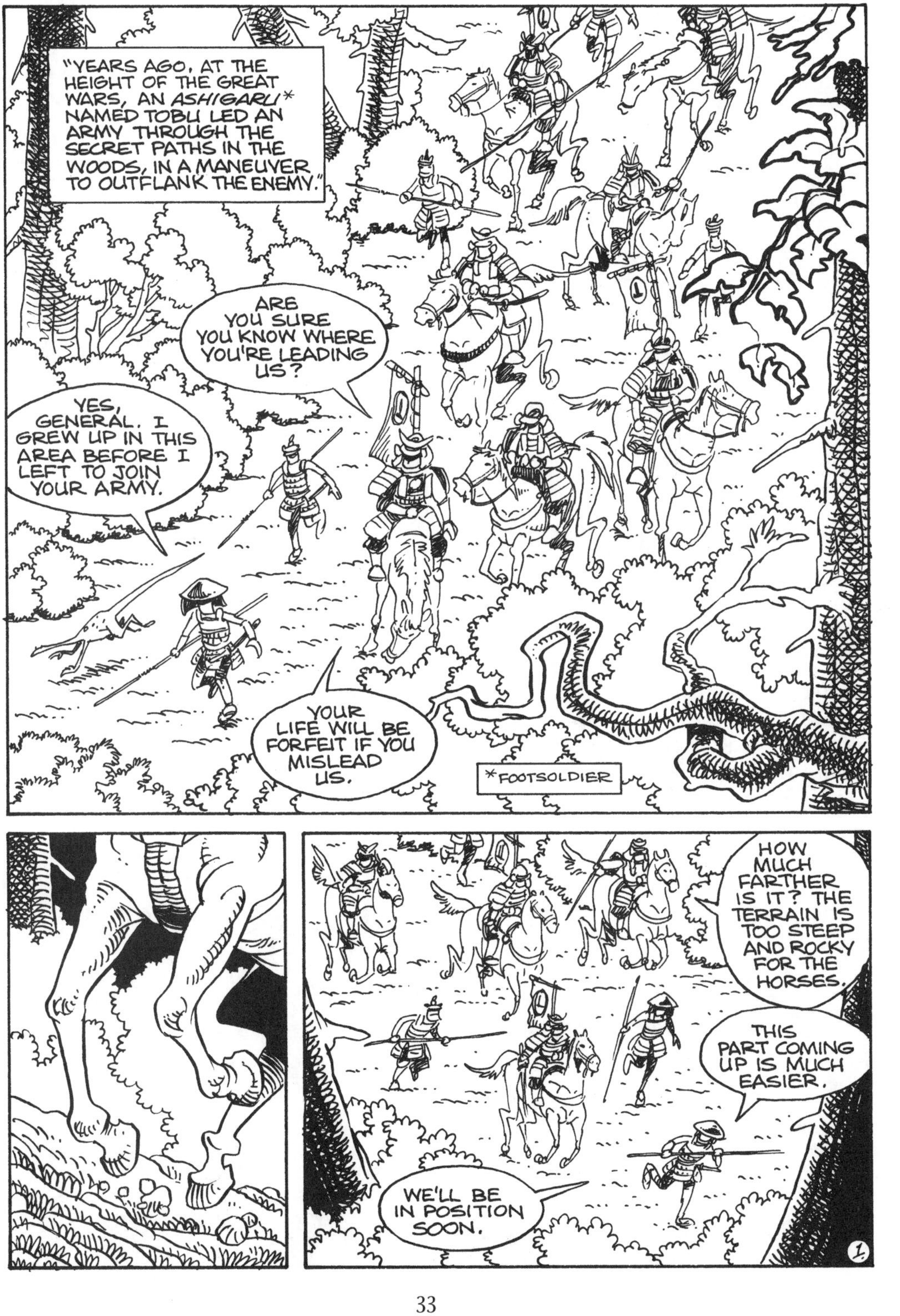
"YEARS AGO, AT THE HEIGHT OF THE GREAT WARS, AN *ASHIGARU** NAMED TOBU LED AN ARMY THROUGH THE SECRET PATHS IN THE WOODS, IN A MANEUVER TO OUTFLANK THE ENEMY."
ARE YOU SURE YOU KNOW WHERE YOU'RE LEADING US?
YES, GENERAL. I GREW UP IN THIS AREA BEFORE I LEFT TO JOIN YOUR ARMY.
YOUR LIFE WILL BE FORFEIT IF YOU MISLEAD US.
*FOOTSOLDIER
HOW MUCH FARTHER IS IT? THE TERRAIN IS TOO STEEP AND ROCKY FOR THE HORSES.
THIS PART COMING UP IS MUCH EASIER.
WE'LL BE IN POSITION SOON.
1.

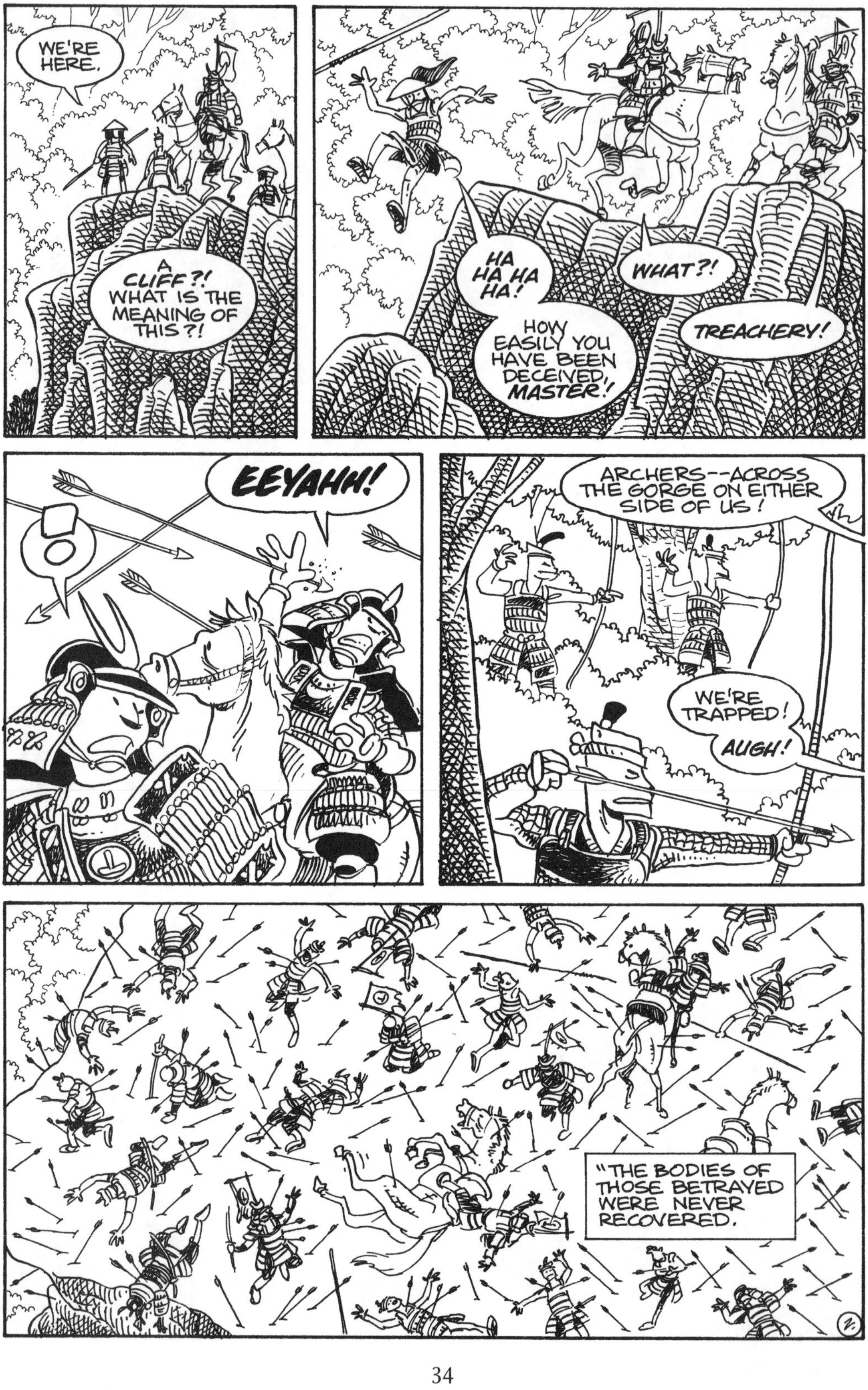
WE'RE HERE.
A CLIFF?! WHAT IS THE MEANING OF THIS?!
HA HA HA HA!
HOW EASILY YOU HAVE BEEN DECEIVED, MASTER!
WHAT?!
TREACHERY!
EEYAHH!
ARCHERS--ACROSS THE GORGE ON EITHER SIDE OF US!
WE'RE TRAPPED!
AUGH!
"THE BODIES OF THOSE BETRAYED WERE NEVER RECOVERED.

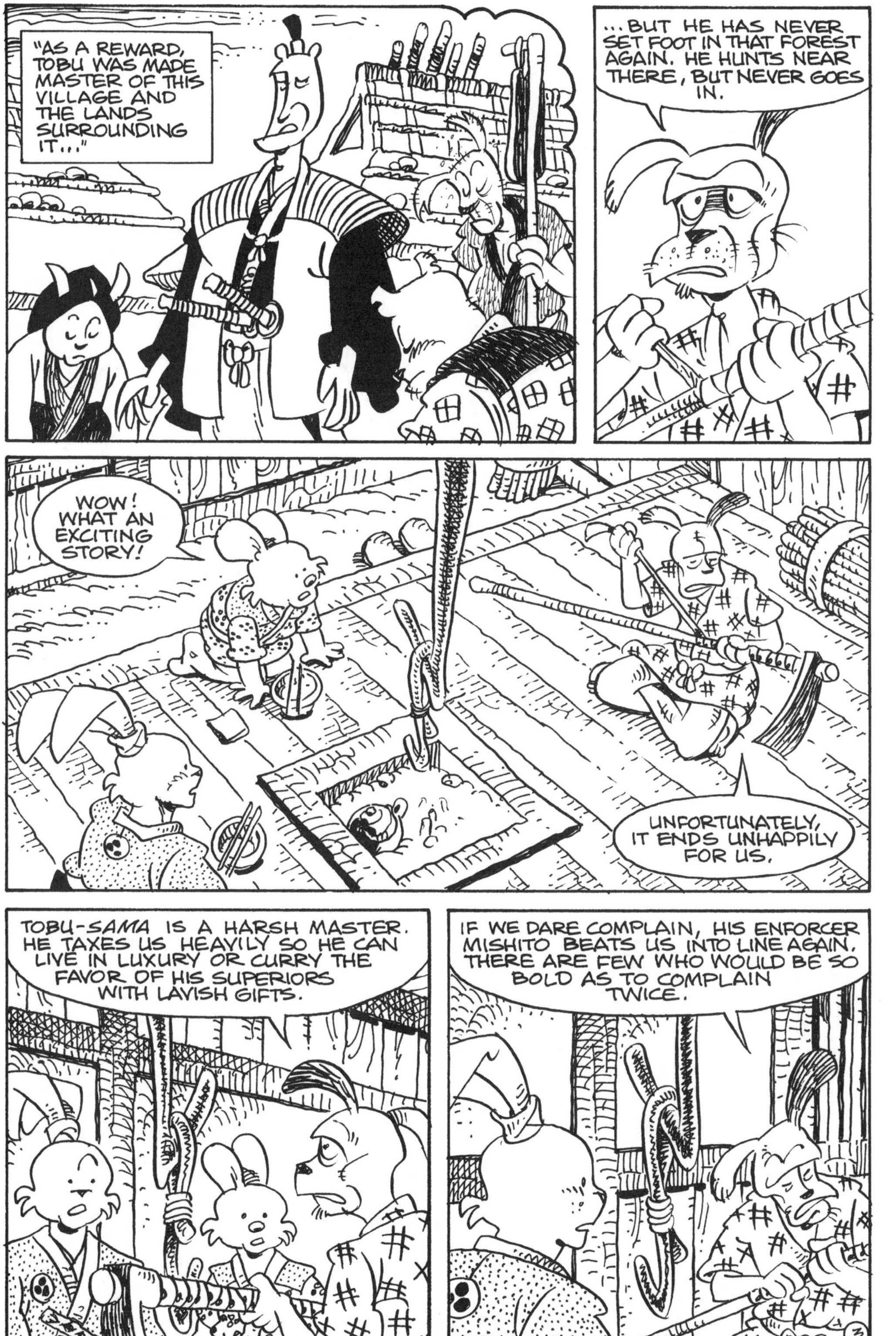
"AS A REWARD, TOBU WAS MADE MASTER OF THIS VILLAGE AND THE LANDS SURROUNDING IT..."
...BUT HE HAS NEVER SET FOOT IN THAT FOREST AGAIN. HE HUNTS NEAR THERE, BUT NEVER GOES IN.
WOW! WHAT AN EXCITING STORY!
UNFORTUNATELY, IT ENDS UNHAPPILY FOR US.
TOBU-*SAMA* IS A HARSH MASTER. HE TAXES US HEAVILY SO HE CAN LIVE IN LUXURY OR CURRY THE FAVOR OF HIS SUPERIORS WITH LAVISH GIFTS.
IF WE DARE COMPLAIN, HIS ENFORCER MISHITO BEATS US INTO LINE AGAIN. THERE ARE FEW WHO WOULD BE SO BOLD AS TO COMPLAIN TWICE.

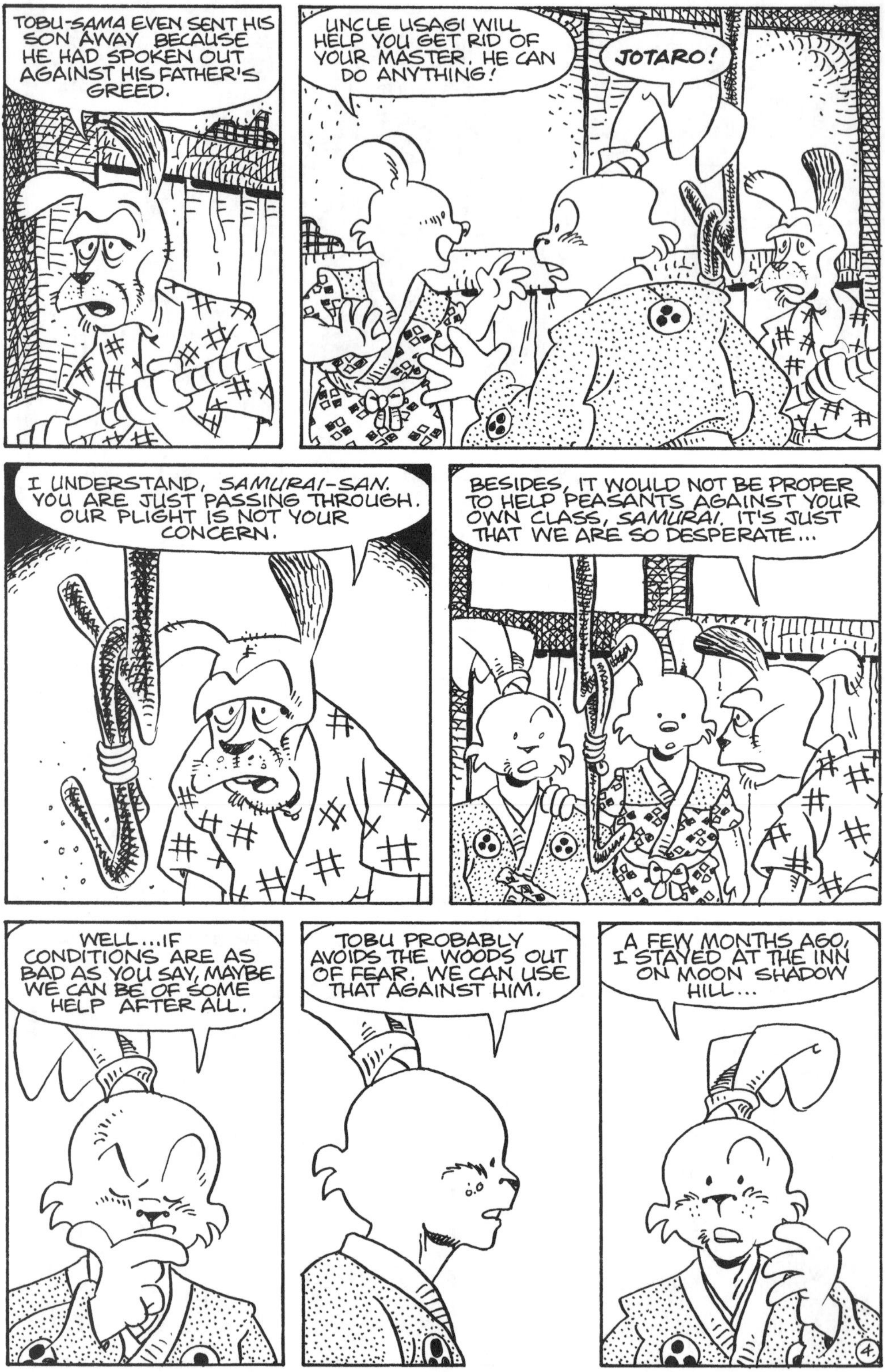
TOBU-SAMA EVEN SENT HIS SON AWAY BECAUSE HE HAD SPOKEN OUT AGAINST HIS FATHER'S GREED.
UNCLE USAGI WILL HELP YOU GET RID OF YOUR MASTER. HE CAN DO ANYTHING!
JOTARO!
I UNDERSTAND, SAMURAI-SAN. YOU ARE JUST PASSING THROUGH. OUR PLIGHT IS NOT YOUR CONCERN.
BESIDES, IT WOULD NOT BE PROPER TO HELP PEASANTS AGAINST YOUR OWN CLASS, SAMURAI. IT'S JUST THAT WE ARE SO DESPERATE...
WELL...IF CONDITIONS ARE AS BAD AS YOU SAY, MAYBE WE CAN BE OF SOME HELP AFTER ALL.
TOBU PROBABLY AVOIDS THE WOODS OUT OF FEAR. WE CAN USE THAT AGAINST HIM.
A FEW MONTHS AGO, I STAYED AT THE INN ON MOON SHADOW HILL...
4

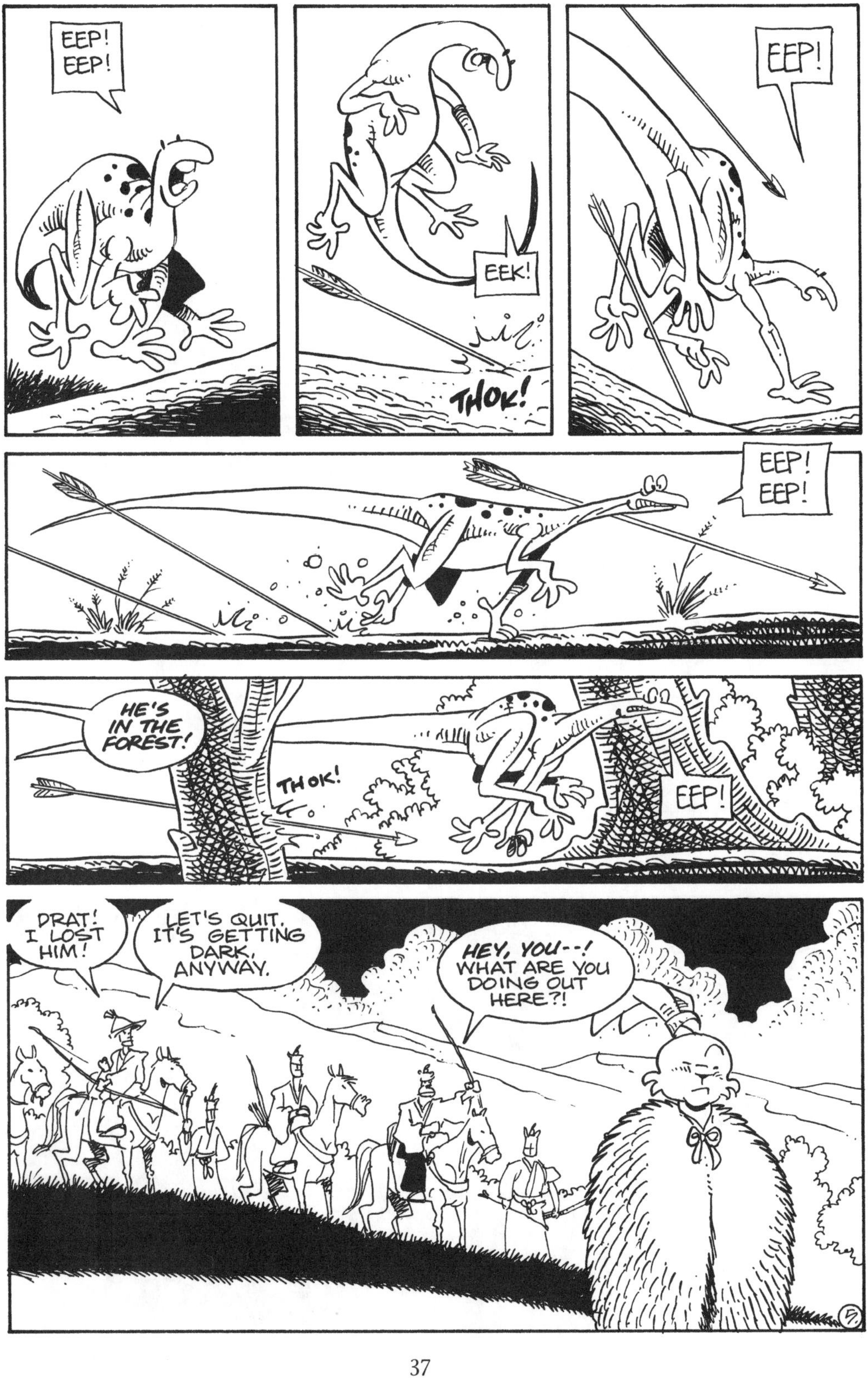
EEP! EEP!
EEK!
THOK!
EEP!
EEP! EEP!
HE'S IN THE FOREST!
THOK!
EEP!
DRAT! I LOST HIM!
LET'S QUIT. IT'S GETTING DARK, ANYWAY.
HEY, YOU--! WHAT ARE YOU DOING OUT HERE?!

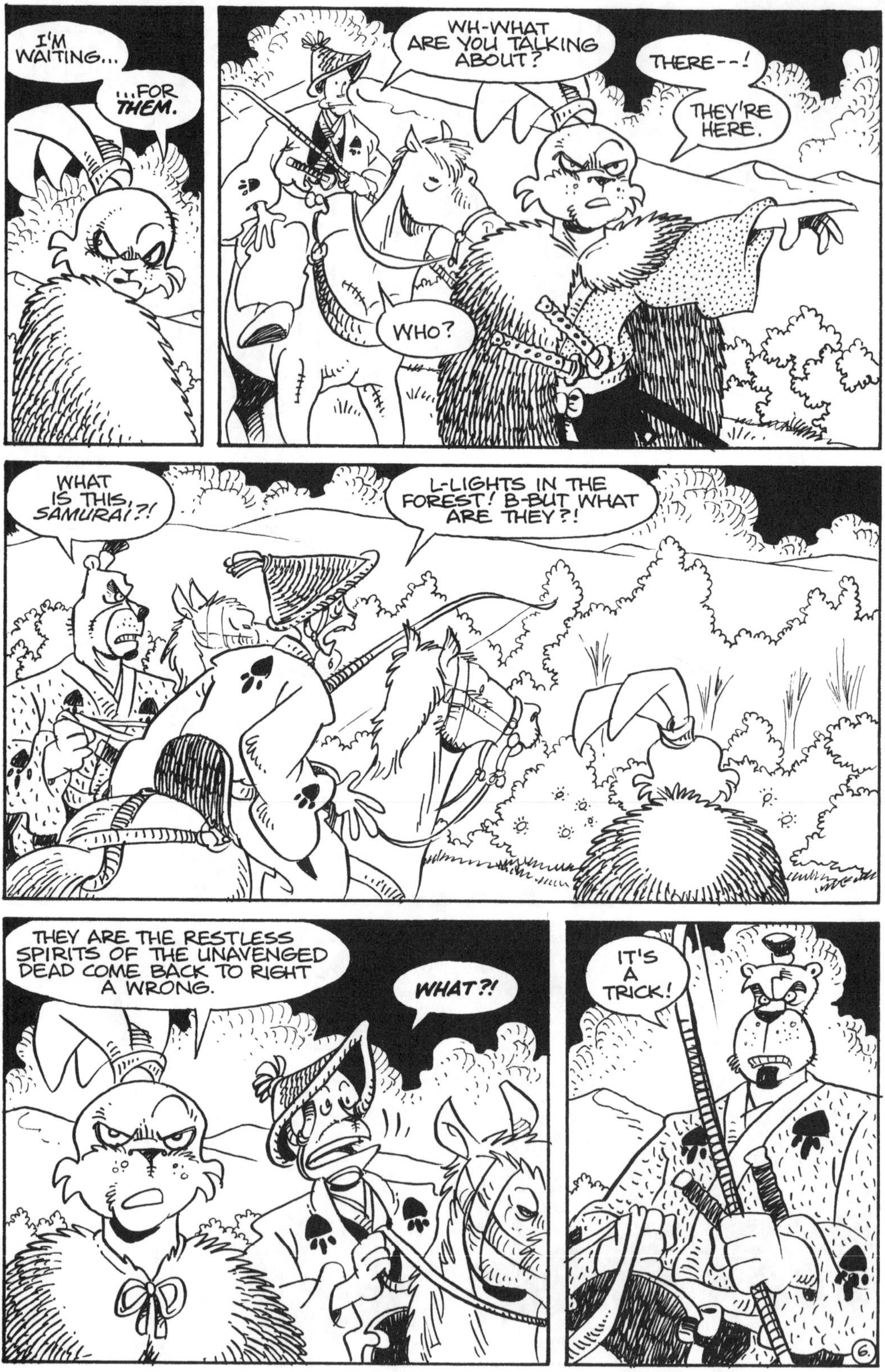
I'M WAITING...
...FOR *THEM.*
WH-WHAT ARE YOU TALKING ABOUT?
THERE--!
THEY'RE HERE.
WHO?
WHAT IS THIS, *SAMURAI?!*
L-LIGHTS IN THE FOREST! B-BUT WHAT ARE THEY?!
THEY ARE THE RESTLESS SPIRITS OF THE UNAVENGED DEAD COME BACK TO RIGHT A WRONG.
WHAT?!
IT'S A TRICK!
6.

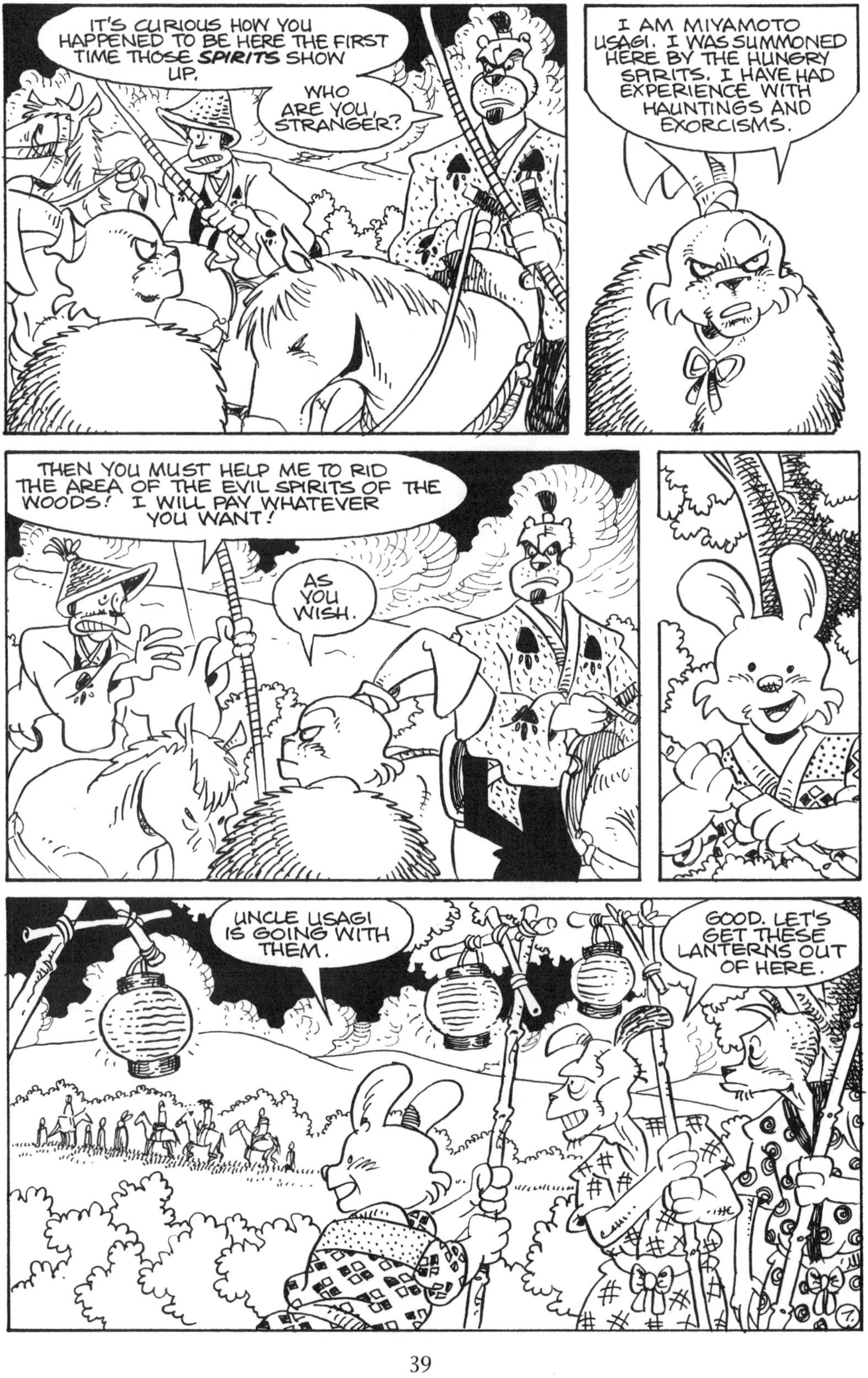
IT'S CURIOUS HOW YOU HAPPENED TO BE HERE THE FIRST TIME THOSE SPIRITS SHOW UP.
WHO ARE YOU, STRANGER?
I AM MIYAMOTO USAGI. I WAS SUMMONED HERE BY THE HUNGRY SPIRITS. I HAVE HAD EXPERIENCE WITH HAUNTINGS AND EXORCISMS.
THEN YOU MUST HELP ME TO RID THE AREA OF THE EVIL SPIRITS OF THE WOODS! I WILL PAY WHATEVER YOU WANT!
AS YOU WISH.
UNCLE USAGI IS GOING WITH THEM.
GOOD. LET'S GET THESE LANTERNS OUT OF HERE.
7.

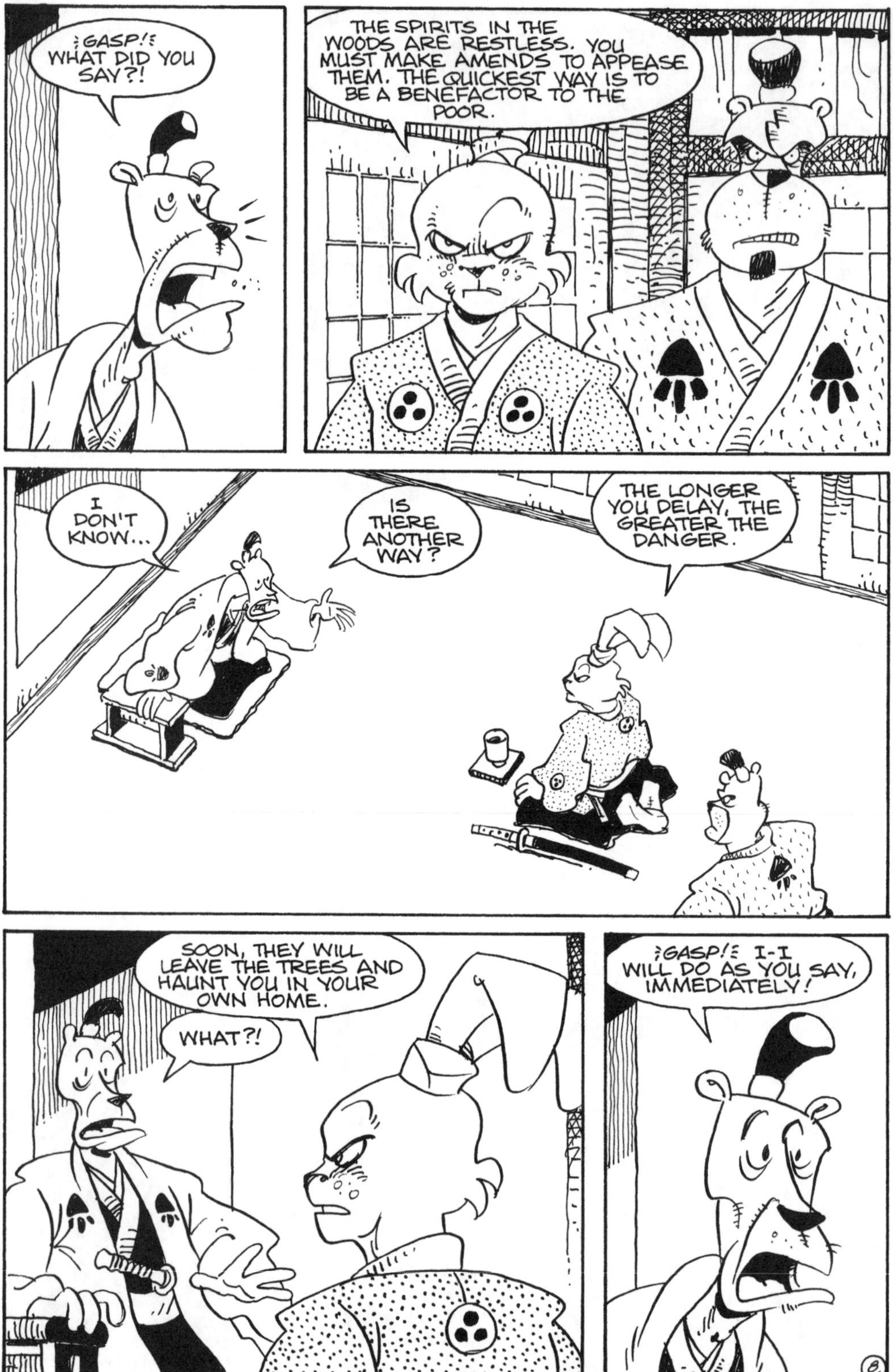

GASP! WHAT DID YOU SAY?!
THE SPIRITS IN THE WOODS ARE RESTLESS. YOU MUST MAKE AMENDS TO APPEASE THEM. THE QUICKEST WAY IS TO BE A BENEFACTOR TO THE POOR.
I DON'T KNOW...
IS THERE ANOTHER WAY?
THE LONGER YOU DELAY, THE GREATER THE DANGER.
SOON, THEY WILL LEAVE THE TREES AND HAUNT YOU IN YOUR OWN HOME.
WHAT?!
GASP! I-I WILL DO AS YOU SAY, IMMEDIATELY!
8.

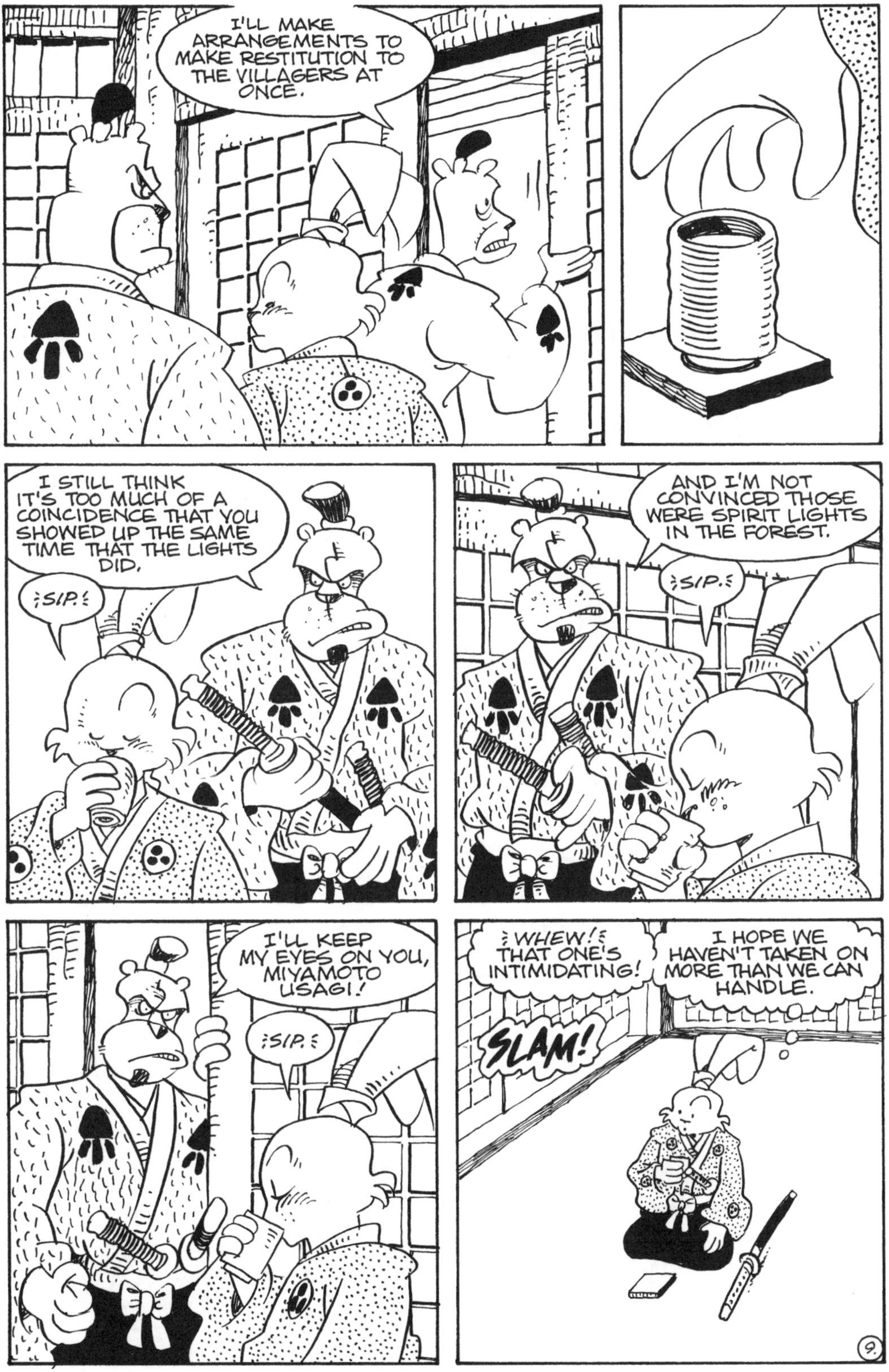

I'LL MAKE ARRANGEMENTS TO MAKE RESTITUTION TO THE VILLAGERS AT ONCE.
I STILL THINK IT'S TOO MUCH OF A COINCIDENCE THAT YOU SHOWED UP THE SAME TIME THAT THE LIGHTS DID,
SIP.
AND I'M NOT CONVINCED THOSE WERE SPIRIT LIGHTS IN THE FOREST.
SIP.
I'LL KEEP MY EYES ON YOU, MIYAMOTO USAGI!
SIP.
SLAM!
WHEW! THAT ONE'S INTIMIDATING!
I HOPE WE HAVEN'T TAKEN ON MORE THAN WE CAN HANDLE.
9.

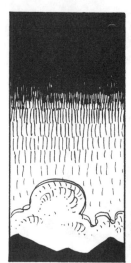

HOI! HOI!

TOBU-SAMA IS IN THE VILLAGE SQUARE GIVING OUT FREE SACKS OF RICE!

REALLY?!

IT LOOKS LIKE YOUR FRIEND'S PLAN IS WORKING!

OF COURSE! UNCLE USAGI CAN DO ANYTHING!

HOI! HOI! FREE FOOD!

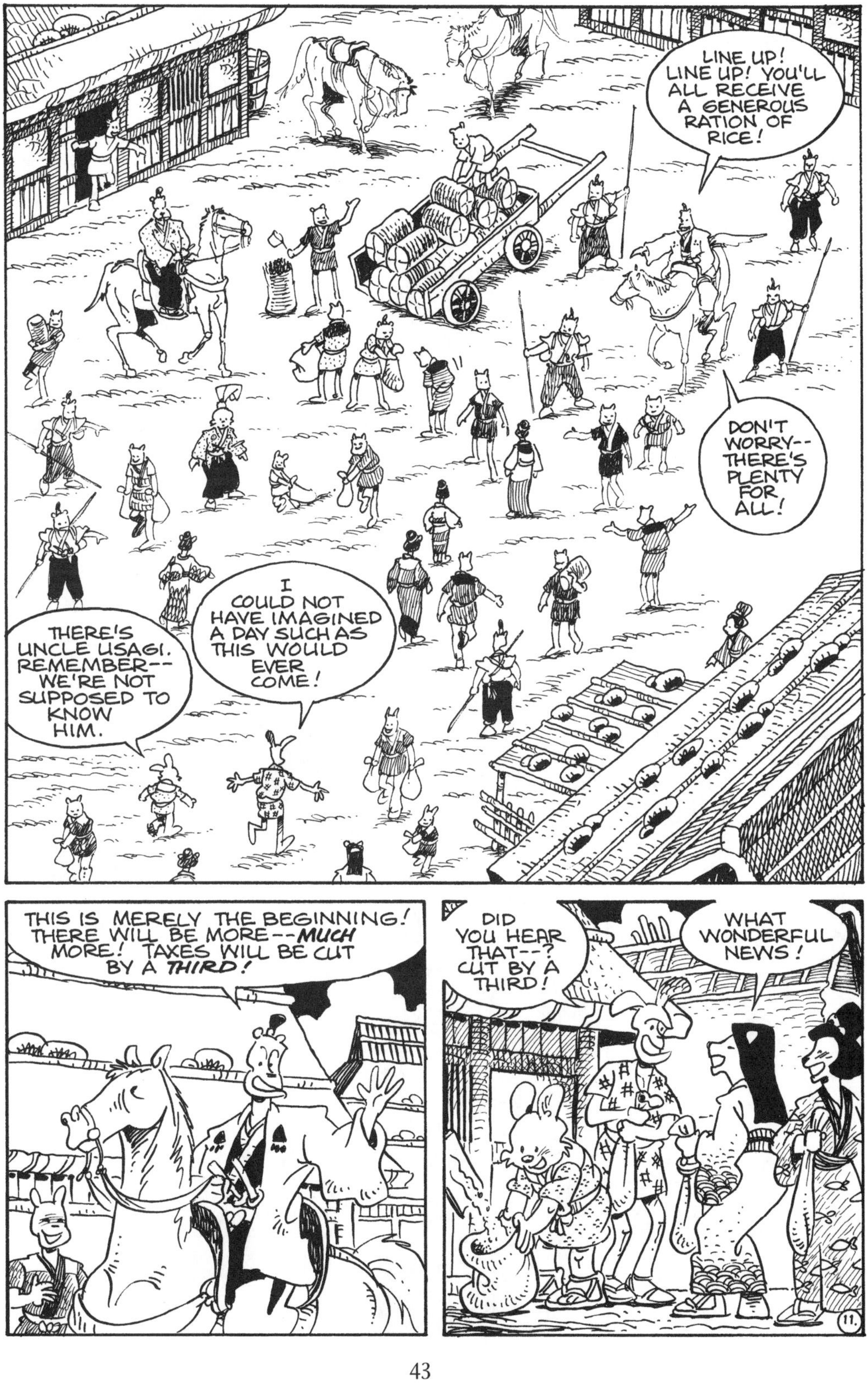
LINE UP! LINE UP! YOU'LL ALL RECEIVE A GENEROUS RATION OF RICE!
DON'T WORRY-- THERE'S PLENTY FOR ALL!
I COULD NOT HAVE IMAGINED A DAY SUCH AS THIS WOULD EVER COME!
THERE'S UNCLE USAGI. REMEMBER-- WE'RE NOT SUPPOSED TO KNOW HIM.
THIS IS MERELY THE BEGINNING! THERE WILL BE MORE--MUCH MORE! TAXES WILL BE CUT BY A THIRD!
DID YOU HEAR THAT--? CUT BY A THIRD!
WHAT WONDERFUL NEWS!
11.

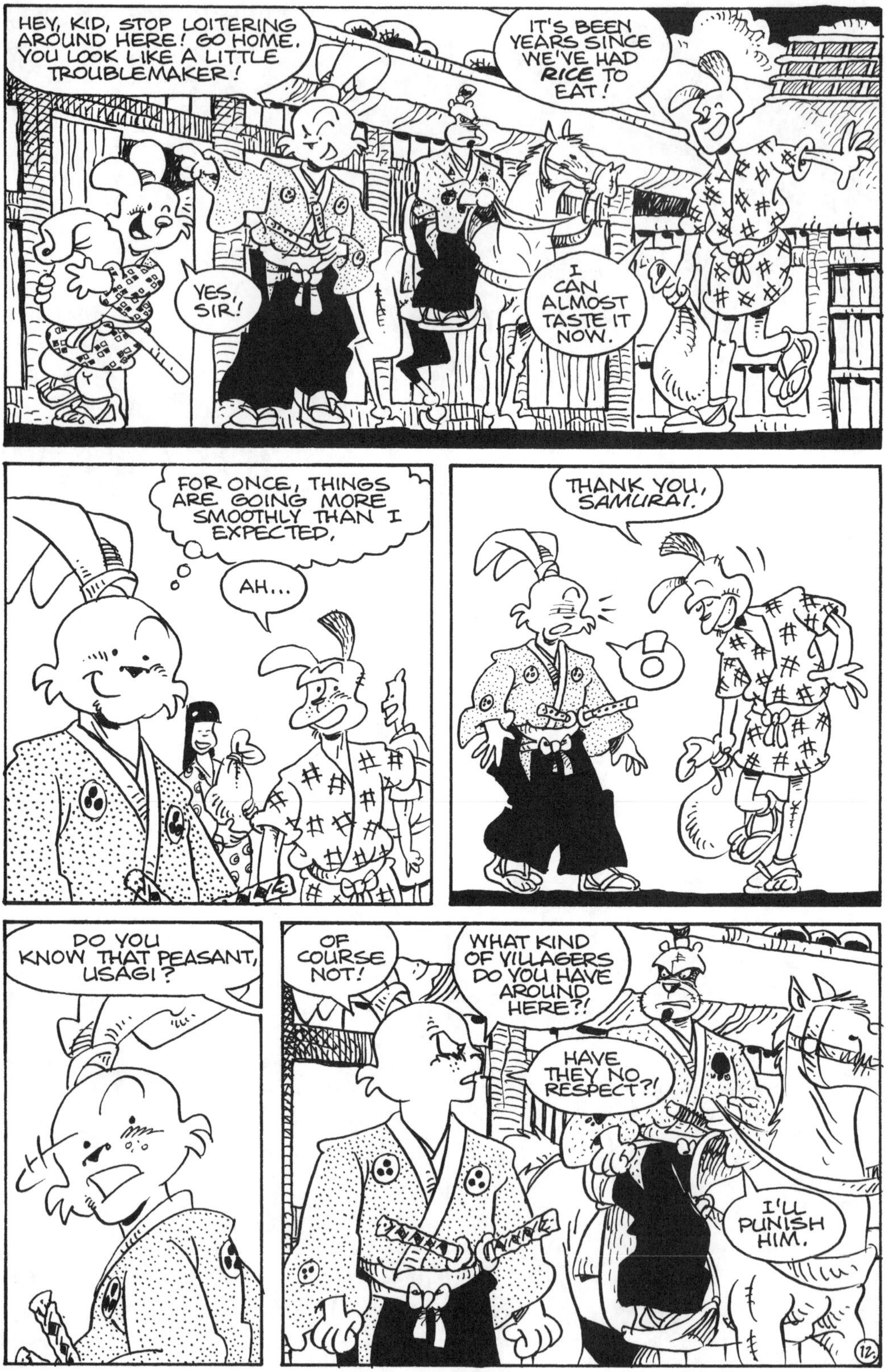
HEY, KID, STOP LOITERING AROUND HERE! GO HOME. YOU LOOK LIKE A LITTLE TROUBLEMAKER!
YES, SIR!
IT'S BEEN YEARS SINCE WE'VE HAD RICE TO EAT!
I CAN ALMOST TASTE IT NOW.
FOR ONCE, THINGS ARE GOING MORE SMOOTHLY THAN I EXPECTED.
AH...
THANK YOU, SAMURAI.
!
DO YOU KNOW THAT PEASANT, USAGI?
OF COURSE NOT!
WHAT KIND OF VILLAGERS DO YOU HAVE AROUND HERE?!
HAVE THEY NO RESPECT?!
I'LL PUNISH HIM.
12

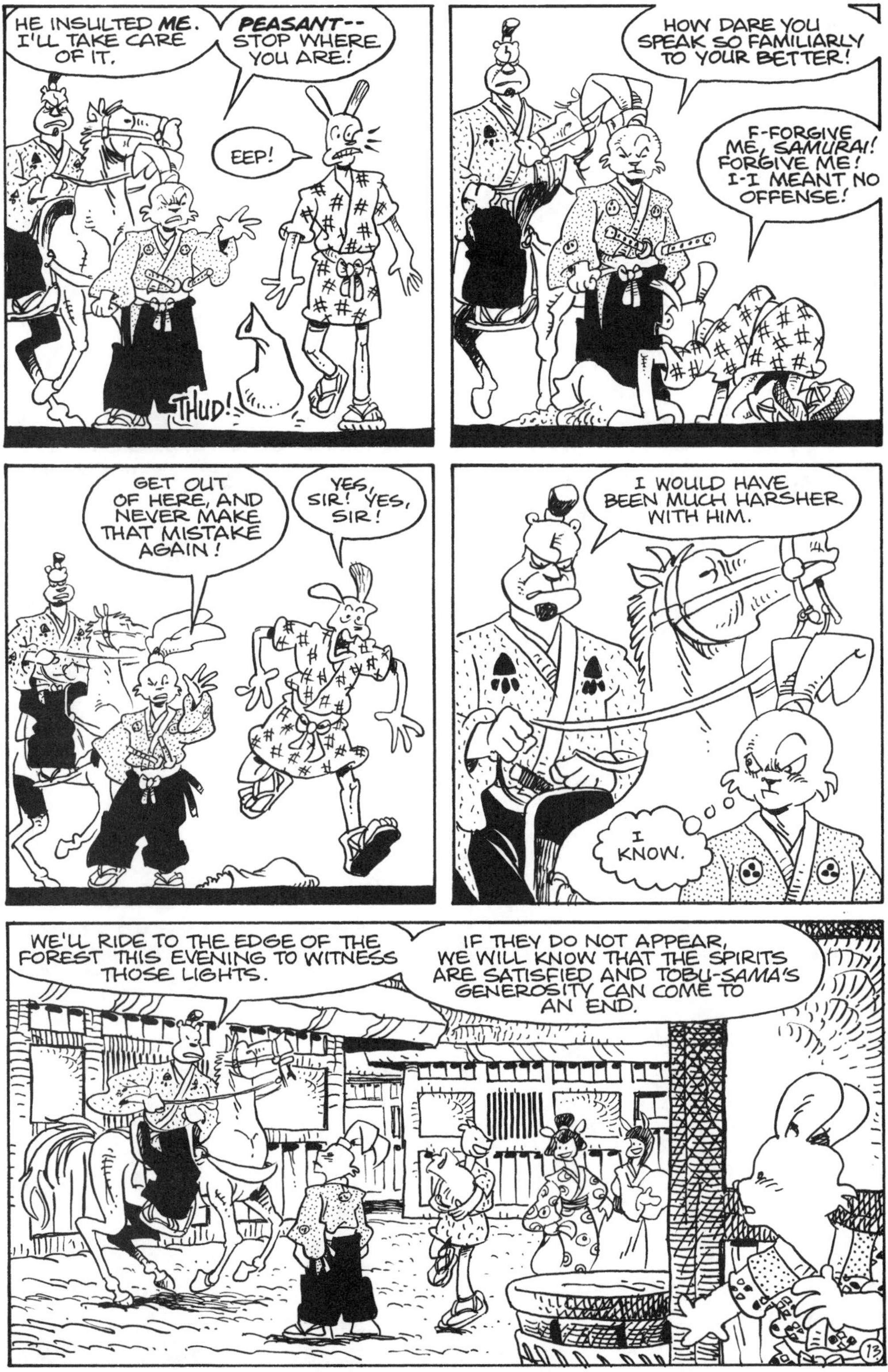
HE INSULTED ME. I'LL TAKE CARE OF IT.
PEASANT-- STOP WHERE YOU ARE!
EEP!
THUD!
HOW DARE YOU SPEAK SO FAMILIARLY TO YOUR BETTER!
F-FORGIVE ME, SAMURAI! FORGIVE ME! I-I MEANT NO OFFENSE!
GET OUT OF HERE, AND NEVER MAKE THAT MISTAKE AGAIN!
YES, SIR! YES, SIR!
I WOULD HAVE BEEN MUCH HARSHER WITH HIM.
I KNOW.
WE'LL RIDE TO THE EDGE OF THE FOREST THIS EVENING TO WITNESS THOSE LIGHTS.
IF THEY DO NOT APPEAR, WE WILL KNOW THAT THE SPIRITS ARE SATISFIED AND TOBU-SAMA'S GENEROSITY CAN COME TO AN END.
13

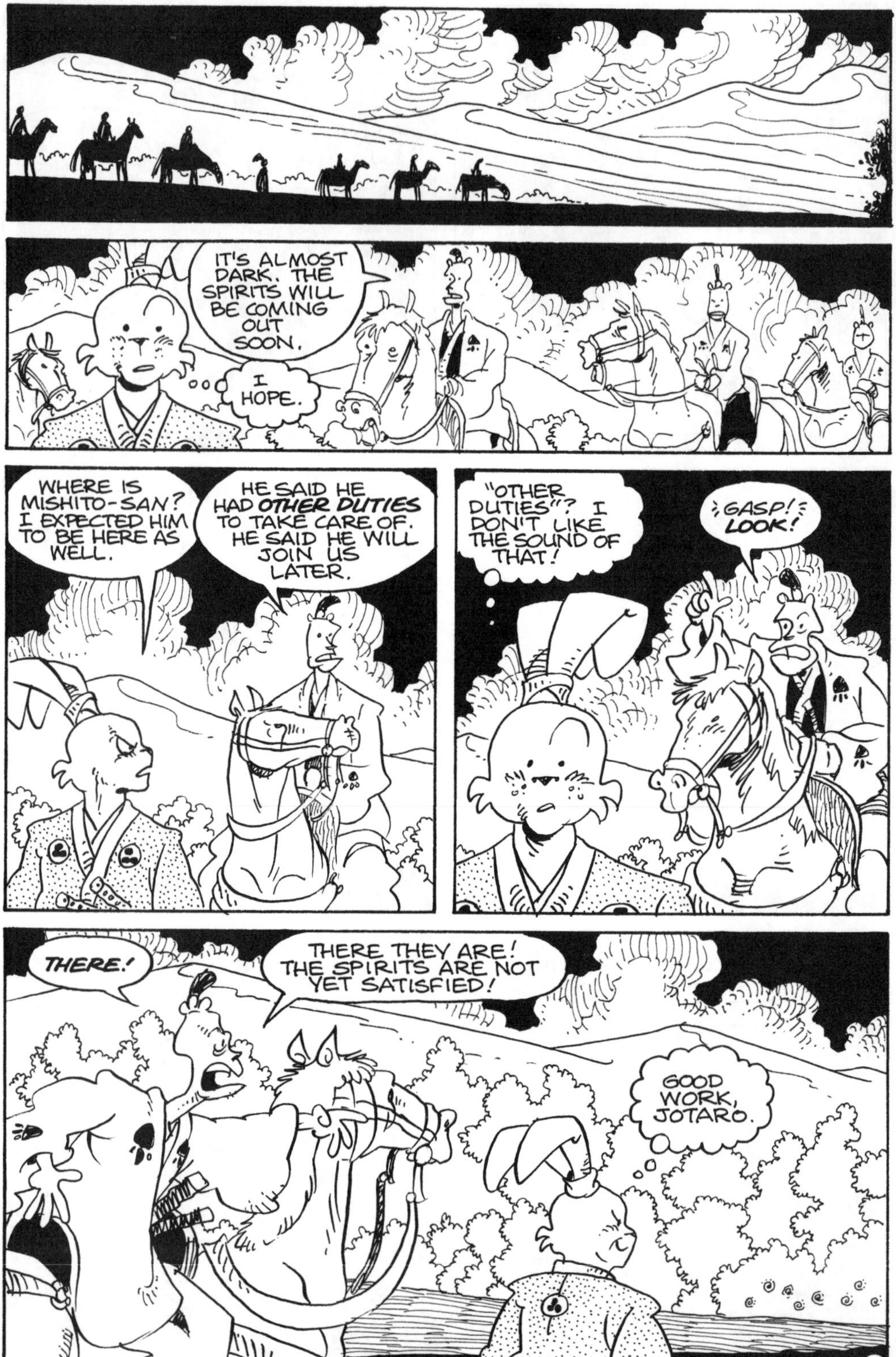
IT'S ALMOST DARK. THE SPIRITS WILL BE COMING OUT SOON.
I HOPE.
WHERE IS MISHITO-SAN? I EXPECTED HIM TO BE HERE AS WELL.
HE SAID HE HAD **OTHER DUTIES** TO TAKE CARE OF. HE SAID HE WILL JOIN US LATER.
"OTHER DUTIES"? I DON'T LIKE THE SOUND OF THAT!
GASP! **LOOK!**
THERE!
THERE THEY ARE! THE SPIRITS ARE NOT YET SATISFIED!
GOOD WORK, JOTARO.
14.

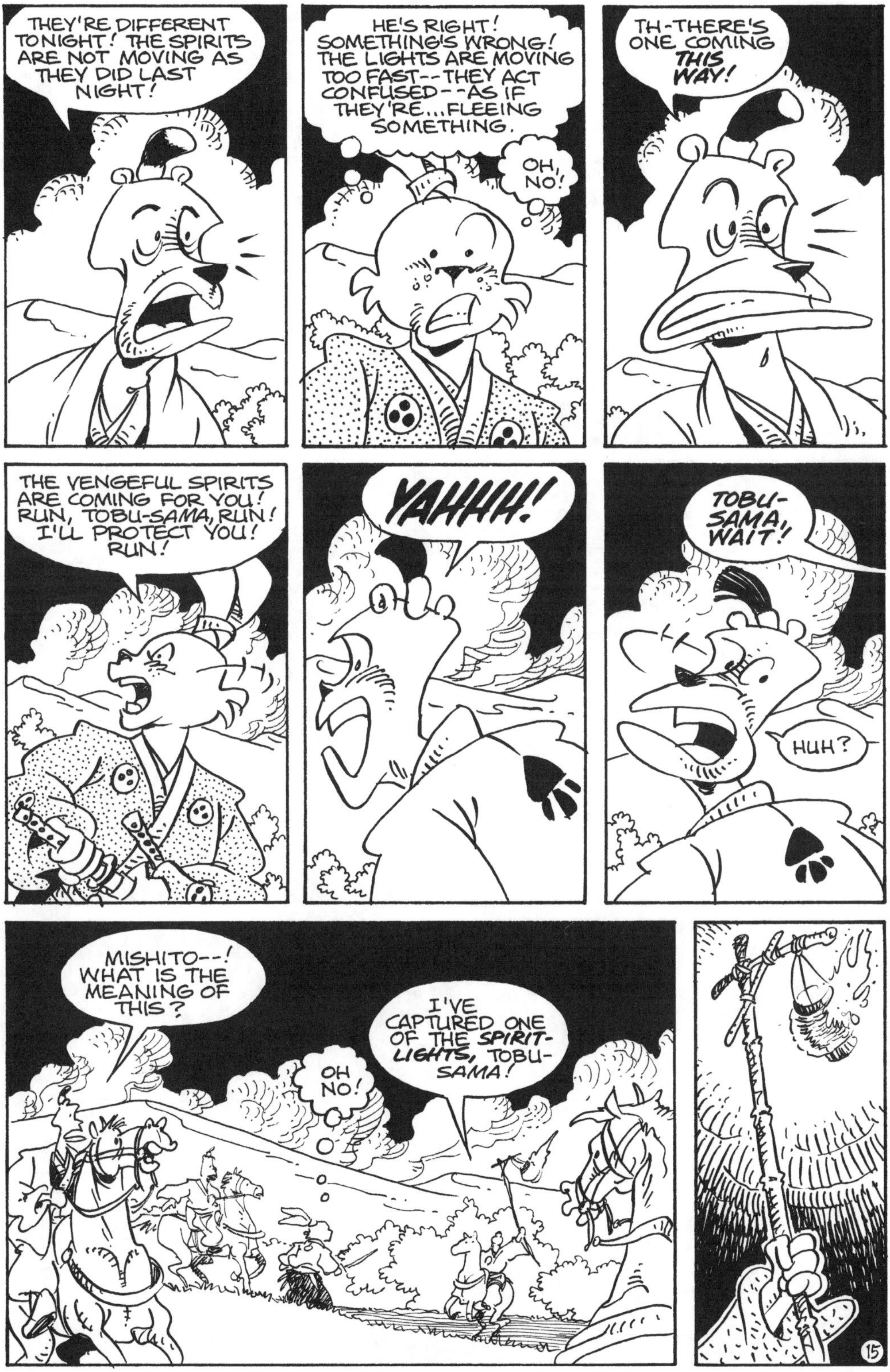
THEY'RE DIFFERENT TONIGHT! THE SPIRITS ARE NOT MOVING AS THEY DID LAST NIGHT!
HE'S RIGHT! SOMETHING'S WRONG! THE LIGHTS ARE MOVING TOO FAST--THEY ACT CONFUSED--AS IF THEY'RE...FLEEING SOMETHING.
OH, NO!
TH-THERE'S ONE COMING THIS WAY!
THE VENGEFUL SPIRITS ARE COMING FOR YOU! RUN, TOBU-SAMA, RUN! I'LL PROTECT YOU! RUN!
YAHHH!
TOBU-SAMA, WAIT!
HUH?
MISHITO--! WHAT IS THE MEANING OF THIS?
OH NO!
I'VE CAPTURED ONE OF THE SPIRIT-LIGHTS, TOBU-SAMA!
15

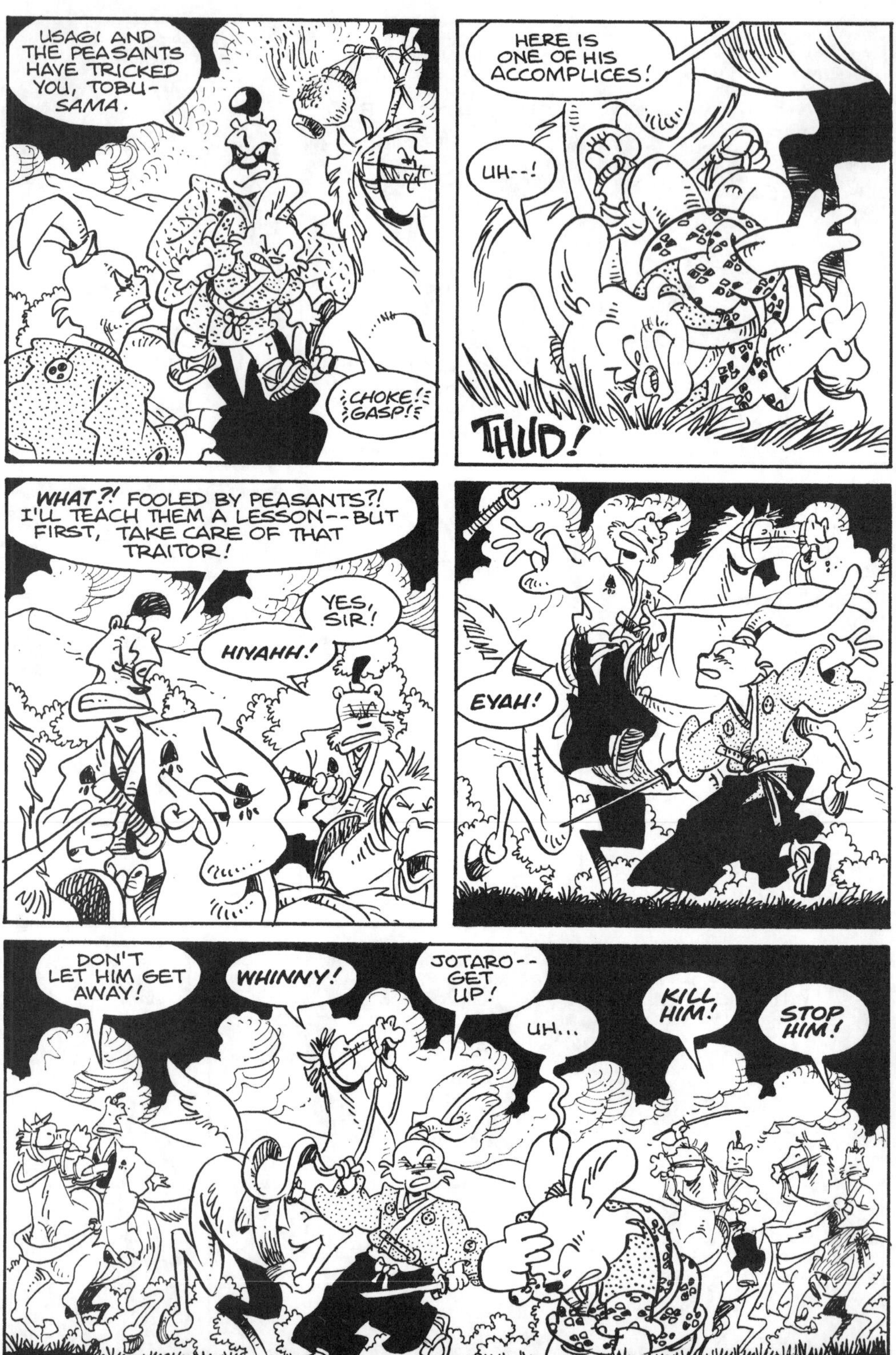
USAGI AND THE PEASANTS HAVE TRICKED YOU, TOBU-SAMA.
CHOKE! GASP!
HERE IS ONE OF HIS ACCOMPLICES!
UH--!
THUD!
WHAT?! FOOLED BY PEASANTS?! I'LL TEACH THEM A LESSON--BUT FIRST, TAKE CARE OF THAT TRAITOR!
YES, SIR!
HIYAHH!
EYAH!
DON'T LET HIM GET AWAY!
WHINNY!
JOTARO--GET UP!
UH...
KILL HIM!
STOP HIM!
16.

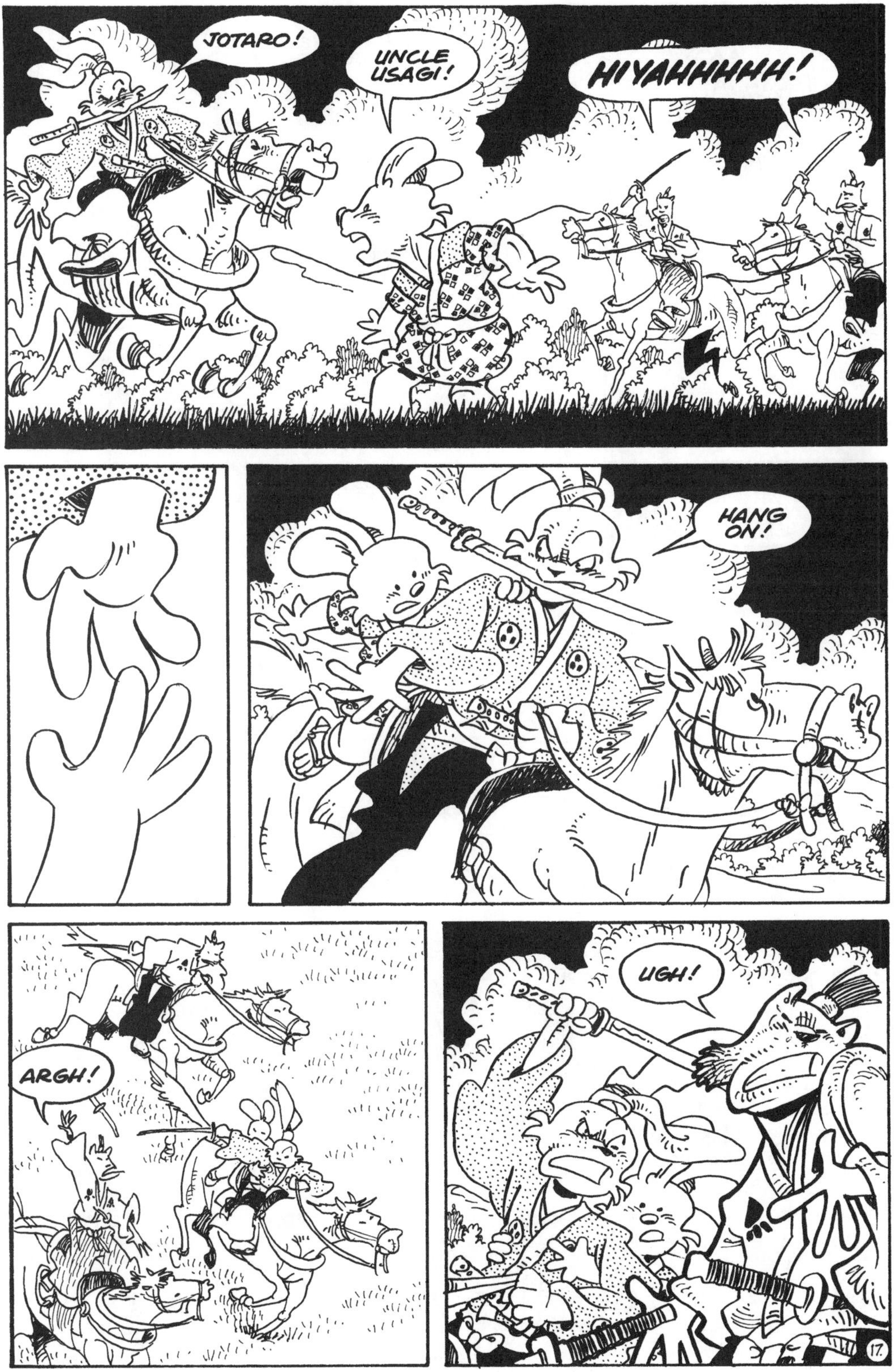
JOTARO!
UNCLE USAGI!
HIYAHHHHH!
HANG ON!
ARGH!
UGH!
17.

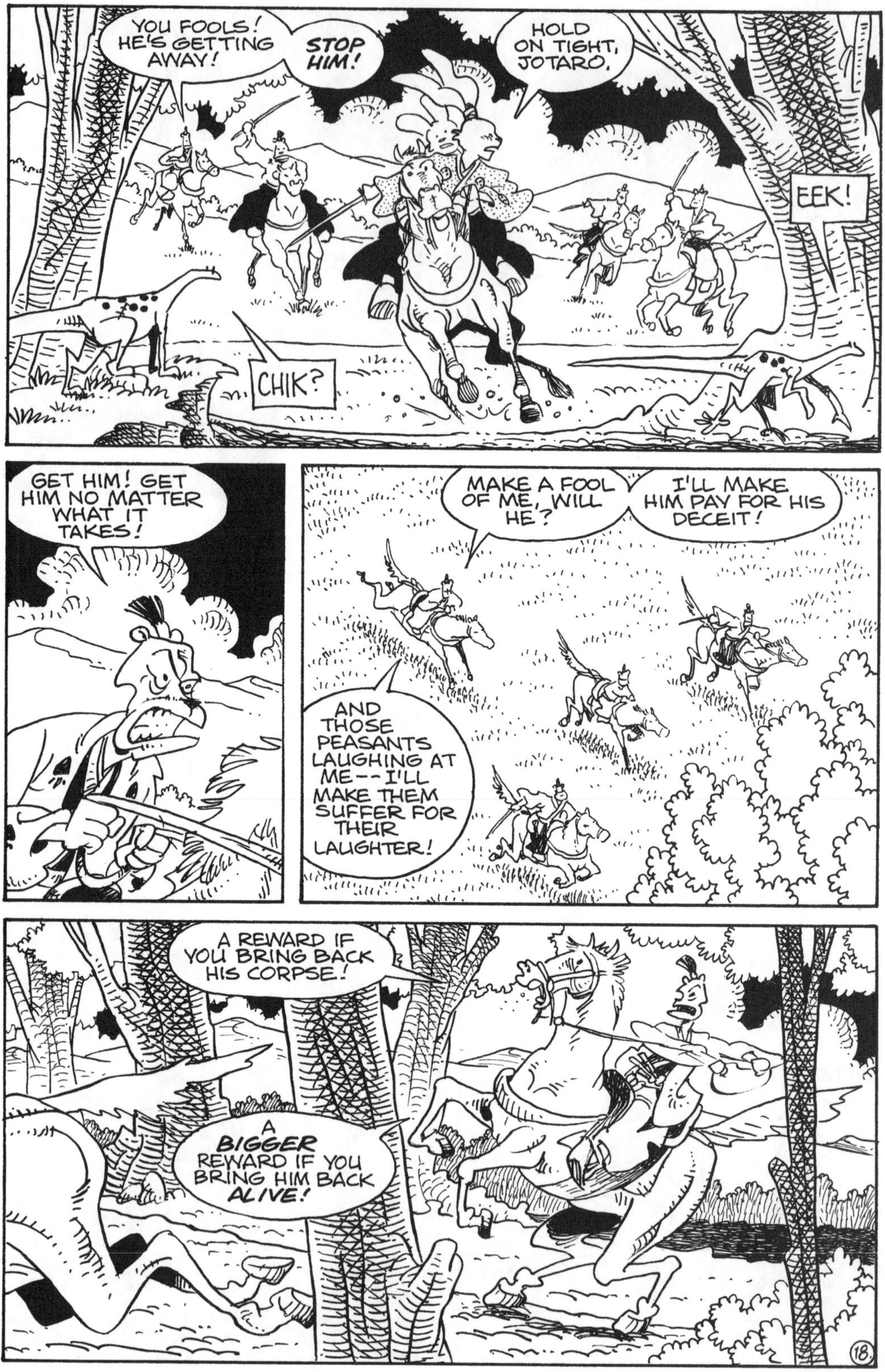
YOU FOOLS! HE'S GETTING AWAY!
STOP HIM!
HOLD ON TIGHT, JOTARO.
EEK!
CHIK?
GET HIM! GET HIM NO MATTER WHAT IT TAKES!
MAKE A FOOL OF ME, WILL HE?
I'LL MAKE HIM PAY FOR HIS DECEIT!
AND THOSE PEASANTS LAUGHING AT ME--I'LL MAKE THEM SUFFER FOR THEIR LAUGHTER!
A REWARD IF YOU BRING BACK HIS CORPSE!
A BIGGER REWARD IF YOU BRING HIM BACK ALIVE!
18

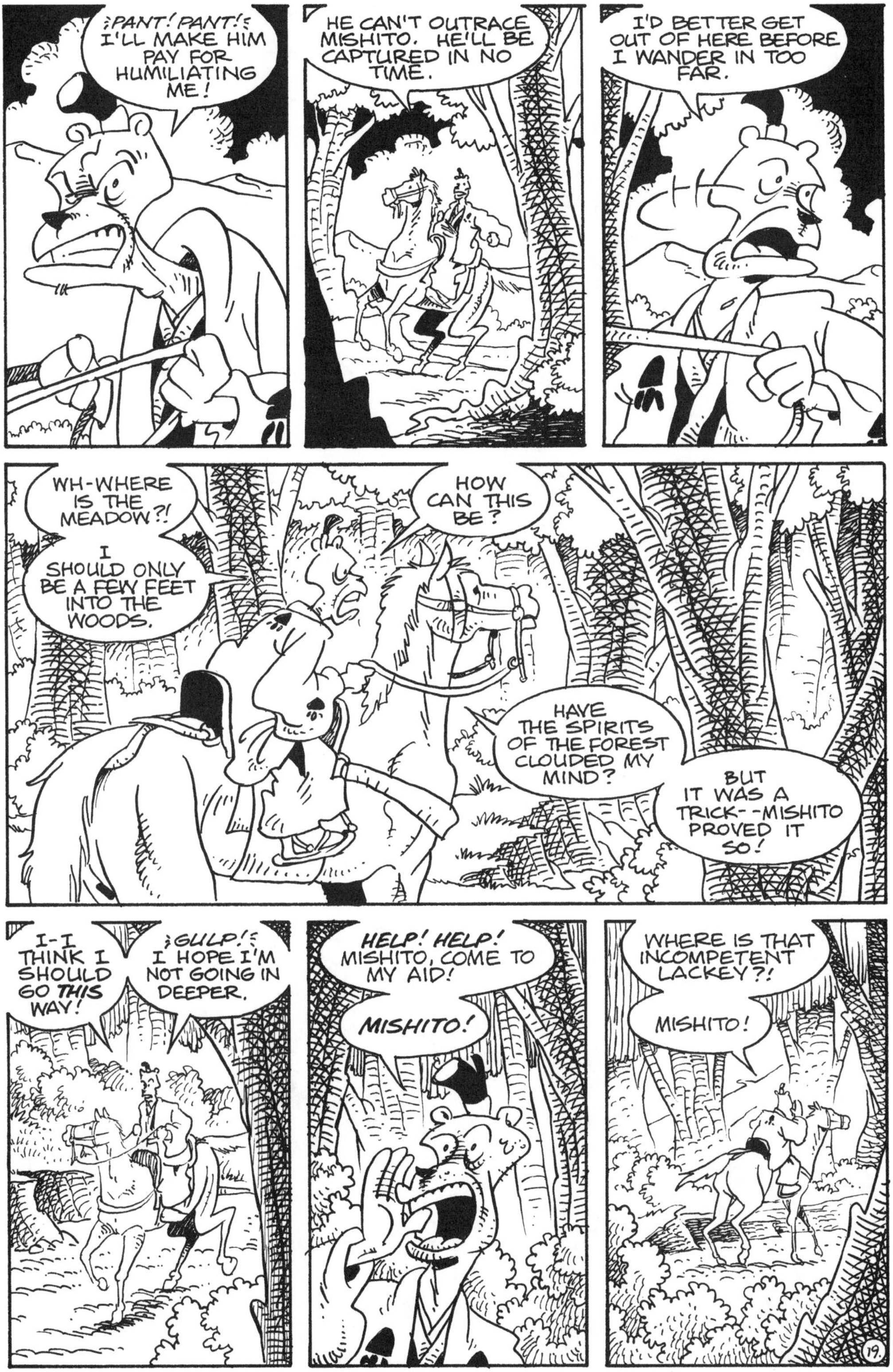

PANT! PANT! I'LL MAKE HIM PAY FOR HUMILIATING ME!
HE CAN'T OUTRACE MISHITO. HE'LL BE CAPTURED IN NO TIME.
I'D BETTER GET OUT OF HERE BEFORE I WANDER IN TOO FAR.
WH-WHERE IS THE MEADOW?!
I SHOULD ONLY BE A FEW FEET INTO THE WOODS.
HOW CAN THIS BE?
HAVE THE SPIRITS OF THE FOREST CLOUDED MY MIND?
BUT IT WAS A TRICK--MISHITO PROVED IT SO!
I-I THINK I SHOULD GO THIS WAY!
GULP! I HOPE I'M NOT GOING IN DEEPER.
HELP! HELP! MISHITO, COME TO MY AID!
MISHITO!
WHERE IS THAT INCOMPETENT LACKEY?!
MISHITO!
19.

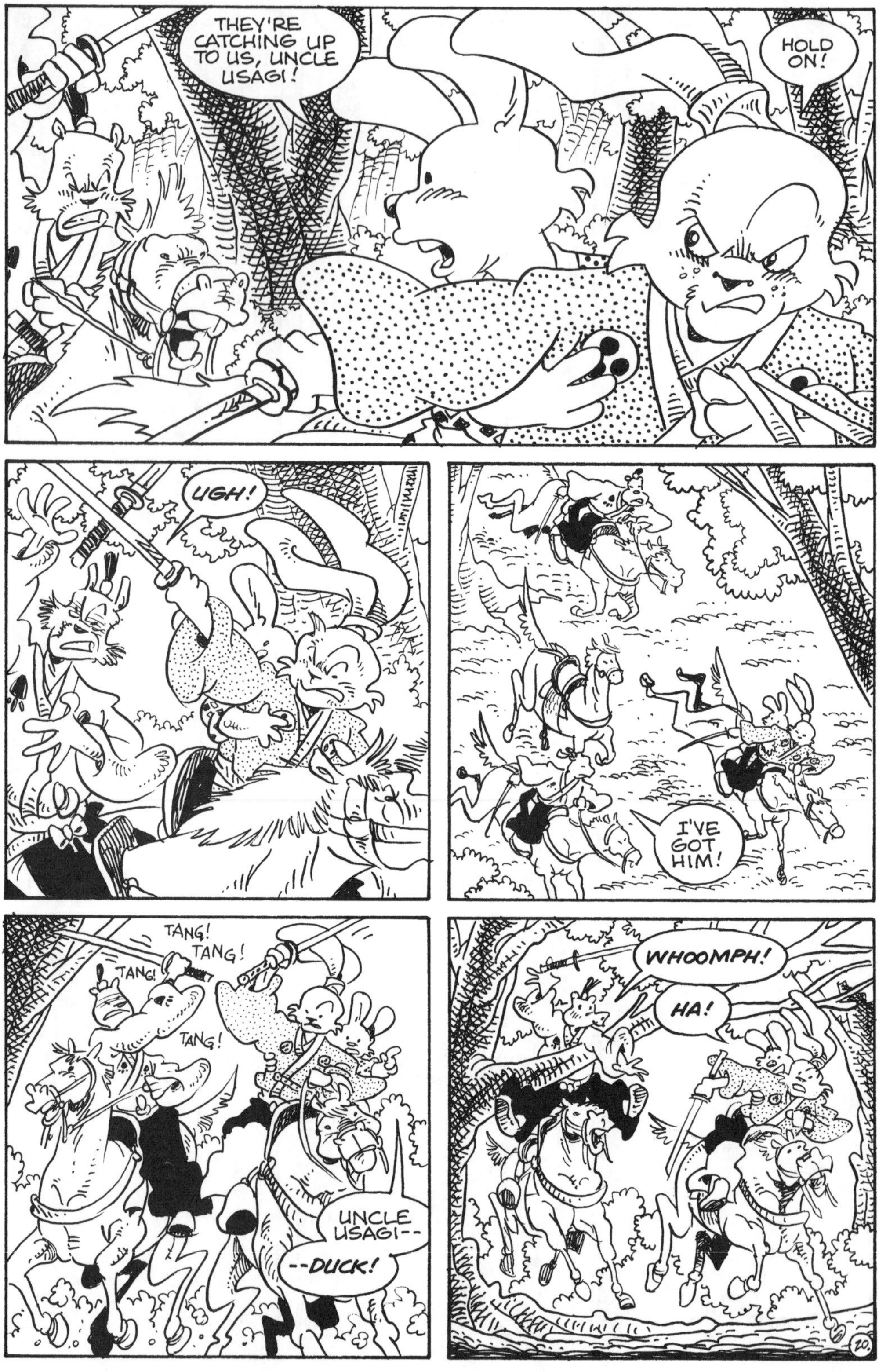
THEY'RE CATCHING UP TO US, UNCLE USAGI!
HOLD ON!
UGH!
I'VE GOT HIM!
TANG! TANG!
TANG!
TANG!
UNCLE USAGI--
--DUCK!
WHOOMPH!
HA!
20.

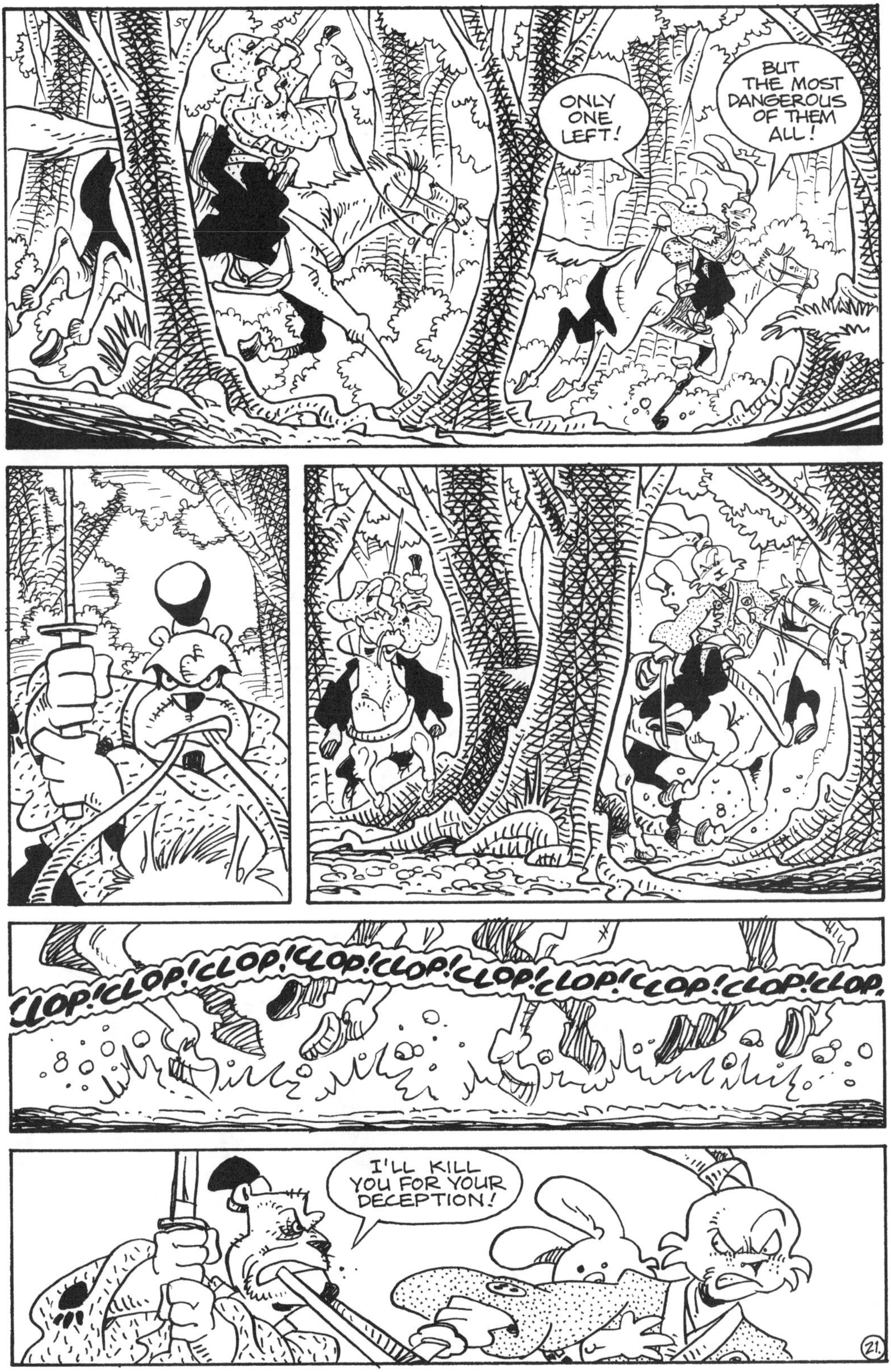
ONLY ONE LEFT!
BUT THE MOST DANGEROUS OF THEM ALL!
CLOP! CLOP! CLOP! CLOP! CLOP! CLOP! CLOP! CLOP! CLOP!
I'LL KILL YOU FOR YOUR DECEPTION!
21.

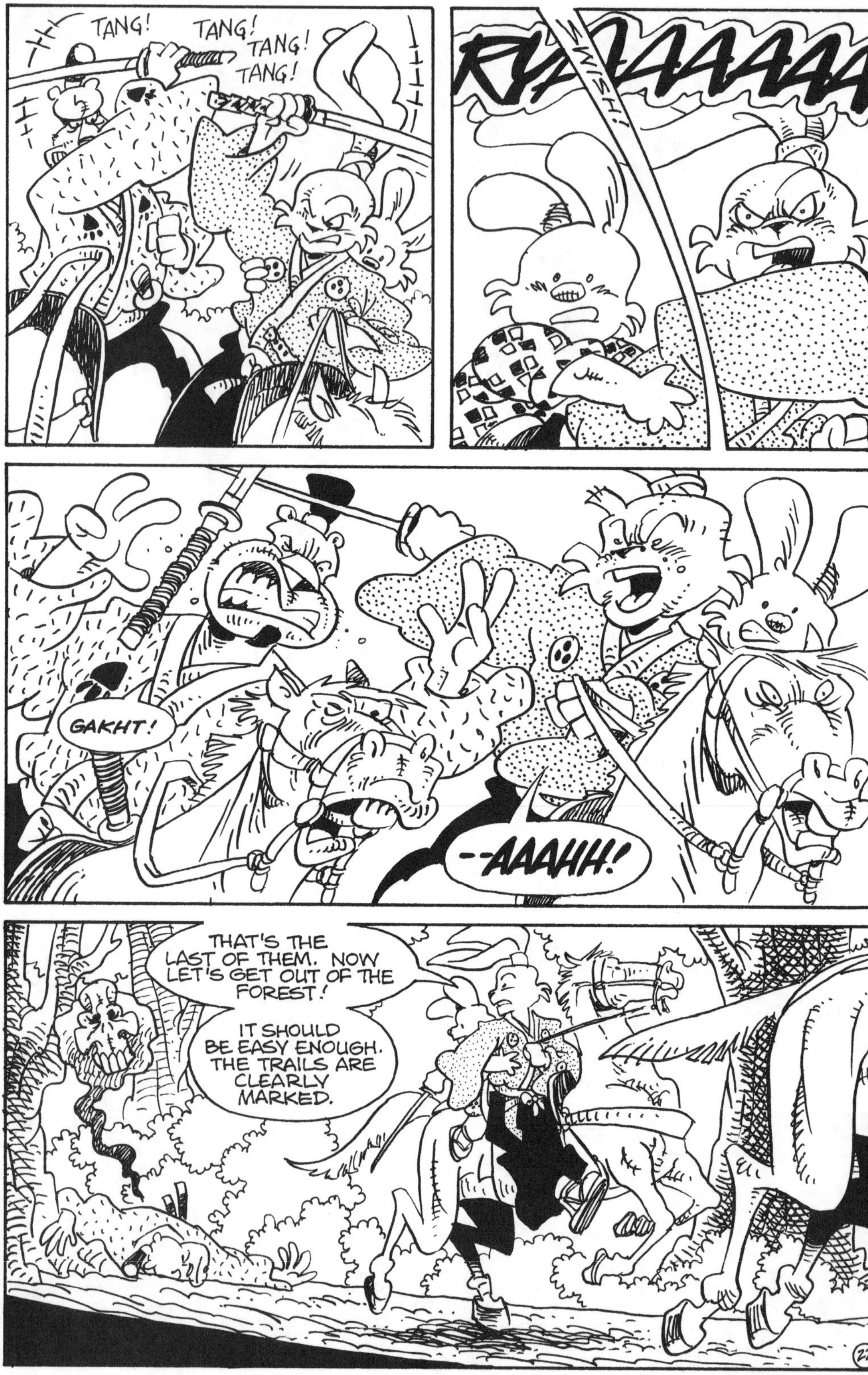
TANG!
TANG!
TANG!
TANG!
RYAAAAAAA
SWISH!
GAKHT!
--AAAHH!
THAT'S THE LAST OF THEM. NOW LET'S GET OUT OF THE FOREST!
IT SHOULD BE EASY ENOUGH. THE TRAILS ARE CLEARLY MARKED.
22

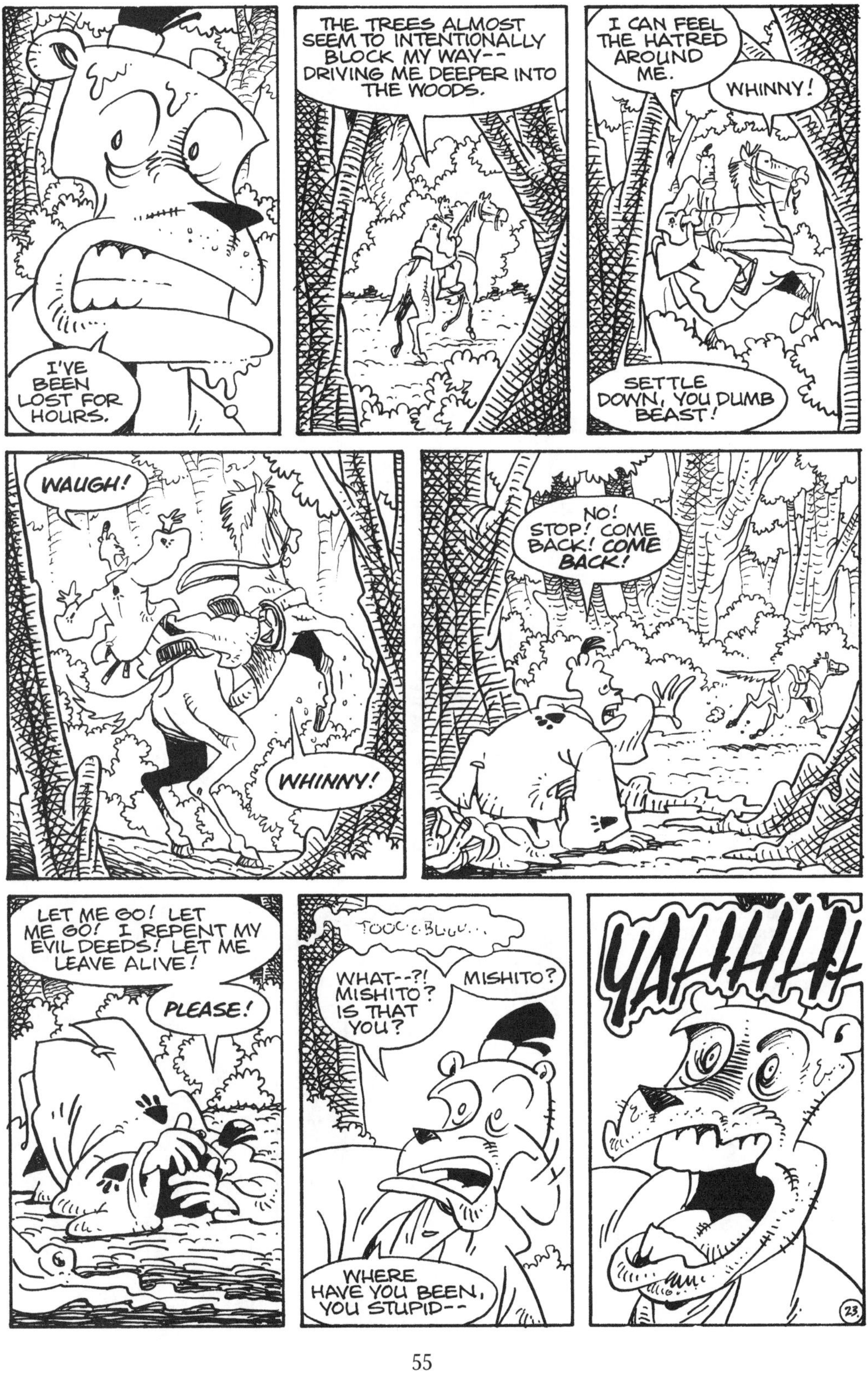
I'VE BEEN LOST FOR HOURS.
THE TREES ALMOST SEEM TO INTENTIONALLY BLOCK MY WAY-- DRIVING ME DEEPER INTO THE WOODS.
I CAN FEEL THE HATRED AROUND ME.
WHINNY!
SETTLE DOWN, YOU DUMB BEAST!
WAUGH!
WHINNY!
NO! STOP! COME BACK! COME BACK!
LET ME GO! LET ME GO! I REPENT MY EVIL DEEDS! LET ME LEAVE ALIVE!
PLEASE!
WHAT--?! MISHITO? IS THAT YOU?
MISHITO?
WHERE HAVE YOU BEEN, YOU STUPID--
YAHHHH
23.

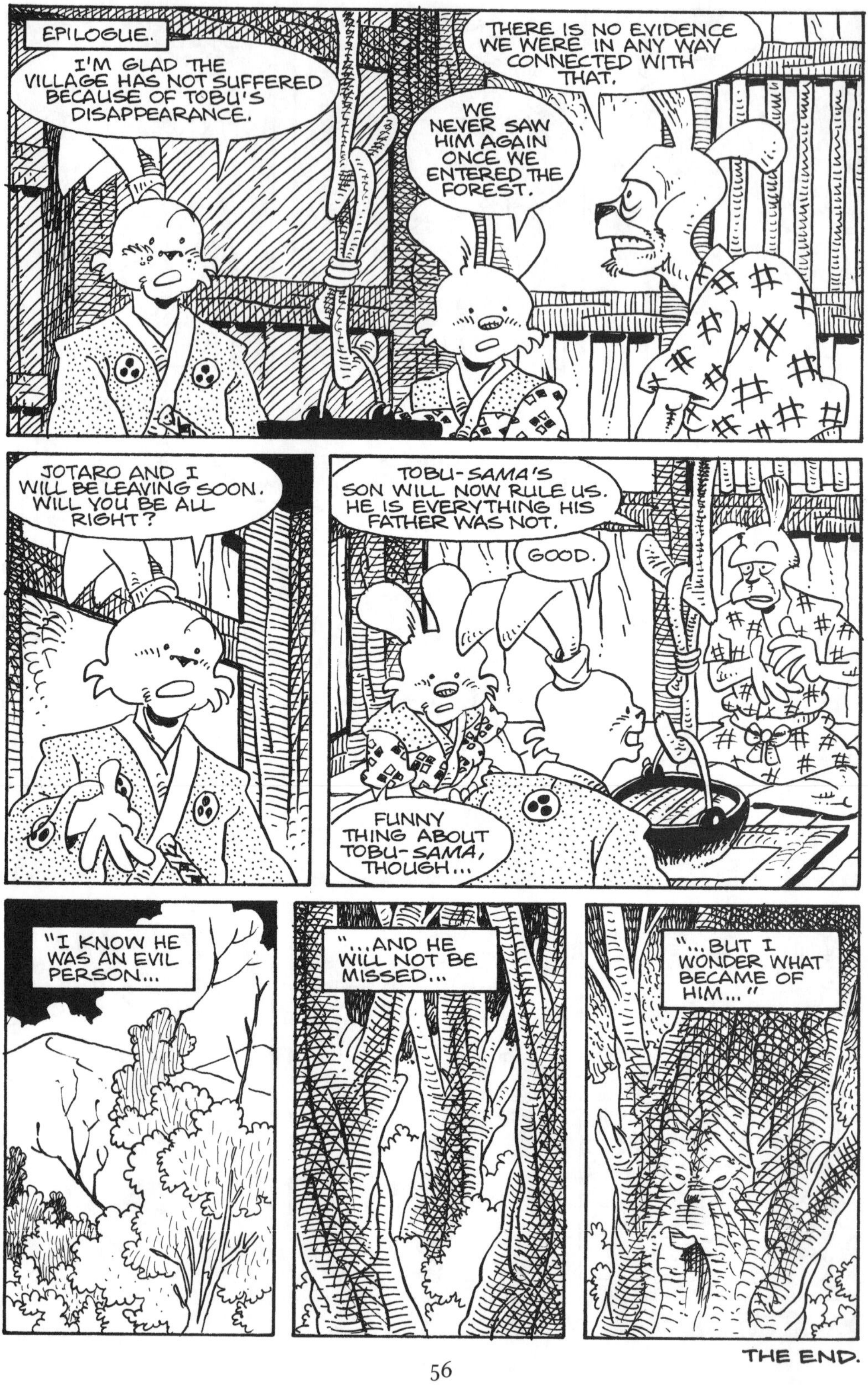
EPILOGUE.
I'M GLAD THE VILLAGE HAS NOT SUFFERED BECAUSE OF TOBU'S DISAPPEARANCE.
THERE IS NO EVIDENCE WE WERE IN ANY WAY CONNECTED WITH THAT.
WE NEVER SAW HIM AGAIN ONCE WE ENTERED THE FOREST.
JOTARO AND I WILL BE LEAVING SOON. WILL YOU BE ALL RIGHT?
TOBU-SAMA'S SON WILL NOW RULE US. HE IS EVERYTHING HIS FATHER WAS NOT.
GOOD.
FUNNY THING ABOUT TOBU-SAMA, THOUGH...
"I KNOW HE WAS AN EVIL PERSON...
"...AND HE WILL NOT BE MISSED...
"...BUT I WONDER WHAT BECAME OF HIM..."
THE END.

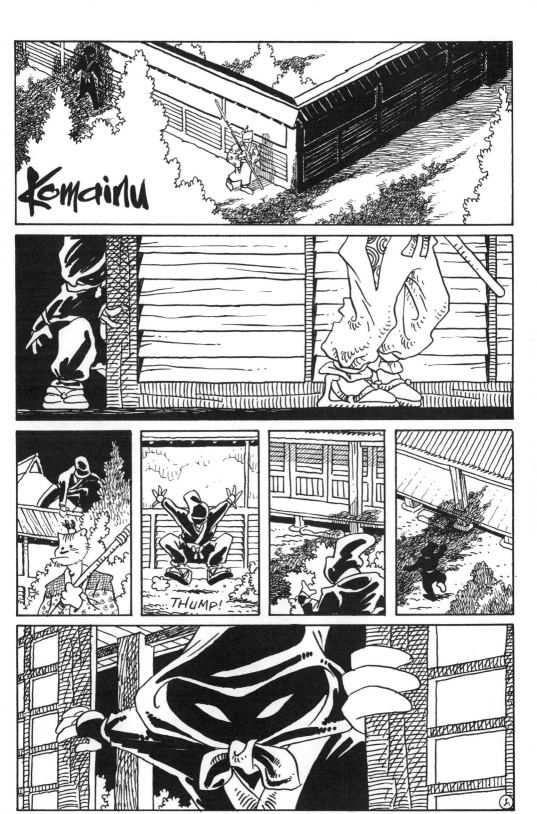

Komainu

THUMP!

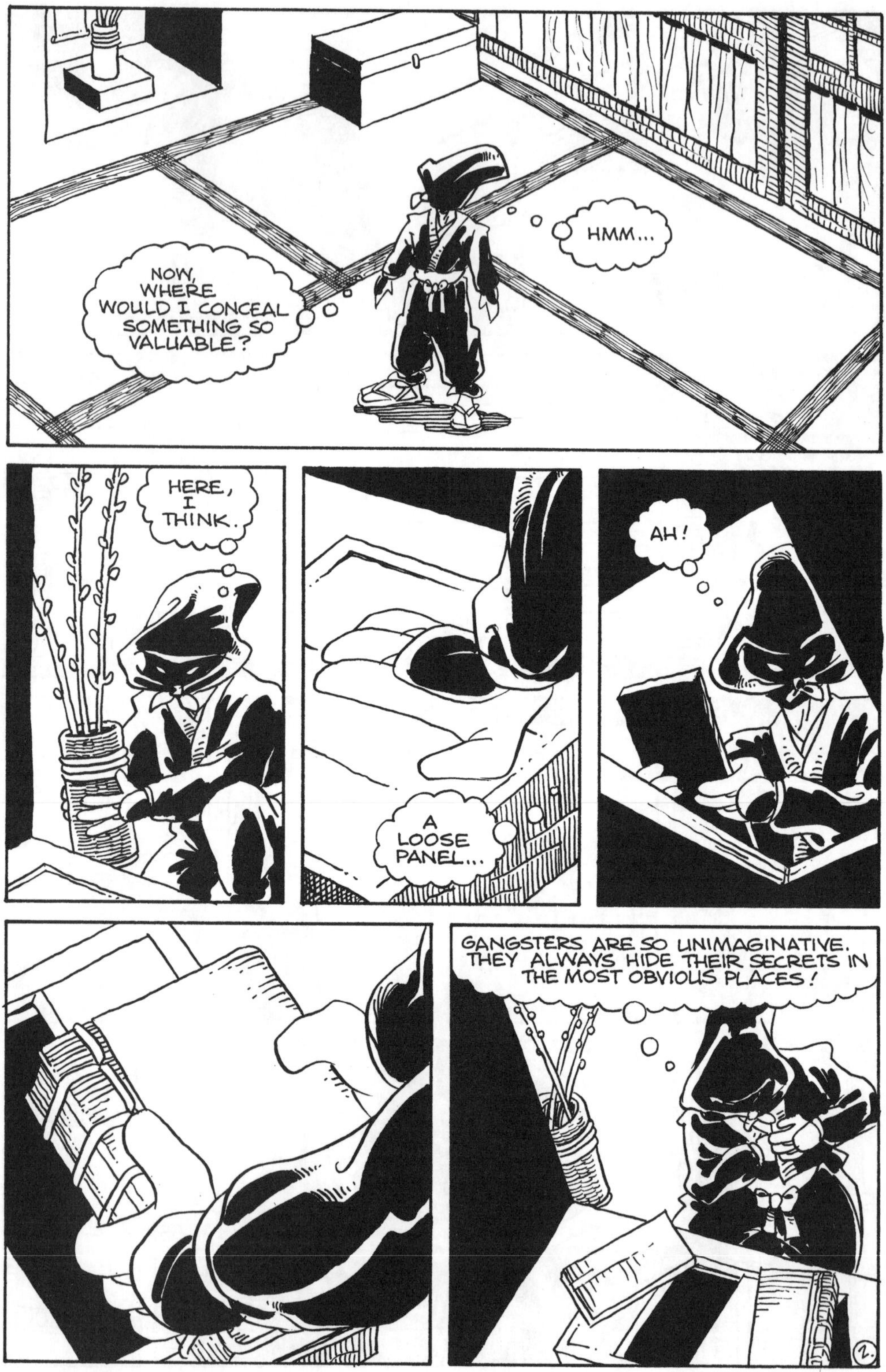
NOW, WHERE WOULD I CONCEAL SOMETHING SO VALUABLE?
HMM...
HERE, I THINK.
A LOOSE PANEL...
AH!
GANGSTERS ARE SO UNIMAGINATIVE. THEY ALWAYS HIDE THEIR SECRETS IN THE MOST OBVIOUS PLACES!
2.

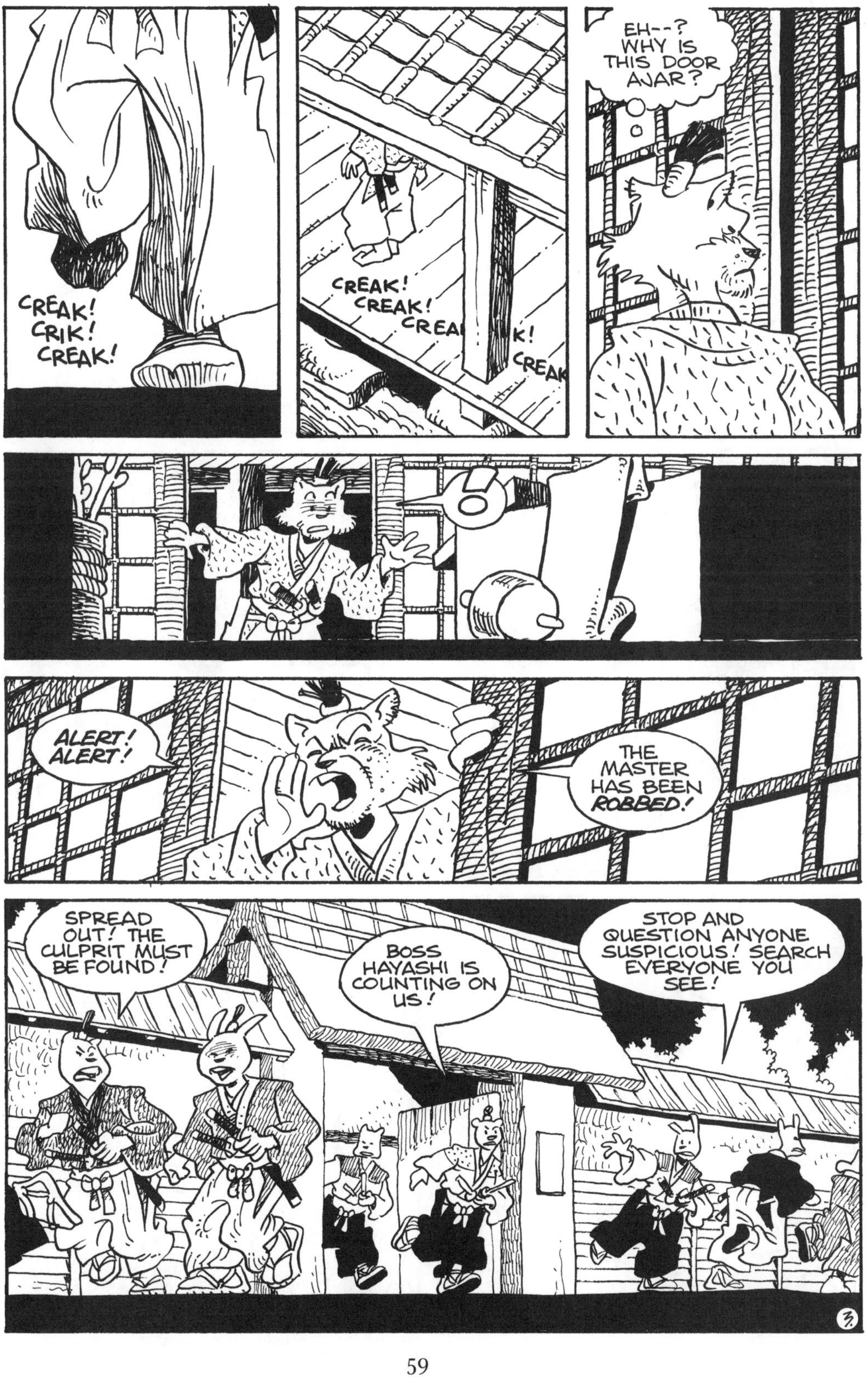
CREAK!
CRIK!
CREAK!
CREAK!
CREAK!
CREAK!
CREAK
EH--? WHY IS THIS DOOR AJAR?
!
ALERT! ALERT!
THE MASTER HAS BEEN *ROBBED*!
SPREAD OUT! THE CULPRIT MUST BE FOUND!
BOSS HAYASHI IS COUNTING ON US!
STOP AND QUESTION ANYONE SUSPICIOUS! SEARCH EVERYONE YOU SEE!
3.

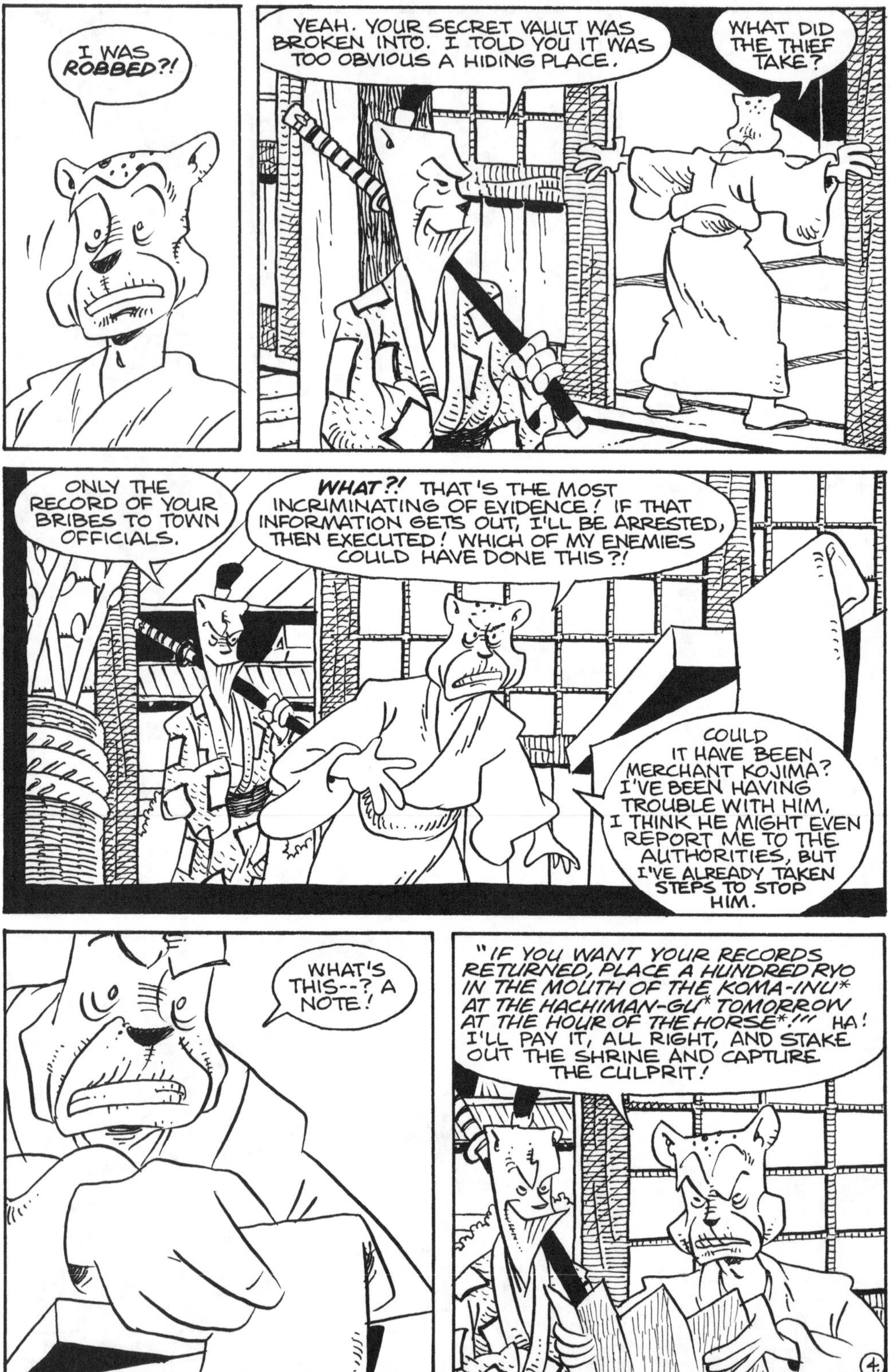
I WAS ROBBED?!
YEAH. YOUR SECRET VAULT WAS BROKEN INTO. I TOLD YOU IT WAS TOO OBVIOUS A HIDING PLACE.
WHAT DID THE THIEF TAKE?
ONLY THE RECORD OF YOUR BRIBES TO TOWN OFFICIALS.
WHAT?! THAT'S THE MOST INCRIMINATING OF EVIDENCE! IF THAT INFORMATION GETS OUT, I'LL BE ARRESTED, THEN EXECUTED! WHICH OF MY ENEMIES COULD HAVE DONE THIS?!
COULD IT HAVE BEEN MERCHANT KOJIMA? I'VE BEEN HAVING TROUBLE WITH HIM, I THINK HE MIGHT EVEN REPORT ME TO THE AUTHORITIES, BUT I'VE ALREADY TAKEN STEPS TO STOP HIM.
WHAT'S THIS--? A NOTE!
"IF YOU WANT YOUR RECORDS RETURNED, PLACE A HUNDRED RYO IN THE MOUTH OF THE KOMA-INU* AT THE HACHIMAN-GU* TOMORROW AT THE HOUR OF THE HORSE*!" HA! I'LL PAY IT, ALL RIGHT, AND STAKE OUT THE SHRINE AND CAPTURE THE CULPRIT!
4.

*STONE DOG *SHRINE TO THE WAR DEITY *11am-1pm

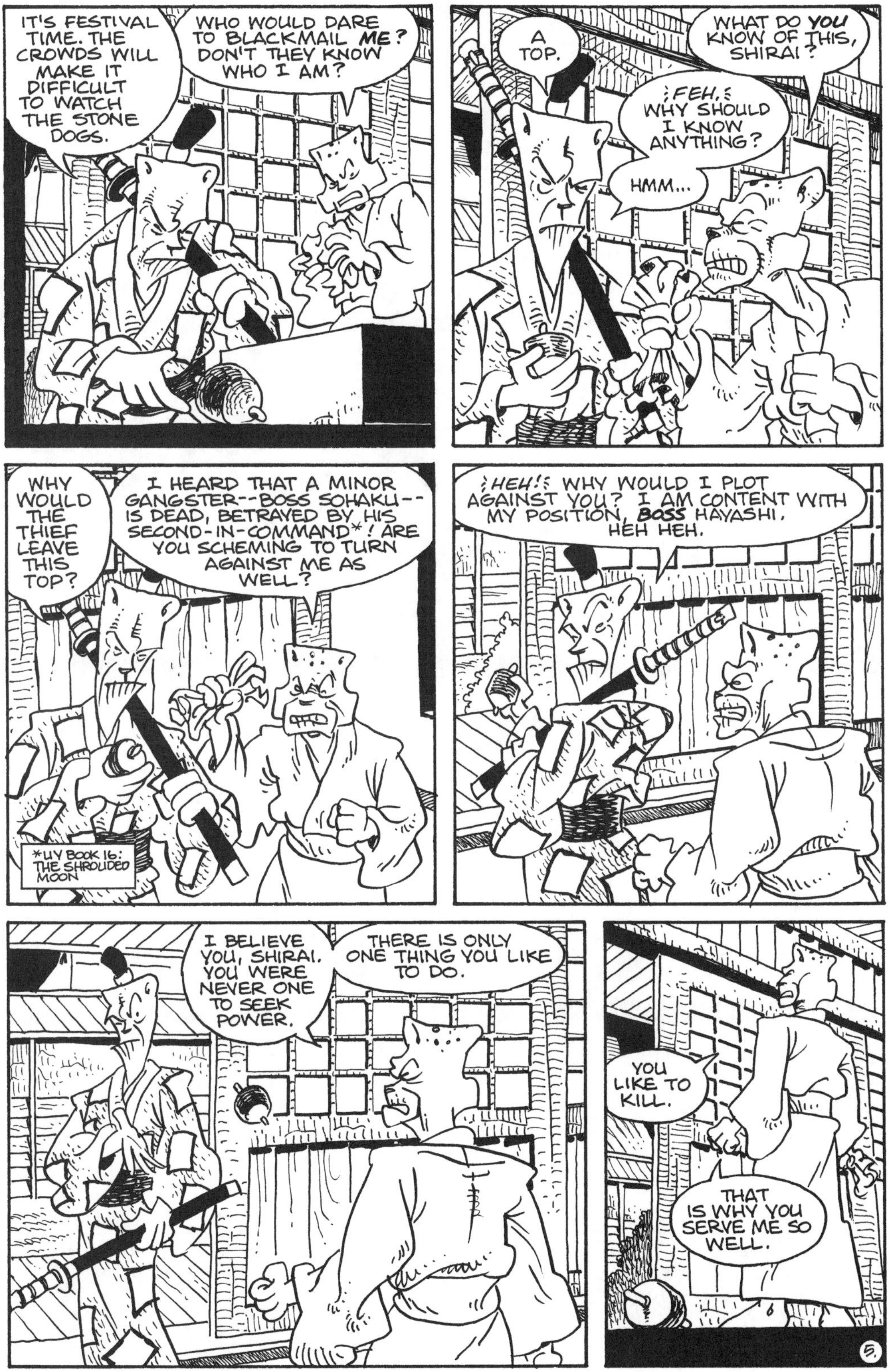
IT'S FESTIVAL TIME. THE CROWDS WILL MAKE IT DIFFICULT TO WATCH THE STONE DOGS.
WHO WOULD DARE TO BLACKMAIL ME? DON'T THEY KNOW WHO I AM?
A TOP.
WHAT DO YOU KNOW OF THIS, SHIRAI?
FEH. WHY SHOULD I KNOW ANYTHING?
HMM...
WHY WOULD THE THIEF LEAVE THIS TOP?
I HEARD THAT A MINOR GANGSTER--BOSS SOHAKU--IS DEAD, BETRAYED BY HIS SECOND-IN-COMMAND*! ARE YOU SCHEMING TO TURN AGAINST ME AS WELL?
*UY BOOK 16: THE SHROUDED MOON
HEH! WHY WOULD I PLOT AGAINST YOU? I AM CONTENT WITH MY POSITION, BOSS HAYASHI. HEH HEH.
I BELIEVE YOU, SHIRAI. YOU WERE NEVER ONE TO SEEK POWER.
THERE IS ONLY ONE THING YOU LIKE TO DO.
YOU LIKE TO KILL.
THAT IS WHY YOU SERVE ME SO WELL.
5.

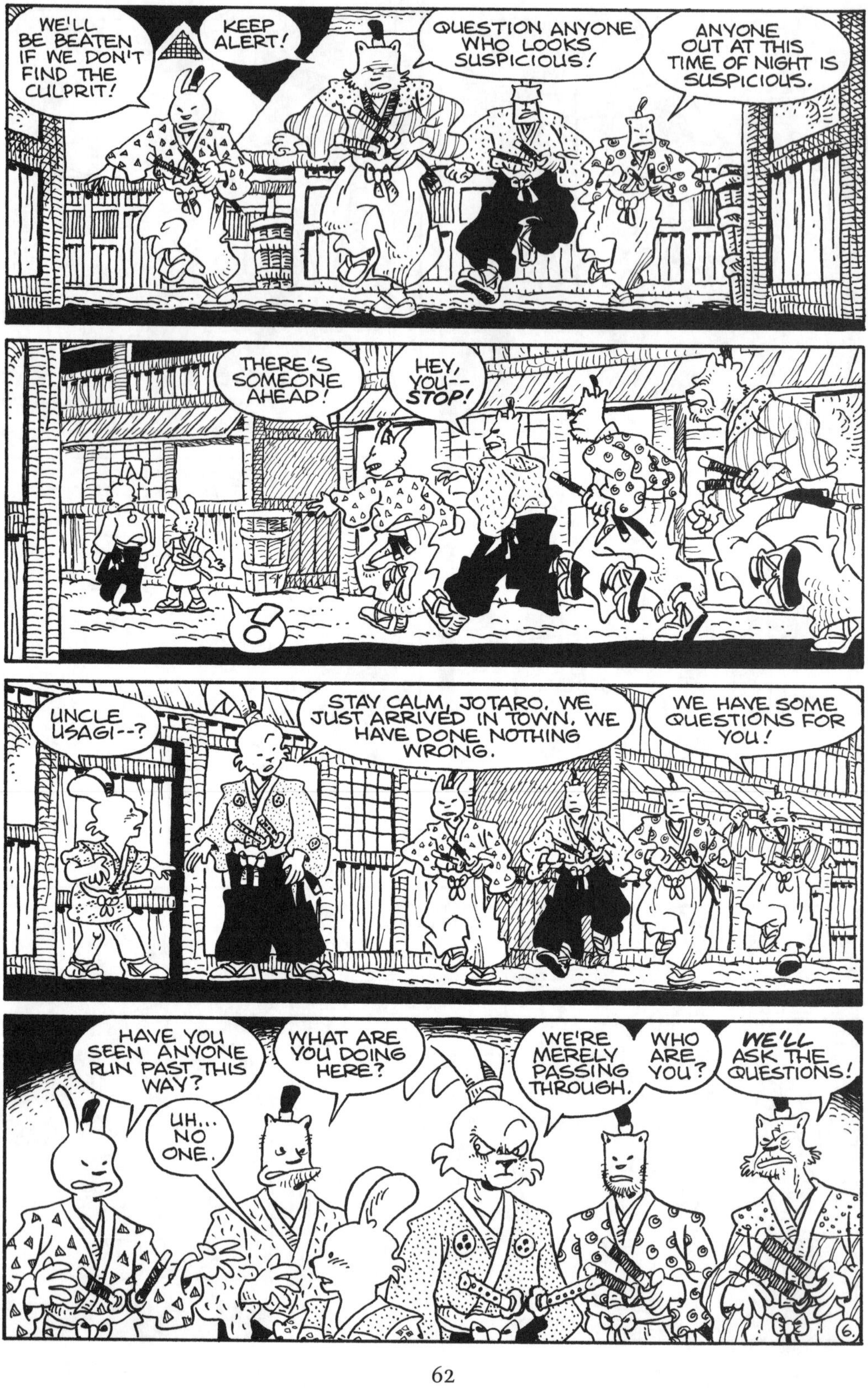
WE'LL BE BEATEN IF WE DON'T FIND THE CULPRIT!
KEEP ALERT!
QUESTION ANYONE WHO LOOKS SUSPICIOUS!
ANYONE OUT AT THIS TIME OF NIGHT IS SUSPICIOUS.
THERE'S SOMEONE AHEAD!
HEY, YOU-- STOP!
UNCLE USAGI--?
STAY CALM, JOTARO. WE JUST ARRIVED IN TOWN. WE HAVE DONE NOTHING WRONG.
WE HAVE SOME QUESTIONS FOR YOU!
HAVE YOU SEEN ANYONE RUN PAST THIS WAY?
UH... NO ONE.
WHAT ARE YOU DOING HERE?
WE'RE MERELY PASSING THROUGH.
WHO ARE YOU?
WE'LL ASK THE QUESTIONS!
6.

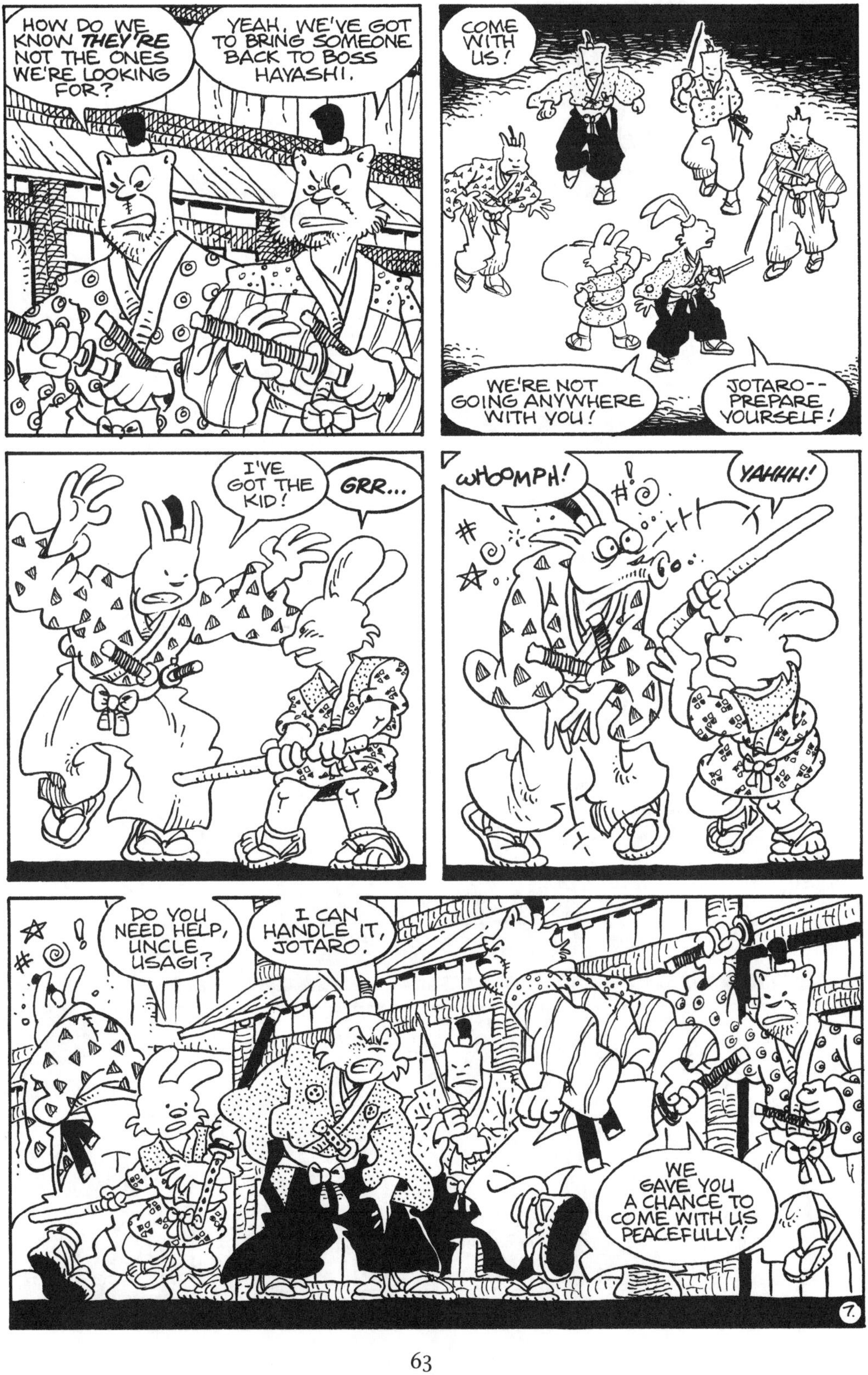
HOW DO WE KNOW THEY'RE NOT THE ONES WE'RE LOOKING FOR?
YEAH, WE'VE GOT TO BRING SOMEONE BACK TO BOSS HAYASHI.
COME WITH US!
WE'RE NOT GOING ANYWHERE WITH YOU!
JOTARO-- PREPARE YOURSELF!
I'VE GOT THE KID!
GRR...
WHOOMPH!
YAHHH!
DO YOU NEED HELP, UNCLE USAGI?
I CAN HANDLE IT, JOTARO.
WE GAVE YOU A CHANCE TO COME WITH US PEACEFULLY!
7.

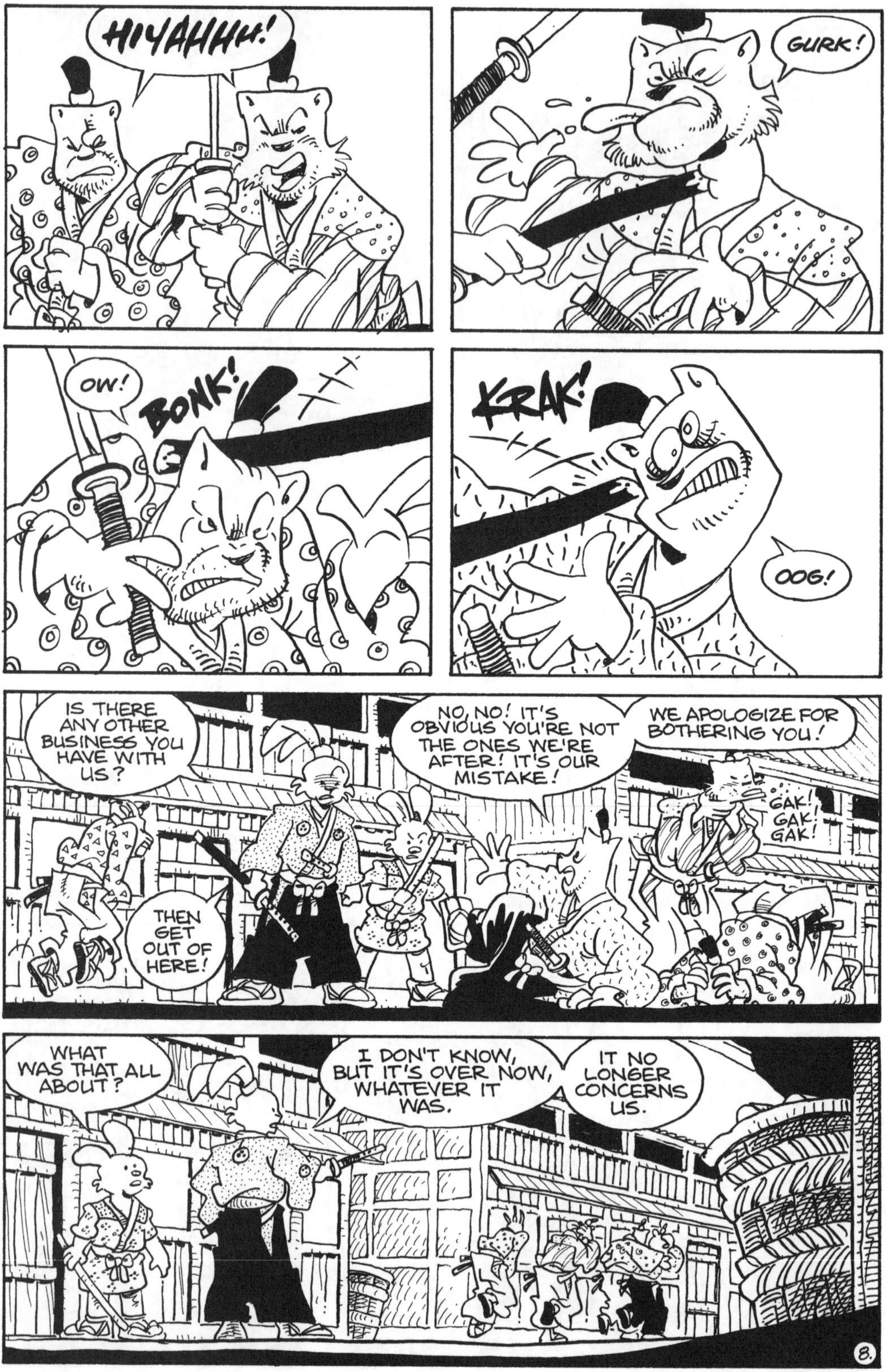
HIYAHHH!
GURK!
OW!
BONK!
KRAK!
OOG!
IS THERE ANY OTHER BUSINESS YOU HAVE WITH US?
NO, NO! IT'S OBVIOUS YOU'RE NOT THE ONES WE'RE AFTER! IT'S OUR MISTAKE!
WE APOLOGIZE FOR BOTHERING YOU!
GAK! GAK! GAK!
THEN GET OUT OF HERE!
WHAT WAS THAT ALL ABOUT?
I DON'T KNOW, BUT IT'S OVER NOW, WHATEVER IT WAS.
IT NO LONGER CONCERNS US.
8.

"...BUT SUSANO-O* WAS UNSTEADY AFTER DRINKING THAT LARGE YAT OF *SAKE**. HE STAGGERED ACROSS THE FIRST BRIDGE..."

WOBBLE!

WOBBLE!

* DEITY of STORMS
* RICE WINE

FLIP!

"...THEN HE CAME TO A SECOND BRIDGE..."

"...AND BARELY MADE IT ACROSS, AS IT WAS AS THIN AS A TIGHTROPE..."

TOK!

FLUP!

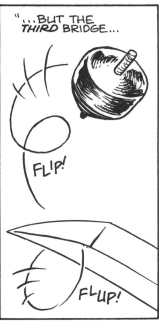

"...BUT THE *THIRD* BRIDGE..."

FLIP!

FLUP!

"...WAS TOO NARROW EVEN FOR HIM!'"

CHOP!

HA HA HA HA HA HA HA HA HA HA HA HA HA HA HA HA HA HA HA HA HA HA

9.

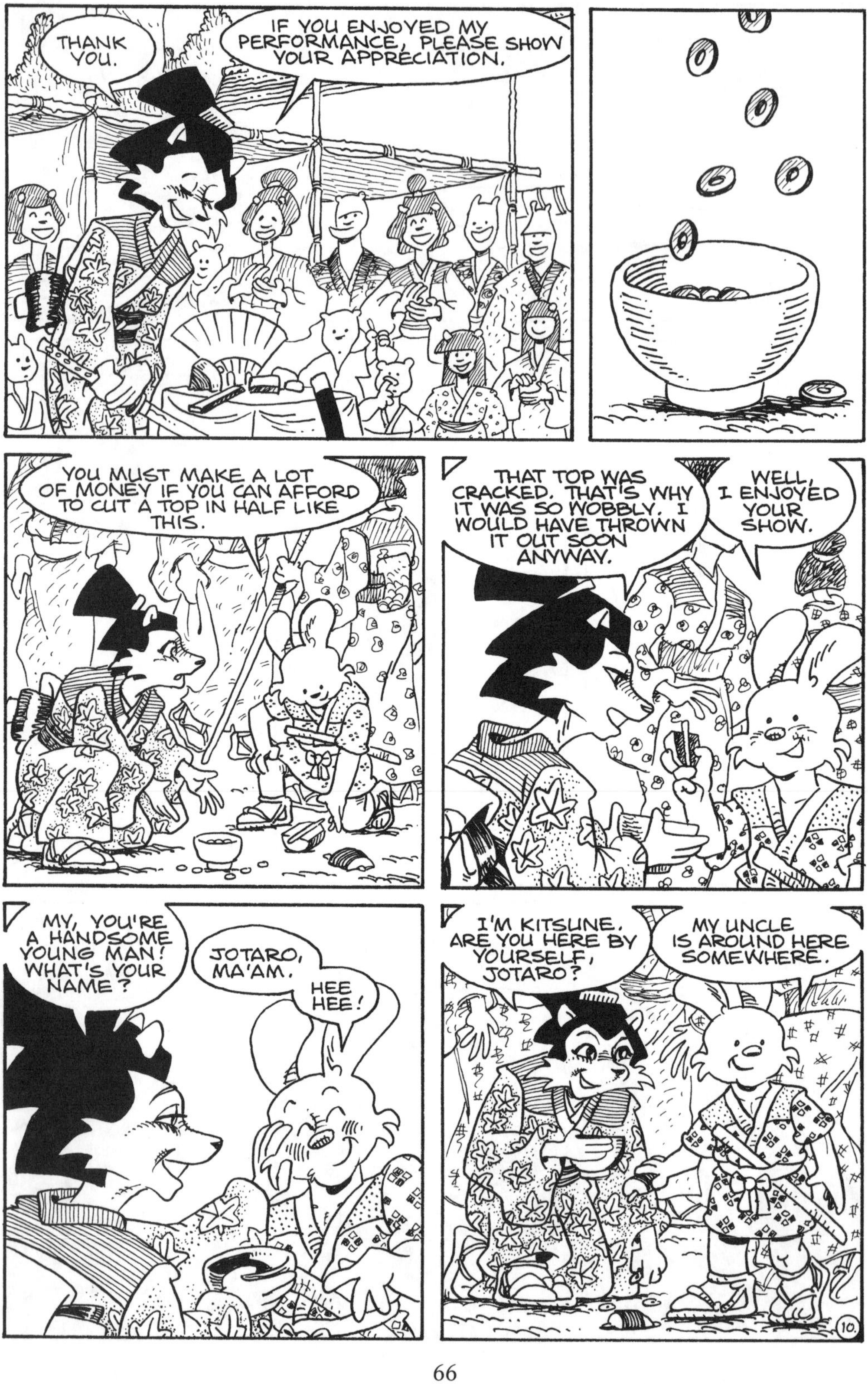
THANK YOU.
IF YOU ENJOYED MY PERFORMANCE, PLEASE SHOW YOUR APPRECIATION.
YOU MUST MAKE A LOT OF MONEY IF YOU CAN AFFORD TO CUT A TOP IN HALF LIKE THIS.
THAT TOP WAS CRACKED. THAT'S WHY IT WAS SO WOBBLY. I WOULD HAVE THROWN IT OUT SOON ANYWAY.
WELL, I ENJOYED YOUR SHOW.
MY, YOU'RE A HANDSOME YOUNG MAN! WHAT'S YOUR NAME?
JOTARO, MA'AM.
HEE HEE!
I'M KITSUNE. ARE YOU HERE BY YOURSELF, JOTARO?
MY UNCLE IS AROUND HERE SOMEWHERE.
10.

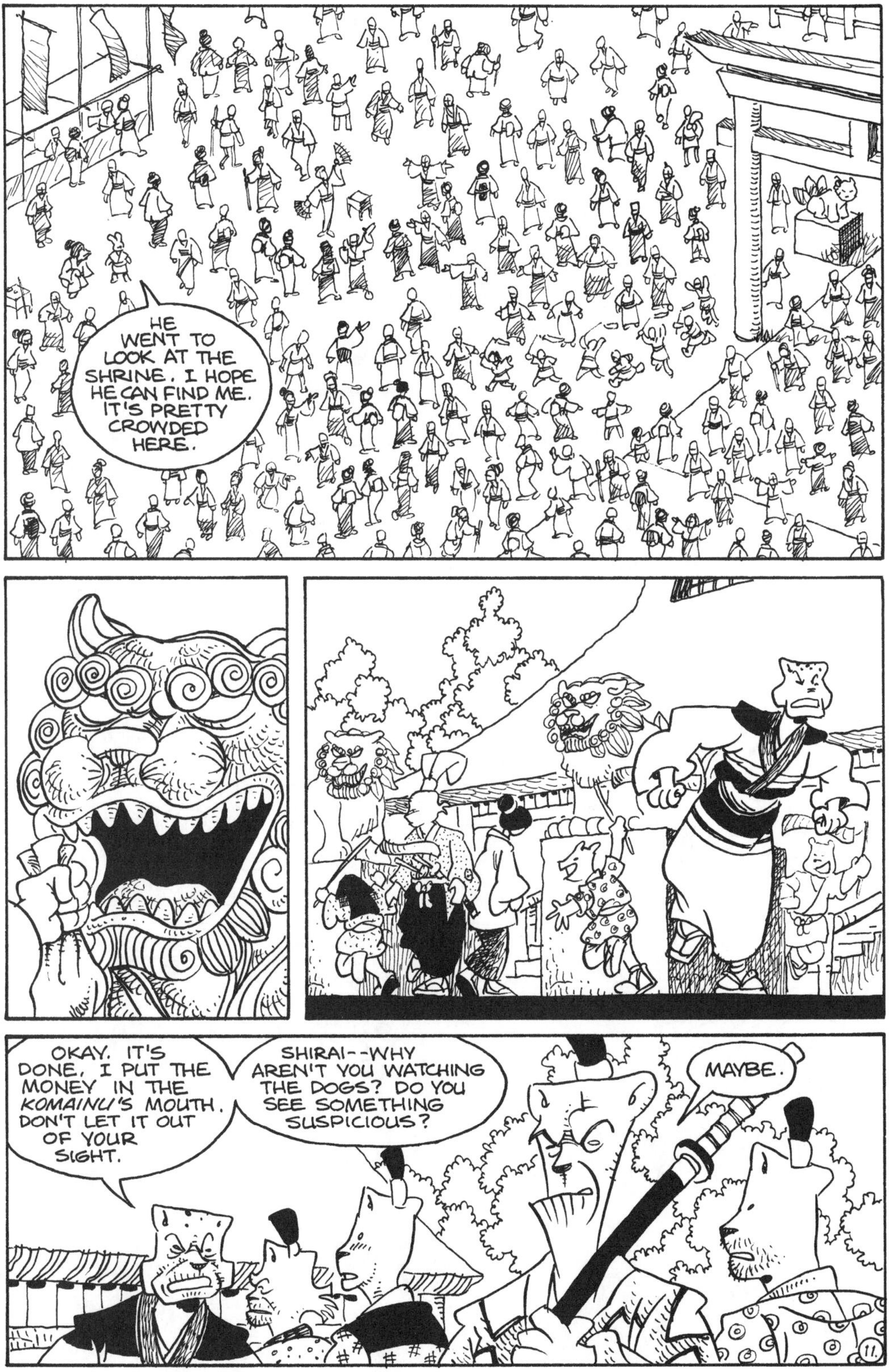
HE WENT TO LOOK AT THE SHRINE. I HOPE HE CAN FIND ME. IT'S PRETTY CROWDED HERE.
OKAY. IT'S DONE. I PUT THE MONEY IN THE *KOMAINU*'S MOUTH. DON'T LET IT OUT OF YOUR SIGHT.
SHIRAI--WHY AREN'T YOU WATCHING THE DOGS? DO YOU SEE SOMETHING SUSPICIOUS?
MAYBE.
11.

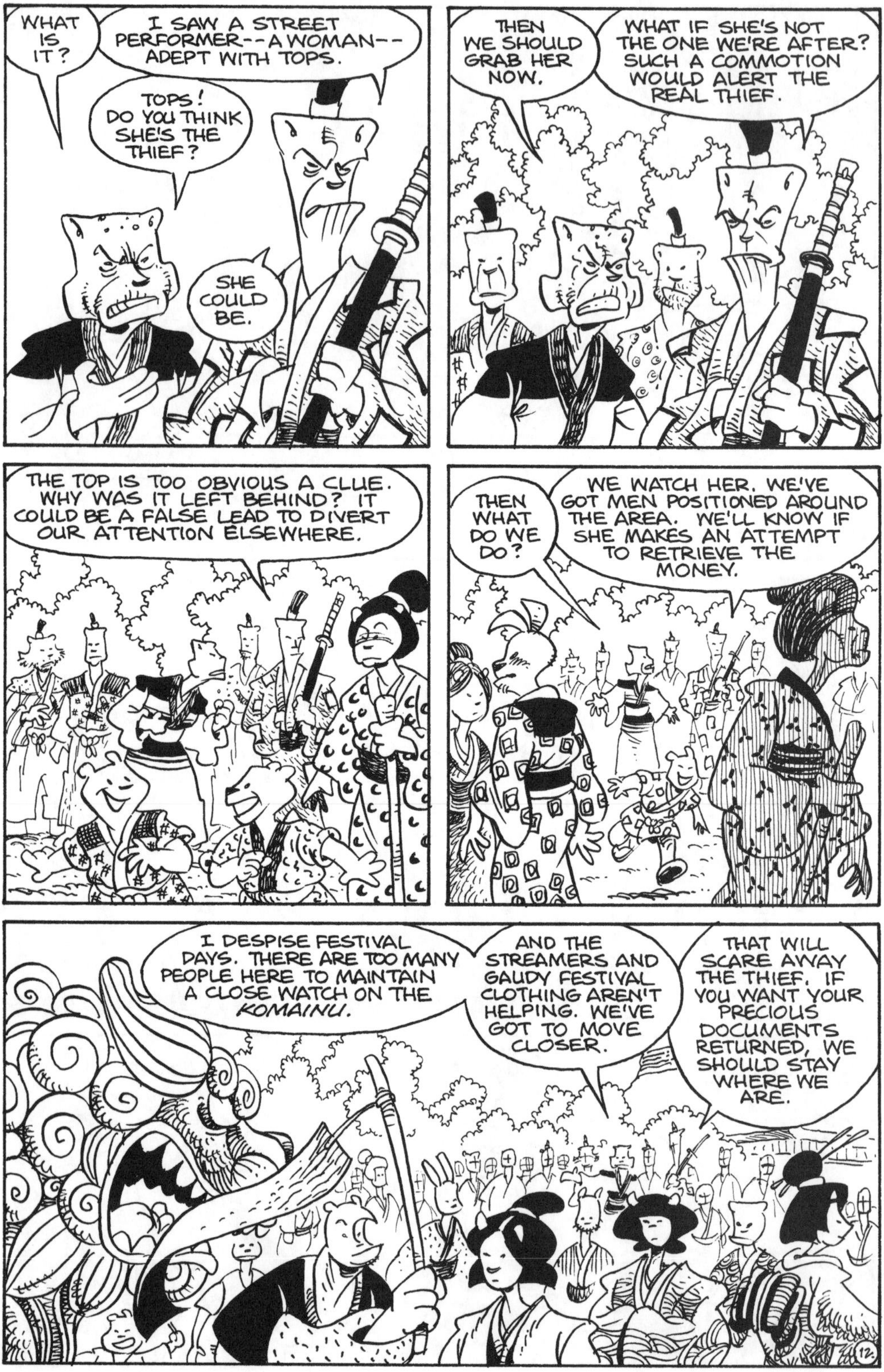
WHAT IS IT?
I SAW A STREET PERFORMER--A WOMAN--ADEPT WITH TOPS.
TOPS! DO YOU THINK SHE'S THE THIEF?
SHE COULD BE.
THEN WE SHOULD GRAB HER NOW.
WHAT IF SHE'S NOT THE ONE WE'RE AFTER? SUCH A COMMOTION WOULD ALERT THE REAL THIEF.
THE TOP IS TOO OBVIOUS A CLUE. WHY WAS IT LEFT BEHIND? IT COULD BE A FALSE LEAD TO DIVERT OUR ATTENTION ELSEWHERE.
THEN WHAT DO WE DO?
WE WATCH HER. WE'VE GOT MEN POSITIONED AROUND THE AREA. WE'LL KNOW IF SHE MAKES AN ATTEMPT TO RETRIEVE THE MONEY.
I DESPISE FESTIVAL DAYS. THERE ARE TOO MANY PEOPLE HERE TO MAINTAIN A CLOSE WATCH ON THE *KOMAINU*.
AND THE STREAMERS AND GAUDY FESTIVAL CLOTHING AREN'T HELPING. WE'VE GOT TO MOVE CLOSER.
THAT WILL SCARE AWAY THE THIEF. IF YOU WANT YOUR PRECIOUS DOCUMENTS RETURNED, WE SHOULD STAY WHERE WE ARE.
12.

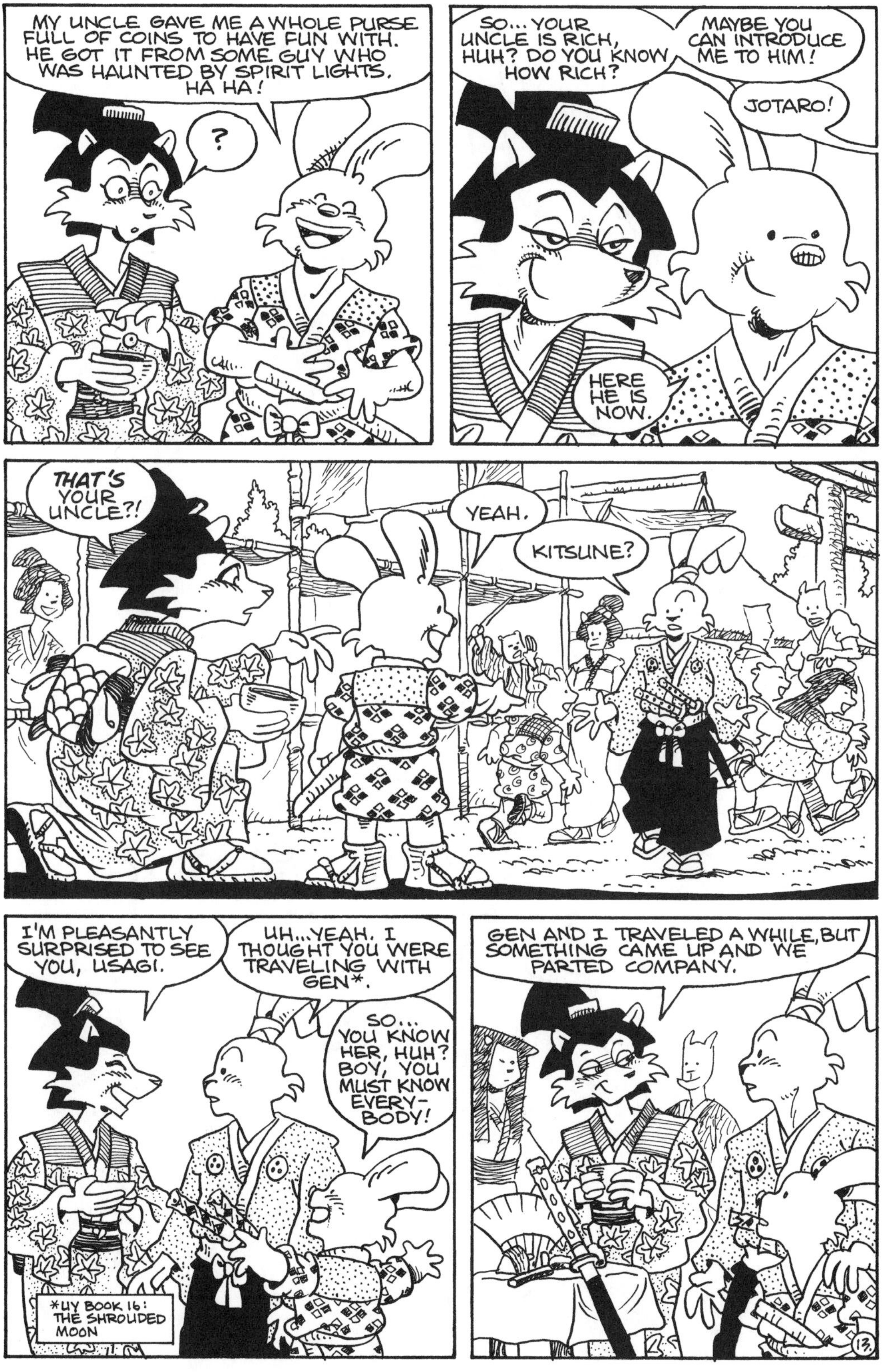
MY UNCLE GAVE ME A WHOLE PURSE FULL OF COINS TO HAVE FUN WITH. HE GOT IT FROM SOME GUY WHO WAS HAUNTED BY SPIRIT LIGHTS. HA HA!
?
SO... YOUR UNCLE IS RICH, HUH? DO YOU KNOW HOW RICH?
MAYBE YOU CAN INTRODUCE ME TO HIM!
JOTARO!
HERE HE IS NOW.
THAT'S YOUR UNCLE?!
YEAH.
KITSUNE?
I'M PLEASANTLY SURPRISED TO SEE YOU, USAGI.
UH...YEAH. I THOUGHT YOU WERE TRAVELING WITH GEN*.
SO... YOU KNOW HER, HUH? BOY, YOU MUST KNOW EVERY-BODY!
*UY BOOK 16: THE SHROUDED MOON
GEN AND I TRAVELED A WHILE, BUT SOMETHING CAME UP AND WE PARTED COMPANY.
13.

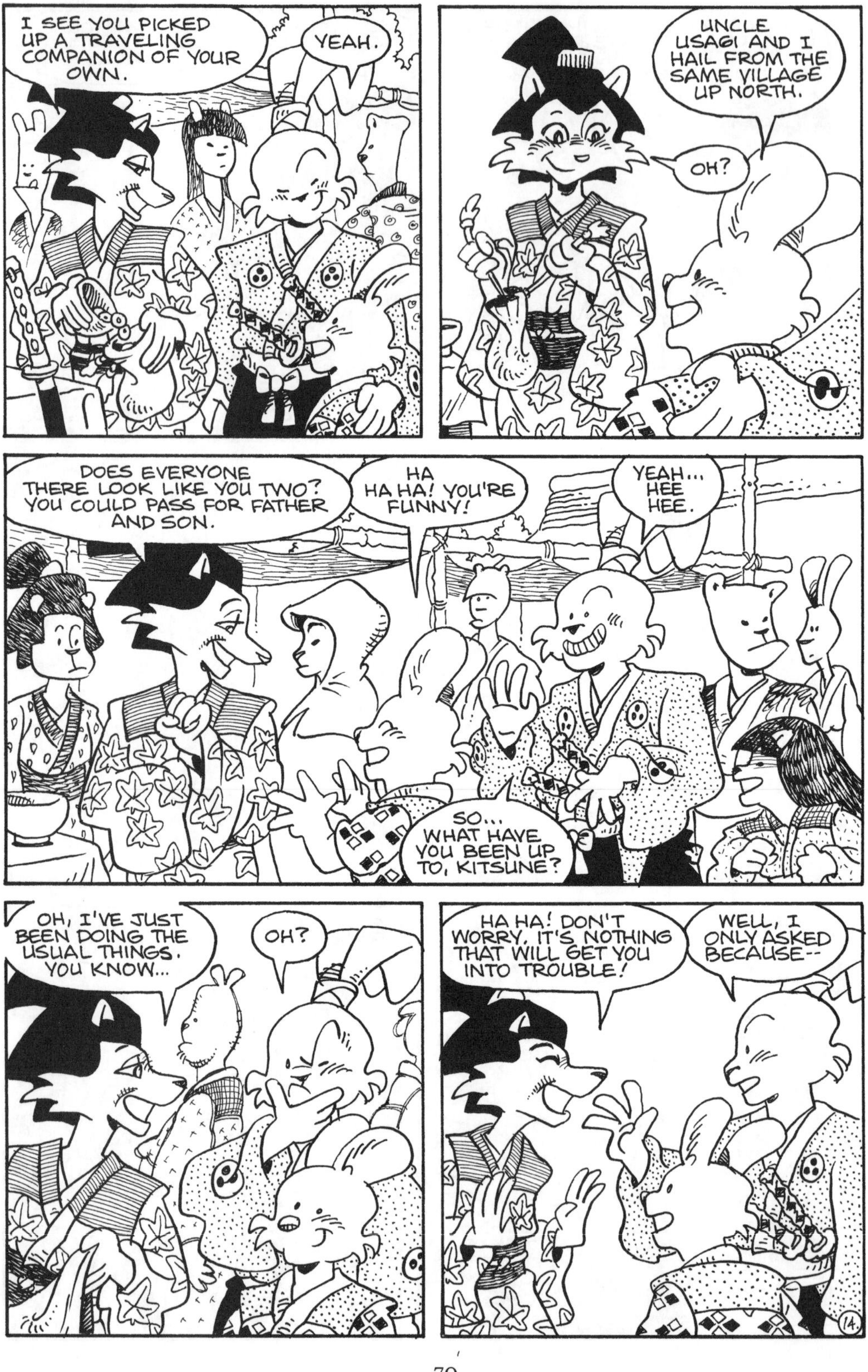
I SEE YOU PICKED UP A TRAVELING COMPANION OF YOUR OWN.
YEAH.
UNCLE USAGI AND I HAIL FROM THE SAME VILLAGE UP NORTH.
OH?
DOES EVERYONE THERE LOOK LIKE YOU TWO? YOU COULD PASS FOR FATHER AND SON.
HA HA HA! YOU'RE FUNNY!
YEAH... HEE HEE.
SO... WHAT HAVE YOU BEEN UP TO, KITSUNE?
OH, I'VE JUST BEEN DOING THE USUAL THINGS. YOU KNOW...
OH?
HA HA! DON'T WORRY. IT'S NOTHING THAT WILL GET YOU INTO TROUBLE!
WELL, I ONLY ASKED BECAUSE--
14.

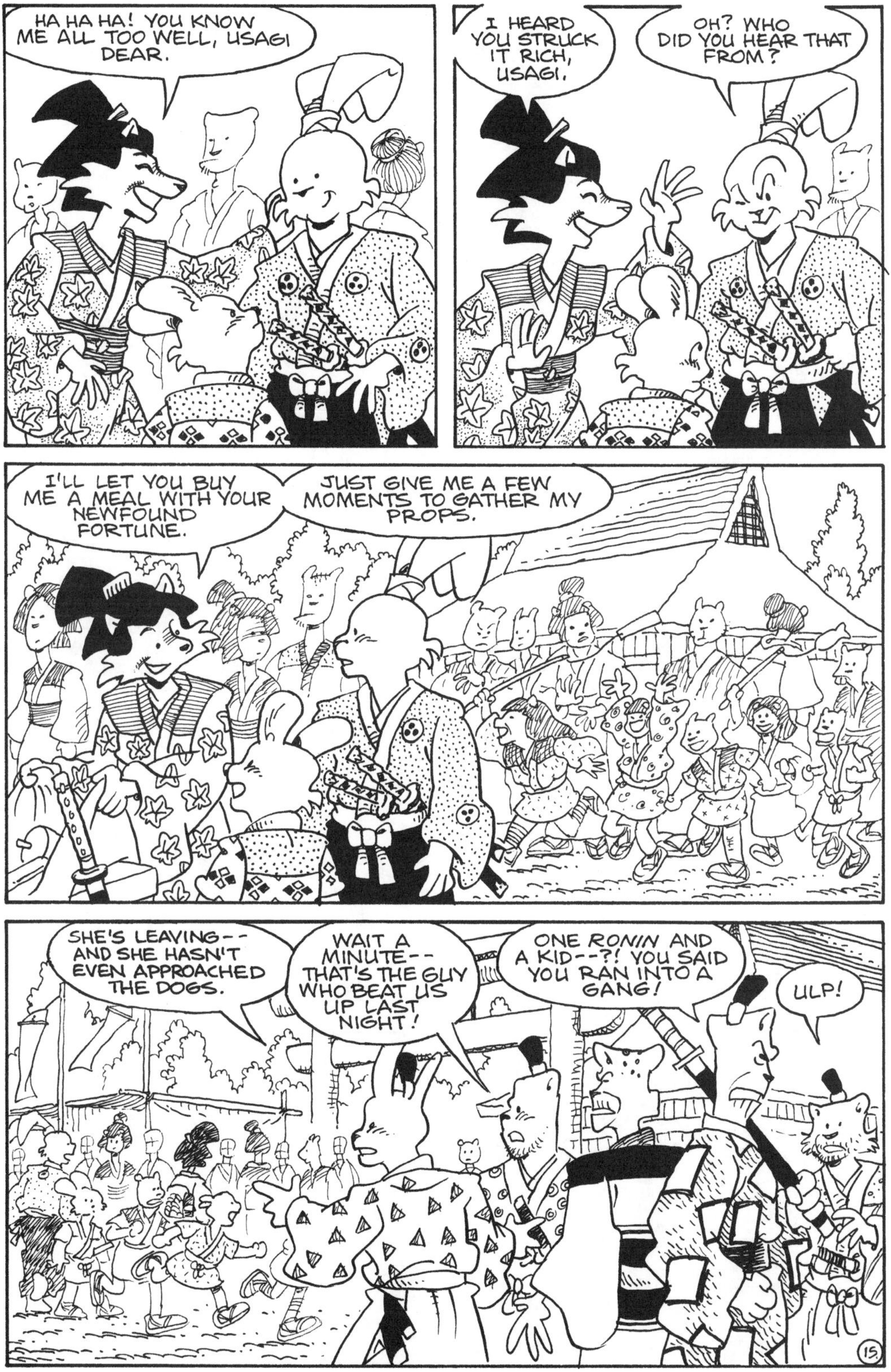
HA HA HA! YOU KNOW ME ALL TOO WELL, USAGI DEAR.
I HEARD YOU STRUCK IT RICH, USAGI.
OH? WHO DID YOU HEAR THAT FROM?
I'LL LET YOU BUY ME A MEAL WITH YOUR NEWFOUND FORTUNE.
JUST GIVE ME A FEW MOMENTS TO GATHER MY PROPS.
SHE'S LEAVING-- AND SHE HASN'T EVEN APPROACHED THE DOGS.
WAIT A MINUTE-- THAT'S THE GUY WHO BEAT US UP LAST NIGHT!
ONE *RONIN* AND A KID--?! YOU SAID YOU RAN INTO A GANG!
ULP!
15

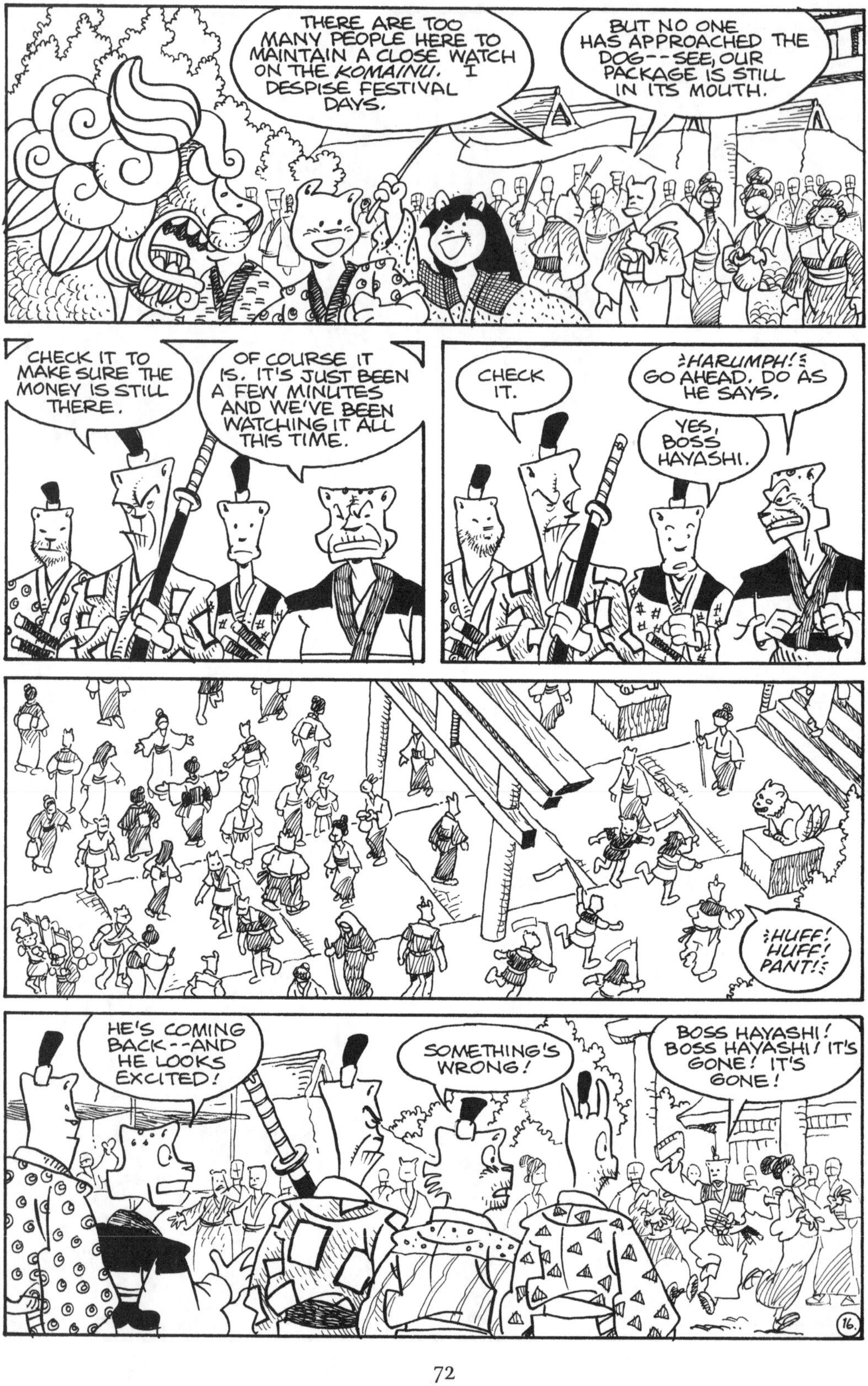
THERE ARE TOO MANY PEOPLE HERE TO MAINTAIN A CLOSE WATCH ON THE *KOMAINU*. I DESPISE FESTIVAL DAYS.
BUT NO ONE HAS APPROACHED THE DOG--SEE, OUR PACKAGE IS STILL IN ITS MOUTH.
CHECK IT TO MAKE SURE THE MONEY IS STILL THERE.
OF COURSE IT IS. IT'S JUST BEEN A FEW MINUTES AND WE'VE BEEN WATCHING IT ALL THIS TIME.
CHECK IT.
HARUMPH! GO AHEAD. DO AS HE SAYS.
YES, BOSS HAYASHI.
HUFF! HUFF! PANT!
HE'S COMING BACK--AND HE LOOKS EXCITED!
SOMETHING'S WRONG!
BOSS HAYASHI! BOSS HAYASHI! IT'S GONE! IT'S GONE!
16.

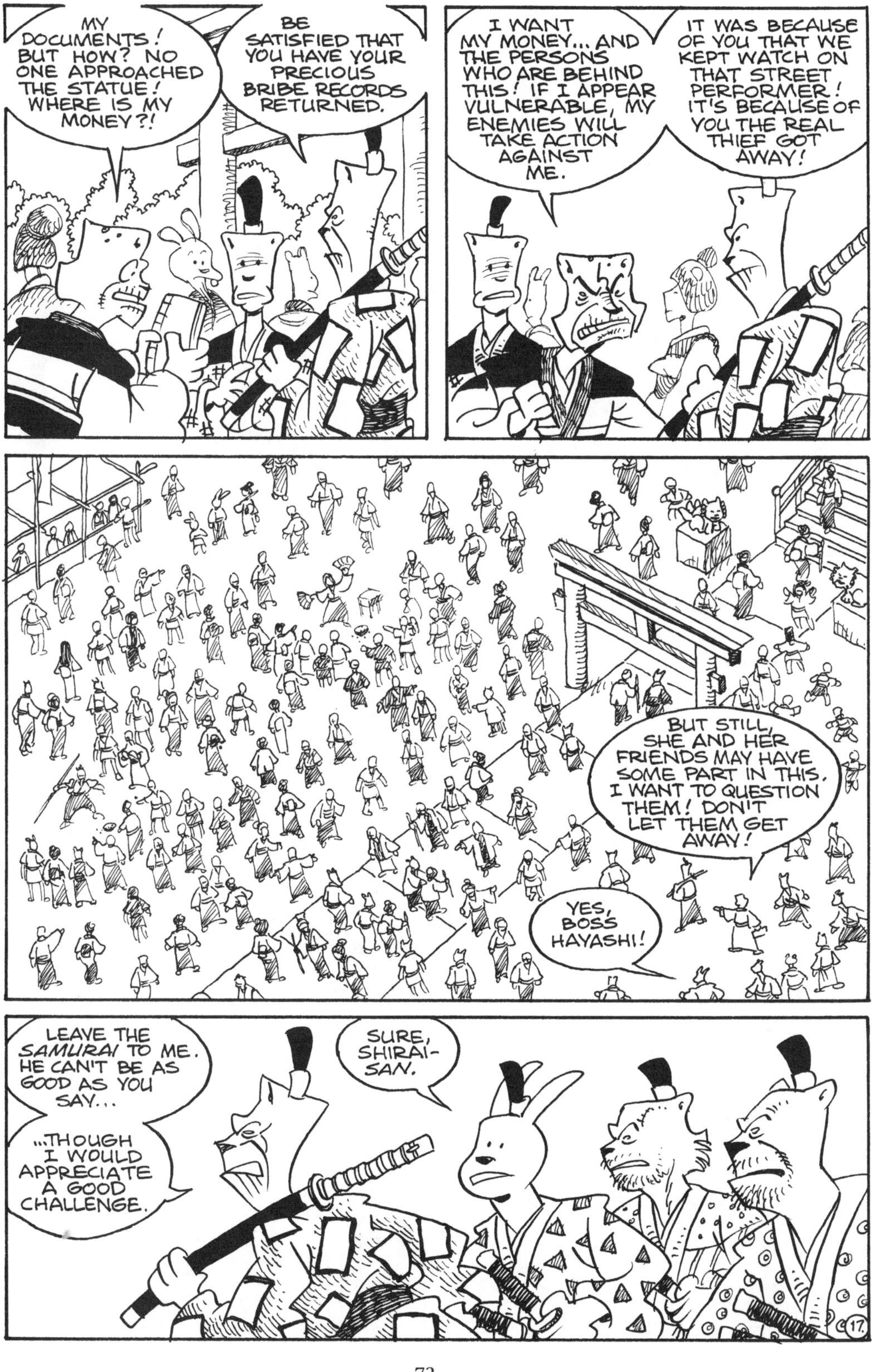
MY DOCUMENTS! BUT HOW? NO ONE APPROACHED THE STATUE! WHERE IS MY MONEY?!
BE SATISFIED THAT YOU HAVE YOUR PRECIOUS BRIBE RECORDS RETURNED.
I WANT MY MONEY... AND THE PERSONS WHO ARE BEHIND THIS! IF I APPEAR VULNERABLE, MY ENEMIES WILL TAKE ACTION AGAINST ME.
IT WAS BECAUSE OF YOU THAT WE KEPT WATCH ON THAT STREET PERFORMER! IT'S BECAUSE OF YOU THE REAL THIEF GOT AWAY!
BUT STILL, SHE AND HER FRIENDS MAY HAVE SOME PART IN THIS. I WANT TO QUESTION THEM! DON'T LET THEM GET AWAY!
YES, BOSS HAYASHI!
LEAVE THE *SAMURAI* TO ME. HE CAN'T BE AS GOOD AS YOU SAY...
...THOUGH I WOULD APPRECIATE A GOOD CHALLENGE.
SURE, SHIRAI-SAN.
17.

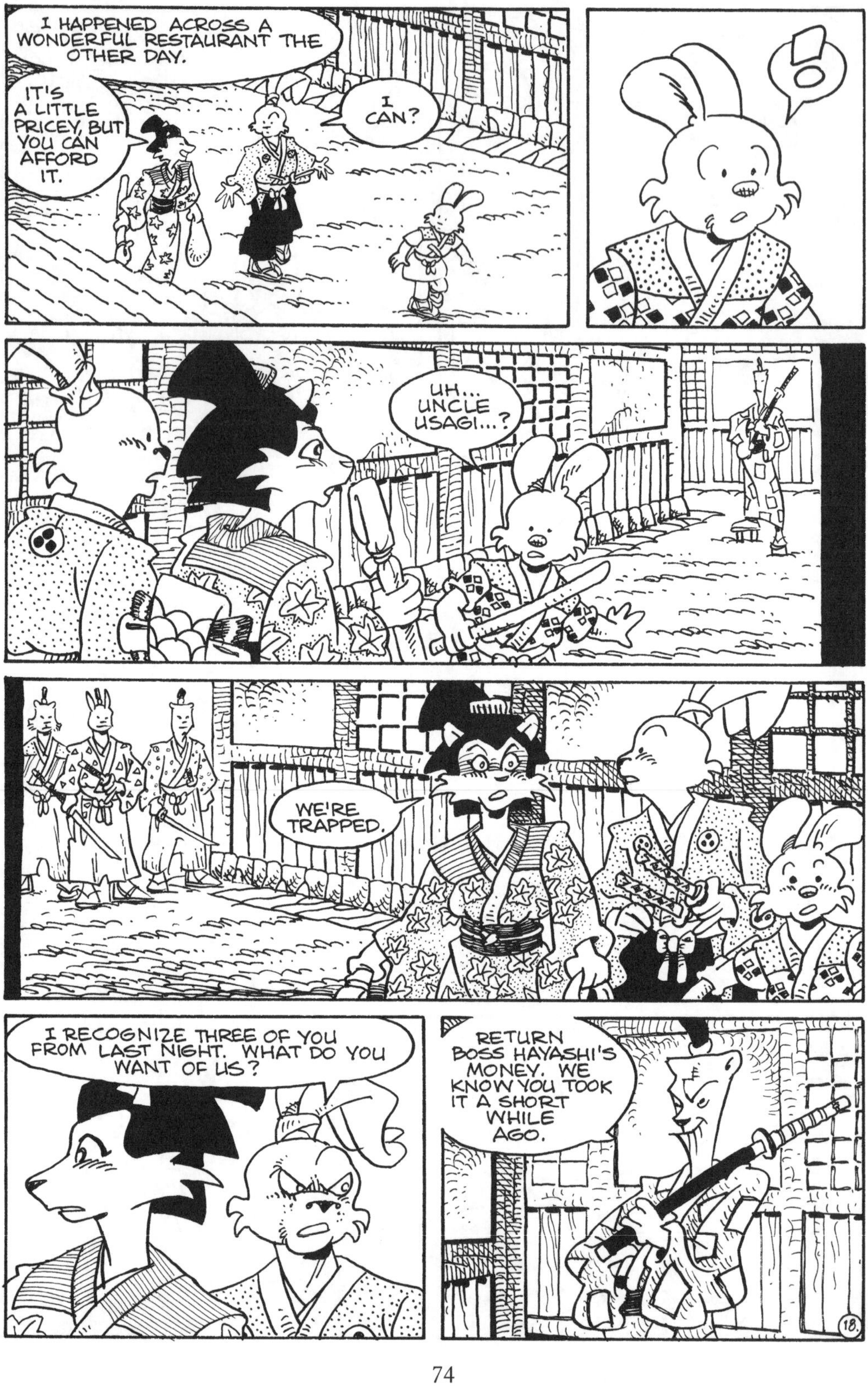
I HAPPENED ACROSS A WONDERFUL RESTAURANT THE OTHER DAY.
IT'S A LITTLE PRICEY, BUT YOU CAN AFFORD IT.
I CAN?
!
UH... UNCLE USAGI...?
WE'RE TRAPPED.
I RECOGNIZE THREE OF YOU FROM LAST NIGHT. WHAT DO YOU WANT OF US?
RETURN BOSS HAYASHI'S MONEY. WE KNOW YOU TOOK IT A SHORT WHILE AGO.
18.

I WOULD THINK THAT YOU WERE A PART OF THIS, KITSUNE, BUT YOU WERE WITH US!

OF COURSE.

GRAB THE GIRL AND THE KID. THE SAMURAI IS MINE TO KILL.

LEAVE THE BRAT TO ME. I'VE GOT A SCORE TO SETTLE FOR WHAT HE DID TO ME LAST NIGHT.

THIS TIME I WON'T BE SO EASY ON HIM.

UGH!

BONK!

STAND STILL, KID! THE BOSS WANTS YOU ALIVE, BUT HE WON'T MIND IF YOU'RE MISSING AN ARM OR A LEG.

GET HIM! HE'S ONLY A KID!

OOF!

19.

75

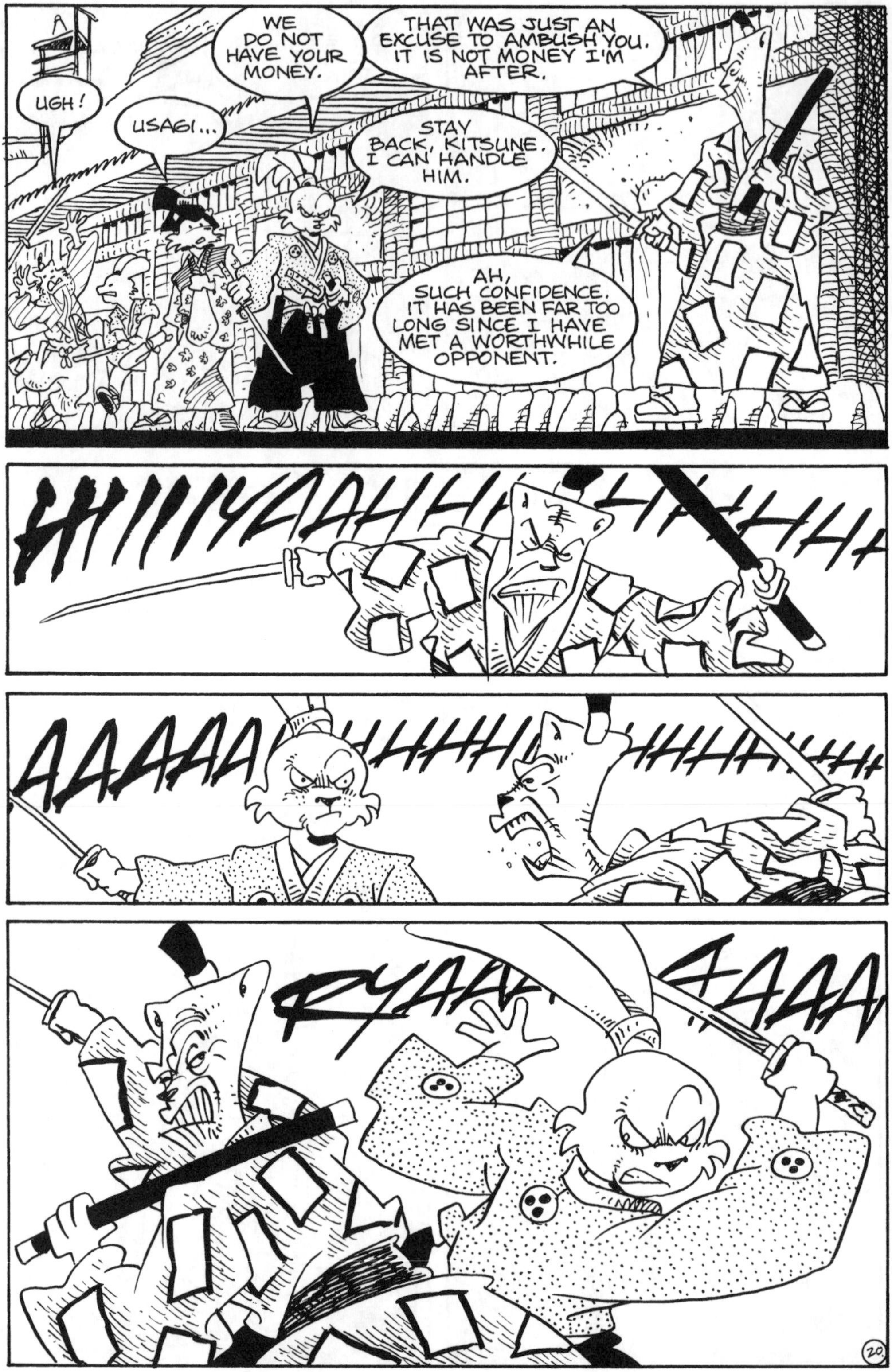
UGH!
USAGI...
WE DO NOT HAVE YOUR MONEY.
THAT WAS JUST AN EXCUSE TO AMBUSH YOU. IT IS NOT MONEY I'M AFTER.
STAY BACK, KITSUNE. I CAN HANDLE HIM.
AH, SUCH CONFIDENCE. IT HAS BEEN FAR TOO LONG SINCE I HAVE MET A WORTHWHILE OPPONENT.
SHIIIYAAHHHHHHHHHHH
AAAAAHHHHHHHHHHHHHHHHH
RYAAAAAAAA
20

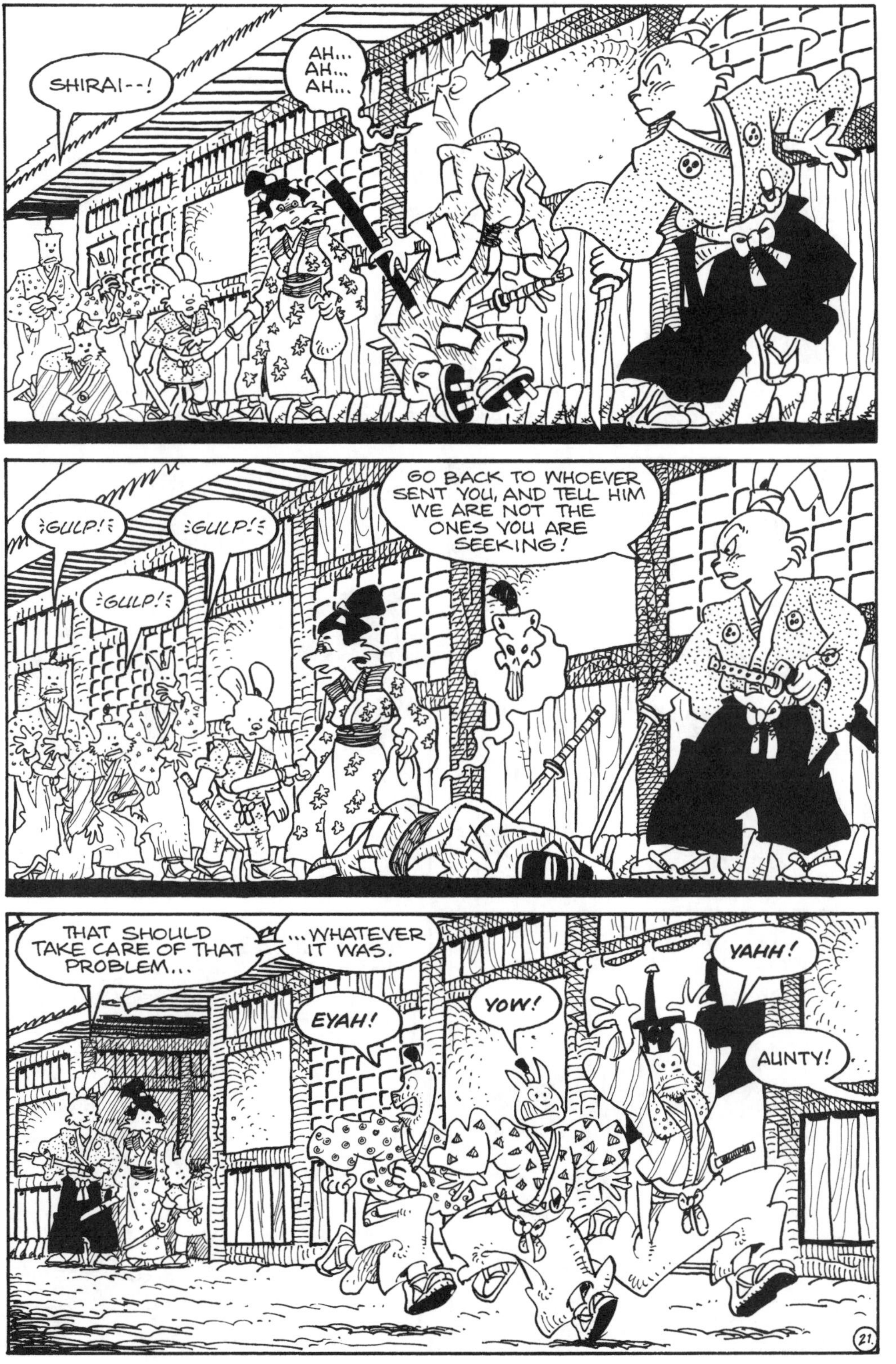
SHIRAI--!
AH... AH... AH...
GULP!
GULP!
GULP!
GO BACK TO WHOEVER SENT YOU, AND TELL HIM WE ARE NOT THE ONES YOU ARE SEEKING!
THAT SHOULD TAKE CARE OF THAT PROBLEM...
...WHATEVER IT WAS.
EYAH!
YOW!
YAHH!
AUNTY!
21.

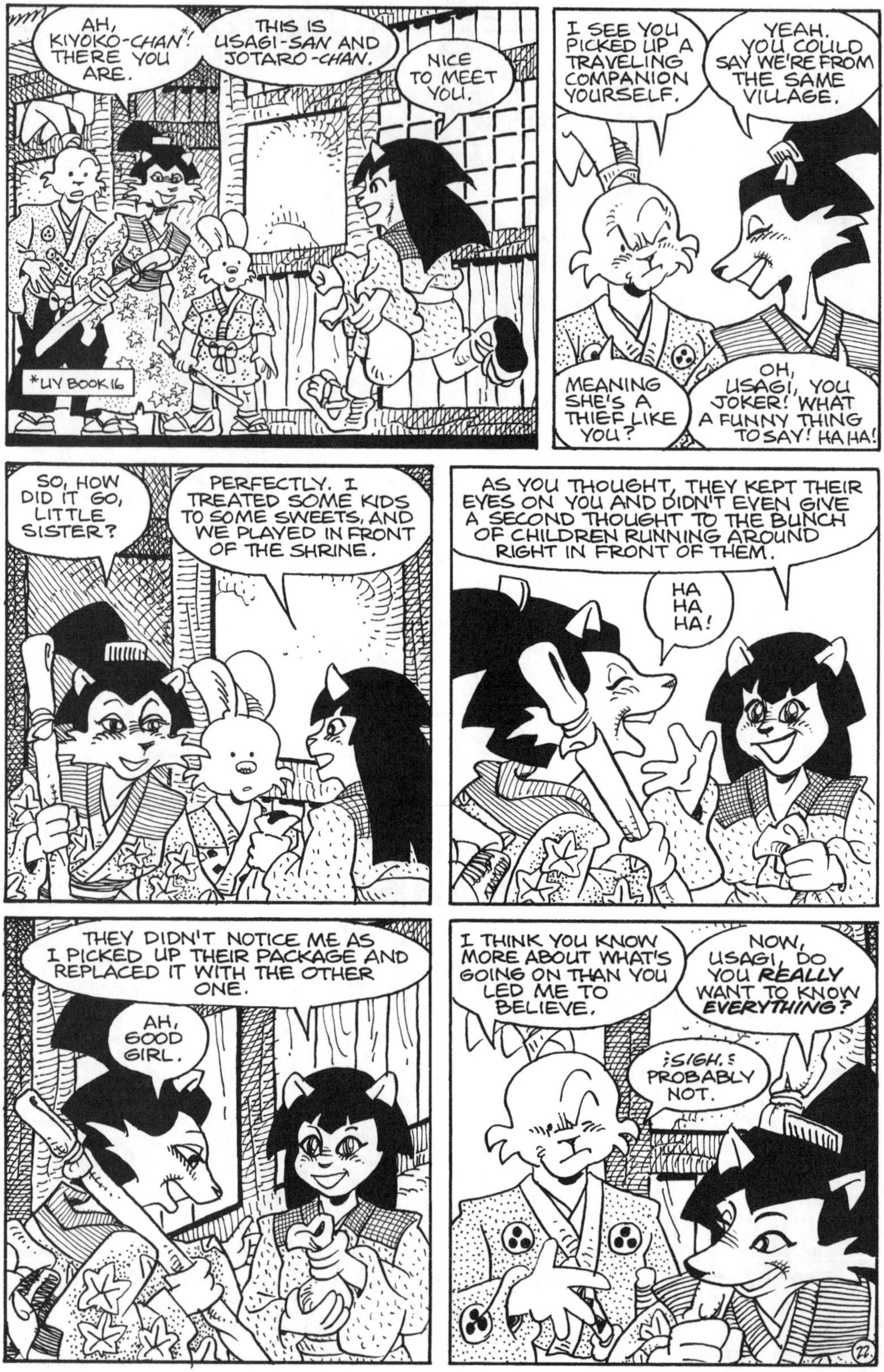
AH, KIYOKO-CHAN!* THERE YOU ARE.
THIS IS USAGI-SAN AND JOTARO-CHAN.
NICE TO MEET YOU.
*UY BOOK 16
I SEE YOU PICKED UP A TRAVELING COMPANION YOURSELF.
YEAH. YOU COULD SAY WE'RE FROM THE SAME VILLAGE.
MEANING SHE'S A THIEF LIKE YOU?
OH, USAGI, YOU JOKER! WHAT A FUNNY THING TO SAY! HA HA!
SO, HOW DID IT GO, LITTLE SISTER?
PERFECTLY. I TREATED SOME KIDS TO SOME SWEETS, AND WE PLAYED IN FRONT OF THE SHRINE.
AS YOU THOUGHT, THEY KEPT THEIR EYES ON YOU AND DIDN'T EVEN GIVE A SECOND THOUGHT TO THE BUNCH OF CHILDREN RUNNING AROUND RIGHT IN FRONT OF THEM.
HA HA HA!
THEY DIDN'T NOTICE ME AS I PICKED UP THEIR PACKAGE AND REPLACED IT WITH THE OTHER ONE.
AH, GOOD GIRL.
I THINK YOU KNOW MORE ABOUT WHAT'S GOING ON THAN YOU LED ME TO BELIEVE.
NOW, USAGI, DO YOU REALLY WANT TO KNOW EVERYTHING?
SIGH. PROBABLY NOT.
22.

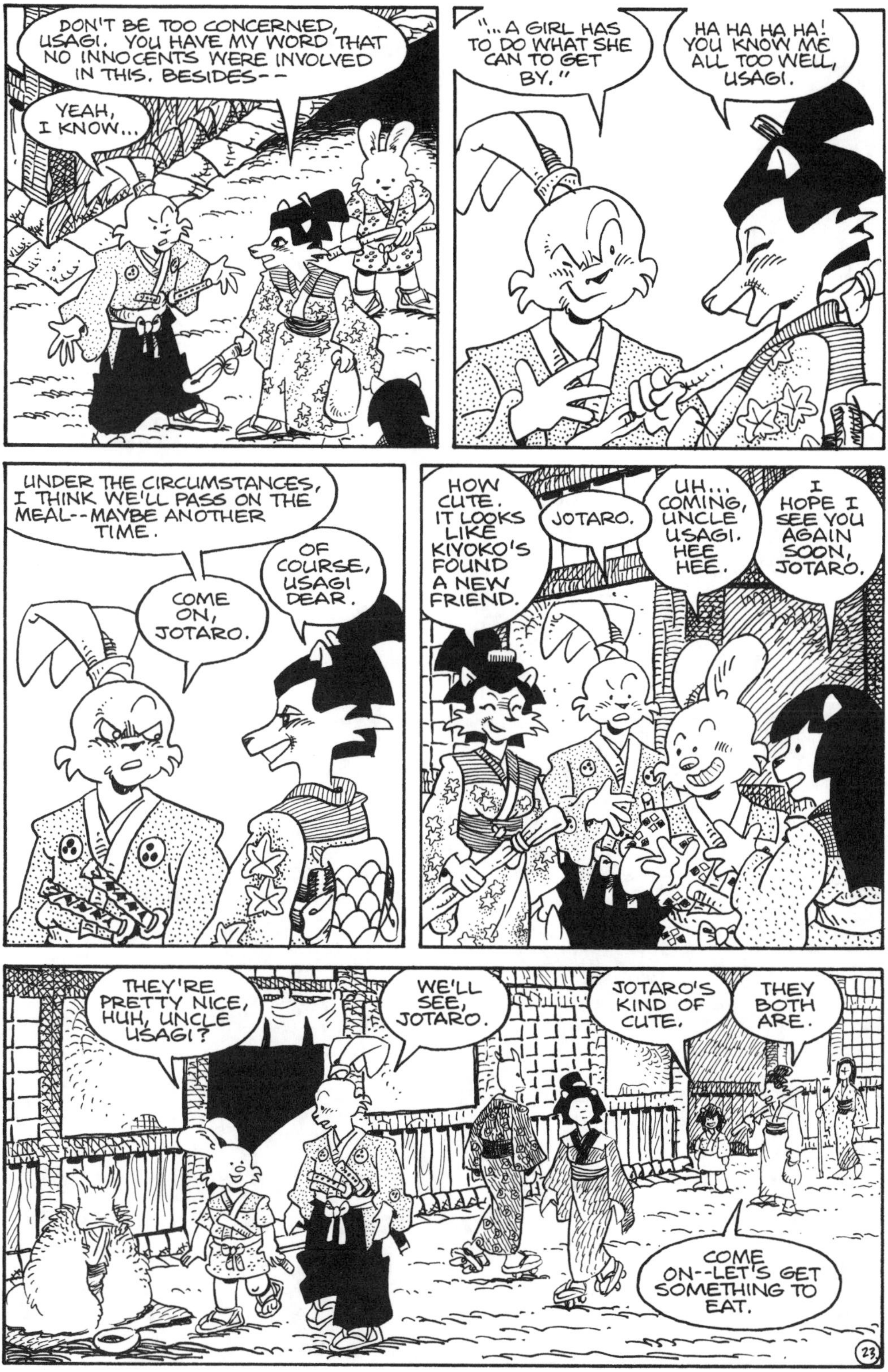
DON'T BE TOO CONCERNED, USAGI. YOU HAVE MY WORD THAT NO INNOCENTS WERE INVOLVED IN THIS. BESIDES--
YEAH, I KNOW...
"...A GIRL HAS TO DO WHAT SHE CAN TO GET BY."
HA HA HA HA! YOU KNOW ME ALL TOO WELL, USAGI.
UNDER THE CIRCUMSTANCES, I THINK WE'LL PASS ON THE MEAL--MAYBE ANOTHER TIME.
COME ON, JOTARO.
OF COURSE, USAGI DEAR.
HOW CUTE. IT LOOKS LIKE KIYOKO'S FOUND A NEW FRIEND.
JOTARO.
UH... COMING, UNCLE USAGI. HEE HEE.
I HOPE I SEE YOU AGAIN SOON, JOTARO.
THEY'RE PRETTY NICE, HUH, UNCLE USAGI?
WE'LL SEE, JOTARO.
JOTARO'S KIND OF CUTE.
THEY BOTH ARE.
COME ON--LET'S GET SOMETHING TO EAT.
23

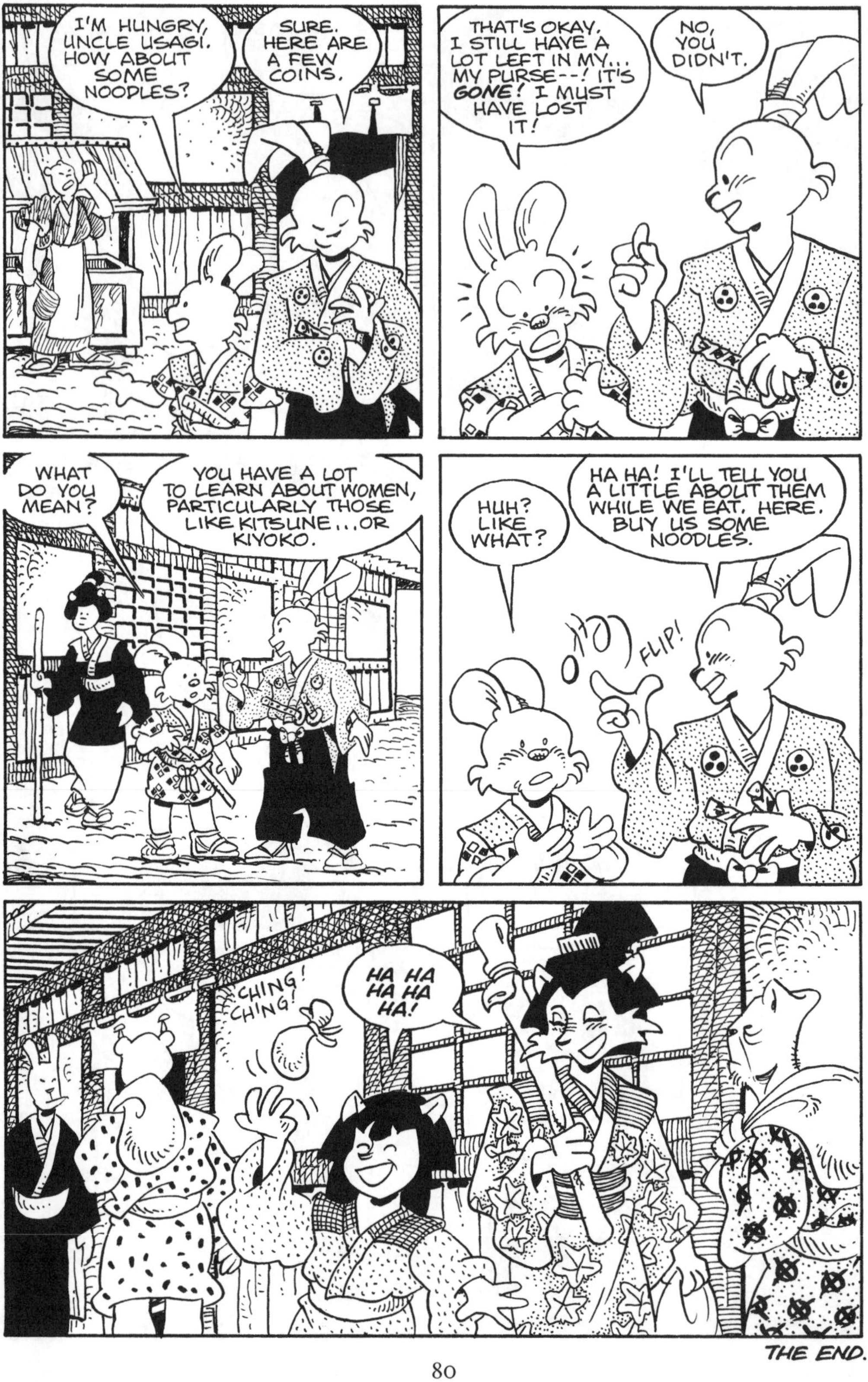

I'M HUNGRY, UNCLE USAGI. HOW ABOUT SOME NOODLES?
SURE. HERE ARE A FEW COINS.
THAT'S OKAY. I STILL HAVE A LOT LEFT IN MY... MY PURSE--! IT'S GONE! I MUST HAVE LOST IT!
NO, YOU DIDN'T.
WHAT DO YOU MEAN?
YOU HAVE A LOT TO LEARN ABOUT WOMEN, PARTICULARLY THOSE LIKE KITSUNE...OR KIYOKO.
HUH? LIKE WHAT?
HA HA! I'LL TELL YOU A LITTLE ABOUT THEM WHILE WE EAT. HERE. BUY US SOME NOODLES.
FLIP!
CHING! CHING!
HA HA HA HA HA!

THE END.

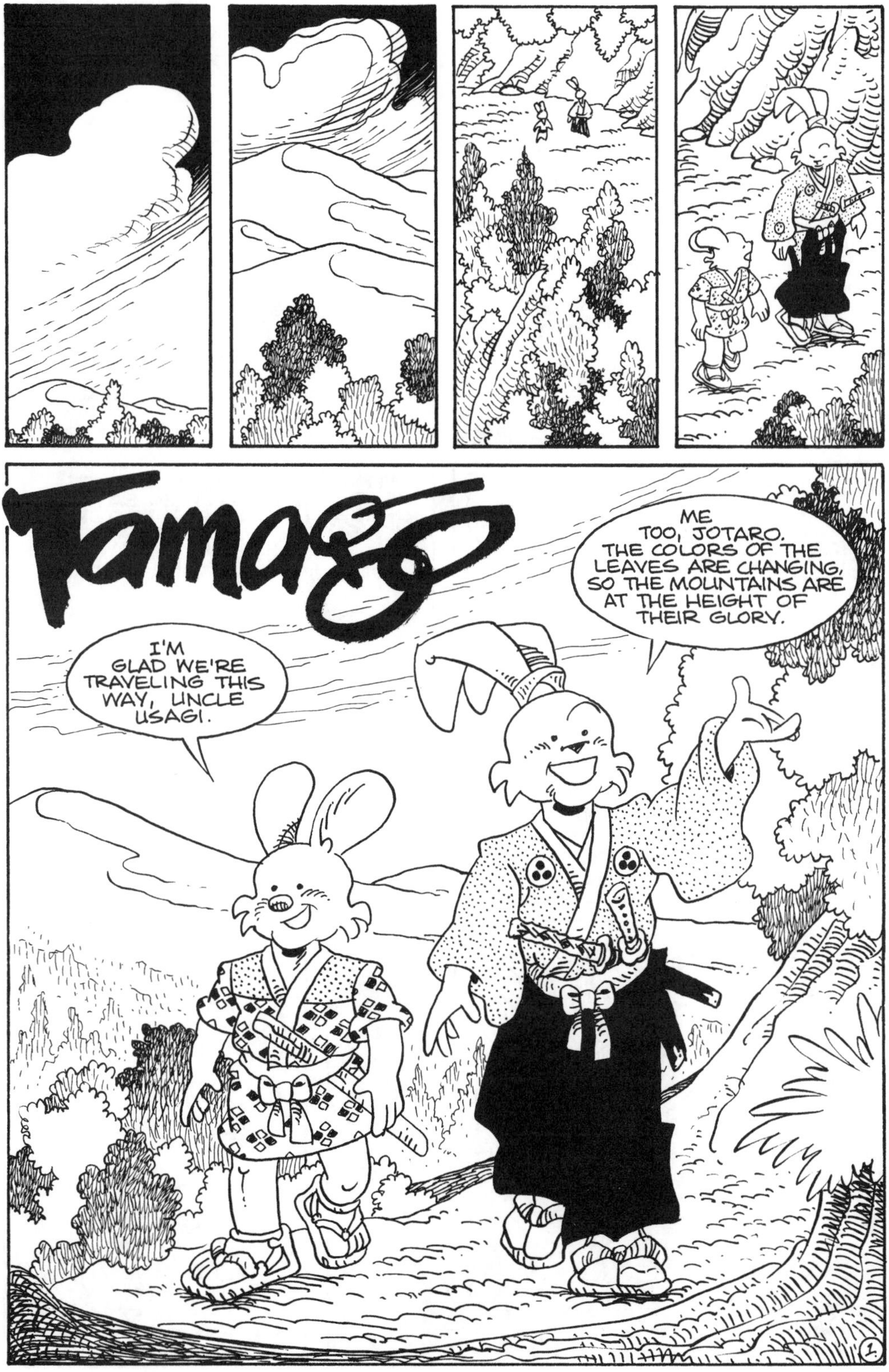
Tamago
I'M GLAD WE'RE TRAVELING THIS WAY, UNCLE USAGI.
ME TOO, JOTARO. THE COLORS OF THE LEAVES ARE CHANGING, SO THE MOUNTAINS ARE AT THE HEIGHT OF THEIR GLORY.
1.

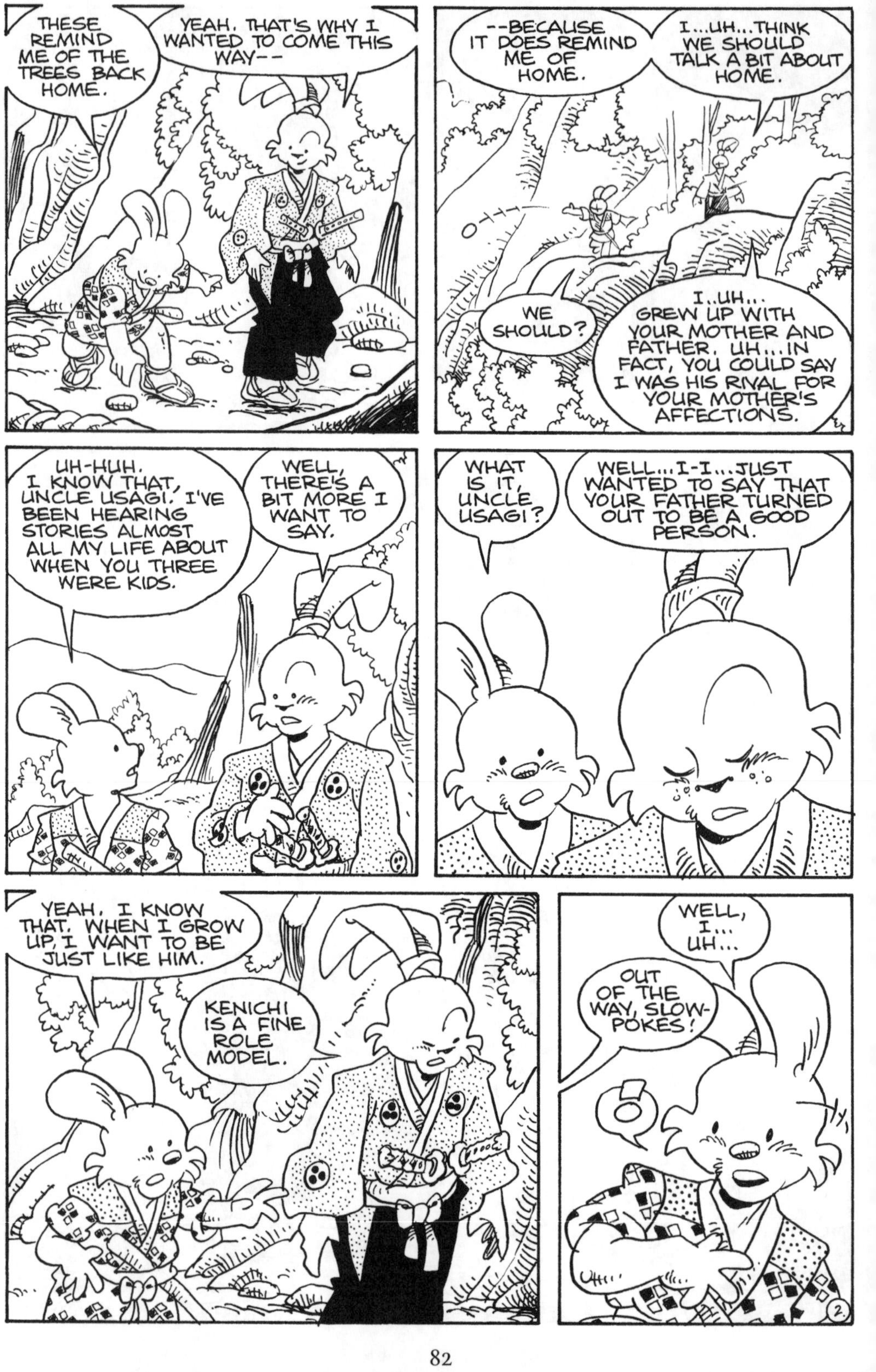

THESE REMIND ME OF THE TREES BACK HOME.
YEAH. THAT'S WHY I WANTED TO COME THIS WAY--
--BECAUSE IT DOES REMIND ME OF HOME.
I...UH...THINK WE SHOULD TALK A BIT ABOUT HOME.
WE SHOULD?
I..UH... GREW UP WITH YOUR MOTHER AND FATHER. UH...IN FACT, YOU COULD SAY I WAS HIS RIVAL FOR YOUR MOTHER'S AFFECTIONS.
UH-HUH. I KNOW THAT, UNCLE USAGI. I'VE BEEN HEARING STORIES ALMOST ALL MY LIFE ABOUT WHEN YOU THREE WERE KIDS.
WELL, THERE'S A BIT MORE I WANT TO SAY.
WHAT IS IT, UNCLE USAGI?
WELL...I-I...JUST WANTED TO SAY THAT YOUR FATHER TURNED OUT TO BE A GOOD PERSON.
YEAH. I KNOW THAT. WHEN I GROW UP, I WANT TO BE JUST LIKE HIM.
KENICHI IS A FINE ROLE MODEL.
WELL, I... UH...
OUT OF THE WAY, SLOW-POKES!
2.

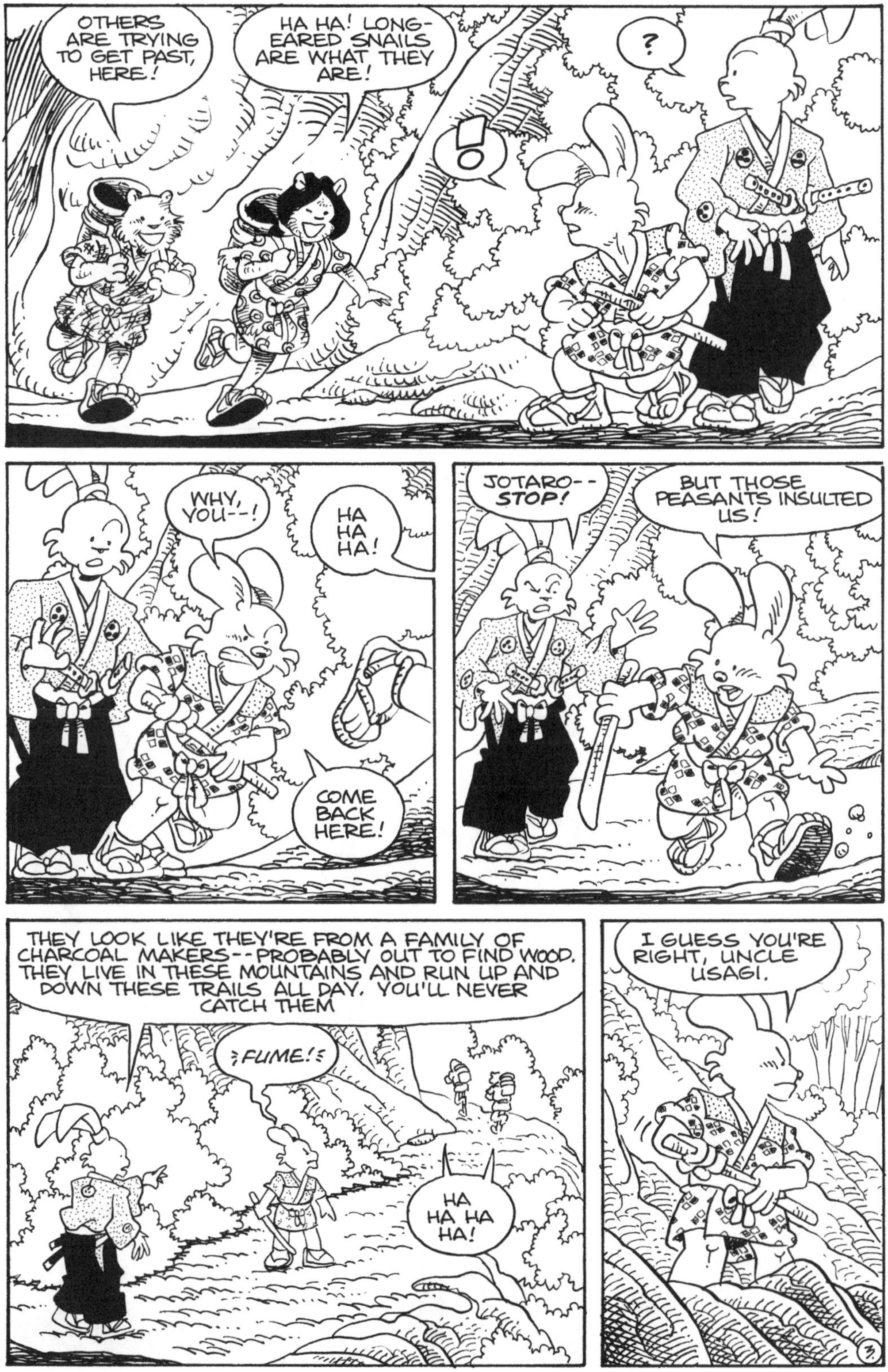
OTHERS ARE TRYING TO GET PAST, HERE!
HA HA! LONG-EARED SNAILS ARE WHAT THEY ARE!
?
!
WHY, YOU--!
HA HA HA!
COME BACK HERE!
JOTARO-- STOP!
BUT THOSE PEASANTS INSULTED US!
THEY LOOK LIKE THEY'RE FROM A FAMILY OF CHARCOAL MAKERS--PROBABLY OUT TO FIND WOOD. THEY LIVE IN THESE MOUNTAINS AND RUN UP AND DOWN THESE TRAILS ALL DAY. YOU'LL NEVER CATCH THEM
FUME!
HA HA HA HA!
I GUESS YOU'RE RIGHT, UNCLE USAGI.
3.

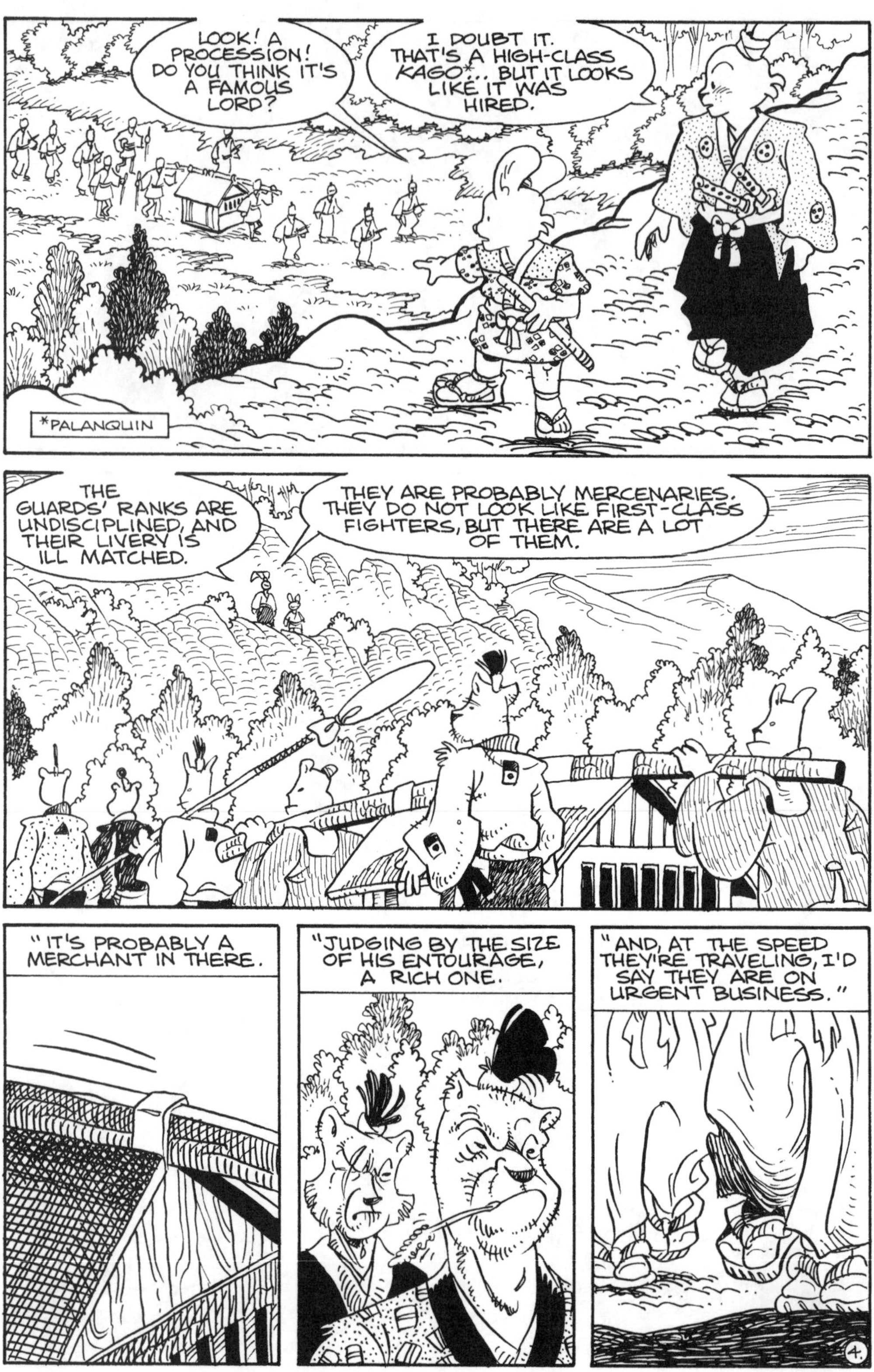
LOOK! A PROCESSION! DO YOU THINK IT'S A FAMOUS LORD?
I DOUBT IT. THAT'S A HIGH-CLASS KAGO*... BUT IT LOOKS LIKE IT WAS HIRED.
*PALANQUIN
THE GUARDS' RANKS ARE UNDISCIPLINED, AND THEIR LIVERY IS ILL MATCHED.
THEY ARE PROBABLY MERCENARIES. THEY DO NOT LOOK LIKE FIRST-CLASS FIGHTERS, BUT THERE ARE A LOT OF THEM.
"IT'S PROBABLY A MERCHANT IN THERE.
"JUDGING BY THE SIZE OF HIS ENTOURAGE, A RICH ONE.
"AND, AT THE SPEED THEY'RE TRAVELING, I'D SAY THEY ARE ON URGENT BUSINESS."
4.

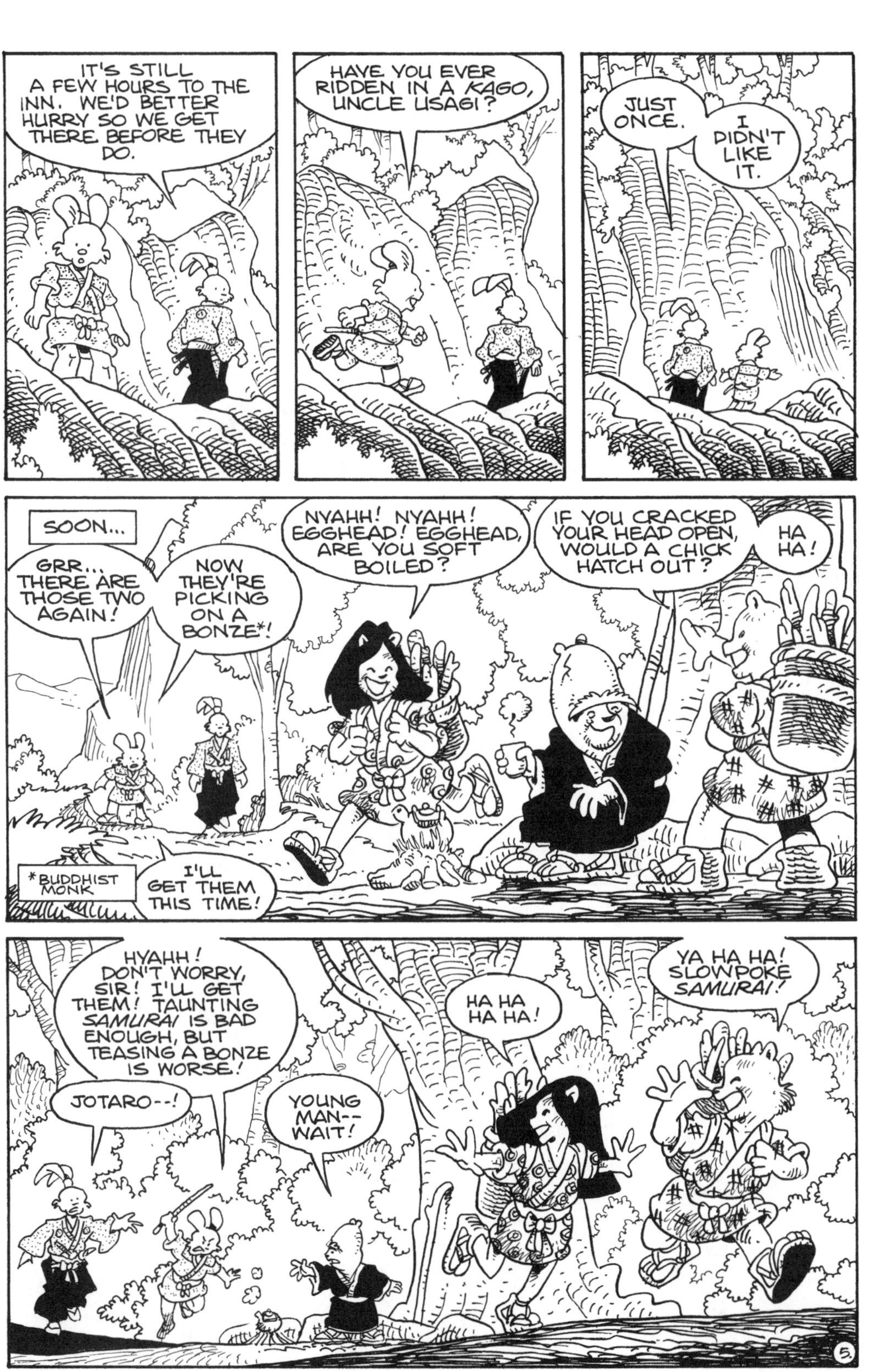
IT'S STILL A FEW HOURS TO THE INN. WE'D BETTER HURRY SO WE GET THERE BEFORE THEY DO.
HAVE YOU EVER RIDDEN IN A *KAGO*, UNCLE USAGI?
JUST ONCE.
I DIDN'T LIKE IT.
SOON...
GRR... THERE ARE THOSE TWO AGAIN!
NOW THEY'RE PICKING ON A BONZE*!
NYAHH! NYAHH! EGGHEAD! EGGHEAD, ARE YOU SOFT BOILED?
IF YOU CRACKED YOUR HEAD OPEN, WOULD A CHICK HATCH OUT?
HA HA!
*BUDDHIST MONK
I'LL GET THEM THIS TIME!
HYAHH! DON'T WORRY, SIR! I'LL GET THEM! TAUNTING *SAMURAI* IS BAD ENOUGH, BUT TEASING A BONZE IS WORSE!
JOTARO--!
YOUNG MAN-- WAIT!
HA HA HA HA!
YA HA HA! SLOWPOKE *SAMURAI*!
5.

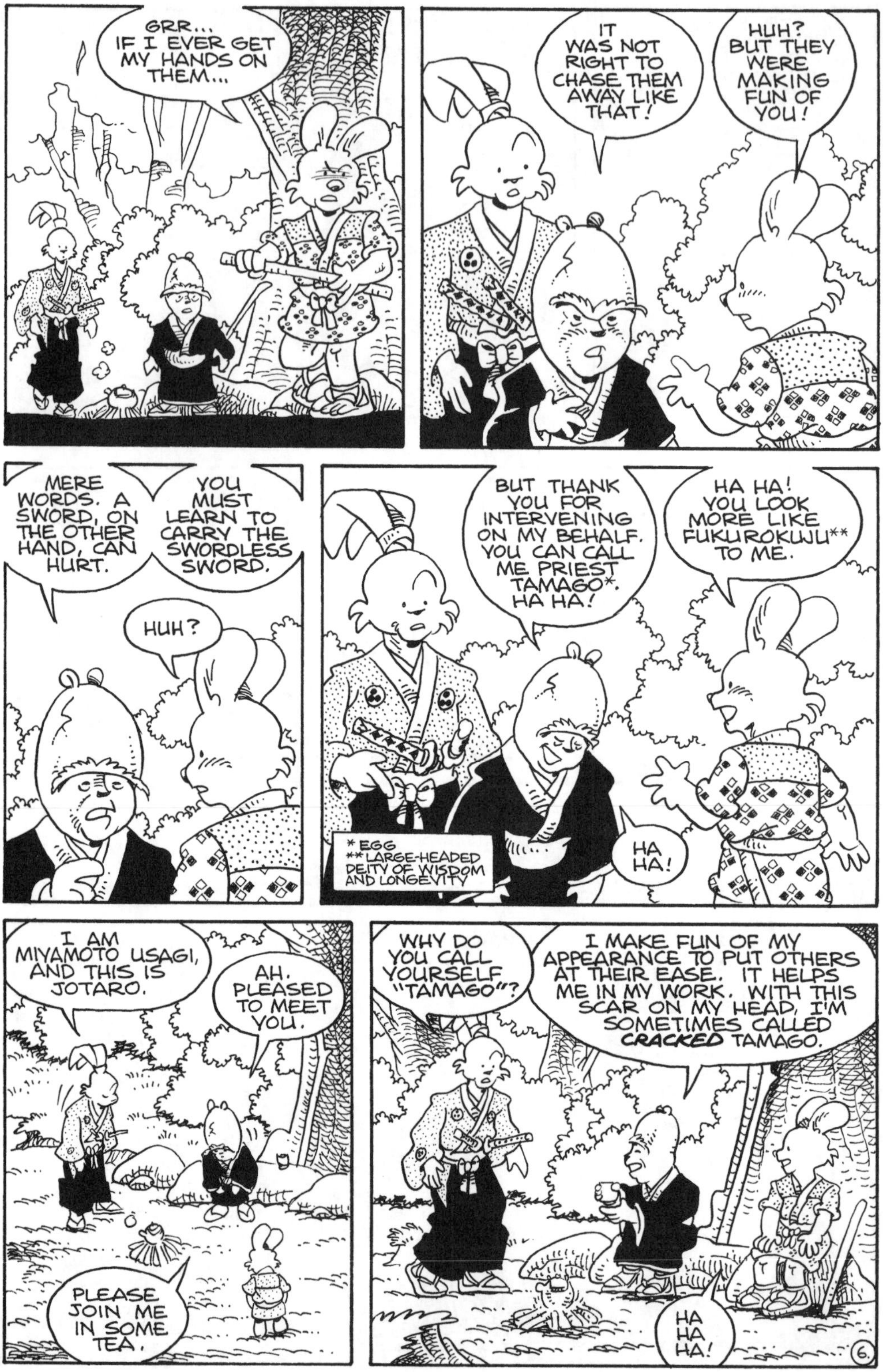
GRR... IF I EVER GET MY HANDS ON THEM...
IT WAS NOT RIGHT TO CHASE THEM AWAY LIKE THAT!
HUH? BUT THEY WERE MAKING FUN OF YOU!
MERE WORDS. A SWORD, ON THE OTHER HAND, CAN HURT.
YOU MUST LEARN TO CARRY THE SWORDLESS SWORD.
HUH?
BUT THANK YOU FOR INTERVENING ON MY BEHALF. YOU CAN CALL ME PRIEST TAMAGO*. HA HA!
HA HA! YOU LOOK MORE LIKE FUKUROKUJU** TO ME.
HA HA!
* EGG
** LARGE-HEADED DEITY OF WISDOM AND LONGEVITY
I AM MIYAMOTO USAGI, AND THIS IS JOTARO.
AH. PLEASED TO MEET YOU.
PLEASE JOIN ME IN SOME TEA.
WHY DO YOU CALL YOURSELF "TAMAGO"?
I MAKE FUN OF MY APPEARANCE TO PUT OTHERS AT THEIR EASE. IT HELPS ME IN MY WORK. WITH THIS SCAR ON MY HEAD, I'M SOMETIMES CALLED CRACKED TAMAGO.
HA HA HA!
6.

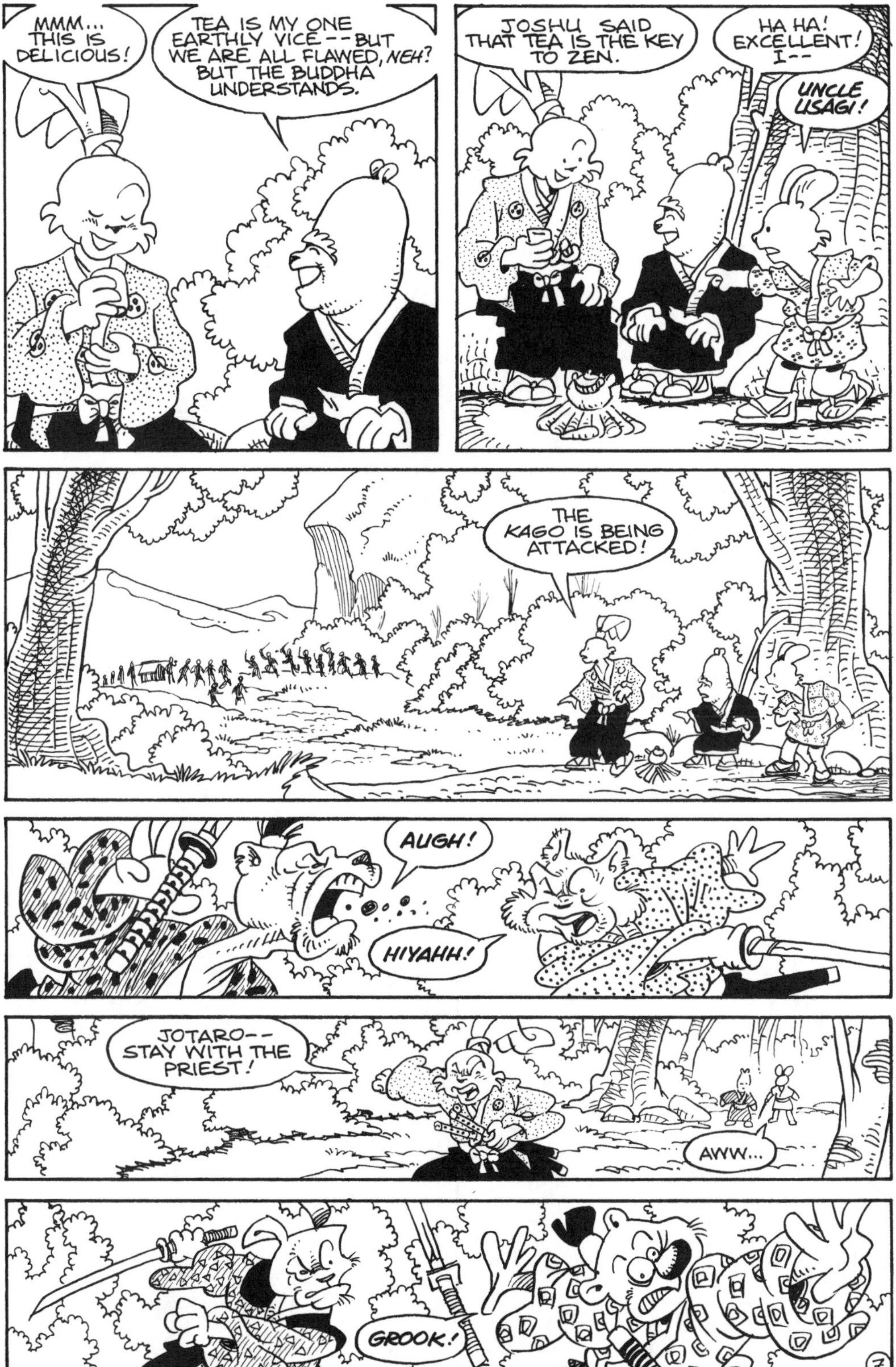
MMM... THIS IS DELICIOUS!
TEA IS MY ONE EARTHLY VICE--BUT WE ARE ALL FLAWED, NEH? BUT THE BUDDHA UNDERSTANDS.
JOSHU SAID THAT TEA IS THE KEY TO ZEN.
HA HA! EXCELLENT! I--
UNCLE USAGI!
THE KAGO IS BEING ATTACKED!
AUGH!
HIYAHH!
JOTARO--STAY WITH THE PRIEST!
AWW...
GROOK!
7.

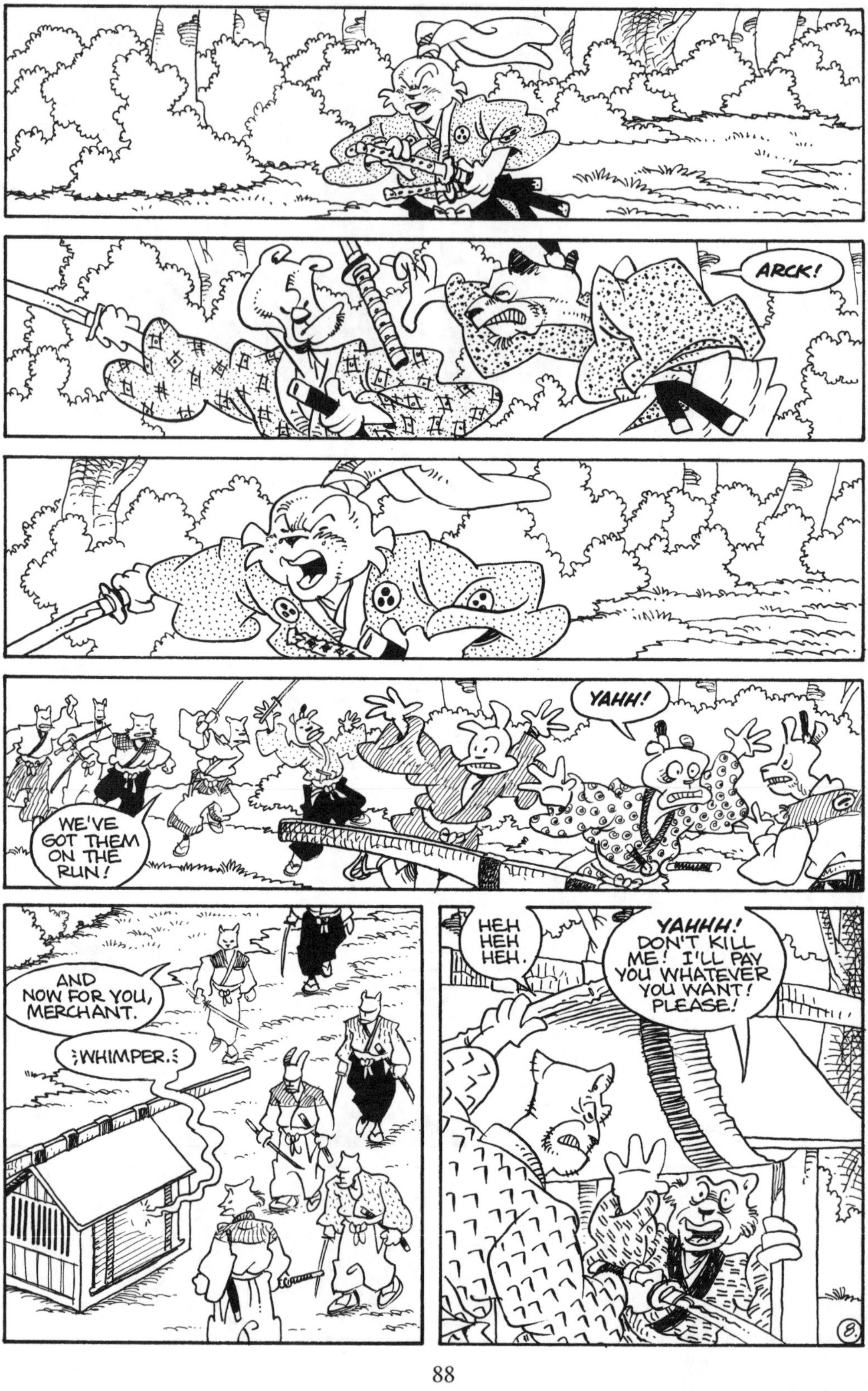
ARCK!
YAHH!
WE'VE GOT THEM ON THE RUN!
AND NOW FOR YOU, MERCHANT.
WHIMPER.
HEH HEH HEH.
YAHHH! DON'T KILL ME! I'LL PAY YOU WHATEVER YOU WANT! PLEASE!
8.

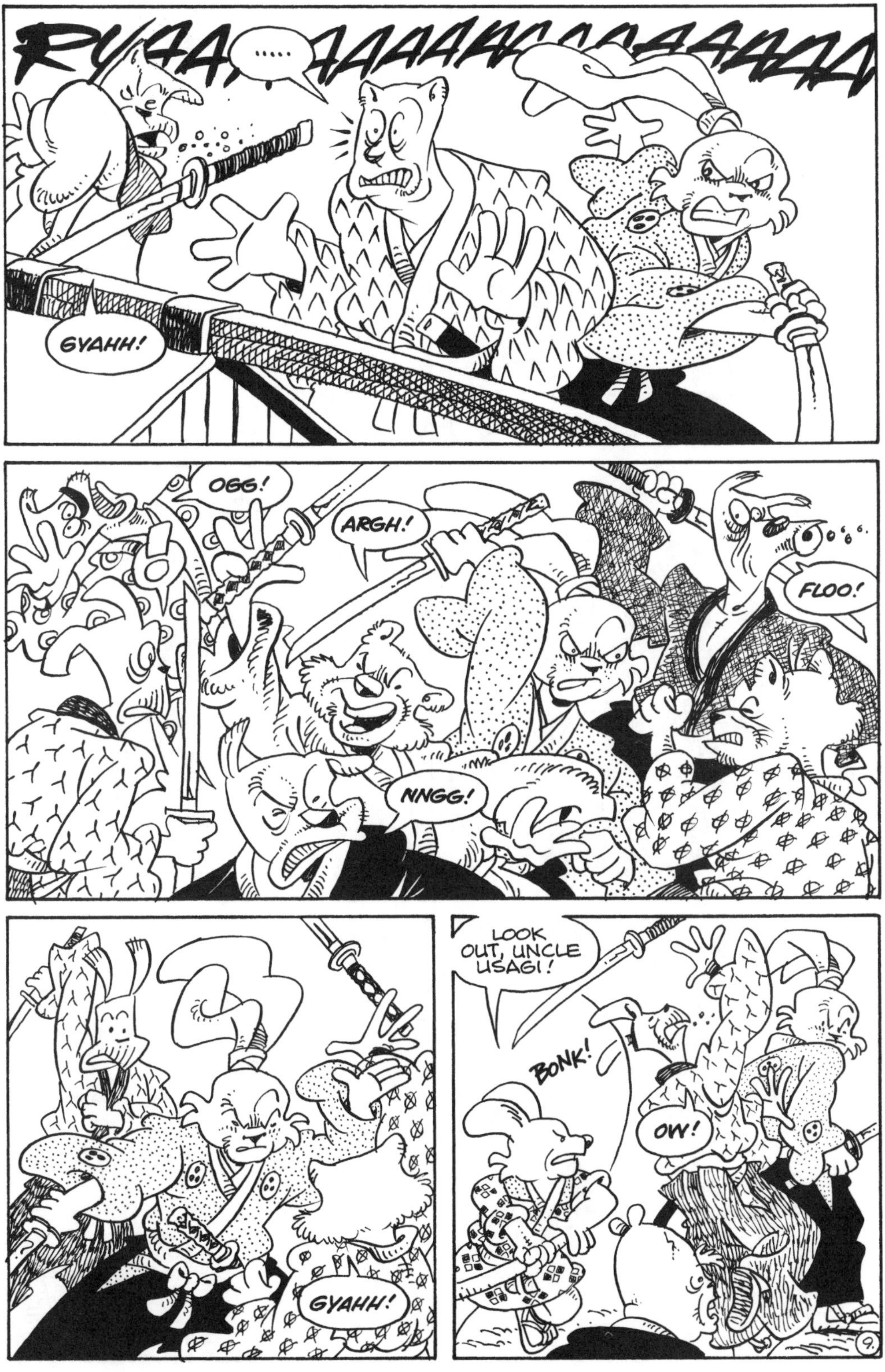

RYAAAAAAAAAAAAAAAAA
.....
GYAHH!
OGG!
ARGH!
FLOO!
NNGG!
GYAHH!
LOOK OUT, UNCLE USAGI!
BONK!
OW!
9.

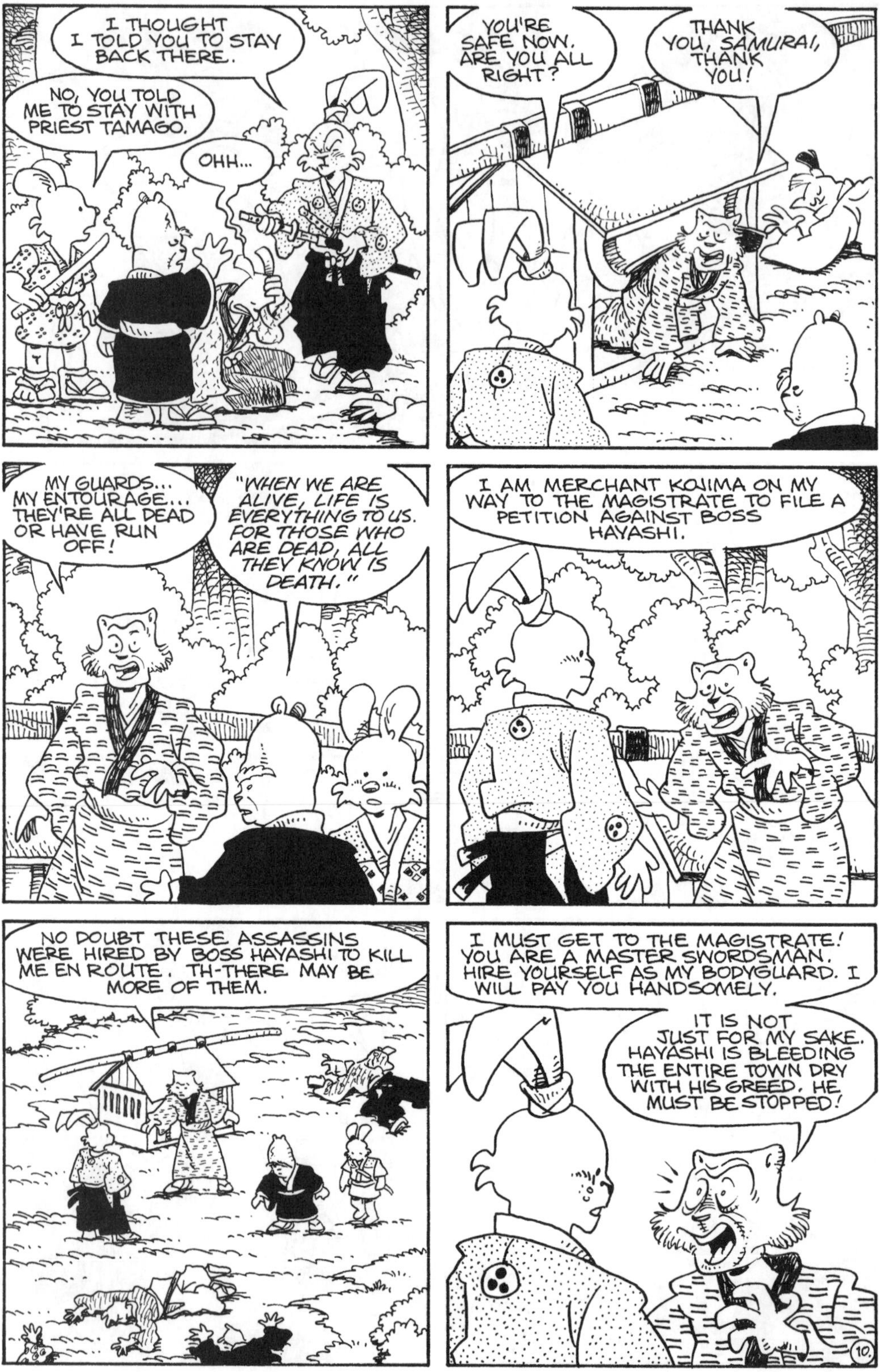
I THOUGHT I TOLD YOU TO STAY BACK THERE.
NO, YOU TOLD ME TO STAY WITH PRIEST TAMAGO.
OHH...
YOU'RE SAFE NOW. ARE YOU ALL RIGHT?
THANK YOU, SAMURAI, THANK YOU!
MY GUARDS... MY ENTOURAGE... THEY'RE ALL DEAD OR HAVE RUN OFF!
"WHEN WE ARE ALIVE, LIFE IS EVERYTHING TO US. FOR THOSE WHO ARE DEAD, ALL THEY KNOW IS DEATH."
I AM MERCHANT KOJIMA ON MY WAY TO THE MAGISTRATE TO FILE A PETITION AGAINST BOSS HAYASHI.
NO DOUBT THESE ASSASSINS WERE HIRED BY BOSS HAYASHI TO KILL ME EN ROUTE. TH-THERE MAY BE MORE OF THEM.
I MUST GET TO THE MAGISTRATE! YOU ARE A MASTER SWORDSMAN. HIRE YOURSELF AS MY BODYGUARD. I WILL PAY YOU HANDSOMELY.
IT IS NOT JUST FOR MY SAKE. HAYASHI IS BLEEDING THE ENTIRE TOWN DRY WITH HIS GREED. HE MUST BE STOPPED!
10.

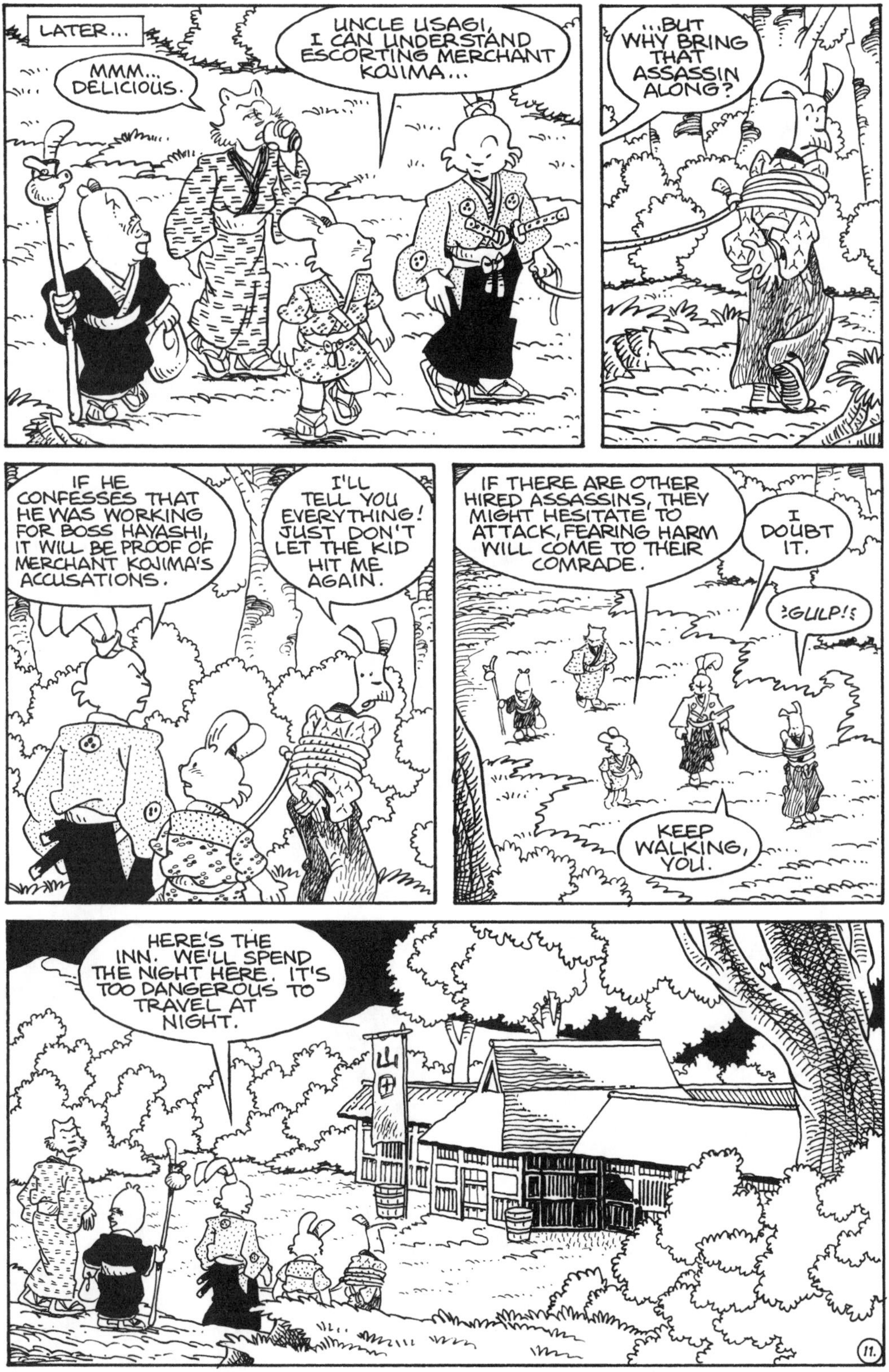
LATER...
MMM... DELICIOUS.
UNCLE USAGI, I CAN UNDERSTAND ESCORTING MERCHANT KOJIMA...
...BUT WHY BRING THAT ASSASSIN ALONG?
IF HE CONFESSES THAT HE WAS WORKING FOR BOSS HAYASHI, IT WILL BE PROOF OF MERCHANT KOJIMA'S ACCUSATIONS.
I'LL TELL YOU EVERYTHING! JUST DON'T LET THE KID HIT ME AGAIN.
IF THERE ARE OTHER HIRED ASSASSINS, THEY MIGHT HESITATE TO ATTACK, FEARING HARM WILL COME TO THEIR COMRADE.
I DOUBT IT.
GULP!
KEEP WALKING, YOU.
HERE'S THE INN. WE'LL SPEND THE NIGHT HERE. IT'S TOO DANGEROUS TO TRAVEL AT NIGHT.
山
11.

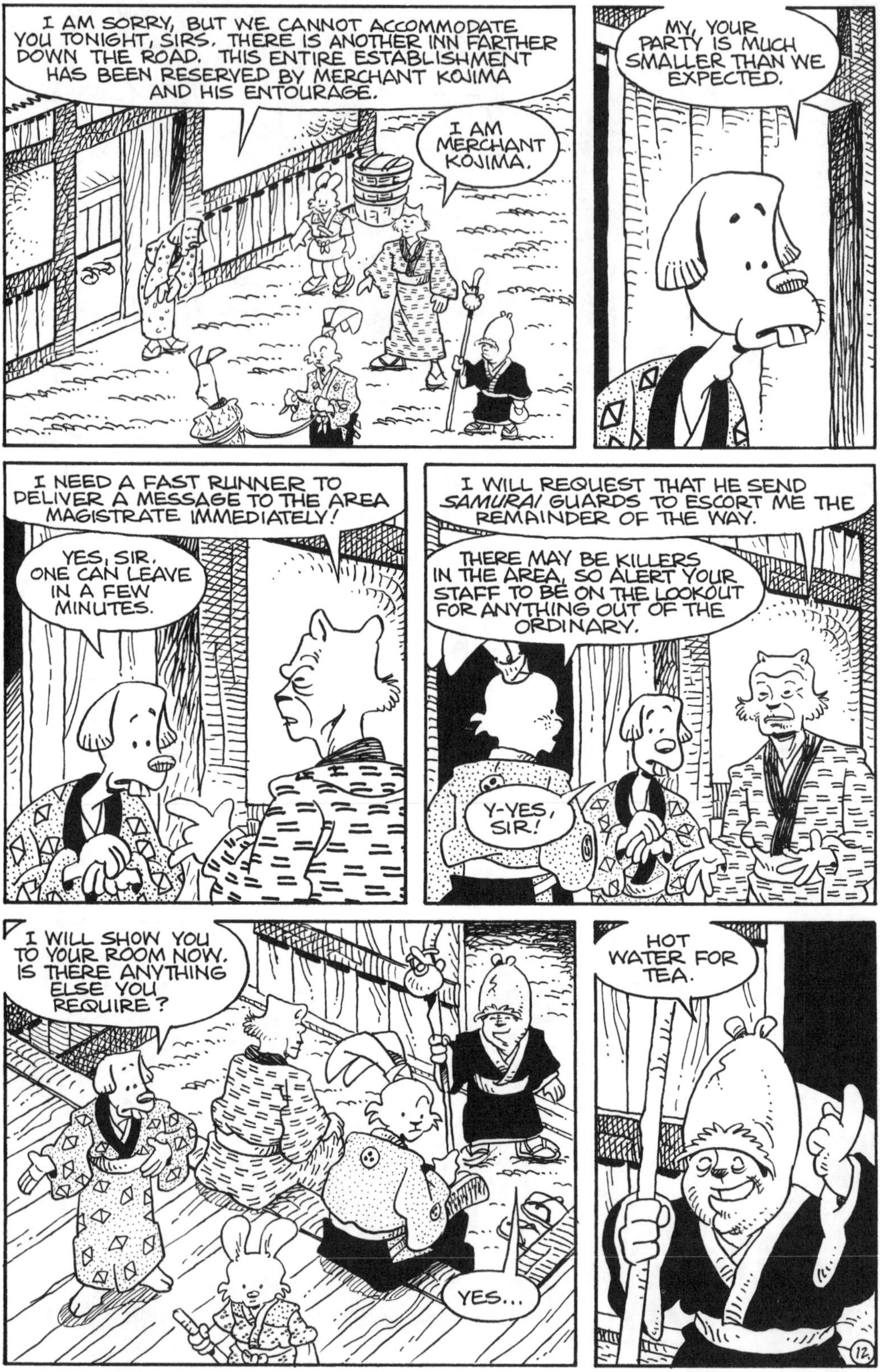
I AM SORRY, BUT WE CANNOT ACCOMMODATE YOU TONIGHT, SIRS. THERE IS ANOTHER INN FARTHER DOWN THE ROAD. THIS ENTIRE ESTABLISHMENT HAS BEEN RESERVED BY MERCHANT KOJIMA AND HIS ENTOURAGE.
I AM MERCHANT KOJIMA.
MY, YOUR PARTY IS MUCH SMALLER THAN WE EXPECTED.
I NEED A FAST RUNNER TO DELIVER A MESSAGE TO THE AREA MAGISTRATE IMMEDIATELY!
YES, SIR. ONE CAN LEAVE IN A FEW MINUTES.
I WILL REQUEST THAT HE SEND *SAMURAI* GUARDS TO ESCORT ME THE REMAINDER OF THE WAY.
THERE MAY BE KILLERS IN THE AREA, SO ALERT YOUR STAFF TO BE ON THE LOOKOUT FOR ANYTHING OUT OF THE ORDINARY.
Y-YES, SIR!
I WILL SHOW YOU TO YOUR ROOM NOW. IS THERE ANYTHING ELSE YOU REQUIRE?
YES...
HOT WATER FOR TEA.
12

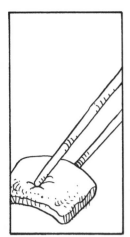

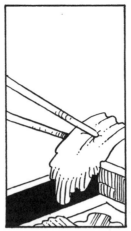

AH... A DELICIOUS MEAL!

HEY, I'M HUNGRY, TOO! I'LL TELL YOU EVERYTHING I KNOW FOR A BOWL OF RICE.

HUH? COME ON.

NO! YOU TRIED TO KILL ME, WHY SHOULD I TREAT YOU WITH ANY CONSIDERATION?

AWWW...

TO BE TIED UP LIKE AN ANIMAL IS BAD ENOUGH. HE SHOULD NOT GO HUNGRY AS WELL.

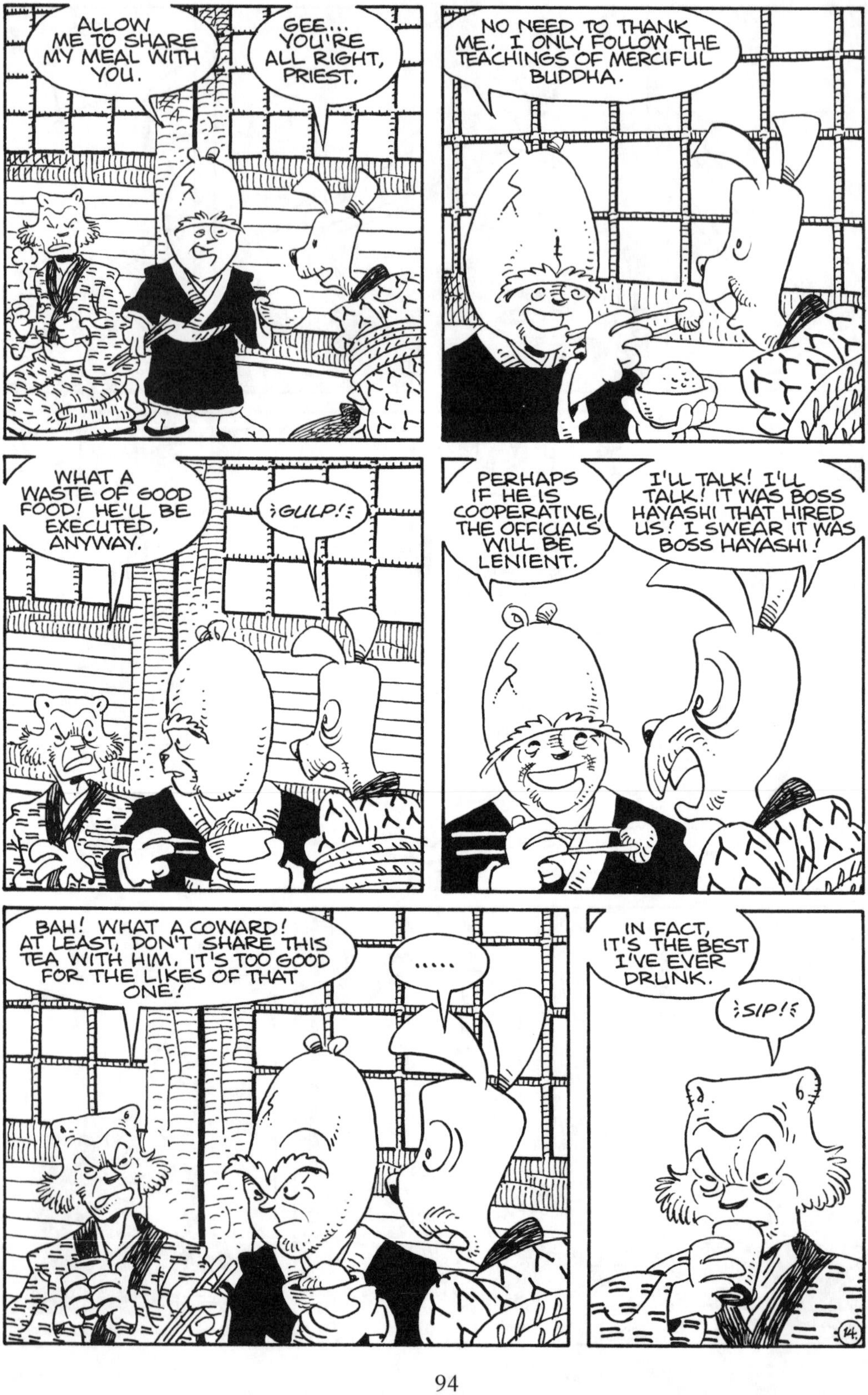
ALLOW ME TO SHARE MY MEAL WITH YOU.
GEE... YOU'RE ALL RIGHT, PRIEST.
NO NEED TO THANK ME. I ONLY FOLLOW THE TEACHINGS OF MERCIFUL BUDDHA.
WHAT A WASTE OF GOOD FOOD! HE'LL BE EXECUTED, ANYWAY.
GULP!
PERHAPS IF HE IS COOPERATIVE, THE OFFICIALS WILL BE LENIENT.
I'LL TALK! I'LL TALK! IT WAS BOSS HAYASHI THAT HIRED US! I SWEAR IT WAS BOSS HAYASHI!
BAH! WHAT A COWARD! AT LEAST, DON'T SHARE THIS TEA WITH HIM. IT'S TOO GOOD FOR THE LIKES OF THAT ONE!
.....
IN FACT, IT'S THE BEST I'VE EVER DRUNK.
SIP!
14.

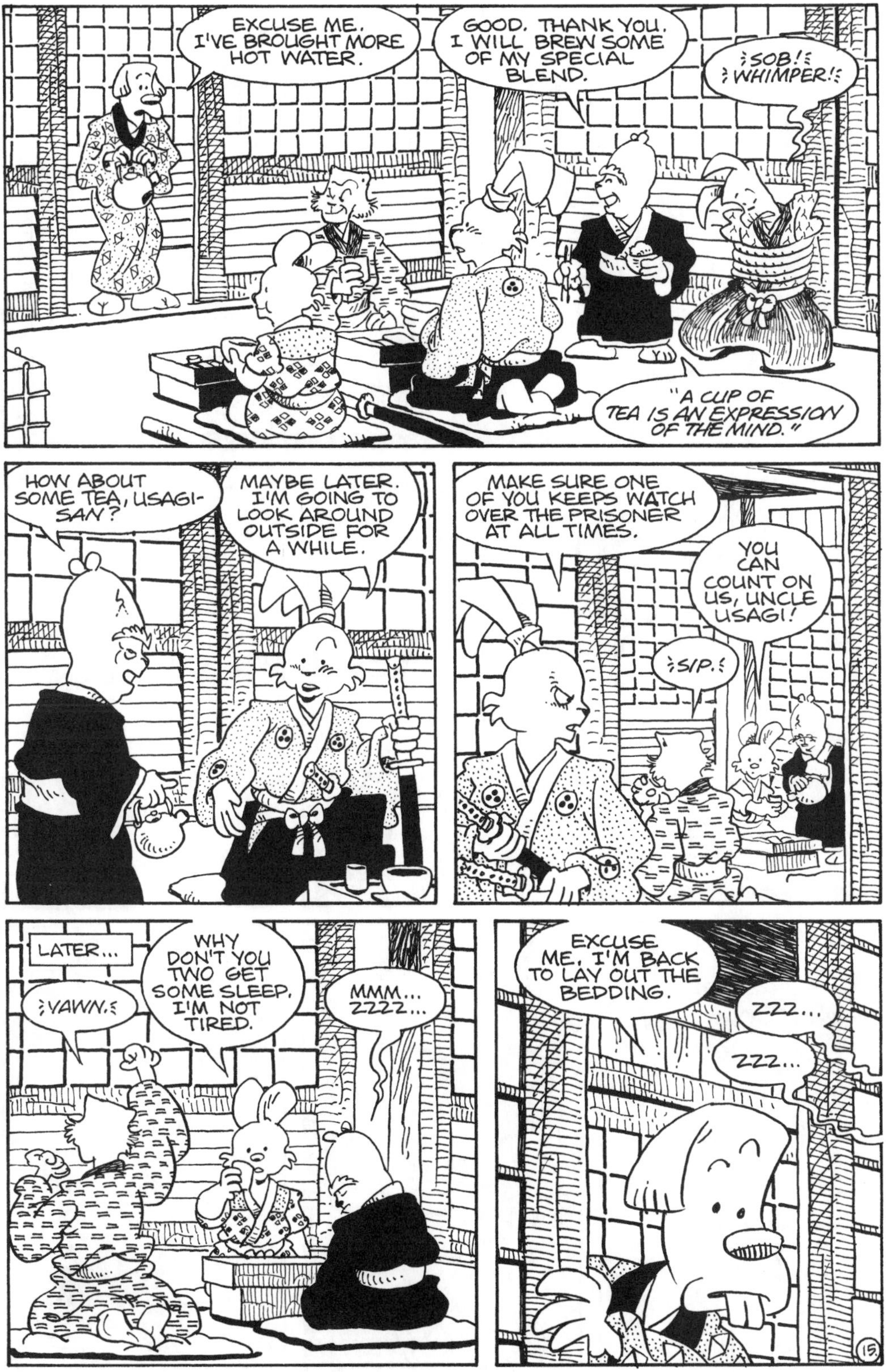
EXCUSE ME. I'VE BROUGHT MORE HOT WATER.
GOOD. THANK YOU. I WILL BREW SOME OF MY SPECIAL BLEND.
SOB! WHIMPER!
"A CUP OF TEA IS AN EXPRESSION OF THE MIND."
HOW ABOUT SOME TEA, USAGI-SAN?
MAYBE LATER. I'M GOING TO LOOK AROUND OUTSIDE FOR A WHILE.
MAKE SURE ONE OF YOU KEEPS WATCH OVER THE PRISONER AT ALL TIMES.
YOU CAN COUNT ON US, UNCLE USAGI!
SIP.
LATER...
YAWN.
WHY DON'T YOU TWO GET SOME SLEEP. I'M NOT TIRED.
MMM... ZZZZ...
EXCUSE ME. I'M BACK TO LAY OUT THE BEDDING.
ZZZ...
ZZZ...
15.

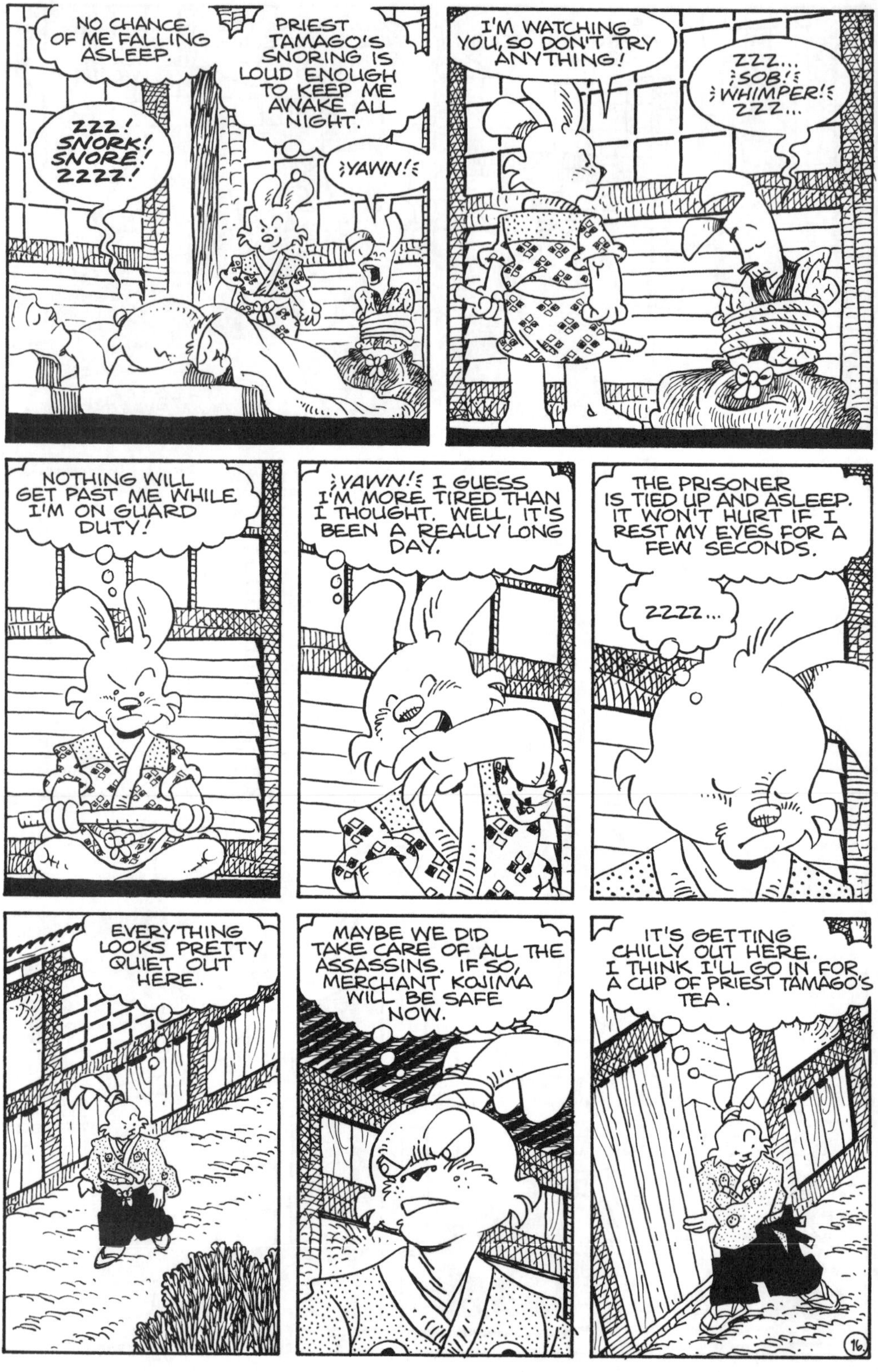
NO CHANCE OF ME FALLING ASLEEP.
PRIEST TAMAGO'S SNORING IS LOUD ENOUGH TO KEEP ME AWAKE ALL NIGHT.
ZZZ! SNORK! SNORE! ZZZZ!
YAWN!
I'M WATCHING YOU, SO DON'T TRY ANYTHING!
ZZZ... SOB! WHIMPER! ZZZ...
NOTHING WILL GET PAST ME WHILE I'M ON GUARD DUTY!
YAWN! I GUESS I'M MORE TIRED THAN I THOUGHT. WELL, IT'S BEEN A REALLY LONG DAY.
THE PRISONER IS TIED UP AND ASLEEP. IT WON'T HURT IF I REST MY EYES FOR A FEW SECONDS.
ZZZZ...
EVERYTHING LOOKS PRETTY QUIET OUT HERE.
MAYBE WE DID TAKE CARE OF ALL THE ASSASSINS. IF SO, MERCHANT KOJIMA WILL BE SAFE NOW.
IT'S GETTING CHILLY OUT HERE. I THINK I'LL GO IN FOR A CUP OF PRIEST TAMAGO'S TEA.
16

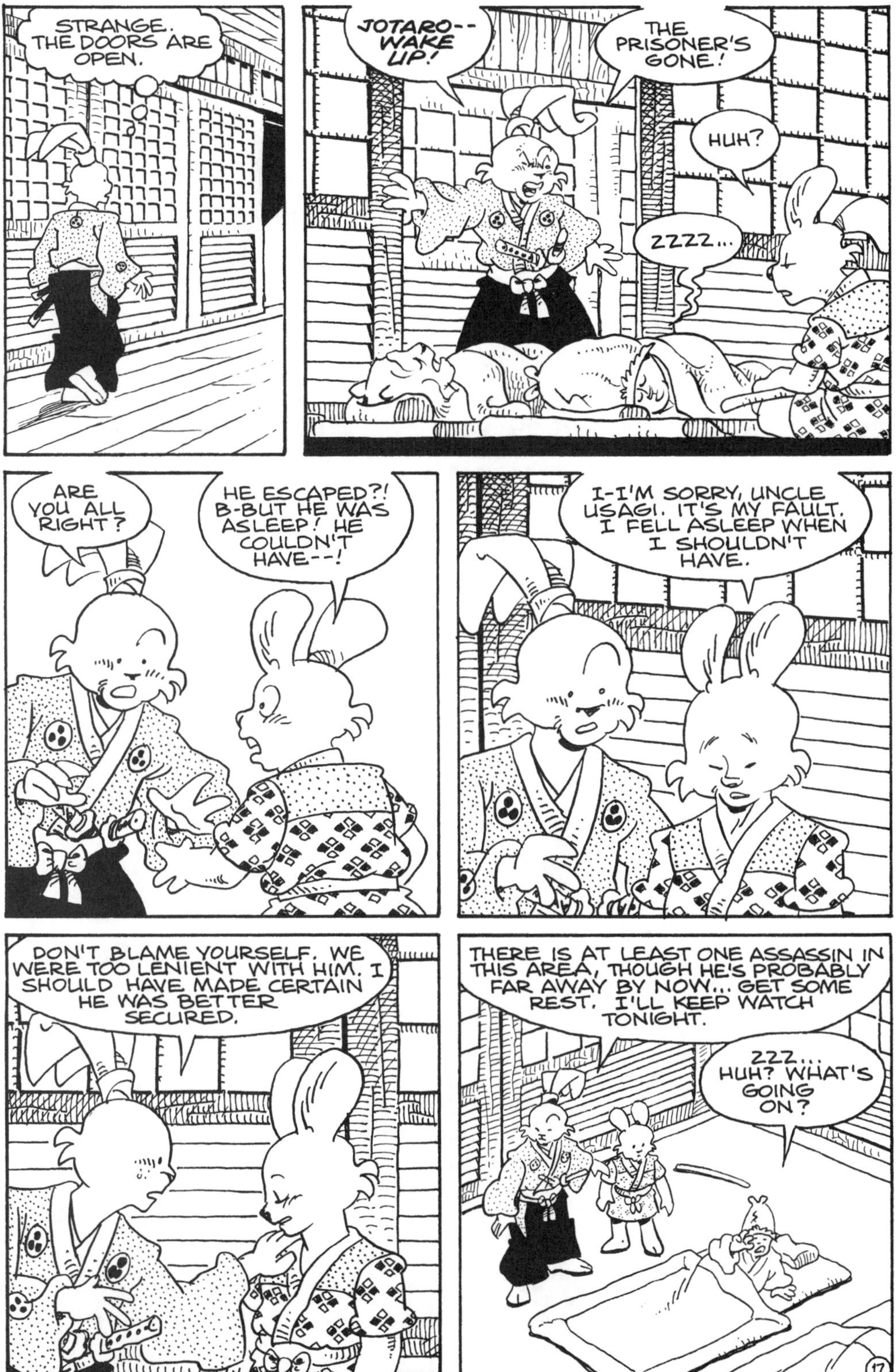
STRANGE. THE DOORS ARE OPEN.
JOTARO-- WAKE UP!
THE PRISONER'S GONE!
HUH?
ZZZZ...
ARE YOU ALL RIGHT?
HE ESCAPED?! B-BUT HE WAS ASLEEP! HE COULDN'T HAVE--!
I-I'M SORRY, UNCLE USAGI. IT'S MY FAULT. I FELL ASLEEP WHEN I SHOULDN'T HAVE.
DON'T BLAME YOURSELF. WE WERE TOO LENIENT WITH HIM. I SHOULD HAVE MADE CERTAIN HE WAS BETTER SECURED.
THERE IS AT LEAST ONE ASSASSIN IN THIS AREA, THOUGH HE'S PROBABLY FAR AWAY BY NOW... GET SOME REST. I'LL KEEP WATCH TONIGHT.
ZZZ... HUH? WHAT'S GOING ON?
17

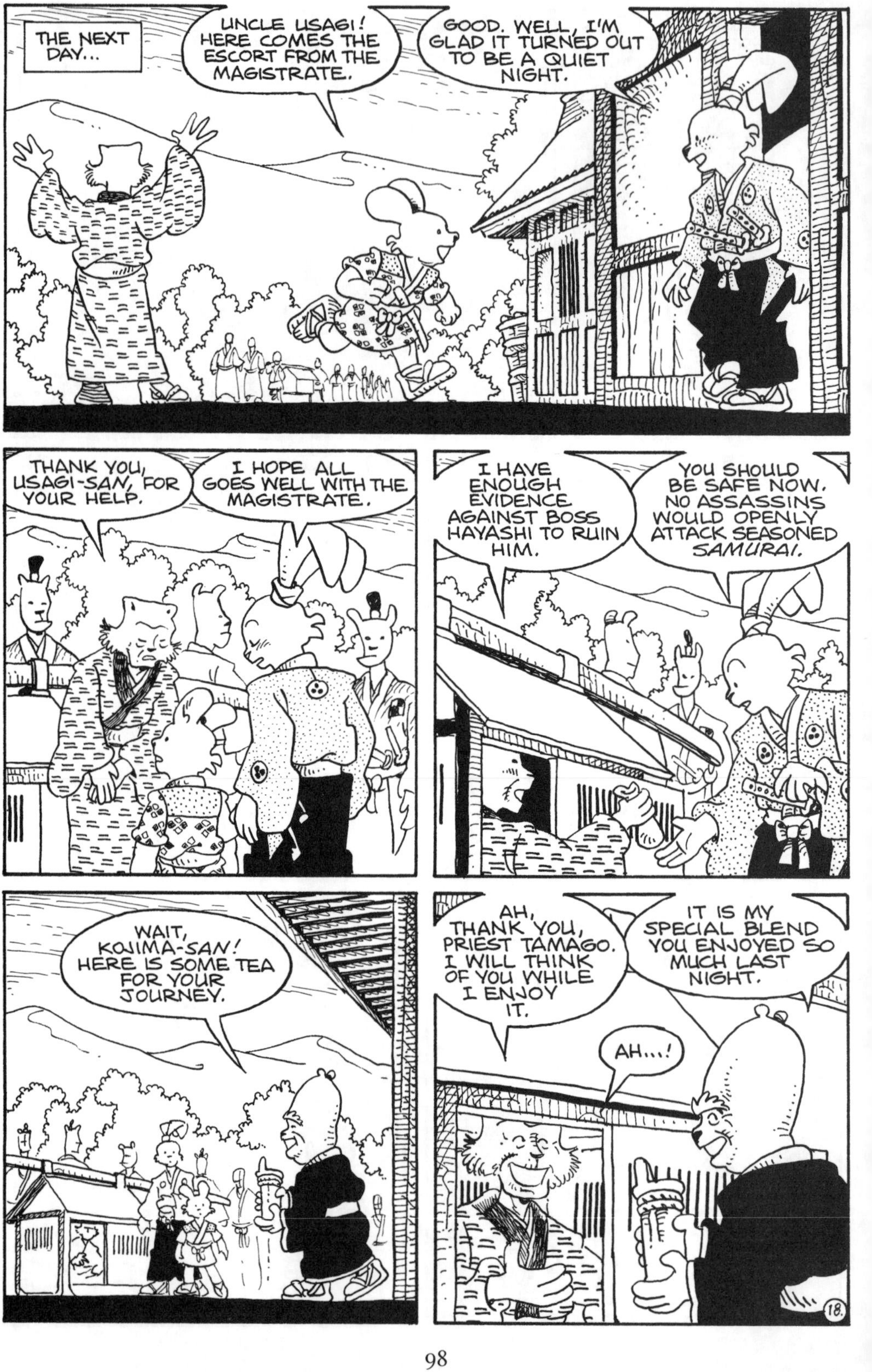
THE NEXT DAY...
UNCLE USAGI! HERE COMES THE ESCORT FROM THE MAGISTRATE.
GOOD. WELL, I'M GLAD IT TURNED OUT TO BE A QUIET NIGHT.
THANK YOU, USAGI-SAN, FOR YOUR HELP.
I HOPE ALL GOES WELL WITH THE MAGISTRATE.
I HAVE ENOUGH EVIDENCE AGAINST BOSS HAYASHI TO RUIN HIM.
YOU SHOULD BE SAFE NOW. NO ASSASSINS WOULD OPENLY ATTACK SEASONED SAMURAI.
WAIT, KOJIMA-SAN! HERE IS SOME TEA FOR YOUR JOURNEY.
AH, THANK YOU, PRIEST TAMAGO. I WILL THINK OF YOU WHILE I ENJOY IT.
IT IS MY SPECIAL BLEND YOU ENJOYED SO MUCH LAST NIGHT.
AH...!
18.

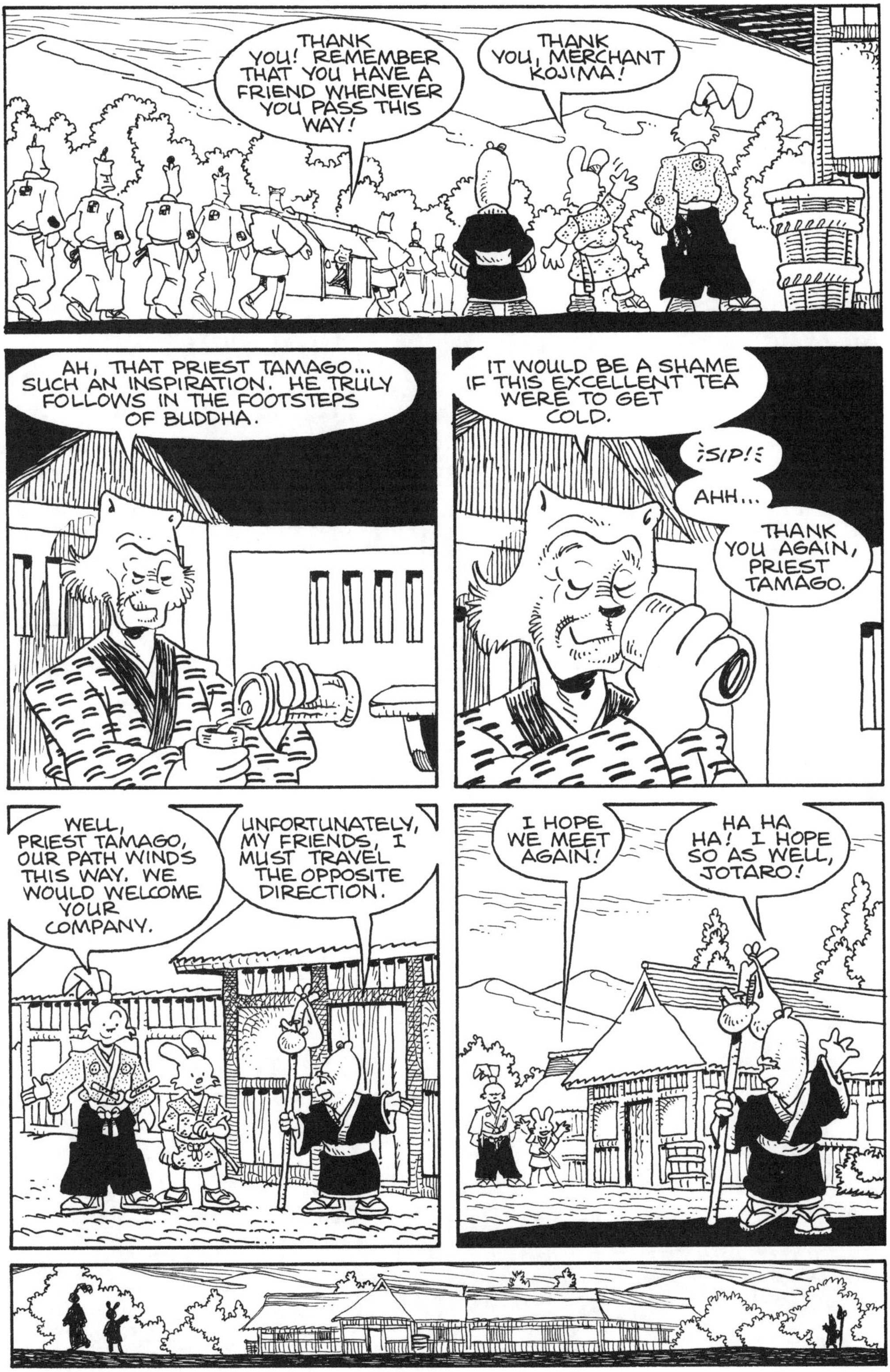
THANK YOU! REMEMBER THAT YOU HAVE A FRIEND WHENEVER YOU PASS THIS WAY!
THANK YOU, MERCHANT KOJIMA!
AH, THAT PRIEST TAMAGO... SUCH AN INSPIRATION. HE TRULY FOLLOWS IN THE FOOTSTEPS OF BUDDHA.
IT WOULD BE A SHAME IF THIS EXCELLENT TEA WERE TO GET COLD.
SIP!
AHH...
THANK YOU AGAIN, PRIEST TAMAGO.
WELL, PRIEST TAMAGO, OUR PATH WINDS THIS WAY. WE WOULD WELCOME YOUR COMPANY.
UNFORTUNATELY, MY FRIENDS, I MUST TRAVEL THE OPPOSITE DIRECTION.
I HOPE WE MEET AGAIN!
HA HA HA! I HOPE SO AS WELL, JOTARO!

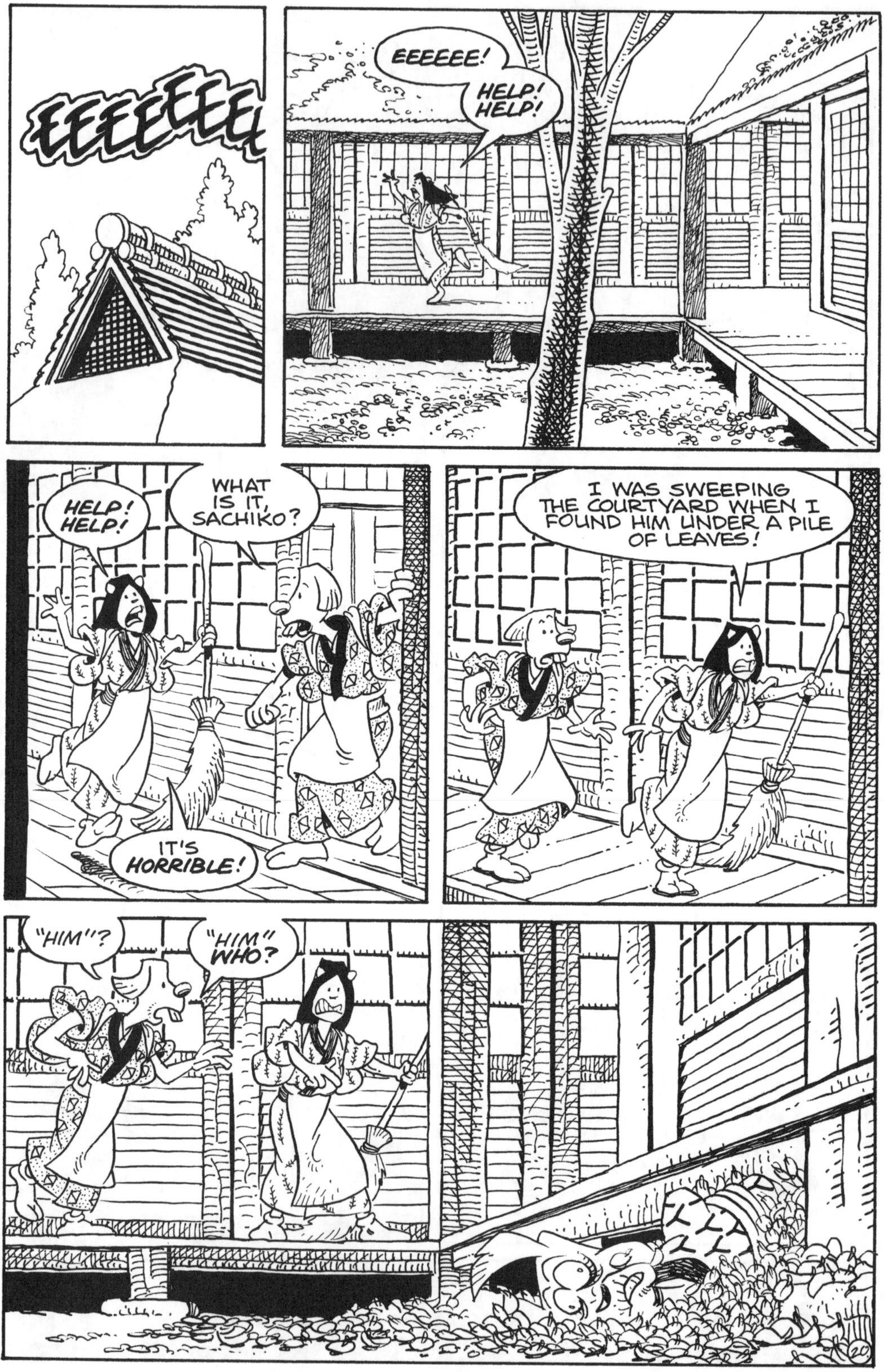
EEEEEEEE
EEEEEE!
HELP! HELP!
HELP! HELP!
WHAT IS IT, SACHIKO?
IT'S HORRIBLE!
I WAS SWEEPING THE COURTYARD WHEN I FOUND HIM UNDER A PILE OF LEAVES!
"HIM"?
"HIM" WHO?
20

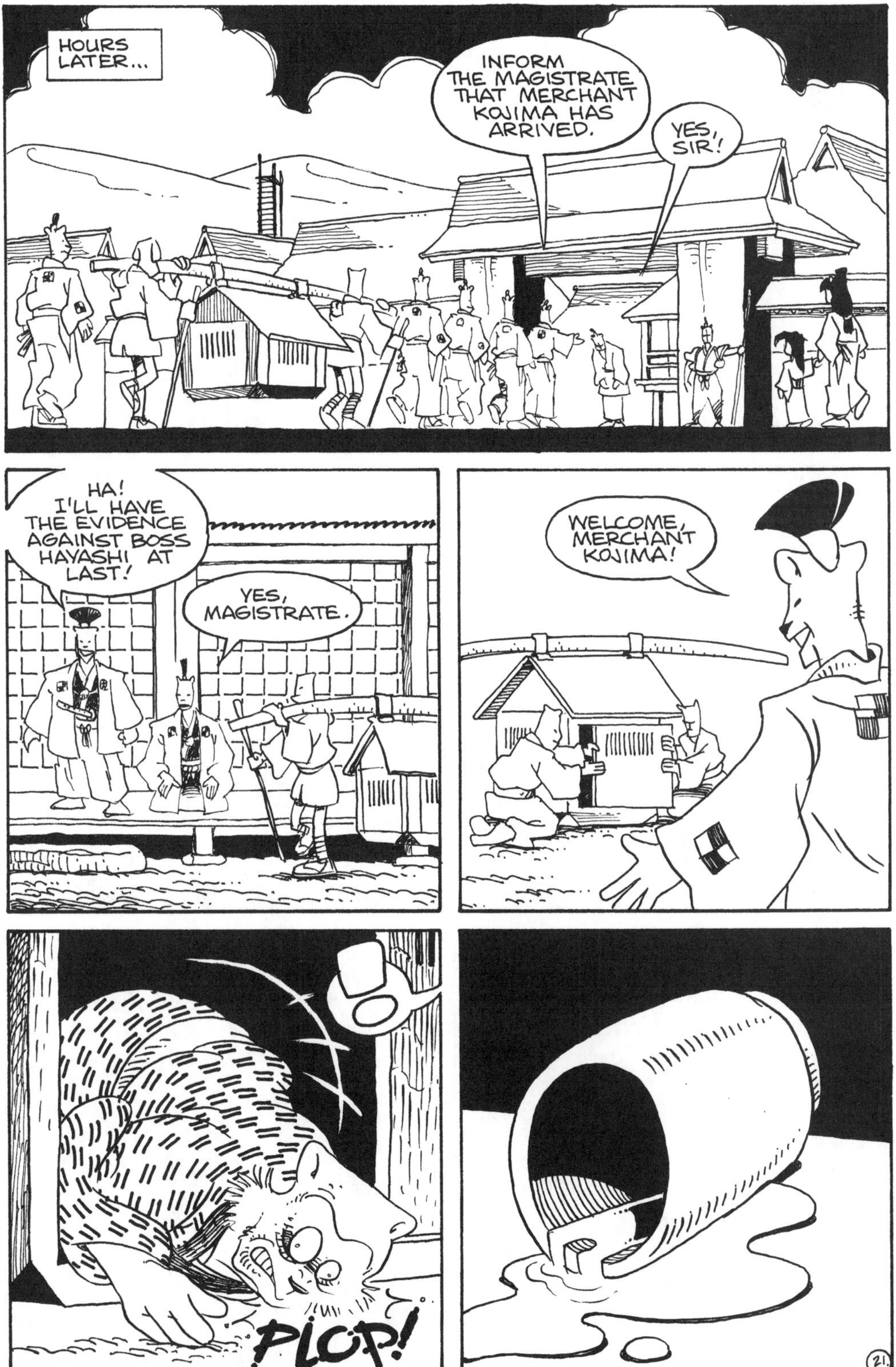
HOURS LATER...
INFORM THE MAGISTRATE THAT MERCHANT KOJIMA HAS ARRIVED.
YES, SIR!
HA! I'LL HAVE THE EVIDENCE AGAINST BOSS HAYASHI AT LAST!
YES, MAGISTRATE.
WELCOME, MERCHANT KOJIMA!
PLOP!
21.

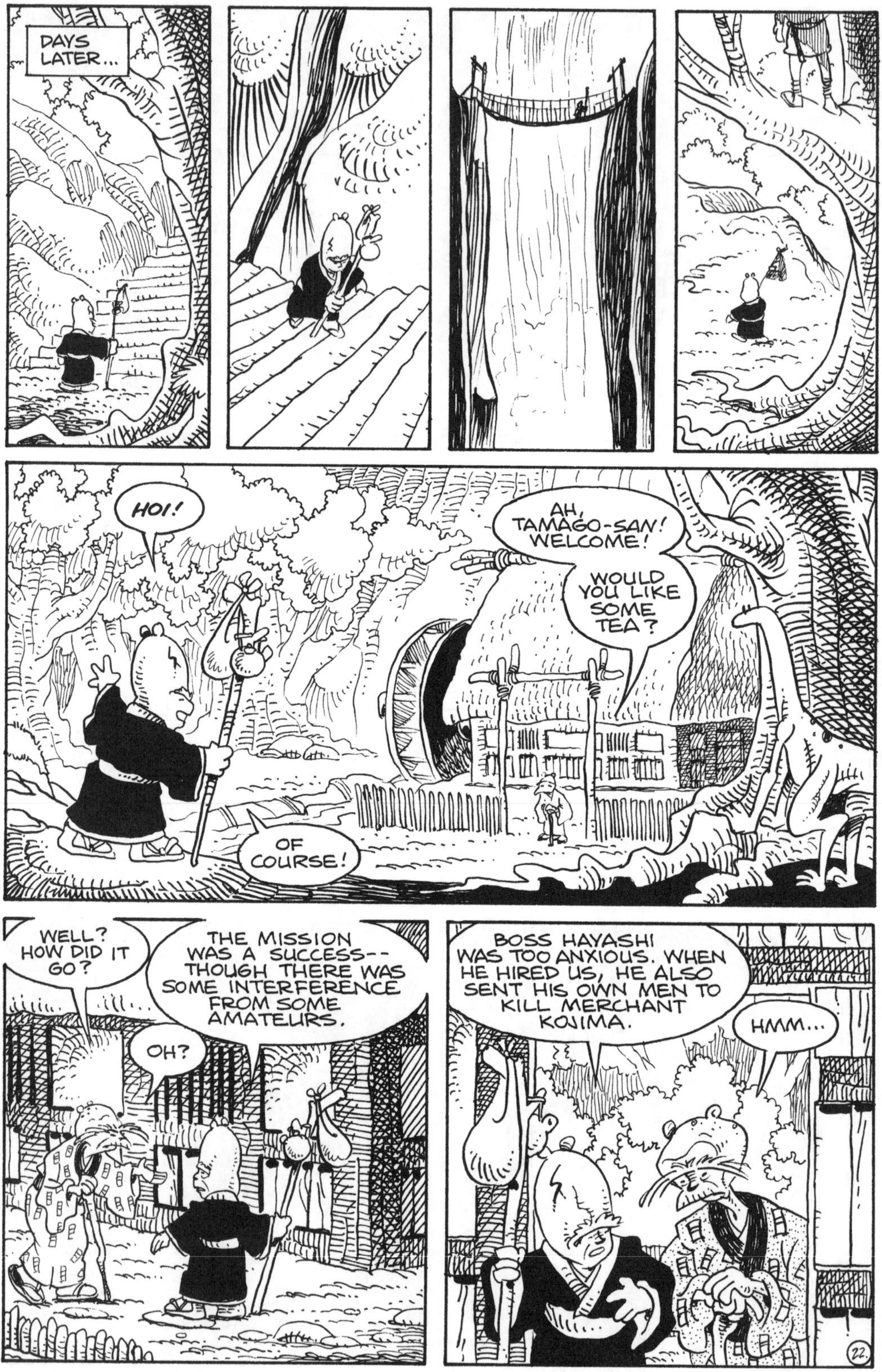
DAYS LATER...
HOI!
AH, TAMAGO-SAN! WELCOME!
WOULD YOU LIKE SOME TEA?
OF COURSE!
WELL? HOW DID IT GO?
THE MISSION WAS A SUCCESS-- THOUGH THERE WAS SOME INTERFERENCE FROM SOME AMATEURS.
OH?
BOSS HAYASHI WAS TOO ANXIOUS. WHEN HE HIRED US, HE ALSO SENT HIS OWN MEN TO KILL MERCHANT KOJIMA.
HMM...
22.

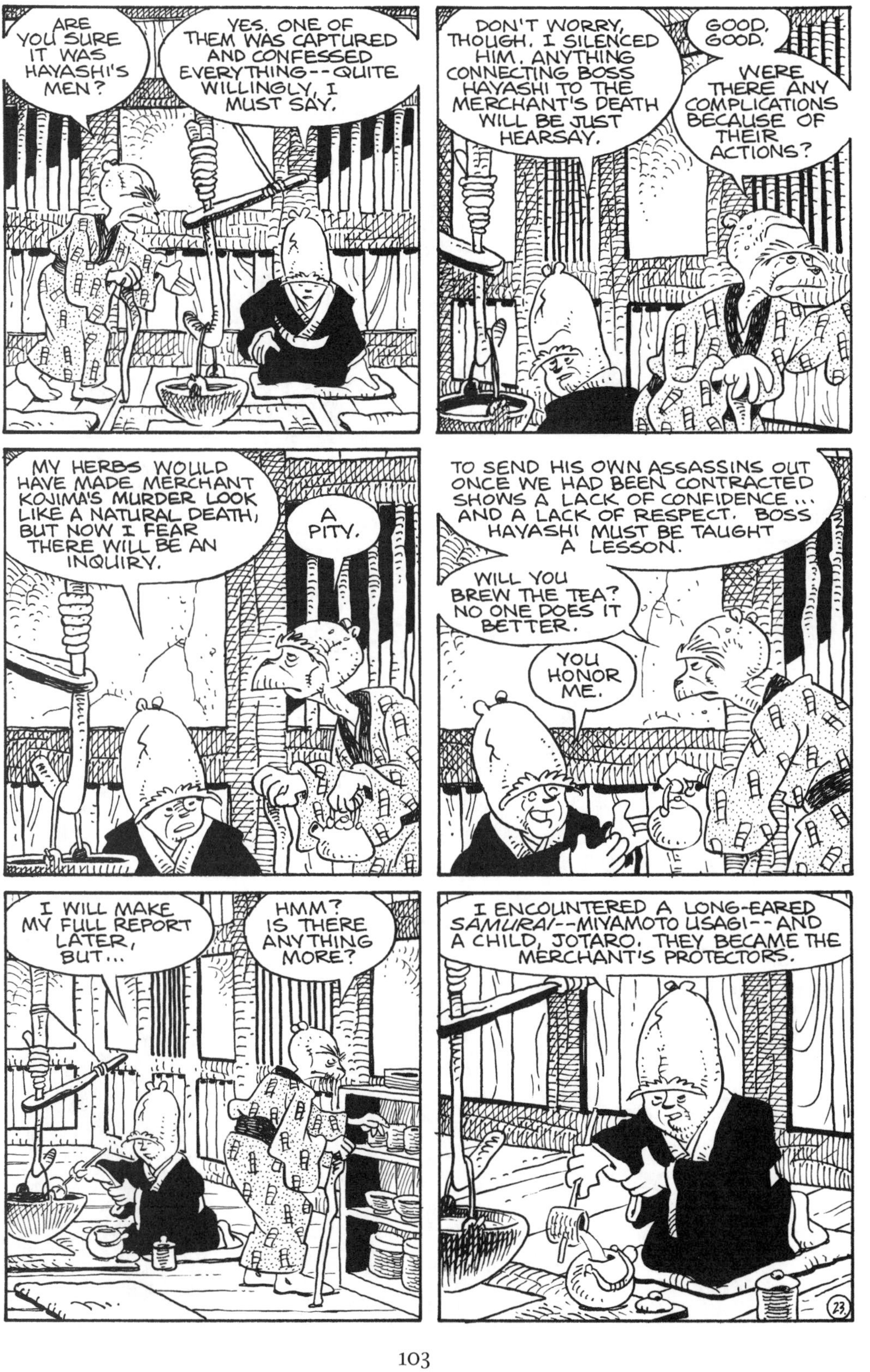
ARE YOU SURE IT WAS HAYASHI'S MEN?
YES. ONE OF THEM WAS CAPTURED AND CONFESSED EVERYTHING--QUITE WILLINGLY, I MUST SAY.
DON'T WORRY, THOUGH. I SILENCED HIM. ANYTHING CONNECTING BOSS HAYASHI TO THE MERCHANT'S DEATH WILL BE JUST HEARSAY.
GOOD, GOOD.
WERE THERE ANY COMPLICATIONS BECAUSE OF THEIR ACTIONS?
MY HERBS WOULD HAVE MADE MERCHANT KOJIMA'S MURDER LOOK LIKE A NATURAL DEATH, BUT NOW I FEAR THERE WILL BE AN INQUIRY.
A PITY.
TO SEND HIS OWN ASSASSINS OUT ONCE WE HAD BEEN CONTRACTED SHOWS A LACK OF CONFIDENCE... AND A LACK OF RESPECT. BOSS HAYASHI MUST BE TAUGHT A LESSON.
WILL YOU BREW THE TEA? NO ONE DOES IT BETTER.
YOU HONOR ME.
I WILL MAKE MY FULL REPORT LATER, BUT...
HMM? IS THERE ANYTHING MORE?
I ENCOUNTERED A LONG-EARED SAMURAI--MIYAMOTO USAGI--AND A CHILD, JOTARO. THEY BECAME THE MERCHANT'S PROTECTORS.
23

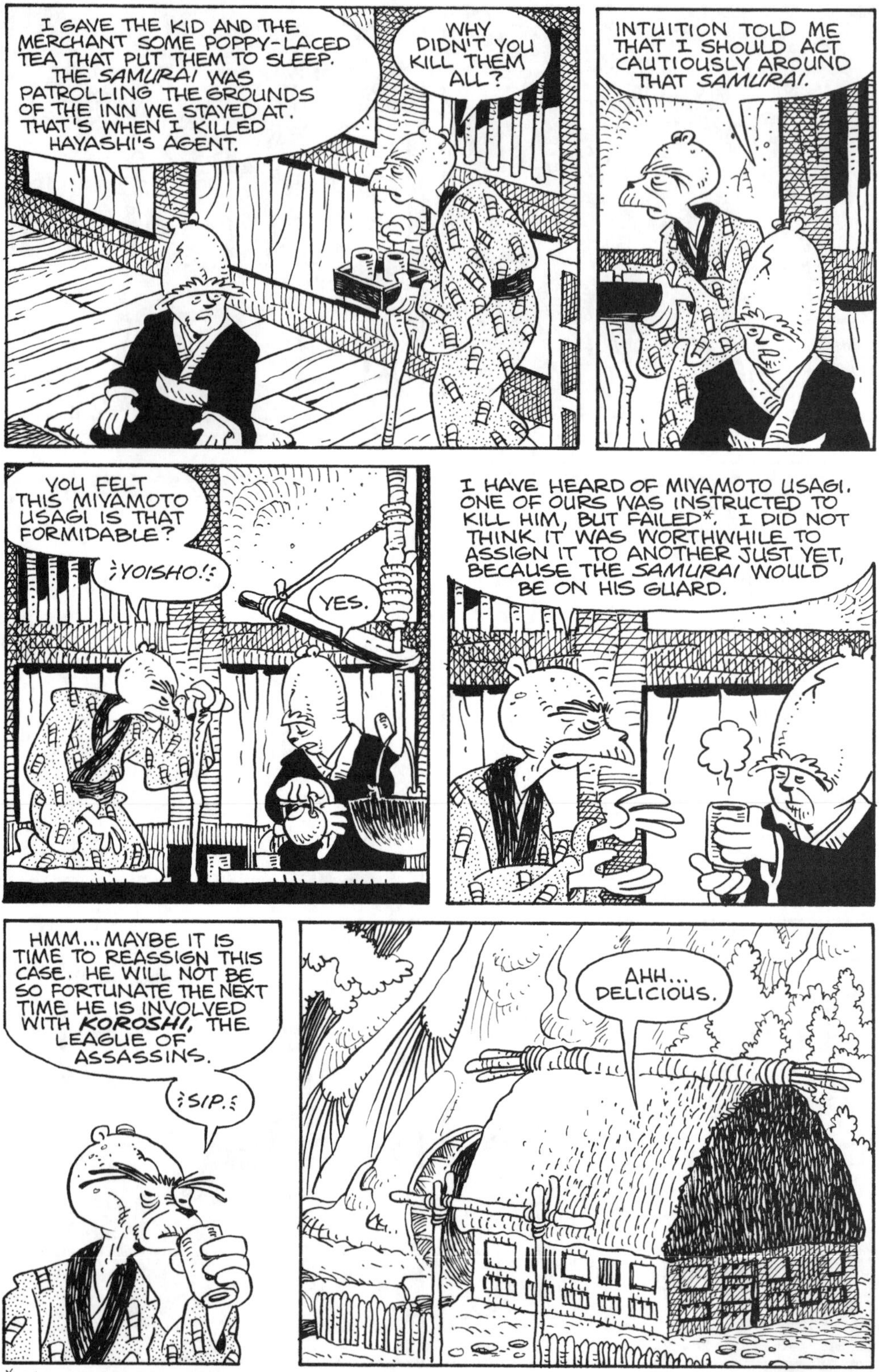
I GAVE THE KID AND THE MERCHANT SOME POPPY-LACED TEA THAT PUT THEM TO SLEEP. THE *SAMURAI* WAS PATROLLING THE GROUNDS OF THE INN WE STAYED AT. THAT'S WHEN I KILLED HAYASHI'S AGENT.
WHY DIDN'T YOU KILL THEM ALL?
INTUITION TOLD ME THAT I SHOULD ACT CAUTIOUSLY AROUND THAT *SAMURAI*.
YOU FELT THIS MIYAMOTO USAGI IS THAT FORMIDABLE?
YOISHO!
YES.
I HAVE HEARD OF MIYAMOTO USAGI. ONE OF OURS WAS INSTRUCTED TO KILL HIM, BUT FAILED*. I DID NOT THINK IT WAS WORTHWHILE TO ASSIGN IT TO ANOTHER JUST YET, BECAUSE THE *SAMURAI* WOULD BE ON HIS GUARD.
HMM... MAYBE IT IS TIME TO REASSIGN THIS CASE. HE WILL NOT BE SO FORTUNATE THE NEXT TIME HE IS INVOLVED WITH ***KOROSHI***, THE LEAGUE OF ASSASSINS.
SIP.
AHH... DELICIOUS.

*UY BOOK 14: DEMON MASK

THE END.

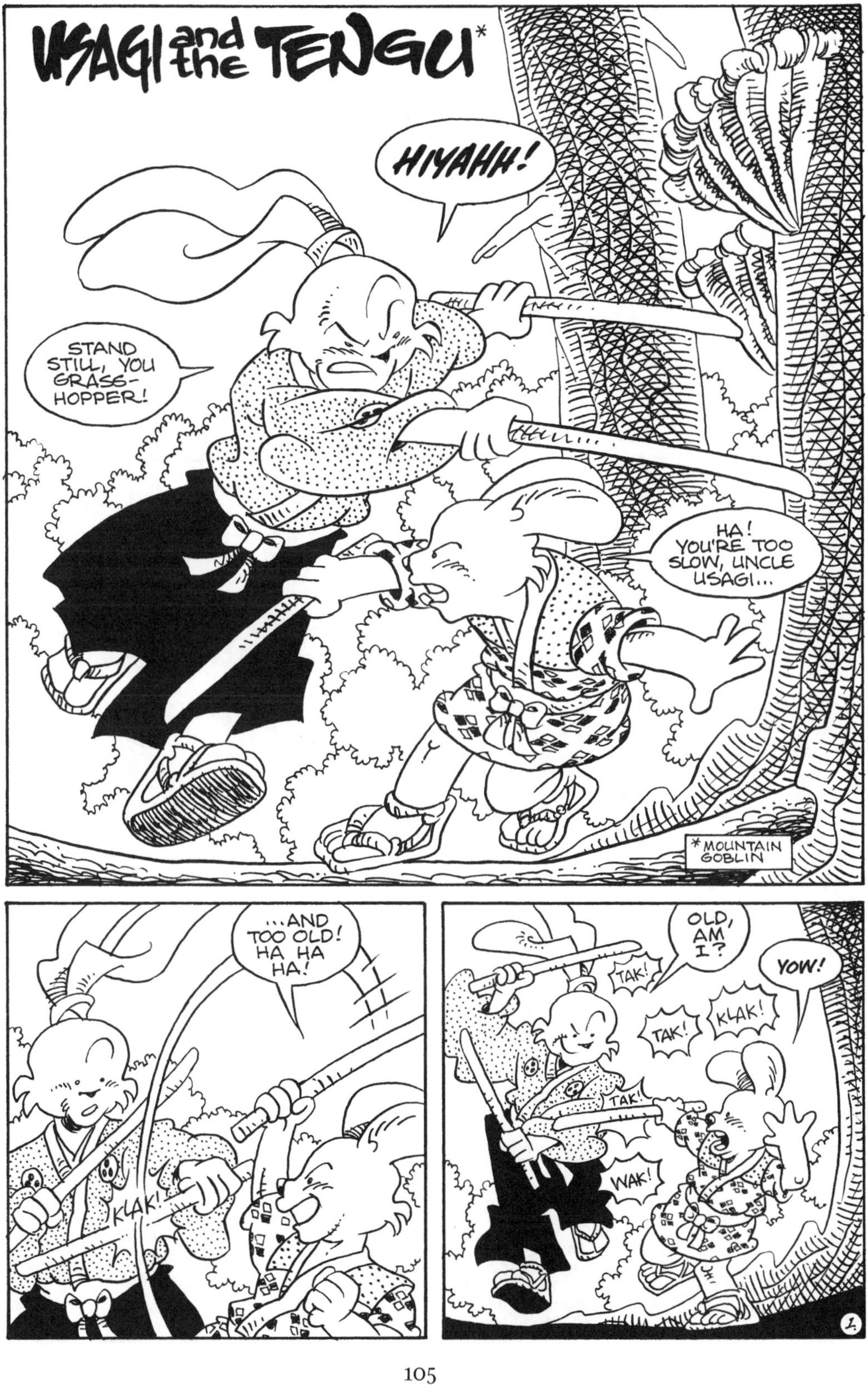
USAGI and the TENGU*
HIYAHH!
STAND STILL, YOU GRASS-HOPPER!
HA! YOU'RE TOO SLOW, UNCLE USAGI...
*MOUNTAIN GOBLIN
...AND TOO OLD! HA HA HA!
KLAK!
OLD, AM I?
TAK!
YOW!
TAK!
KLAK!
TAK!
WAK!
1.

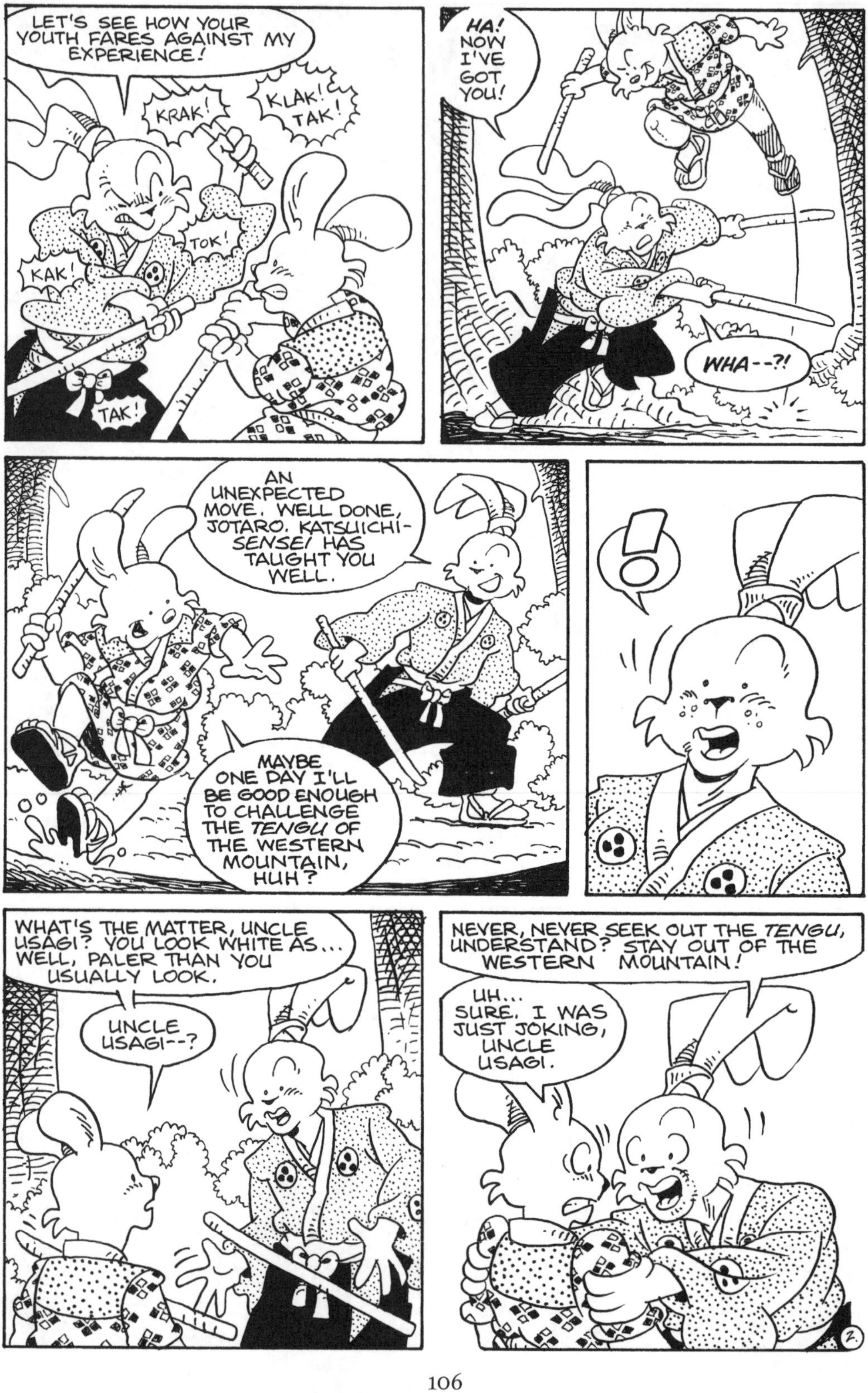
LET'S SEE HOW YOUR YOUTH FARES AGAINST MY EXPERIENCE!
KRAK!
KLAK! TAK!
TOK!
KAK!
TAK!
HA! NOW I'VE GOT YOU!
WHA--?!
AN UNEXPECTED MOVE. WELL DONE, JOTARO. KATSUICHI-SENSEI HAS TAUGHT YOU WELL.
MAYBE ONE DAY I'LL BE GOOD ENOUGH TO CHALLENGE THE TENGU OF THE WESTERN MOUNTAIN, HUH?
!
WHAT'S THE MATTER, UNCLE USAGI? YOU LOOK WHITE AS... WELL, PALER THAN YOU USUALLY LOOK.
UNCLE USAGI--?
NEVER, NEVER SEEK OUT THE TENGU, UNDERSTAND? STAY OUT OF THE WESTERN MOUNTAIN!
UH... SURE. I WAS JUST JOKING, UNCLE USAGI.
2.

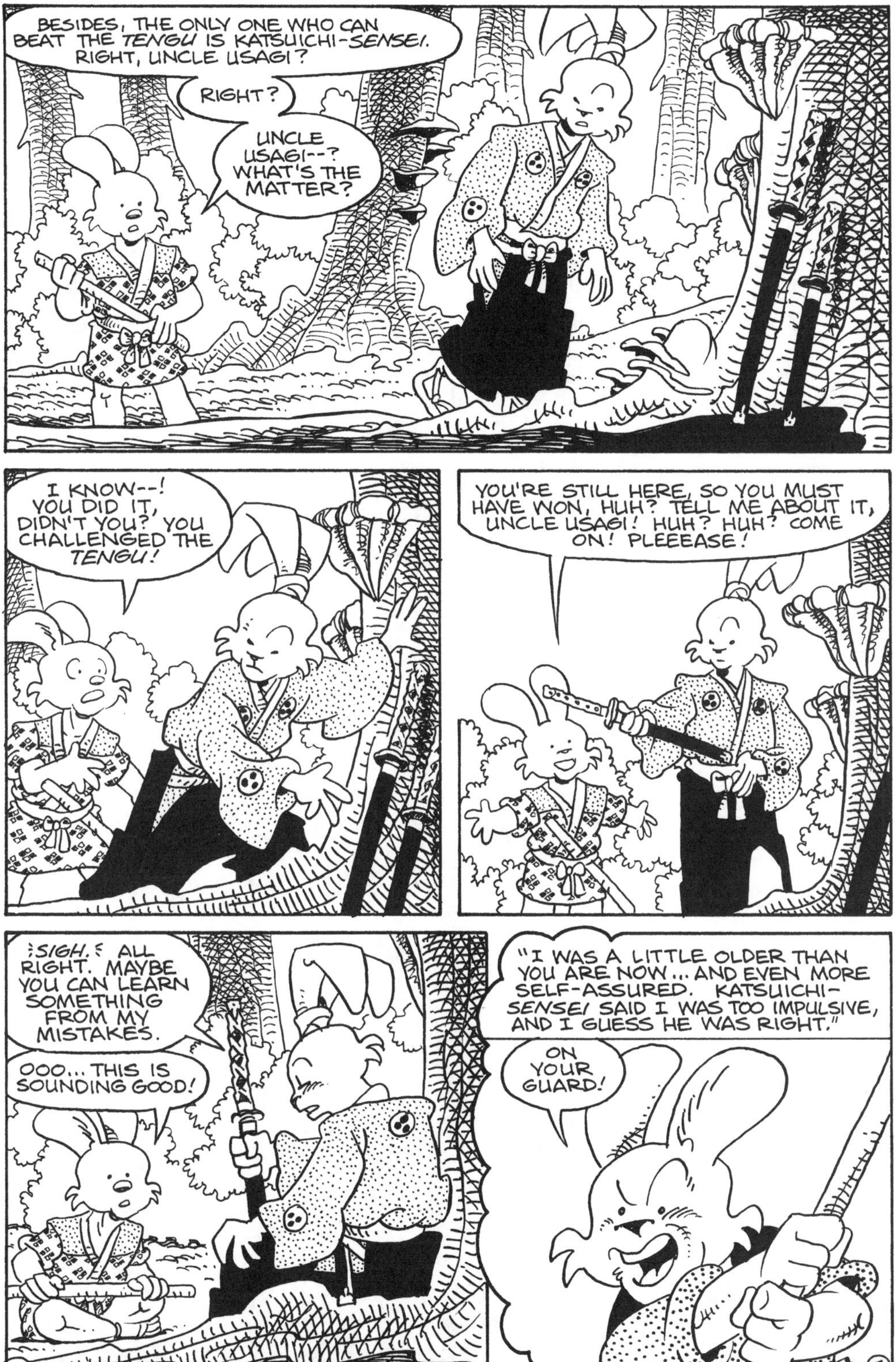

BESIDES, THE ONLY ONE WHO CAN BEAT THE *TENGU* IS KATSUICHI-*SENSEI*. RIGHT, UNCLE USAGI?
RIGHT?
UNCLE USAGI--? WHAT'S THE MATTER?
I KNOW--! YOU DID IT, DIDN'T YOU? YOU CHALLENGED THE *TENGU*!
YOU'RE STILL HERE, SO YOU MUST HAVE WON, HUH? TELL ME ABOUT IT, UNCLE USAGI! HUH? HUH? COME ON! PLEEEASE!
SIGH. ALL RIGHT. MAYBE YOU CAN LEARN SOMETHING FROM MY MISTAKES.
OOO... THIS IS SOUNDING GOOD!
"I WAS A LITTLE OLDER THAN YOU ARE NOW... AND EVEN MORE SELF-ASSURED. KATSUICHI-*SENSEI* SAID I WAS TOO IMPULSIVE, AND I GUESS HE WAS RIGHT."
ON YOUR GUARD!

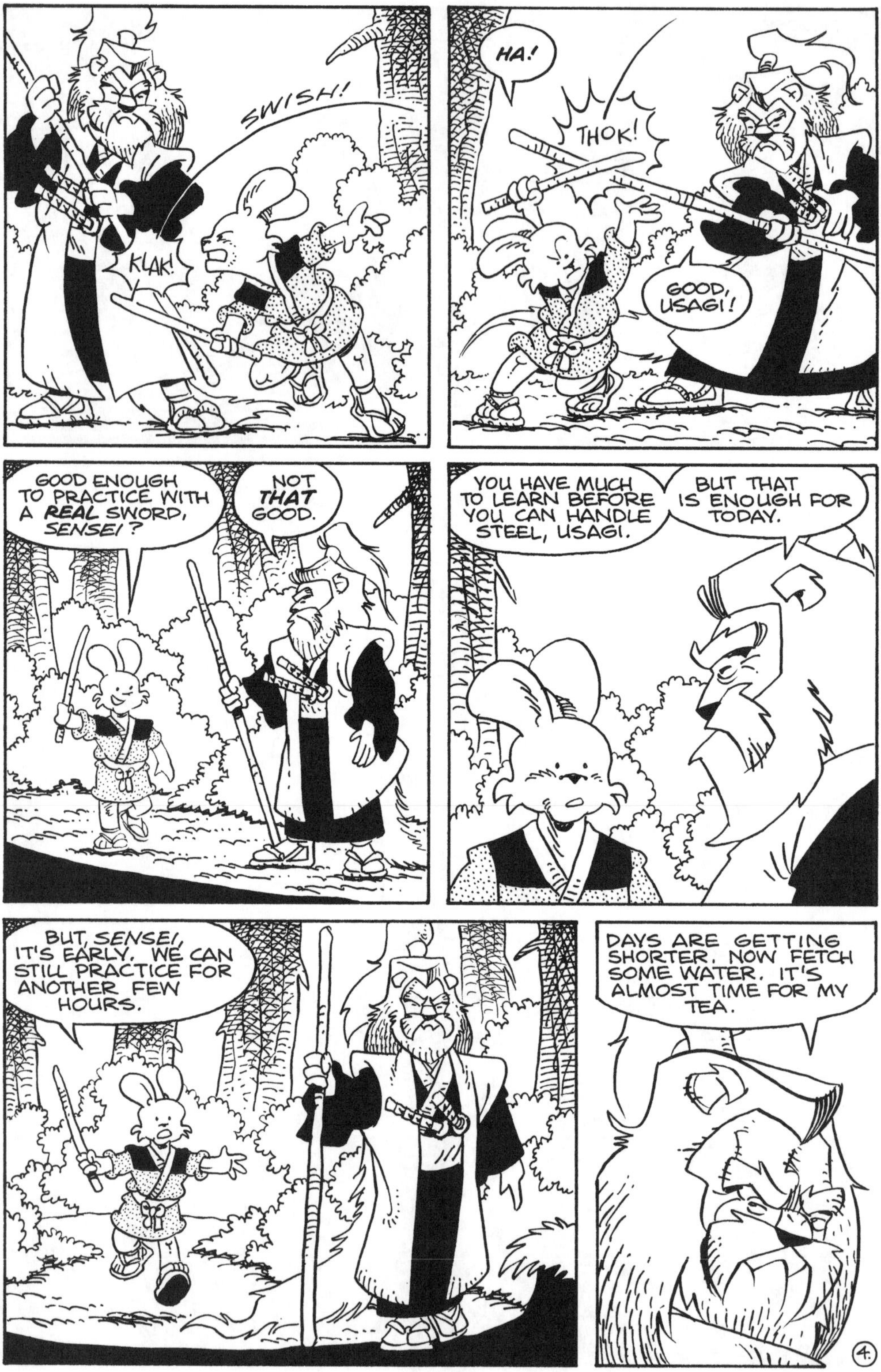
SWISH!
KLAK!
HA!
THOK!
GOOD, USAGI!
GOOD ENOUGH TO PRACTICE WITH A REAL SWORD, SENSEI?
NOT THAT GOOD.
YOU HAVE MUCH TO LEARN BEFORE YOU CAN HANDLE STEEL, USAGI.
BUT THAT IS ENOUGH FOR TODAY.
BUT, SENSEI, IT'S EARLY. WE CAN STILL PRACTICE FOR ANOTHER FEW HOURS.
DAYS ARE GETTING SHORTER. NOW FETCH SOME WATER. IT'S ALMOST TIME FOR MY TEA.
4.

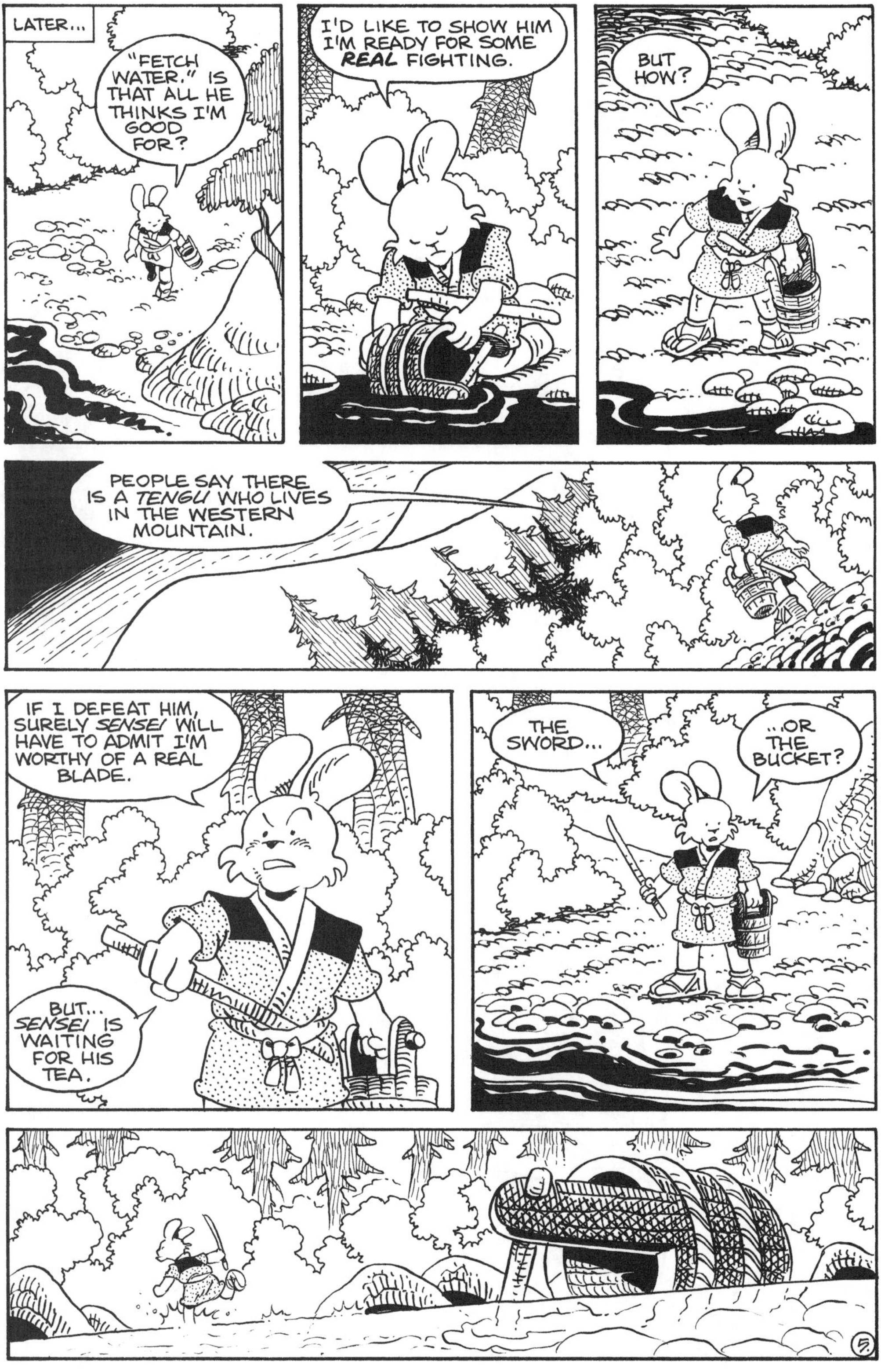
LATER...
"FETCH WATER." IS THAT ALL HE THINKS I'M GOOD FOR?
I'D LIKE TO SHOW HIM I'M READY FOR SOME **REAL** FIGHTING.
BUT HOW?
PEOPLE SAY THERE IS A *TENGU* WHO LIVES IN THE WESTERN MOUNTAIN.
IF I DEFEAT HIM, SURELY *SENSEI* WILL HAVE TO ADMIT I'M WORTHY OF A REAL BLADE.
BUT... *SENSEI* IS WAITING FOR HIS TEA.
THE SWORD...
...OR THE BUCKET?
5

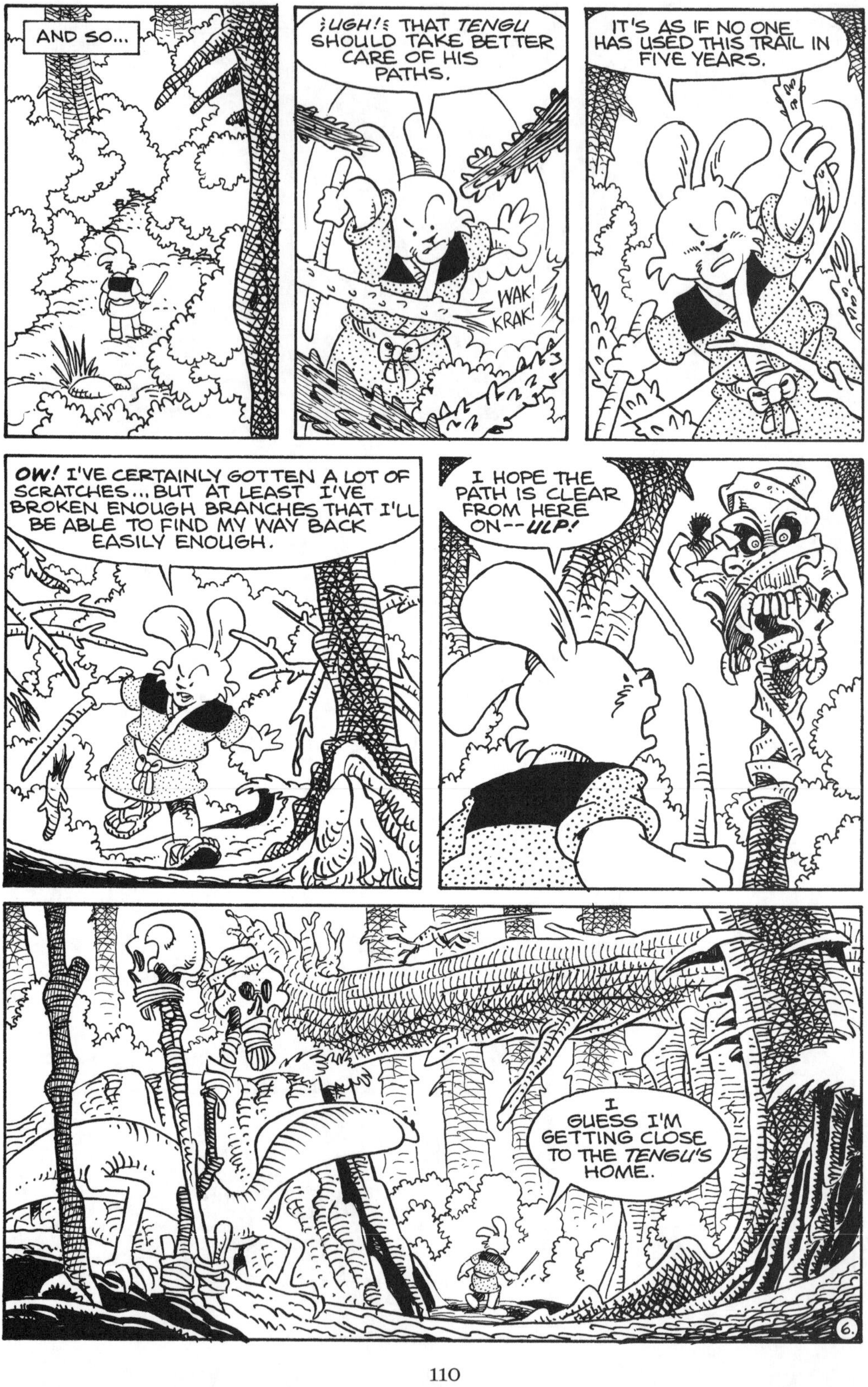
AND SO...
UGH! THAT TENGU SHOULD TAKE BETTER CARE OF HIS PATHS.
WAK! KRAK!
IT'S AS IF NO ONE HAS USED THIS TRAIL IN FIVE YEARS.
OW! I'VE CERTAINLY GOTTEN A LOT OF SCRATCHES... BUT AT LEAST I'VE BROKEN ENOUGH BRANCHES THAT I'LL BE ABLE TO FIND MY WAY BACK EASILY ENOUGH.
I HOPE THE PATH IS CLEAR FROM HERE ON--ULP!
I GUESS I'M GETTING CLOSE TO THE TENGU'S HOME.
6.

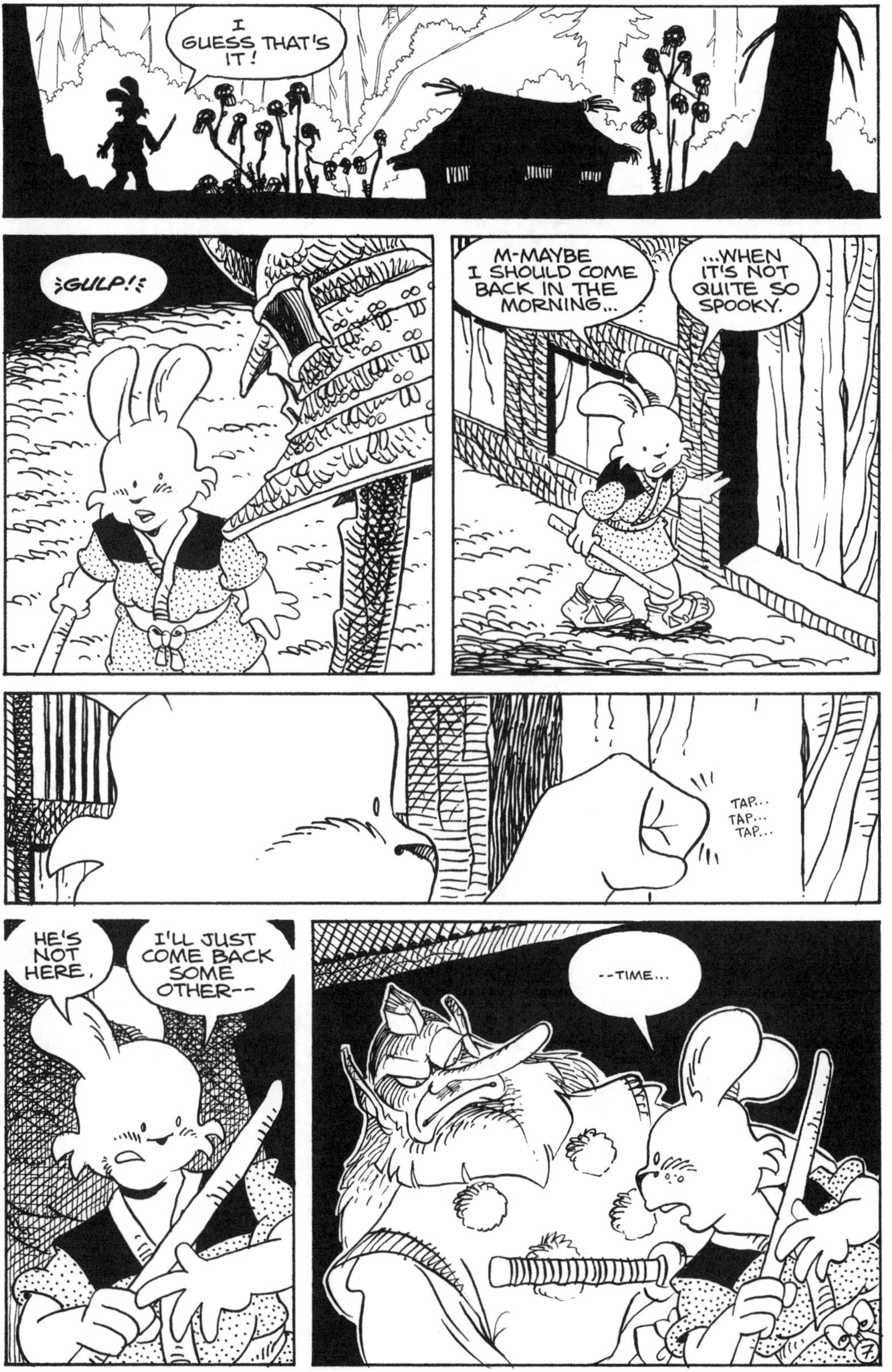
I GUESS THAT'S IT!
;GULP!;
M-MAYBE I SHOULD COME BACK IN THE MORNING...
...WHEN IT'S NOT QUITE SO SPOOKY.
TAP... TAP... TAP...
HE'S NOT HERE.
I'LL JUST COME BACK SOME OTHER--
--TIME...
7.

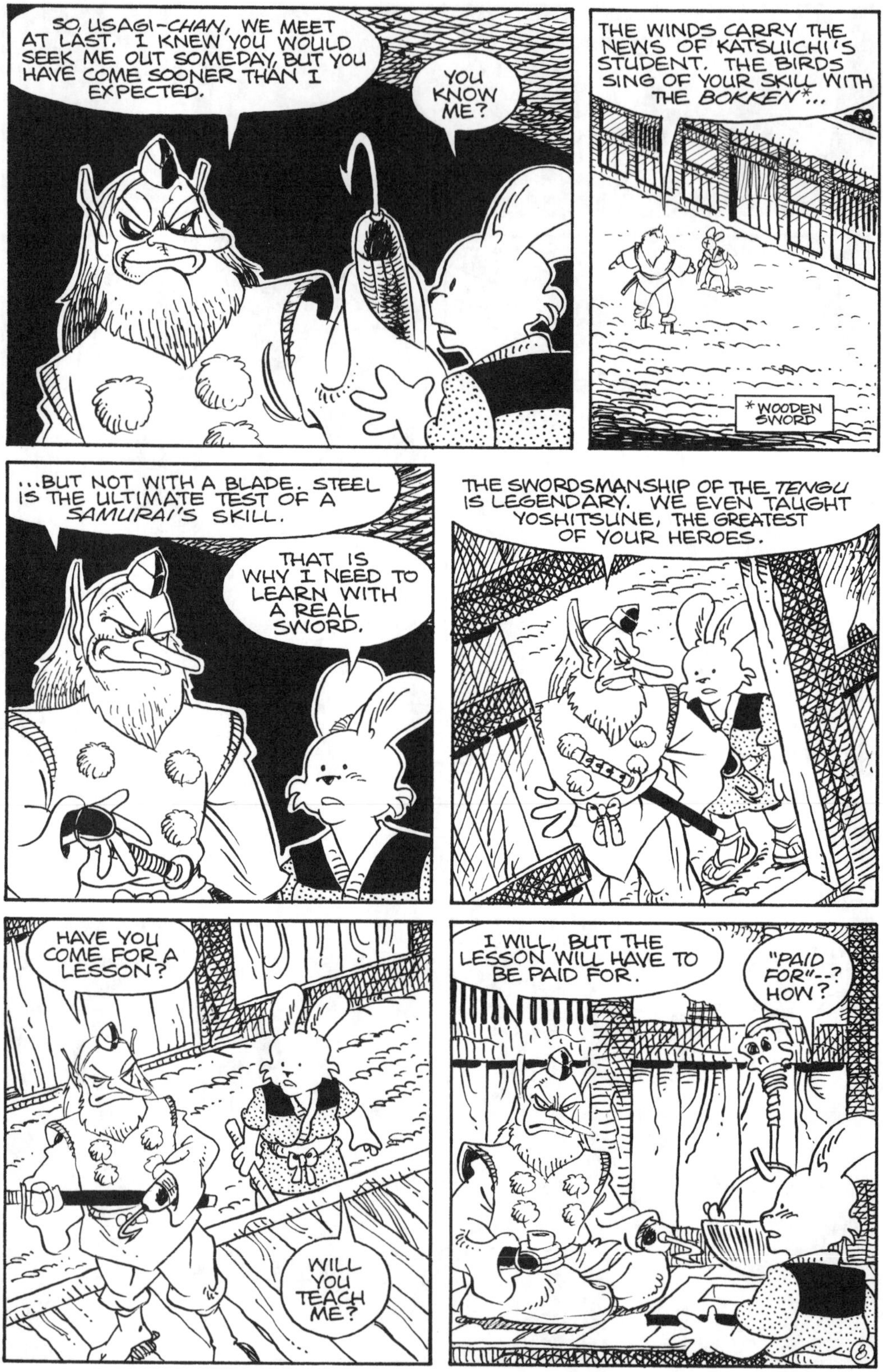
SO, USAGI-*CHAN*, WE MEET AT LAST. I KNEW YOU WOULD SEEK ME OUT SOMEDAY, BUT YOU HAVE COME SOONER THAN I EXPECTED.
YOU KNOW ME?
THE WINDS CARRY THE NEWS OF KATSUICHI'S STUDENT. THE BIRDS SING OF YOUR SKILL WITH THE *BOKKEN**...
*WOODEN SWORD
...BUT NOT WITH A BLADE. STEEL IS THE ULTIMATE TEST OF A *SAMURAI*'S SKILL.
THAT IS WHY I NEED TO LEARN WITH A REAL SWORD.
THE SWORDSMANSHIP OF THE *TENGU* IS LEGENDARY. WE EVEN TAUGHT YOSHITSUNE, THE GREATEST OF YOUR HEROES.
HAVE YOU COME FOR A LESSON?
WILL YOU TEACH ME?
I WILL, BUT THE LESSON WILL HAVE TO BE PAID FOR.
"*PAID FOR*"--? HOW?
8.

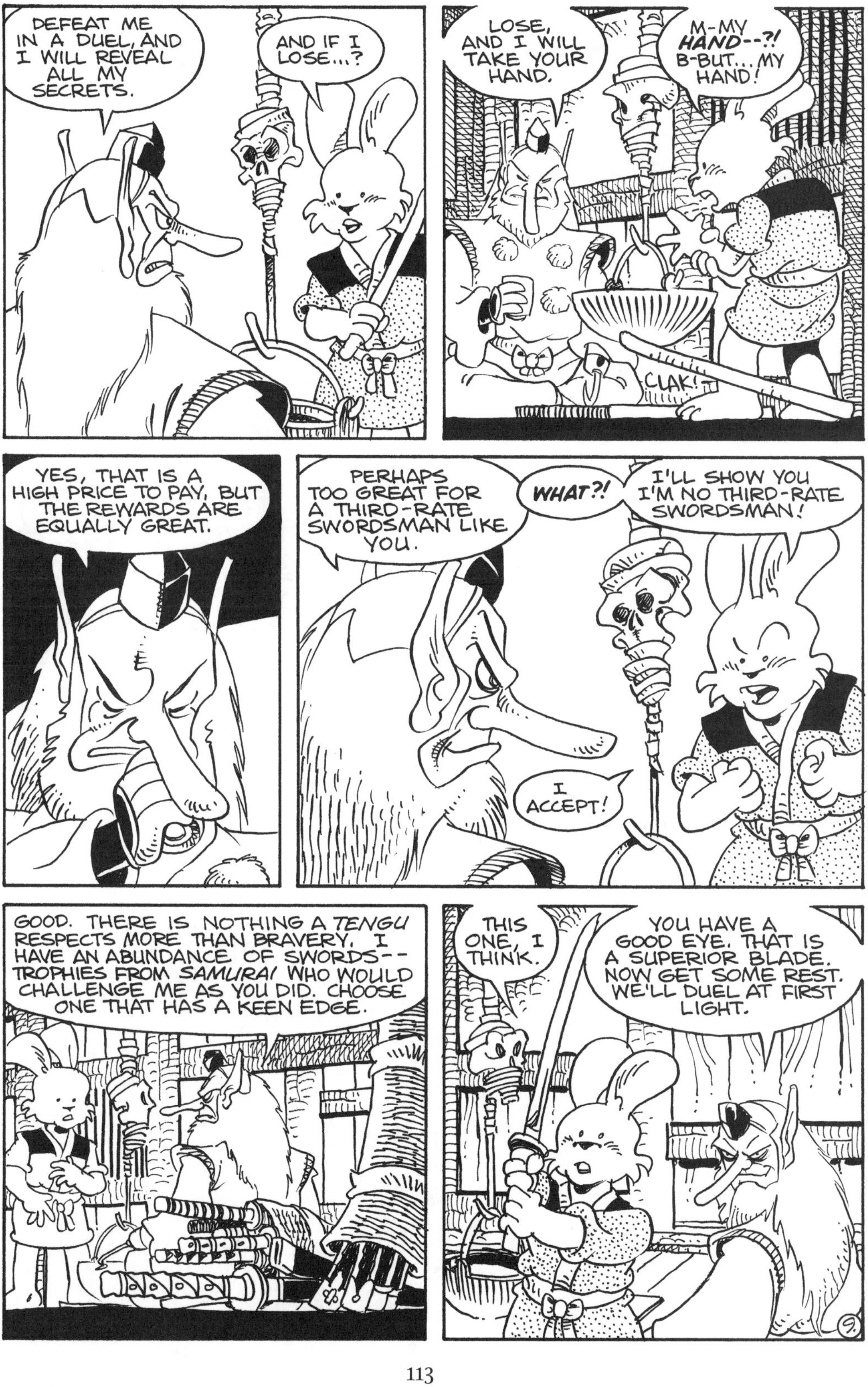
DEFEAT ME IN A DUEL, AND I WILL REVEAL ALL MY SECRETS.
AND IF I LOSE...?
LOSE, AND I WILL TAKE YOUR HAND.
M-MY *HAND*--?! B-BUT... MY HAND!
CLAK!
YES, THAT IS A HIGH PRICE TO PAY, BUT THE REWARDS ARE EQUALLY GREAT.
PERHAPS TOO GREAT FOR A THIRD-RATE SWORDSMAN LIKE YOU.
WHAT?!
I'LL SHOW YOU I'M NO THIRD-RATE SWORDSMAN!
I ACCEPT!
GOOD. THERE IS NOTHING A *TENGU* RESPECTS MORE THAN BRAVERY. I HAVE AN ABUNDANCE OF SWORDS--TROPHIES FROM *SAMURAI* WHO WOULD CHALLENGE ME AS YOU DID. CHOOSE ONE THAT HAS A KEEN EDGE.
THIS ONE, I THINK.
YOU HAVE A GOOD EYE. THAT IS A SUPERIOR BLADE. NOW GET SOME REST. WE'LL DUEL AT FIRST LIGHT.
9.

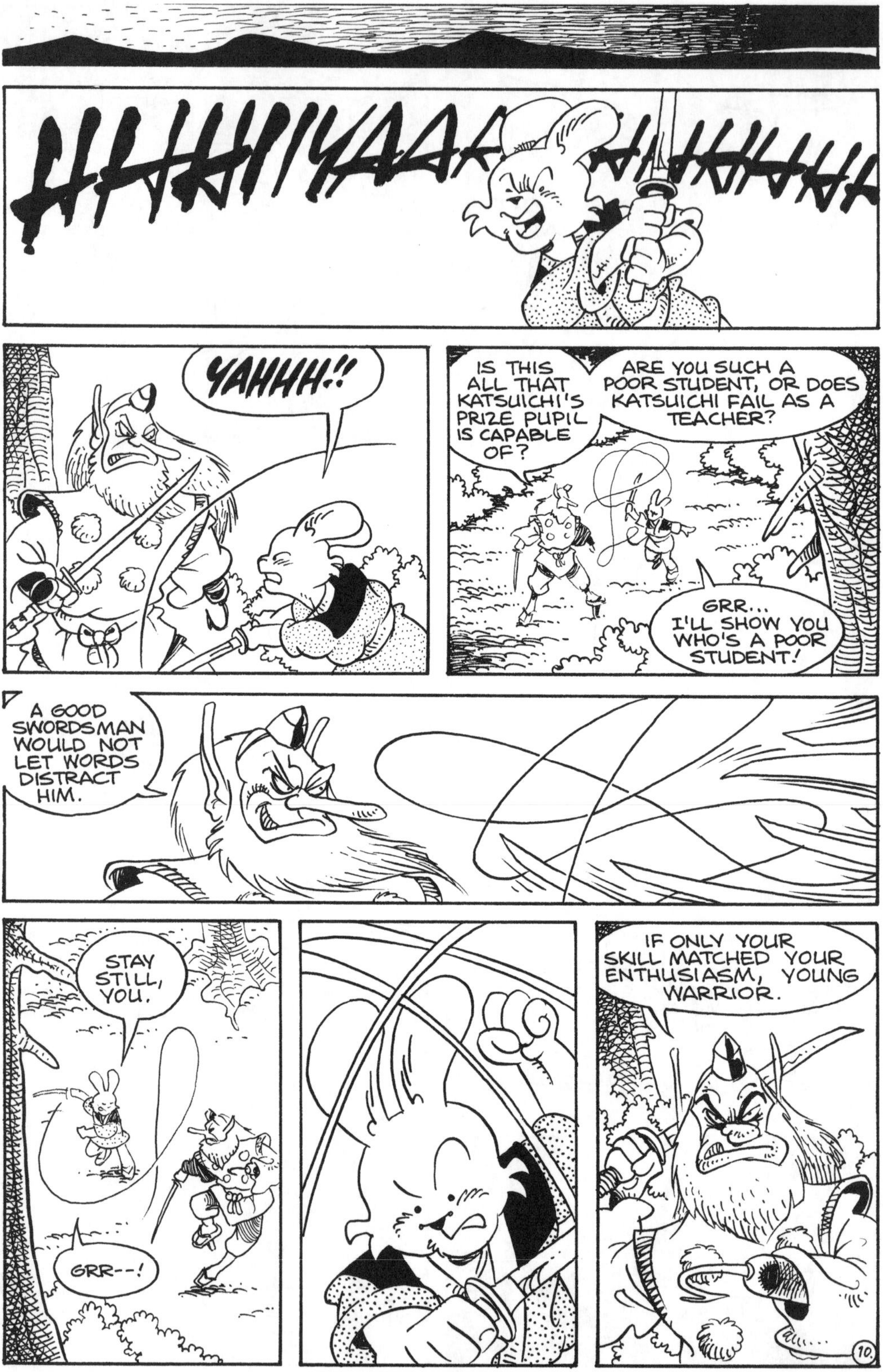

HHHHIYAAAAAAHHHHHHH
YAHHH.!!
IS THIS ALL THAT KATSUICHI'S PRIZE PUPIL IS CAPABLE OF?
ARE YOU SUCH A POOR STUDENT, OR DOES KATSUICHI FAIL AS A TEACHER?
GRR... I'LL SHOW YOU WHO'S A POOR STUDENT!
A GOOD SWORDSMAN WOULD NOT LET WORDS DISTRACT HIM.
STAY STILL, YOU.
GRR--!
IF ONLY YOUR SKILL MATCHED YOUR ENTHUSIASM, YOUNG WARRIOR.
10

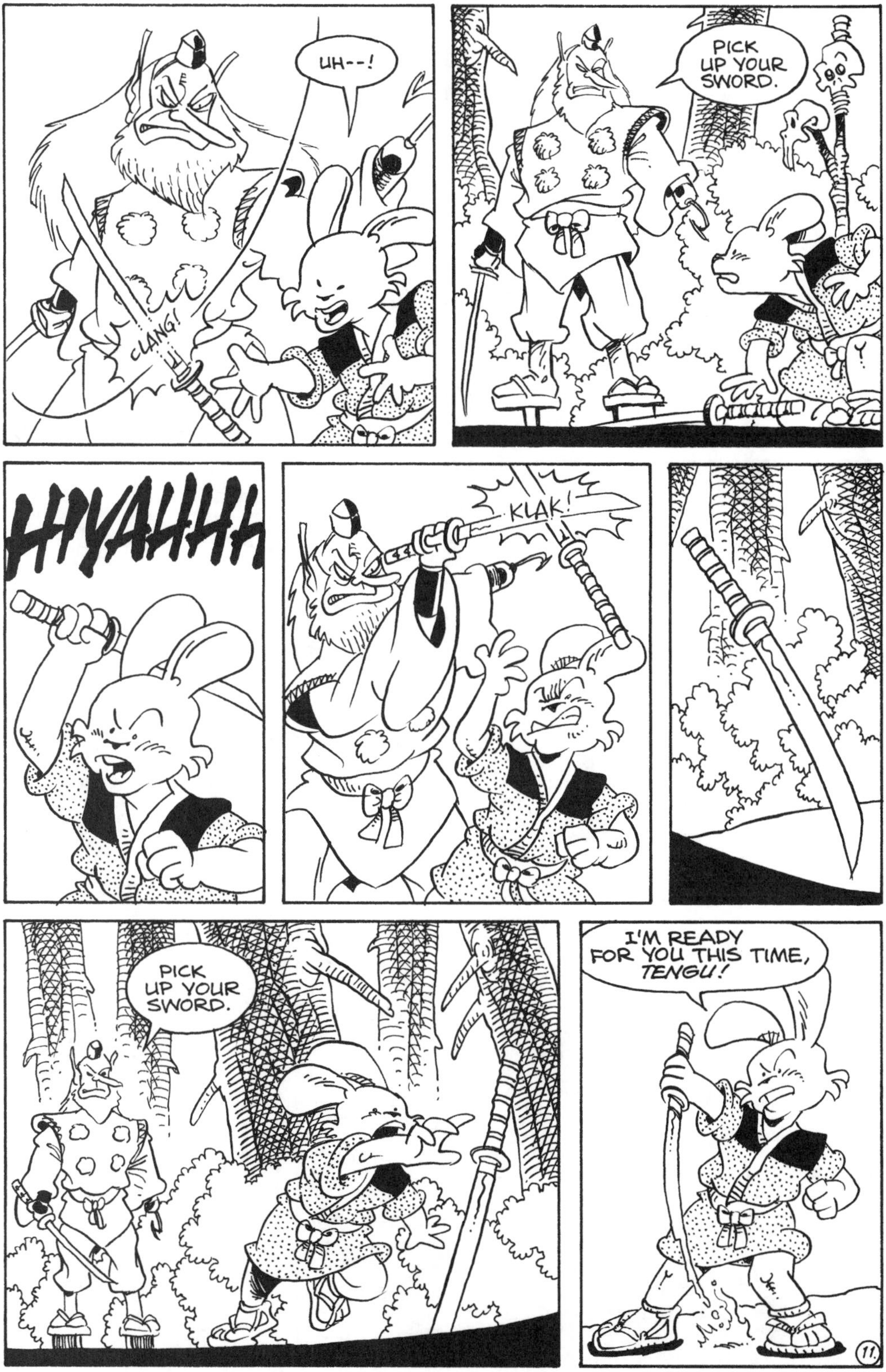
UH--!
CLANG!
PICK UP YOUR SWORD.
HIYAHHH
KLAK!
PICK UP YOUR SWORD.
I'M READY FOR YOU THIS TIME, *TENGU!*
11.

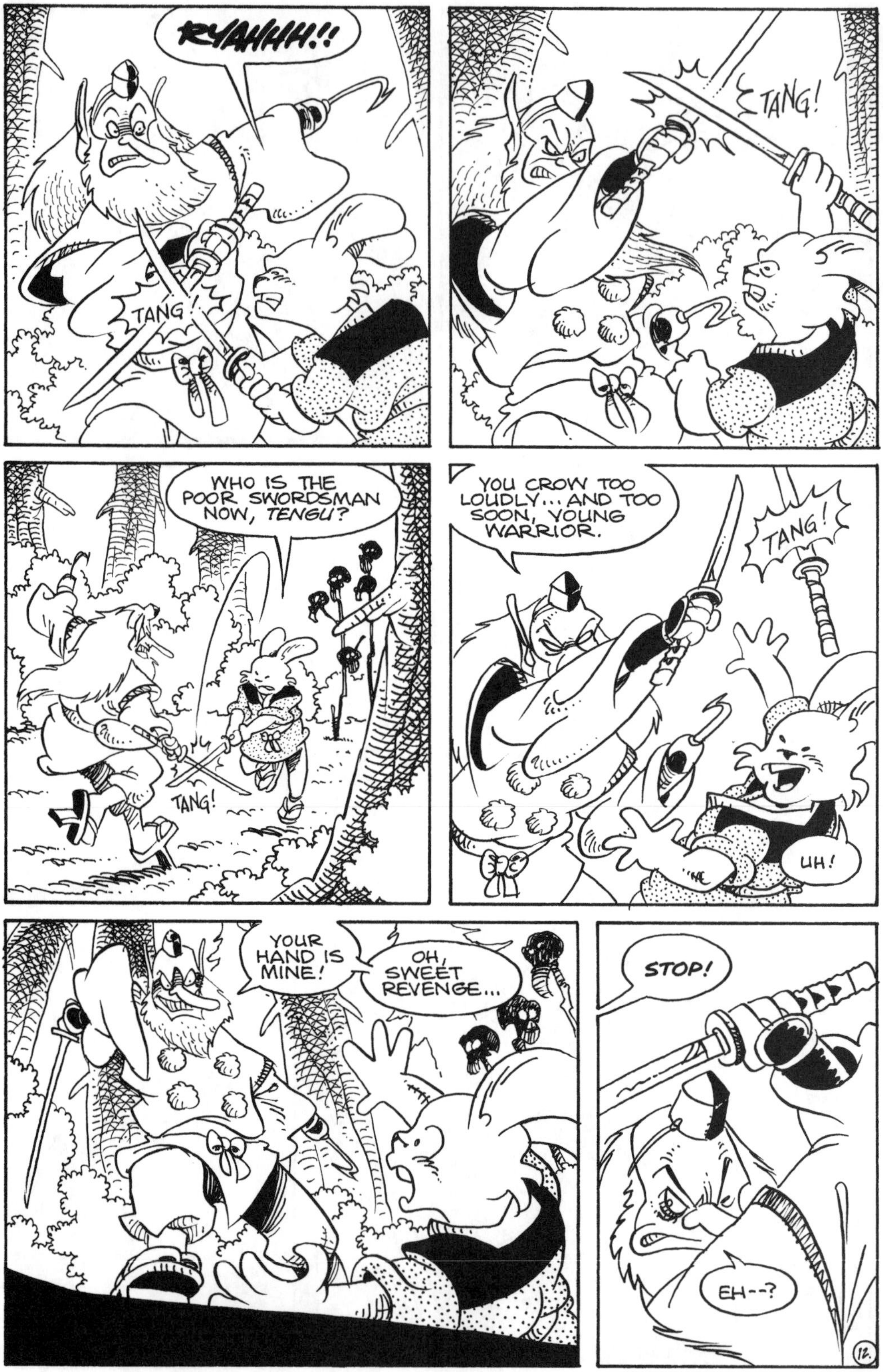
RYAHHH!!
TANG!
TANG!
WHO IS THE POOR SWORDSMAN NOW, TENGU?
TANG!
YOU CROW TOO LOUDLY... AND TOO SOON, YOUNG WARRIOR.
TANG!
UH!
YOUR HAND IS MINE!
OH, SWEET REVENGE...
STOP!
EH--?
12.

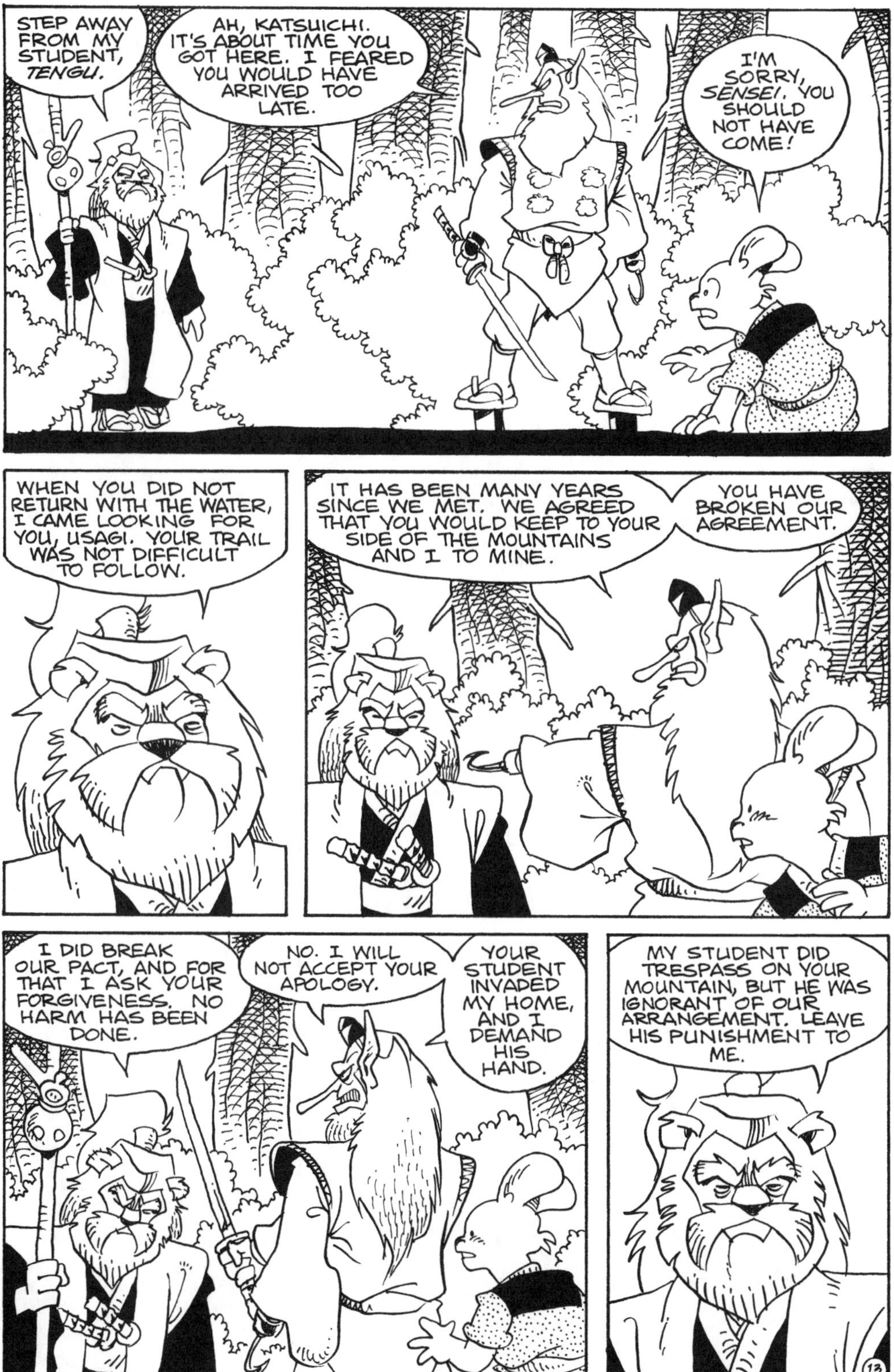
STEP AWAY FROM MY STUDENT, TENGU.
AH, KATSUICHI. IT'S ABOUT TIME YOU GOT HERE. I FEARED YOU WOULD HAVE ARRIVED TOO LATE.
I'M SORRY, SENSEI. YOU SHOULD NOT HAVE COME!
WHEN YOU DID NOT RETURN WITH THE WATER, I CAME LOOKING FOR YOU, USAGI. YOUR TRAIL WAS NOT DIFFICULT TO FOLLOW.
IT HAS BEEN MANY YEARS SINCE WE MET. WE AGREED THAT YOU WOULD KEEP TO YOUR SIDE OF THE MOUNTAINS AND I TO MINE.
YOU HAVE BROKEN OUR AGREEMENT.
I DID BREAK OUR PACT, AND FOR THAT I ASK YOUR FORGIVENESS. NO HARM HAS BEEN DONE.
NO. I WILL NOT ACCEPT YOUR APOLOGY.
YOUR STUDENT INVADED MY HOME, AND I DEMAND HIS HAND.
MY STUDENT DID TRESPASS ON YOUR MOUNTAIN, BUT HE WAS IGNORANT OF OUR ARRANGEMENT. LEAVE HIS PUNISHMENT TO ME.
13

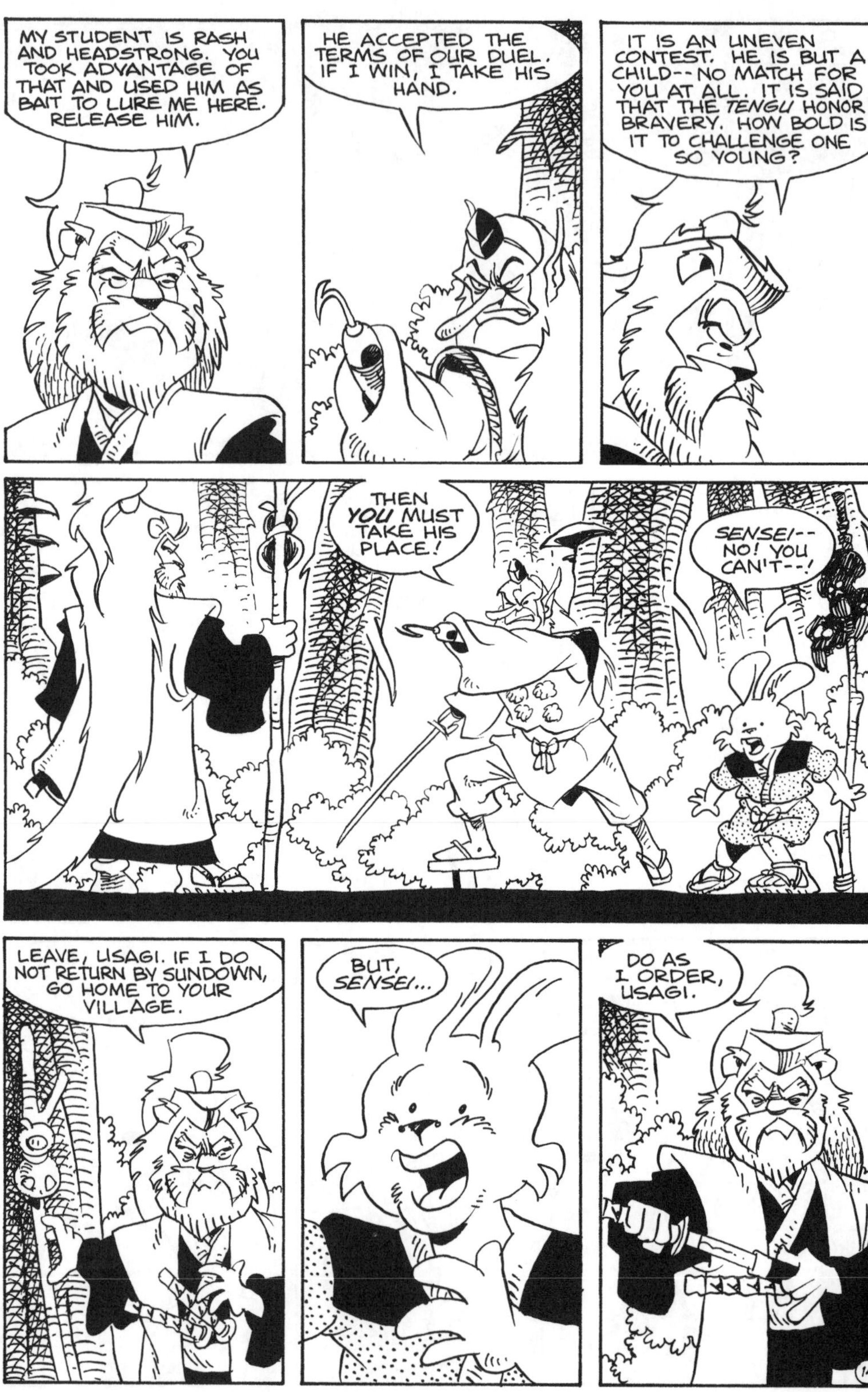
MY STUDENT IS RASH AND HEADSTRONG. YOU TOOK ADVANTAGE OF THAT AND USED HIM AS BAIT TO LURE ME HERE. RELEASE HIM.
HE ACCEPTED THE TERMS OF OUR DUEL. IF I WIN, I TAKE HIS HAND.
IT IS AN UNEVEN CONTEST. HE IS BUT A CHILD--NO MATCH FOR YOU AT ALL. IT IS SAID THAT THE *TENGU* HONOR BRAVERY. HOW BOLD IS IT TO CHALLENGE ONE SO YOUNG?
THEN *YOU* MUST TAKE HIS PLACE!
SENSEI--NO! YOU CAN'T--!
LEAVE, USAGI. IF I DO NOT RETURN BY SUNDOWN, GO HOME TO YOUR VILLAGE.
BUT, *SENSEI*...
DO AS I ORDER, USAGI.
14.

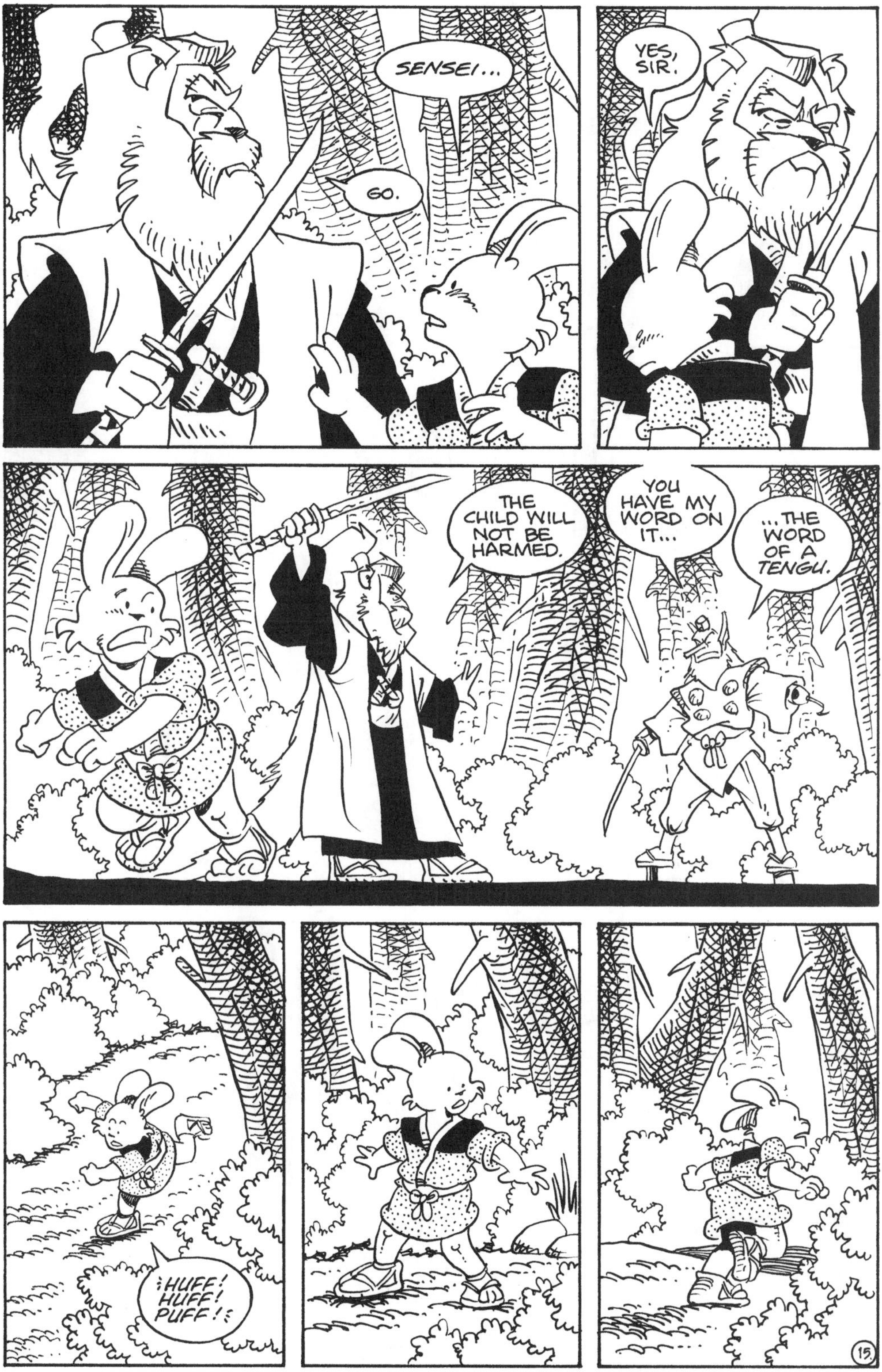
SENSEI...
GO.
YES, SIR.
THE CHILD WILL NOT BE HARMED.
YOU HAVE MY WORD ON IT...
...THE WORD OF A TENGU.
HUFF! HUFF! PUFF!
15

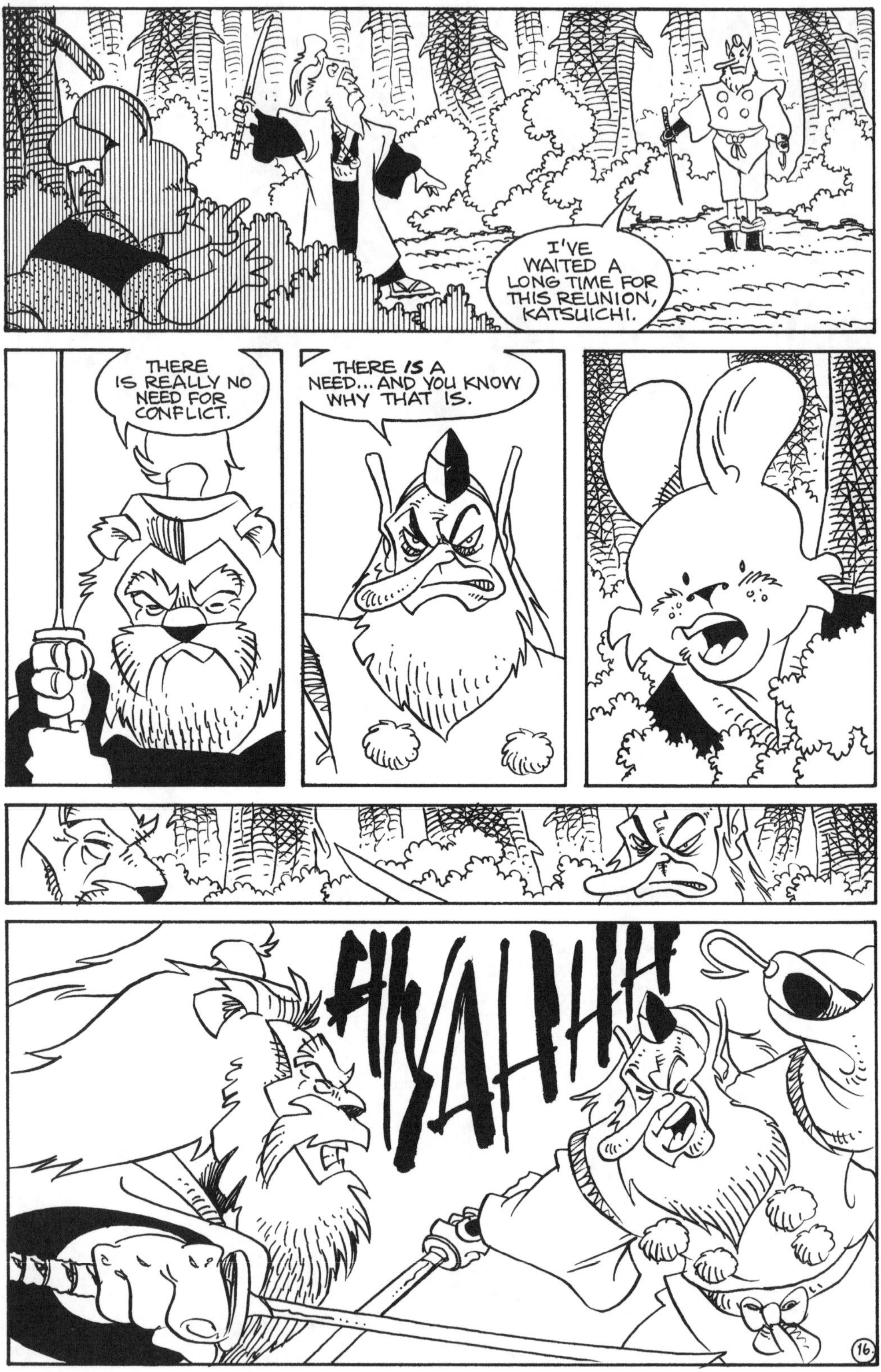
I'VE WAITED A LONG TIME FOR THIS REUNION, KATSUICHI.
THERE IS REALLY NO NEED FOR CONFLICT.
THERE *IS* A NEED... AND YOU KNOW WHY THAT IS.
AKAAHHH!
16

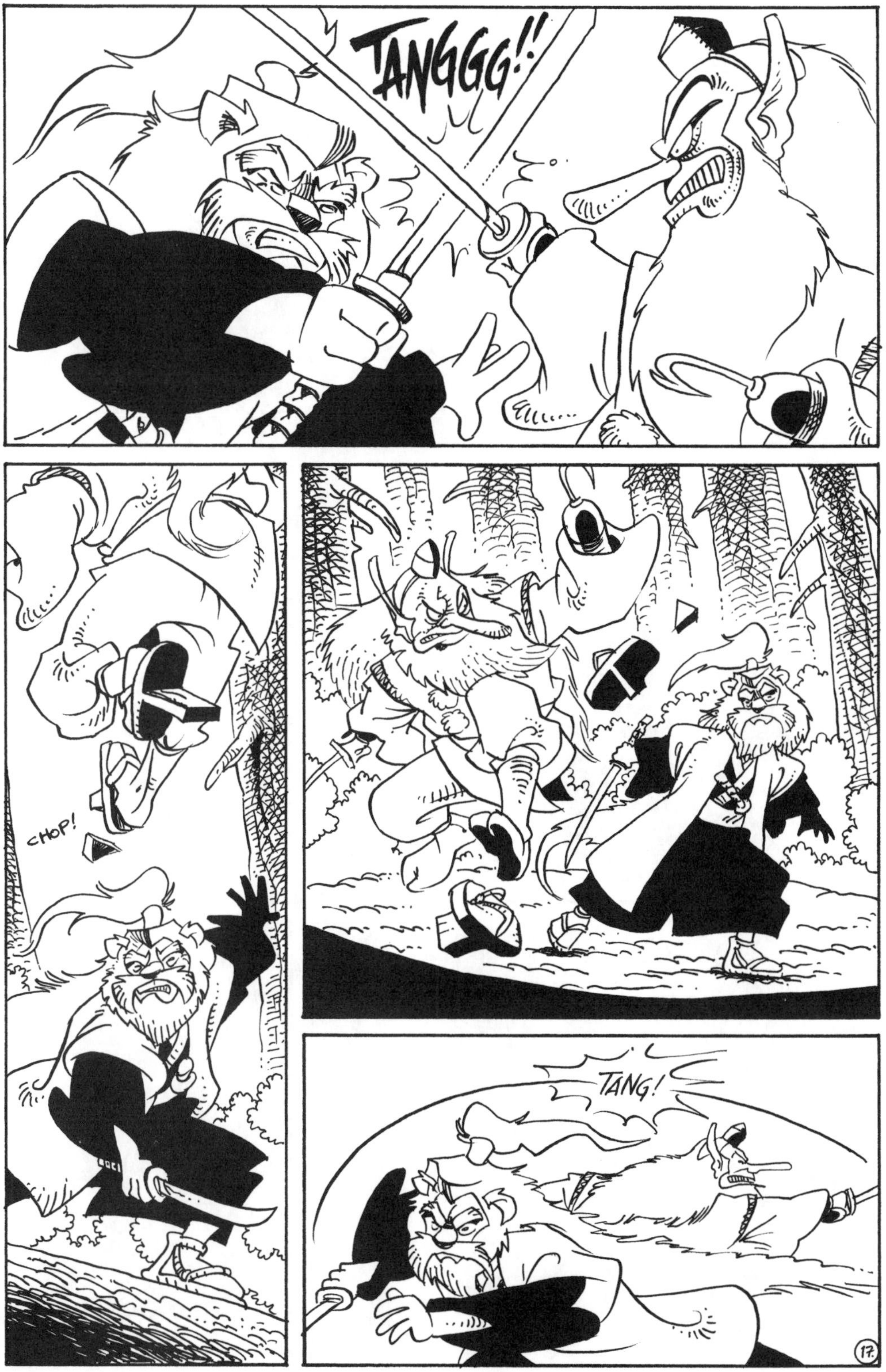
TANGGG!!
CHOP!
TANG!
17.

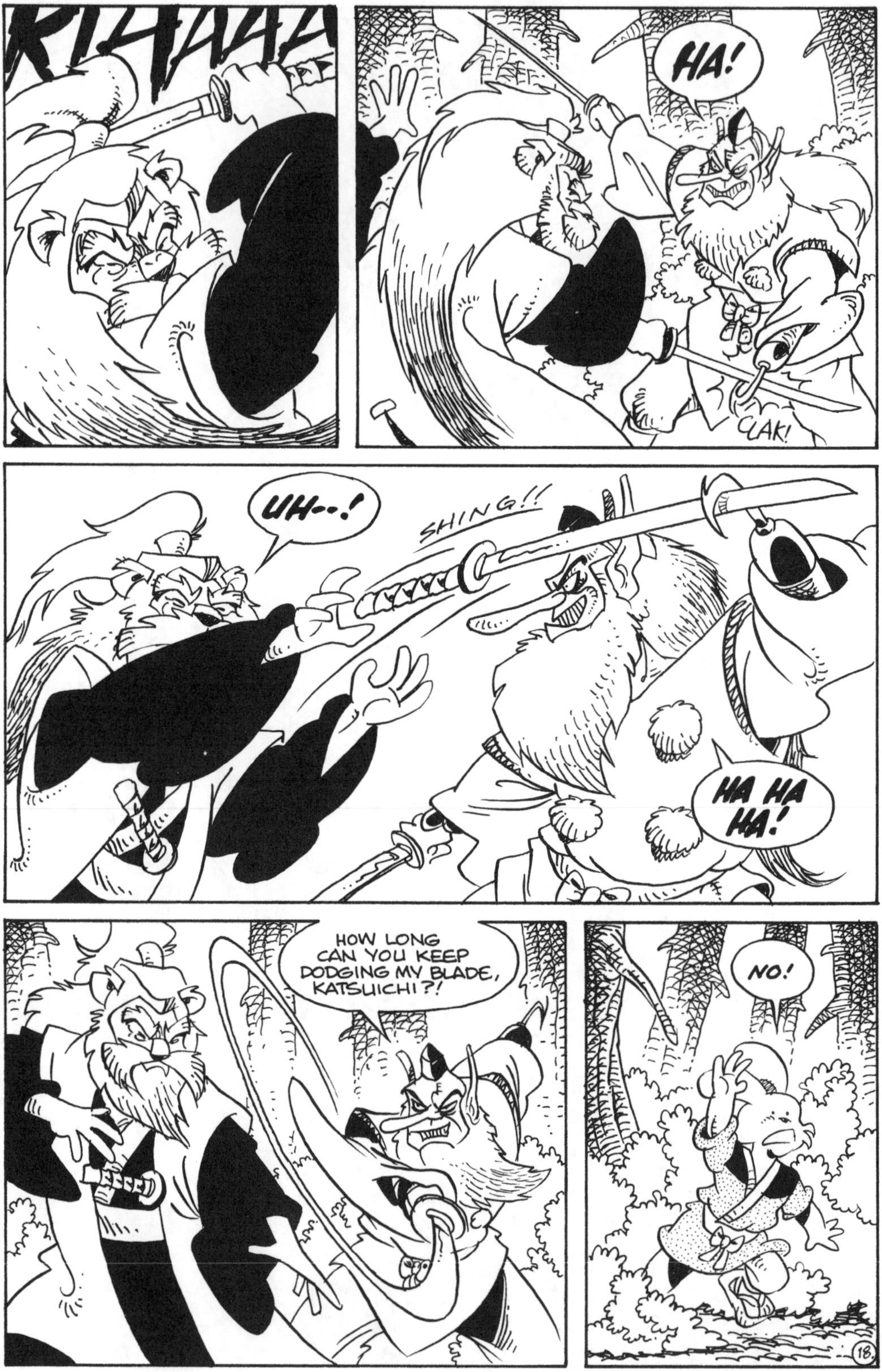
KIHAAA
HA!
CLAK!
UH--!
SHING!!
HA HA HA!
HOW LONG CAN YOU KEEP DODGING MY BLADE, KATSUICHI?!
NO!
18

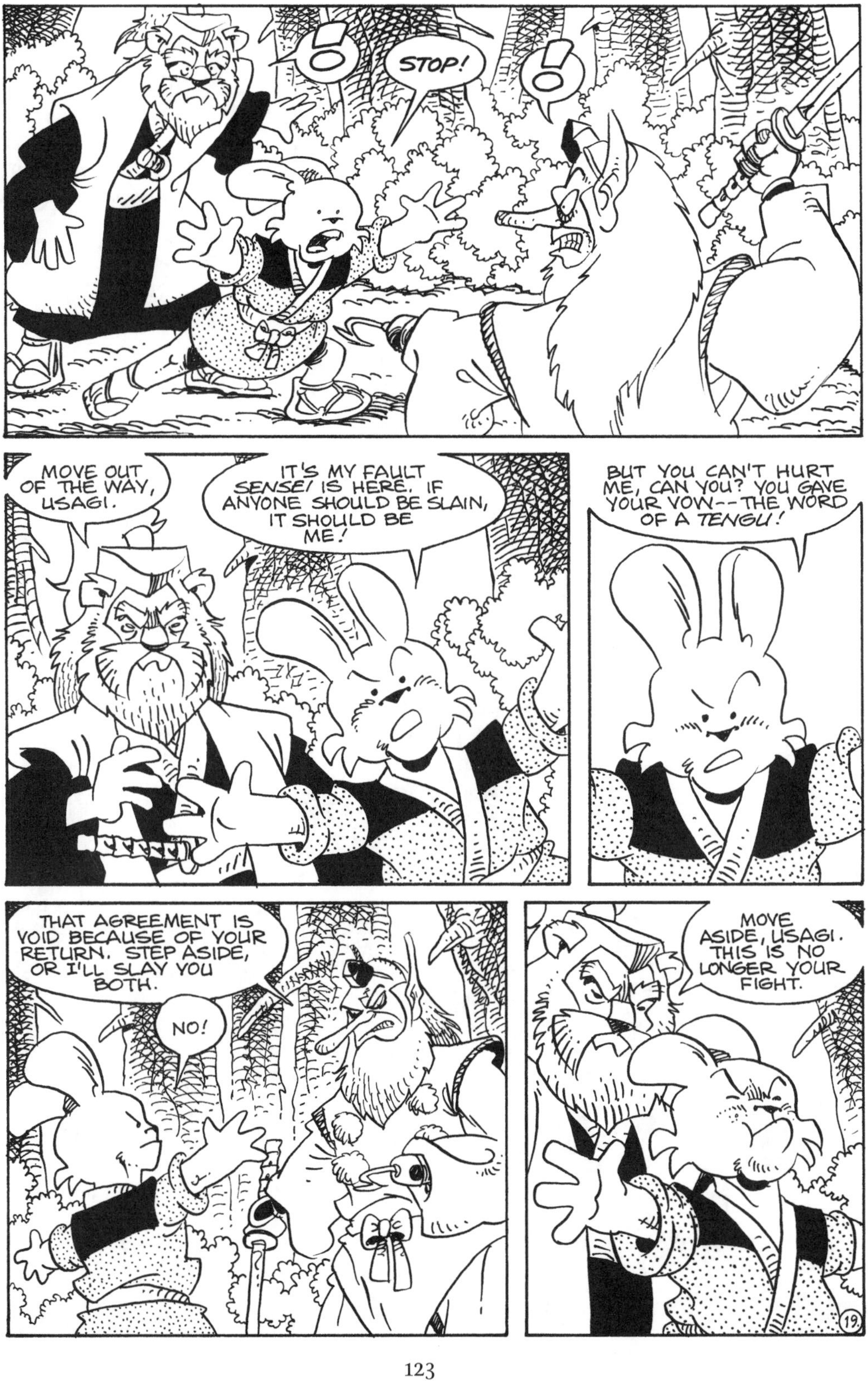
!
STOP!
!
MOVE OUT OF THE WAY, USAGI.
IT'S MY FAULT *SENSEI* IS HERE. IF ANYONE SHOULD BE SLAIN, IT SHOULD BE ME!
BUT YOU CAN'T HURT ME, CAN YOU? YOU GAVE YOUR VOW--THE WORD OF A *TENGU*!
THAT AGREEMENT IS VOID BECAUSE OF YOUR RETURN. STEP ASIDE, OR I'LL SLAY YOU BOTH.
NO!
MOVE ASIDE, USAGI. THIS IS NO LONGER YOUR FIGHT.
19

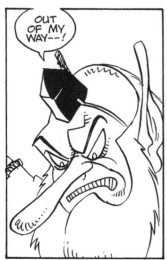

OUT OF MY WAY--!

NO!

NGGGHH--!

HA! HA! HA! HA! HA! HA! HA! HA! HA! HA!

YOU *ARE* RASH AND HEADSTRONG, YOUNG WARRIOR, BUT YOU ALSO HAVE AUDACITY. IF THERE IS ONE THING A *TENGU* RESPECTS, IT IS BRAVERY.

YOU MAY BOTH LEAVE, BUT LISTEN WELL-- I WILL NOT BE SO MAGNANIMOUS SHOULD YOU RETURN.

DO YOU UNDERSTAND ME, KATSUICHI?

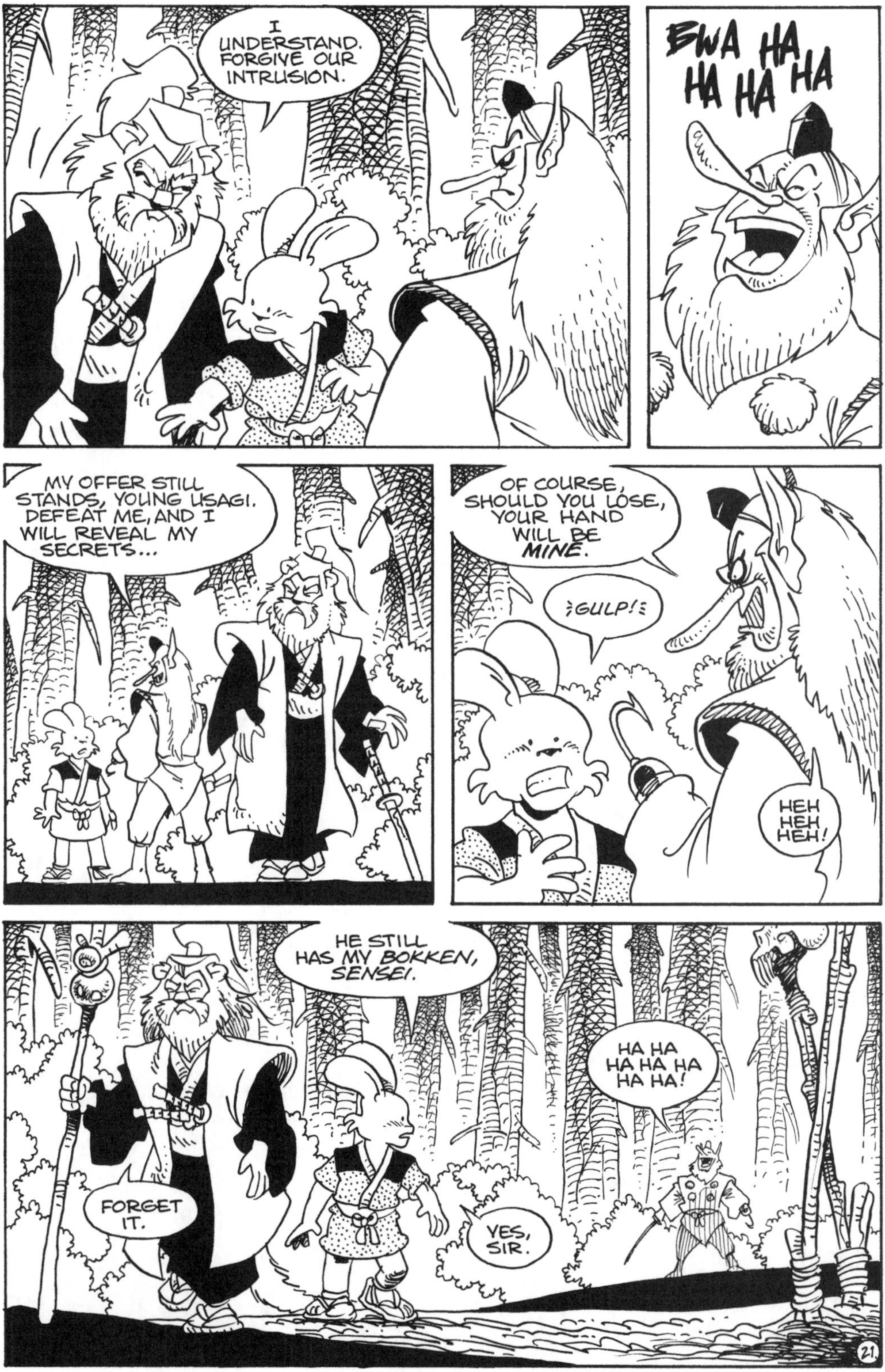
I UNDERSTAND. FORGIVE OUR INTRUSION.
BWA HA HA HA HA HA
MY OFFER STILL STANDS, YOUNG USAGI. DEFEAT ME, AND I WILL REVEAL MY SECRETS...
OF COURSE, SHOULD YOU LOSE, YOUR HAND WILL BE *MINE*.
GULP!
HEH HEH HEH!
HE STILL HAS MY *BOKKEN*, *SENSEI*.
HA HA HA HA HA HA HA!
FORGET IT.
YES, SIR.
21

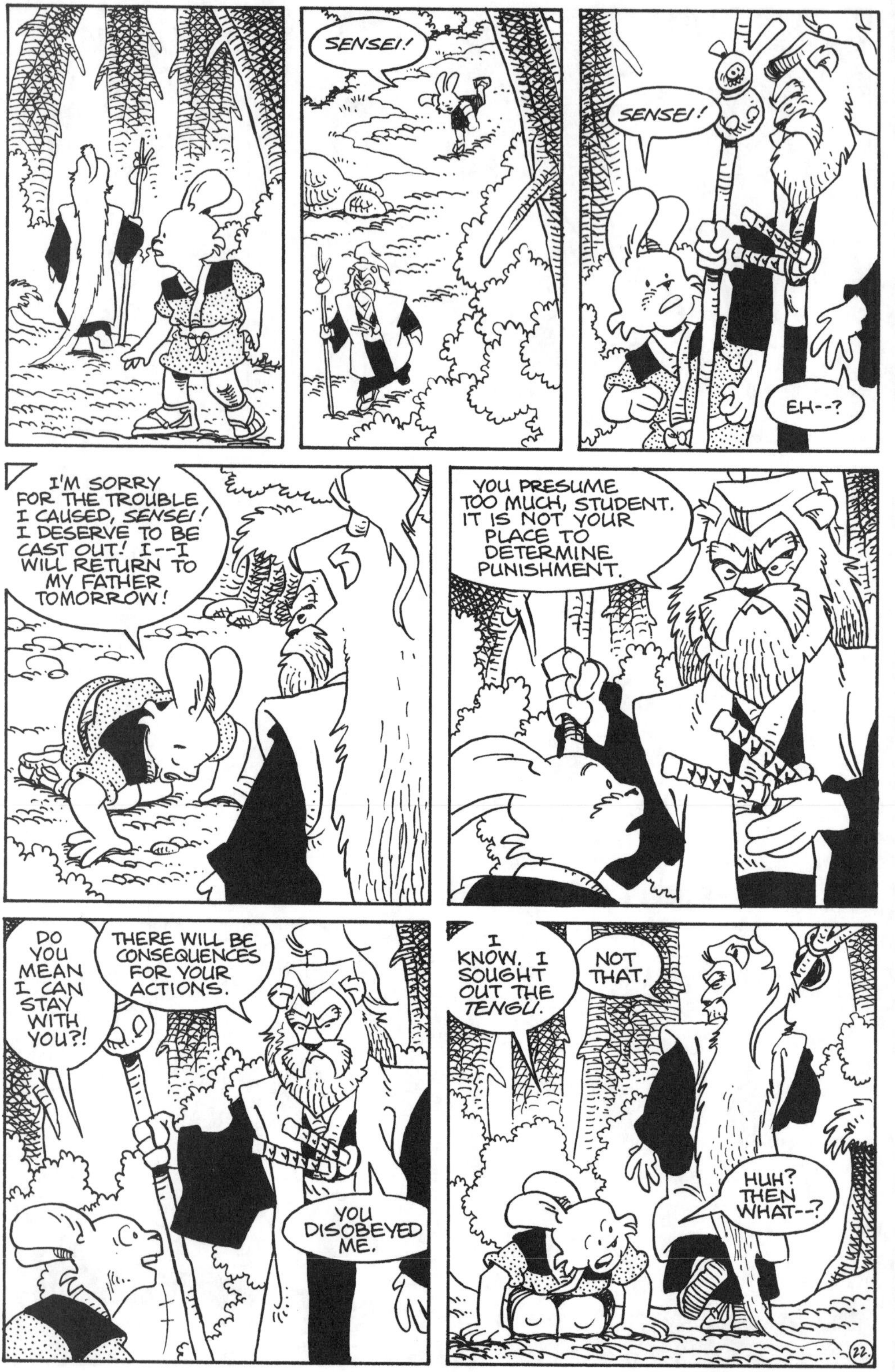
SENSEI!
SENSEI!
EH--?
I'M SORRY FOR THE TROUBLE I CAUSED, SENSEI! I DESERVE TO BE CAST OUT! I--I WILL RETURN TO MY FATHER TOMORROW!
YOU PRESUME TOO MUCH, STUDENT. IT IS NOT YOUR PLACE TO DETERMINE PUNISHMENT.
THERE WILL BE CONSEQUENCES FOR YOUR ACTIONS.
DO YOU MEAN I CAN STAY WITH YOU?!
YOU DISOBEYED ME.
I KNOW. I SOUGHT OUT THE TENGU.
NOT THAT.
HUH? THEN WHAT--?
22.

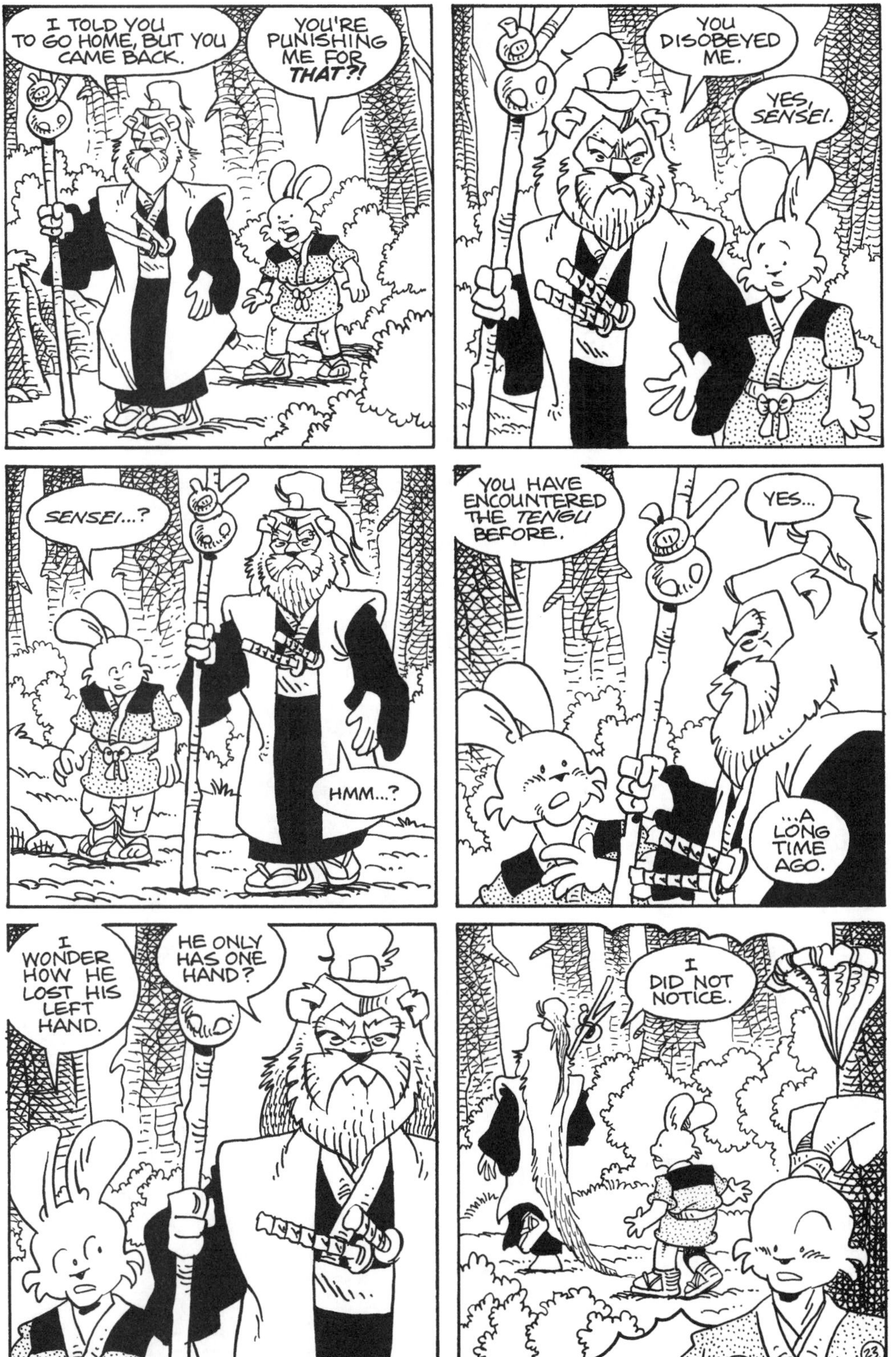
I TOLD YOU TO GO HOME, BUT YOU CAME BACK.
YOU'RE PUNISHING ME FOR *THAT?!*
YOU DISOBEYED ME.
YES, *SENSEI*.
SENSEI...?
HMM...?
YOU HAVE ENCOUNTERED THE *TENGU* BEFORE.
YES...
...A LONG TIME AGO.
I WONDER HOW HE LOST HIS LEFT HAND.
HE ONLY HAS ONE HAND?
I DID NOT NOTICE.
23.

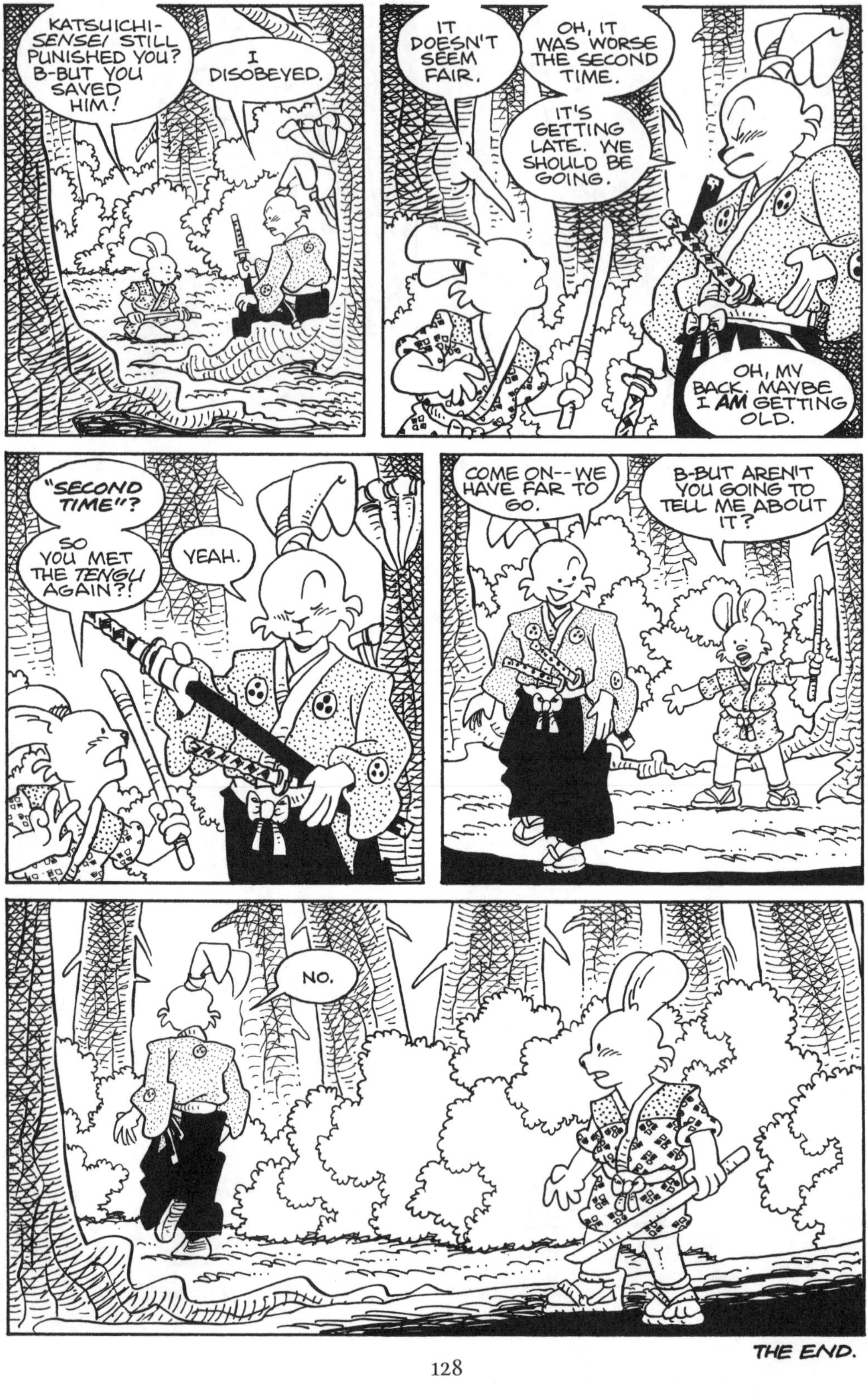
KATSUICHI-SENSEI STILL PUNISHED YOU? B-BUT YOU SAVED HIM!
I DISOBEYED.
IT DOESN'T SEEM FAIR.
OH, IT WAS WORSE THE SECOND TIME.
IT'S GETTING LATE. WE SHOULD BE GOING.
OH, MY BACK. MAYBE I AM GETTING OLD.
"SECOND TIME"?
SO YOU MET THE TENGU AGAIN?!
YEAH.
COME ON--WE HAVE FAR TO GO.
B-BUT AREN'T YOU GOING TO TELL ME ABOUT IT?
NO.
THE END.

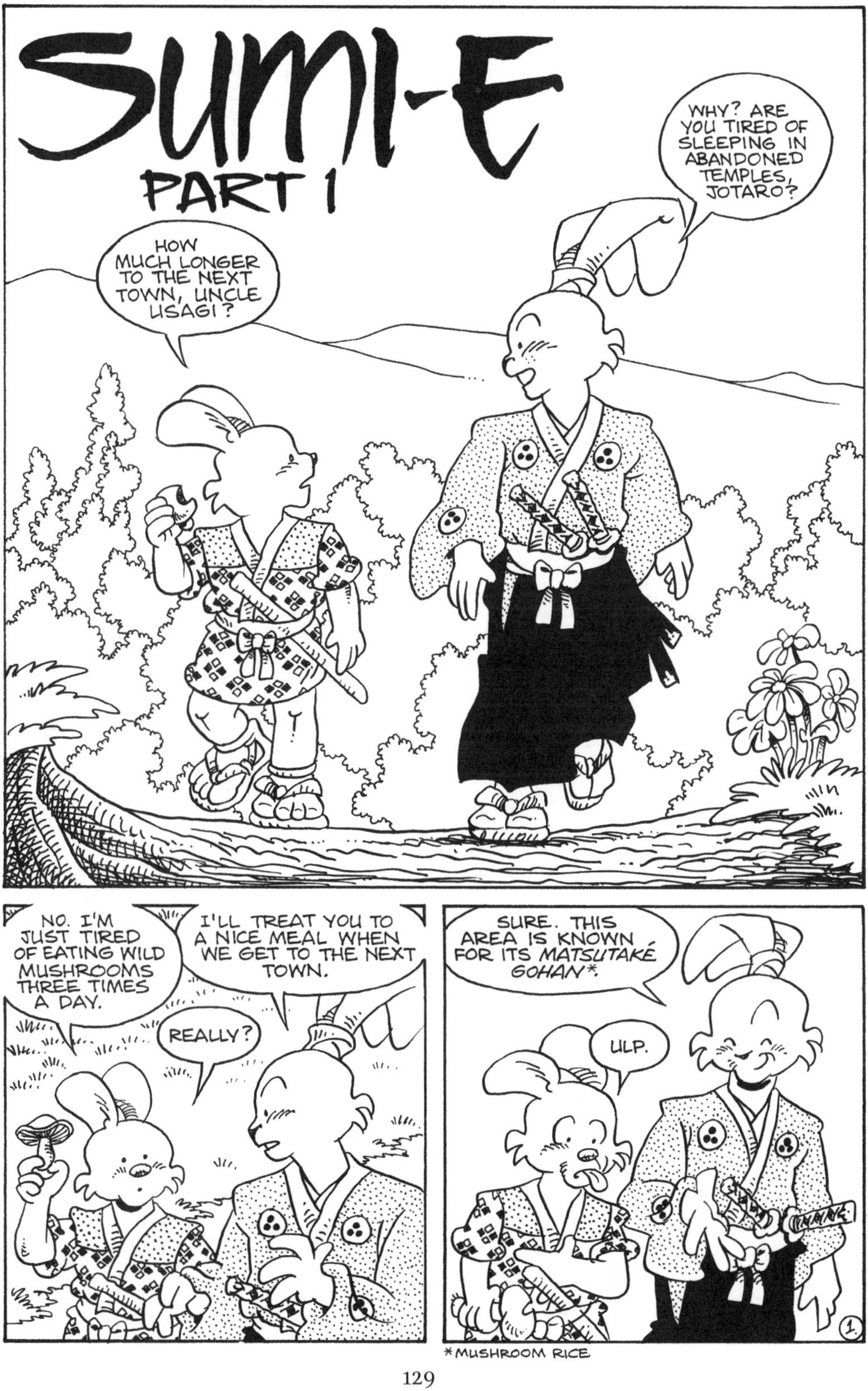
SUMI-E
PART 1
HOW MUCH LONGER TO THE NEXT TOWN, UNCLE USAGI?
WHY? ARE YOU TIRED OF SLEEPING IN ABANDONED TEMPLES, JOTARO?
NO. I'M JUST TIRED OF EATING WILD MUSHROOMS THREE TIMES A DAY.
I'LL TREAT YOU TO A NICE MEAL WHEN WE GET TO THE NEXT TOWN.
REALLY?
SURE. THIS AREA IS KNOWN FOR ITS *MATSUTAKÉ GOHAN**.
ULP.
1.

*MUSHROOM RICE

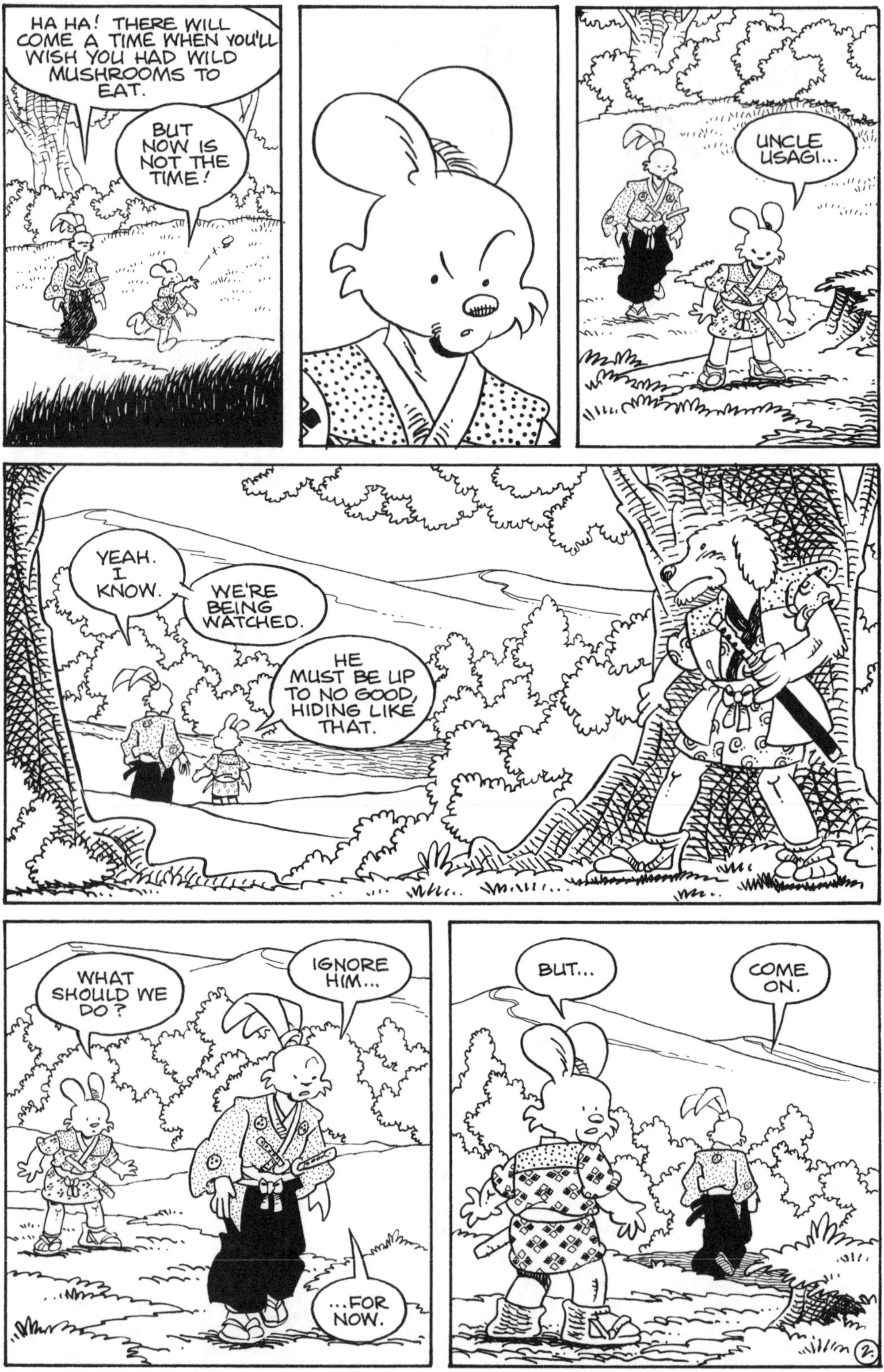
HA HA! THERE WILL COME A TIME WHEN YOU'LL WISH YOU HAD WILD MUSHROOMS TO EAT.
BUT NOW IS NOT THE TIME!
UNCLE USAGI...
YEAH. I KNOW.
WE'RE BEING WATCHED.
HE MUST BE UP TO NO GOOD, HIDING LIKE THAT.
WHAT SHOULD WE DO?
IGNORE HIM...
...FOR NOW.
BUT...
COME ON.
2.

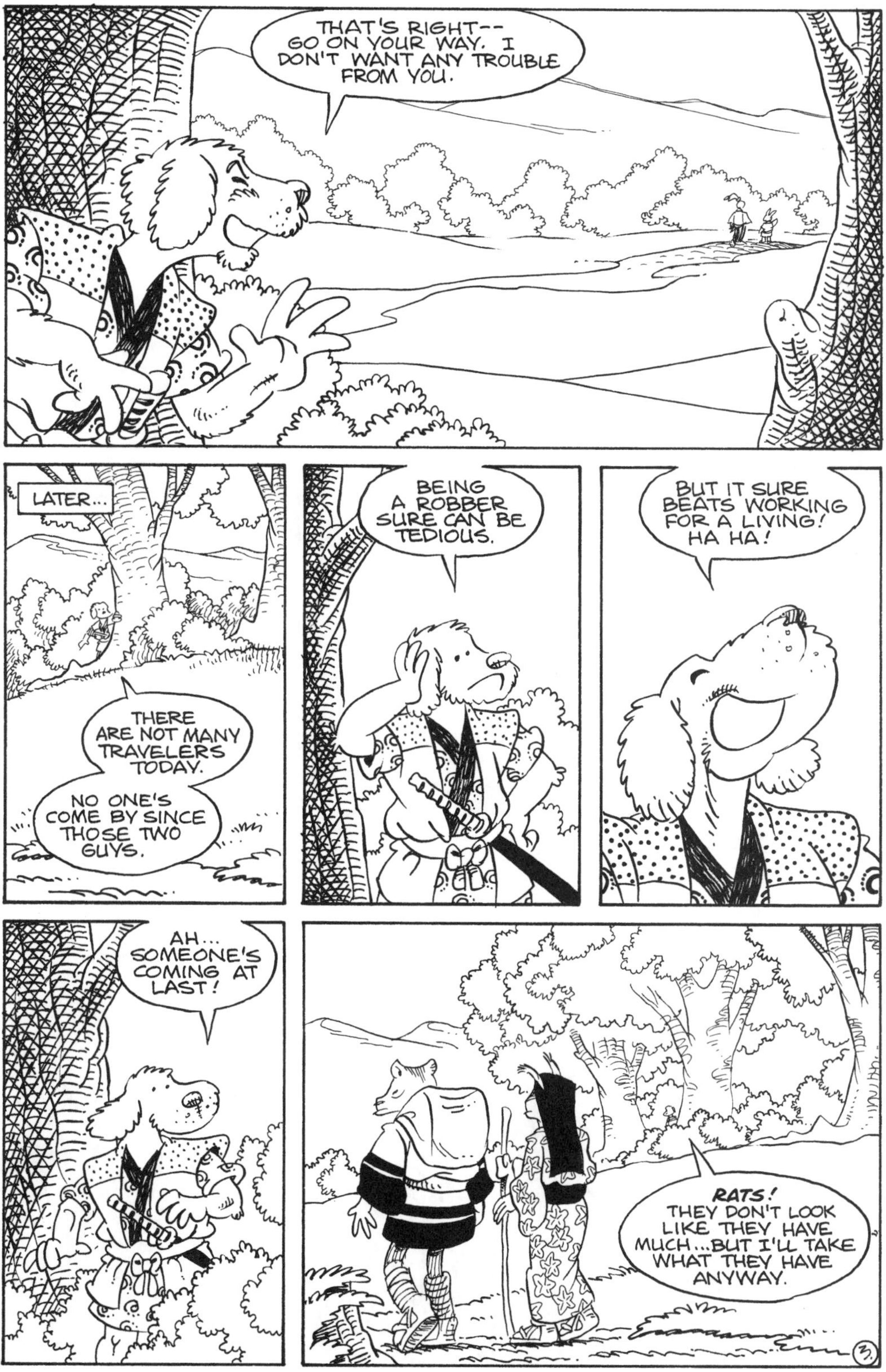
THAT'S RIGHT-- GO ON YOUR WAY. I DON'T WANT ANY TROUBLE FROM YOU.
LATER...
THERE ARE NOT MANY TRAVELERS TODAY.
NO ONE'S COME BY SINCE THOSE TWO GUYS.
BEING A ROBBER SURE CAN BE TEDIOUS.
BUT IT SURE BEATS WORKING FOR A LIVING! HA HA!
AH... SOMEONE'S COMING AT LAST!
RATS! THEY DON'T LOOK LIKE THEY HAVE MUCH...BUT I'LL TAKE WHAT THEY HAVE ANYWAY.
3.

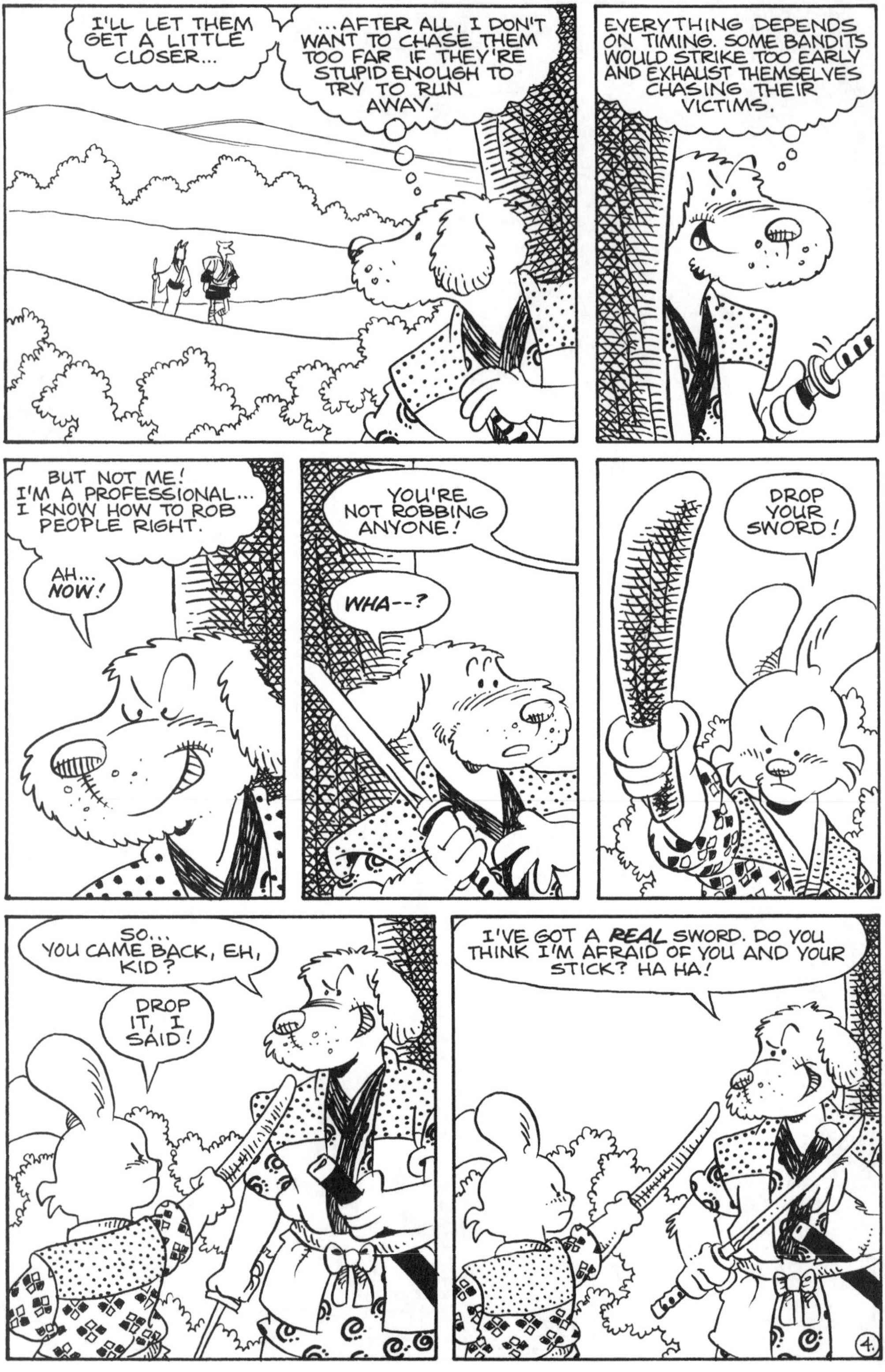
I'LL LET THEM GET A LITTLE CLOSER...
...AFTER ALL, I DON'T WANT TO CHASE THEM TOO FAR IF THEY'RE STUPID ENOUGH TO TRY TO RUN AWAY.
EVERYTHING DEPENDS ON TIMING. SOME BANDITS WOULD STRIKE TOO EARLY AND EXHAUST THEMSELVES CHASING THEIR VICTIMS.
BUT NOT ME! I'M A PROFESSIONAL... I KNOW HOW TO ROB PEOPLE RIGHT.
AH... NOW!
YOU'RE NOT ROBBING ANYONE!
WHA--?
DROP YOUR SWORD!
SO... YOU CAME BACK, EH, KID?
DROP IT, I SAID!
I'VE GOT A REAL SWORD. DO YOU THINK I'M AFRAID OF YOU AND YOUR STICK? HA HA!
4.

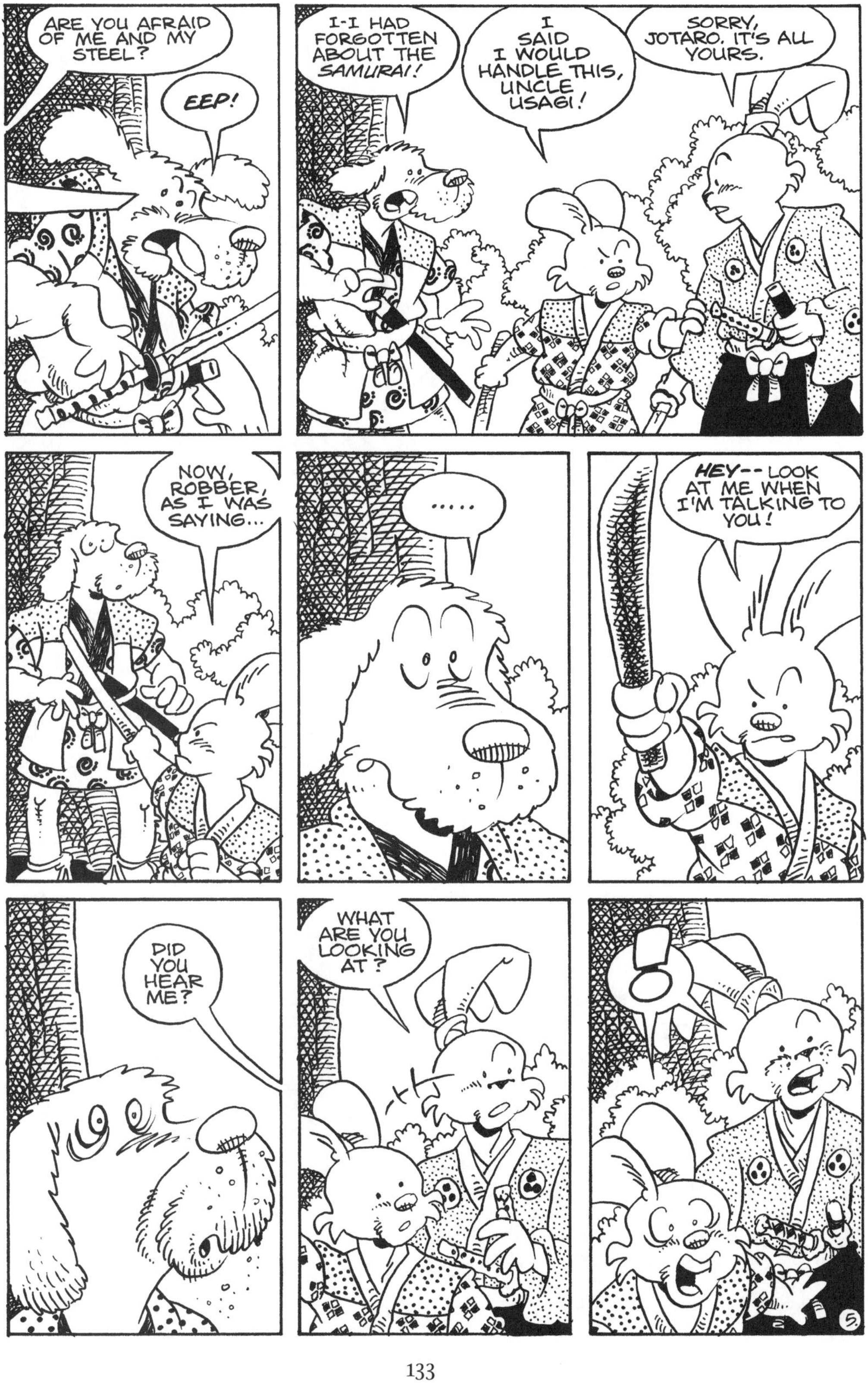
ARE YOU AFRAID OF ME AND MY STEEL?
EEP!
I-I HAD FORGOTTEN ABOUT THE *SAMURAI*!
I SAID I WOULD HANDLE THIS, UNCLE USAGI!
SORRY, JOTARO. IT'S ALL YOURS.
NOW, ROBBER, AS I WAS SAYING...
.....
HEY--LOOK AT ME WHEN I'M TALKING TO YOU!
DID YOU HEAR ME?
WHAT ARE YOU LOOKING AT?
5.

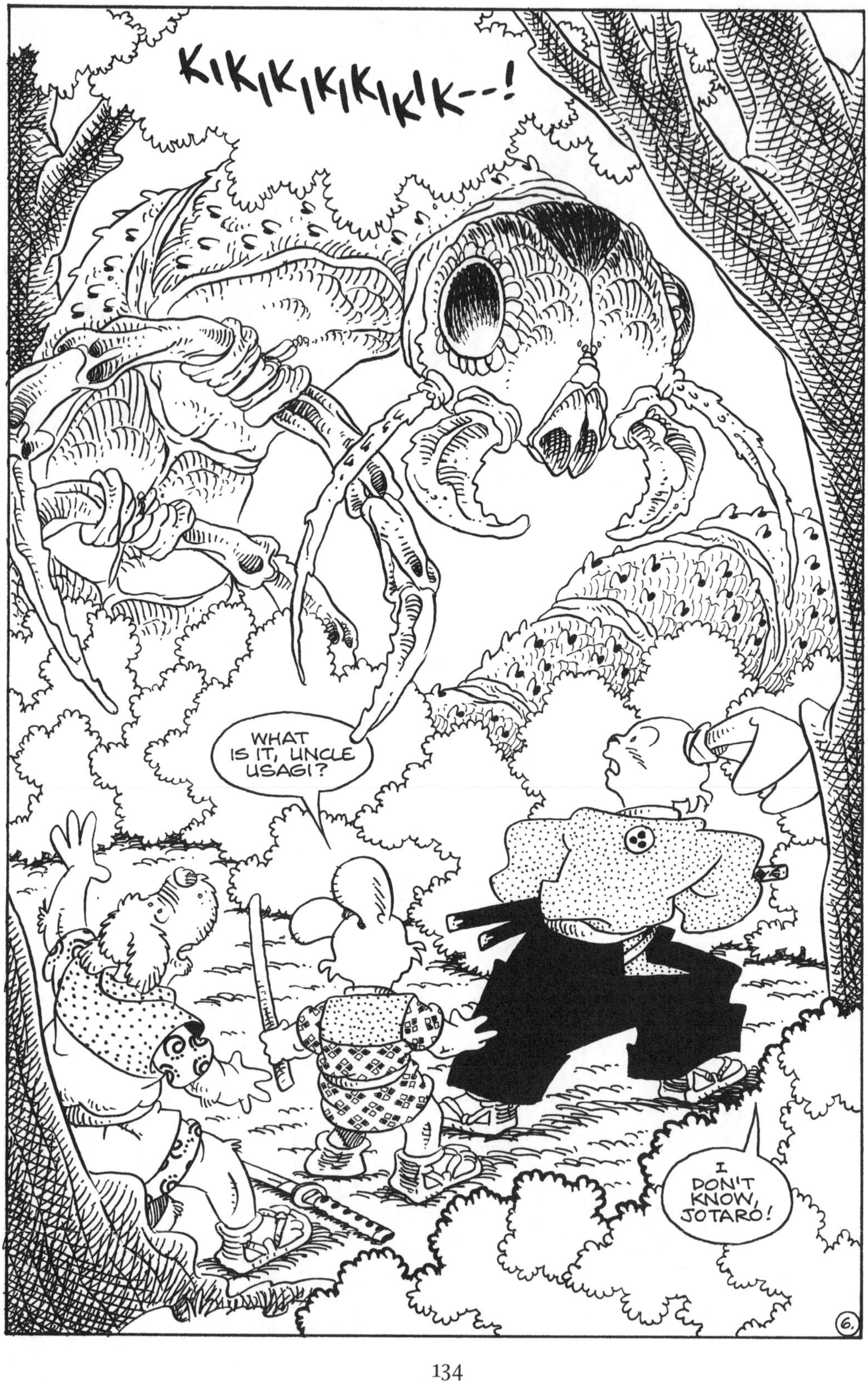
KIKIKIKIKIKIKIK--!
WHAT IS IT, UNCLE USAGI?
I DON'T KNOW, JOTARO!
6.

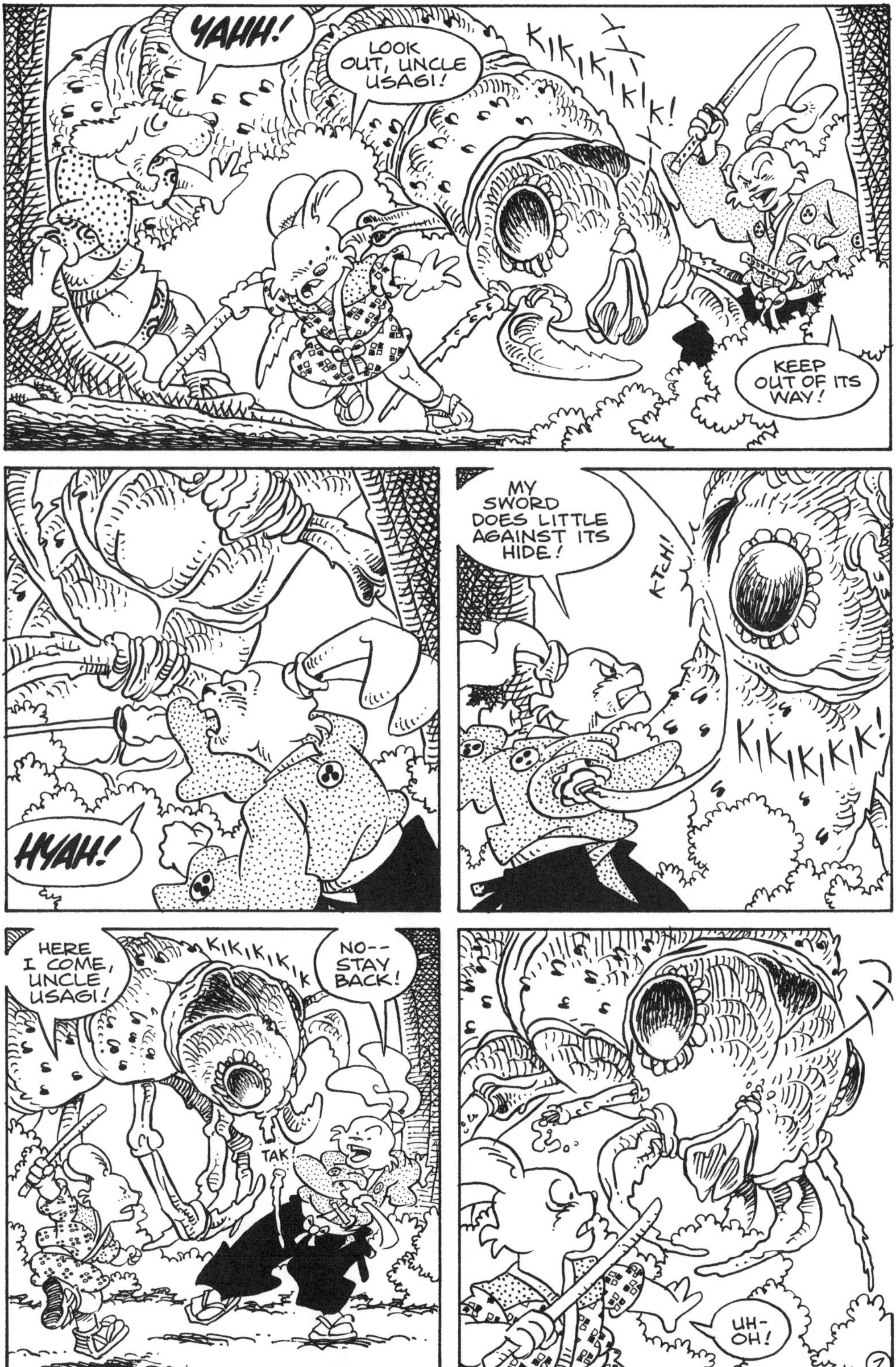
YAHH!
LOOK OUT, UNCLE USAGI!
KIKIKIKIKIK!
KEEP OUT OF ITS WAY!
HYAH!
MY SWORD DOES LITTLE AGAINST ITS HIDE!
K-TCH!
KIKIKIKIKIK!
HERE I COME, UNCLE USAGI!
KIKIKIKIKIK
NO-- STAY BACK!
TAK!
UH-OH!
7.

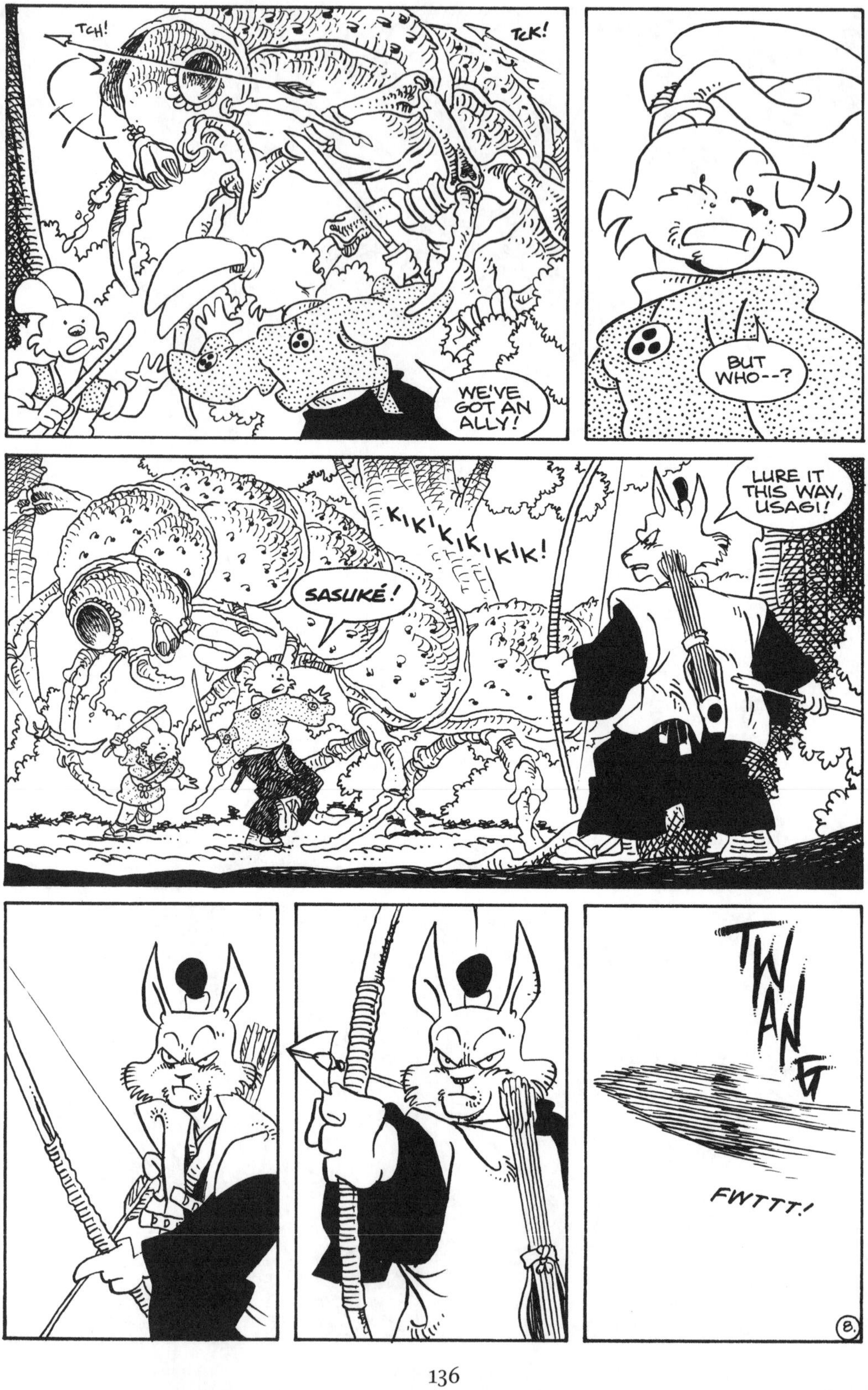
TCH!
TCK!
WE'VE GOT AN ALLY!
BUT WHO--?
KIKIKIKIKIKIK!
SASUKÉ!
LURE IT THIS WAY, USAGI!
TWANG
FWTTT!
8.

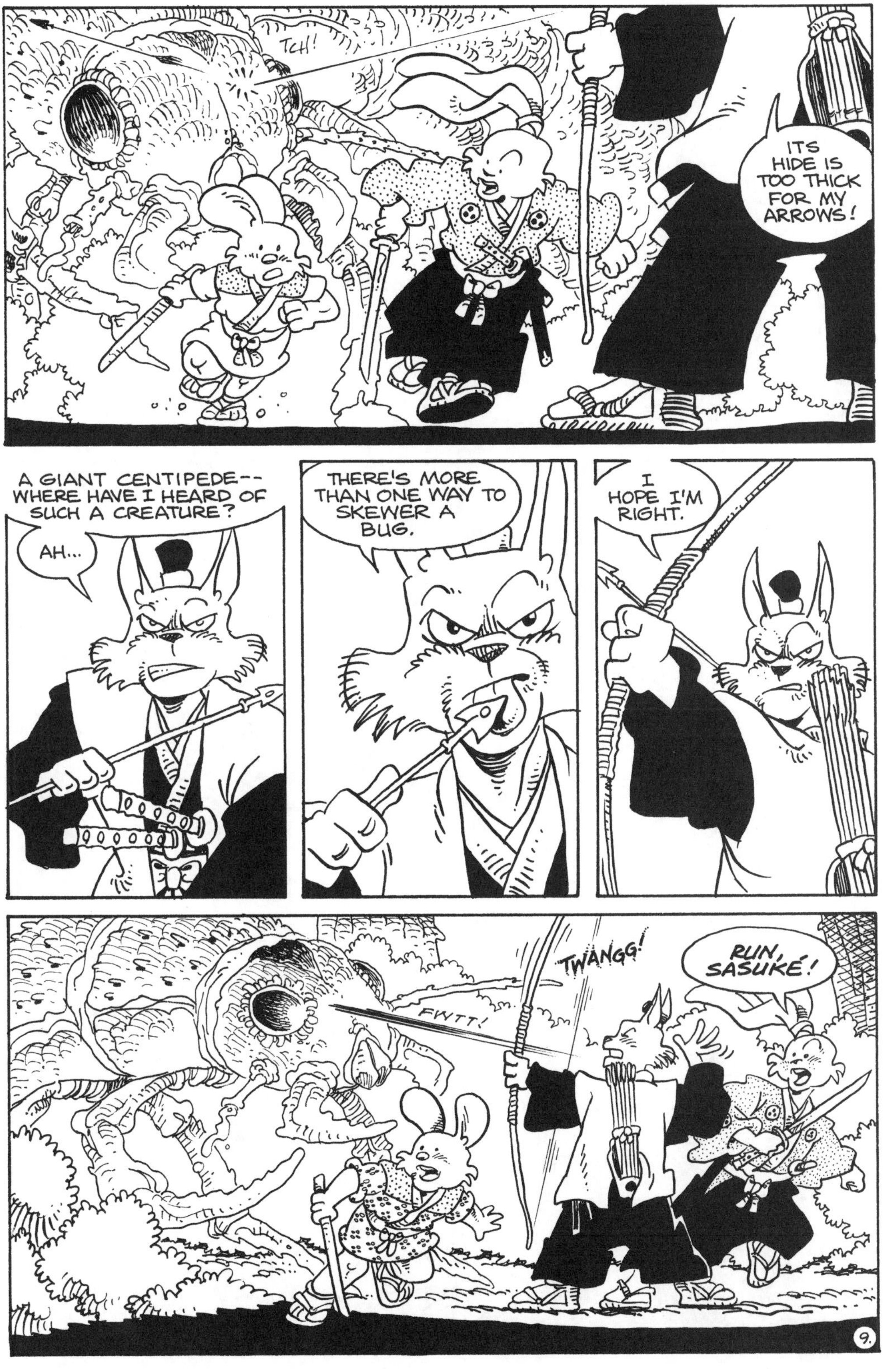
TCH!
ITS HIDE IS TOO THICK FOR MY ARROWS!
A GIANT CENTIPEDE-- WHERE HAVE I HEARD OF SUCH A CREATURE?
AH...
THERE'S MORE THAN ONE WAY TO SKEWER A BUG.
I HOPE I'M RIGHT.
TWANGG!
FWTT!
RUN, SASUKÉ!
9.

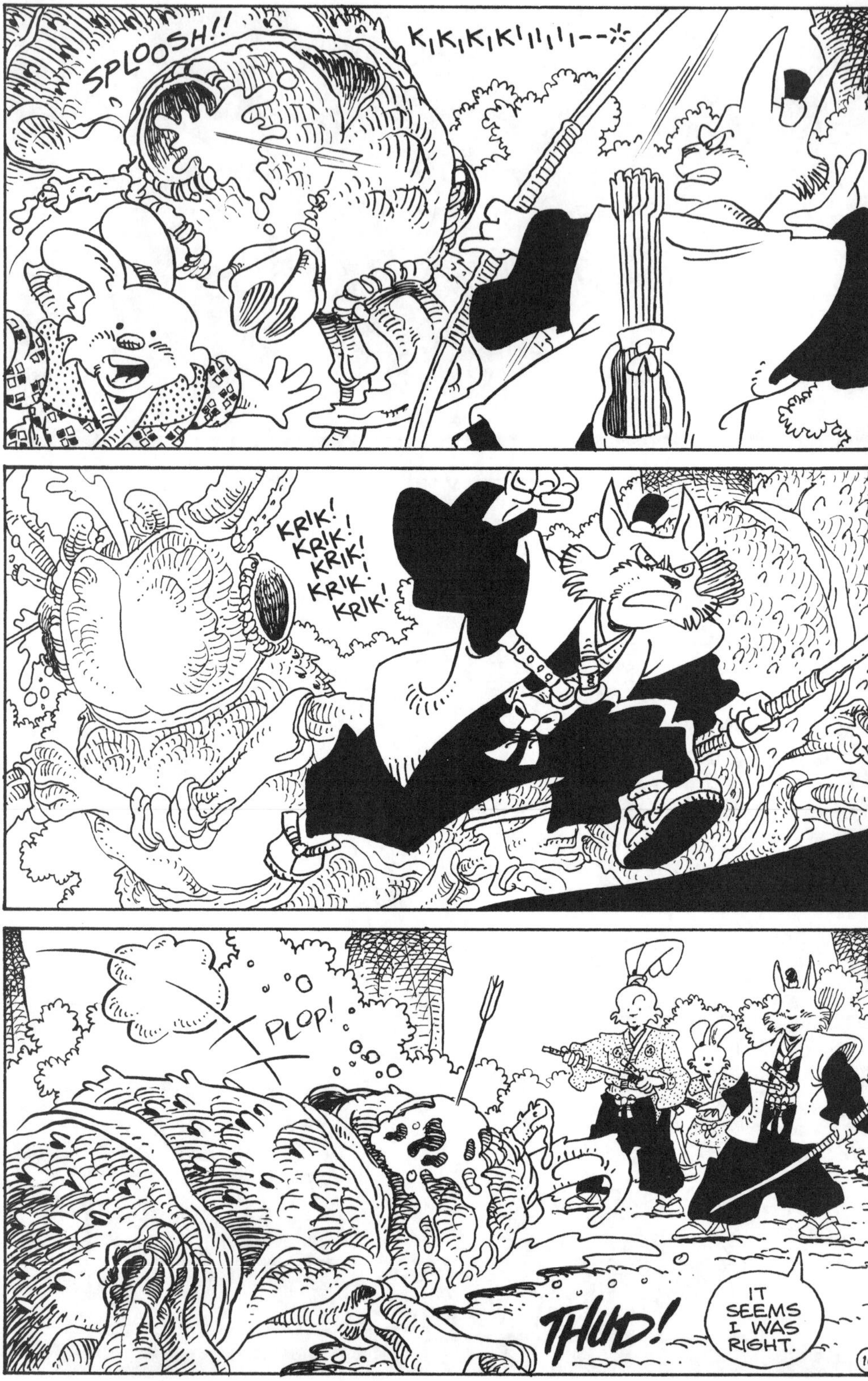
SPLOOSH!!
KIKIKIKIIIIII--
KRIK!
KRIK!
KRIK!
KRIK!
KRIK!
PLOP!
THUD!
IT SEEMS I WAS RIGHT.
10.

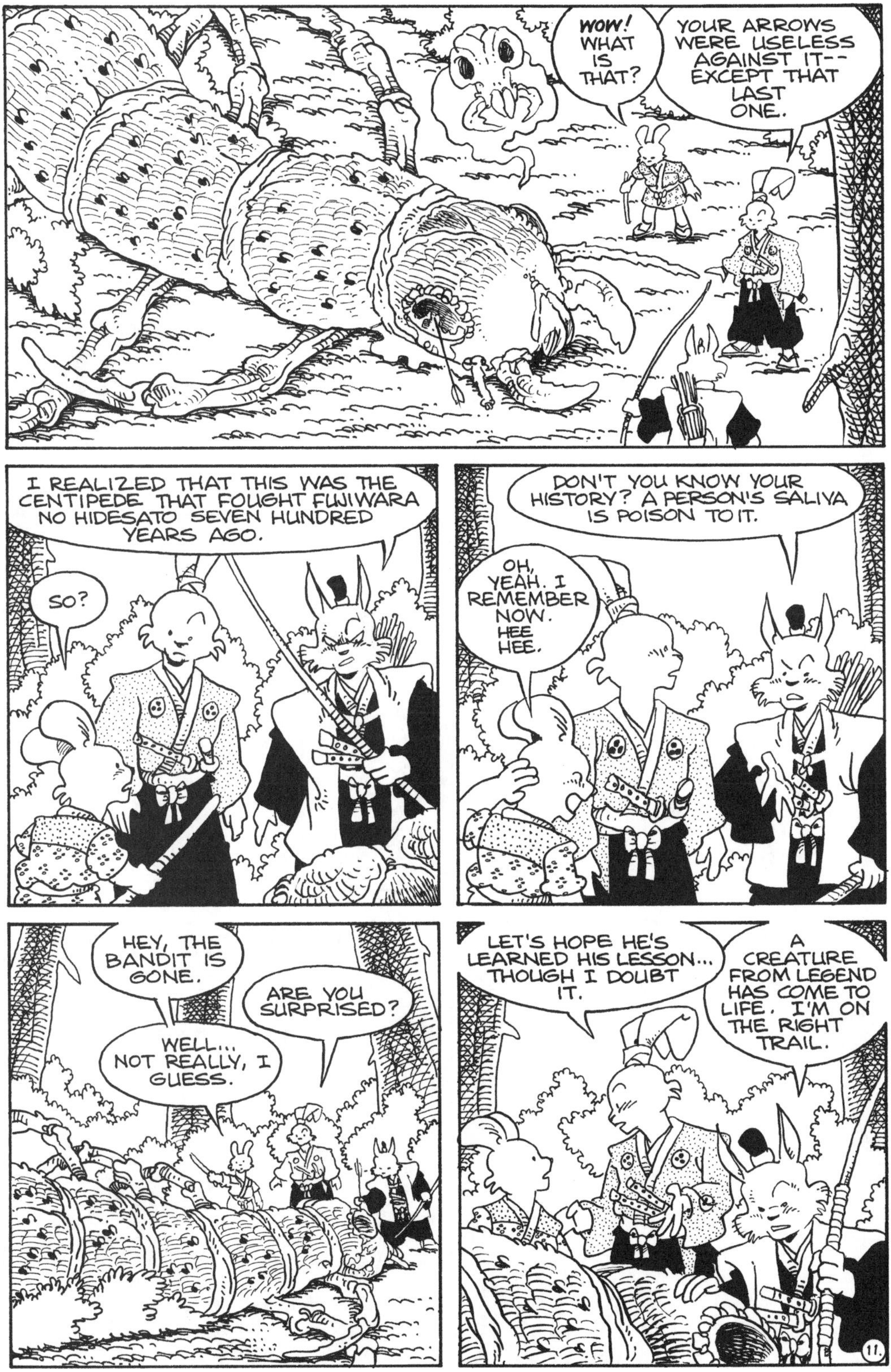
WOW! WHAT IS THAT?
YOUR ARROWS WERE USELESS AGAINST IT-- EXCEPT THAT LAST ONE.
I REALIZED THAT THIS WAS THE CENTIPEDE THAT FOUGHT FUJIWARA NO HIDESATO SEVEN HUNDRED YEARS AGO.
SO?
DON'T YOU KNOW YOUR HISTORY? A PERSON'S SALIVA IS POISON TO IT.
OH, YEAH. I REMEMBER NOW. HEE HEE.
HEY, THE BANDIT IS GONE.
ARE YOU SURPRISED?
WELL... NOT REALLY, I GUESS.
LET'S HOPE HE'S LEARNED HIS LESSON... THOUGH I DOUBT IT.
A CREATURE FROM LEGEND HAS COME TO LIFE. I'M ON THE RIGHT TRAIL.
11.

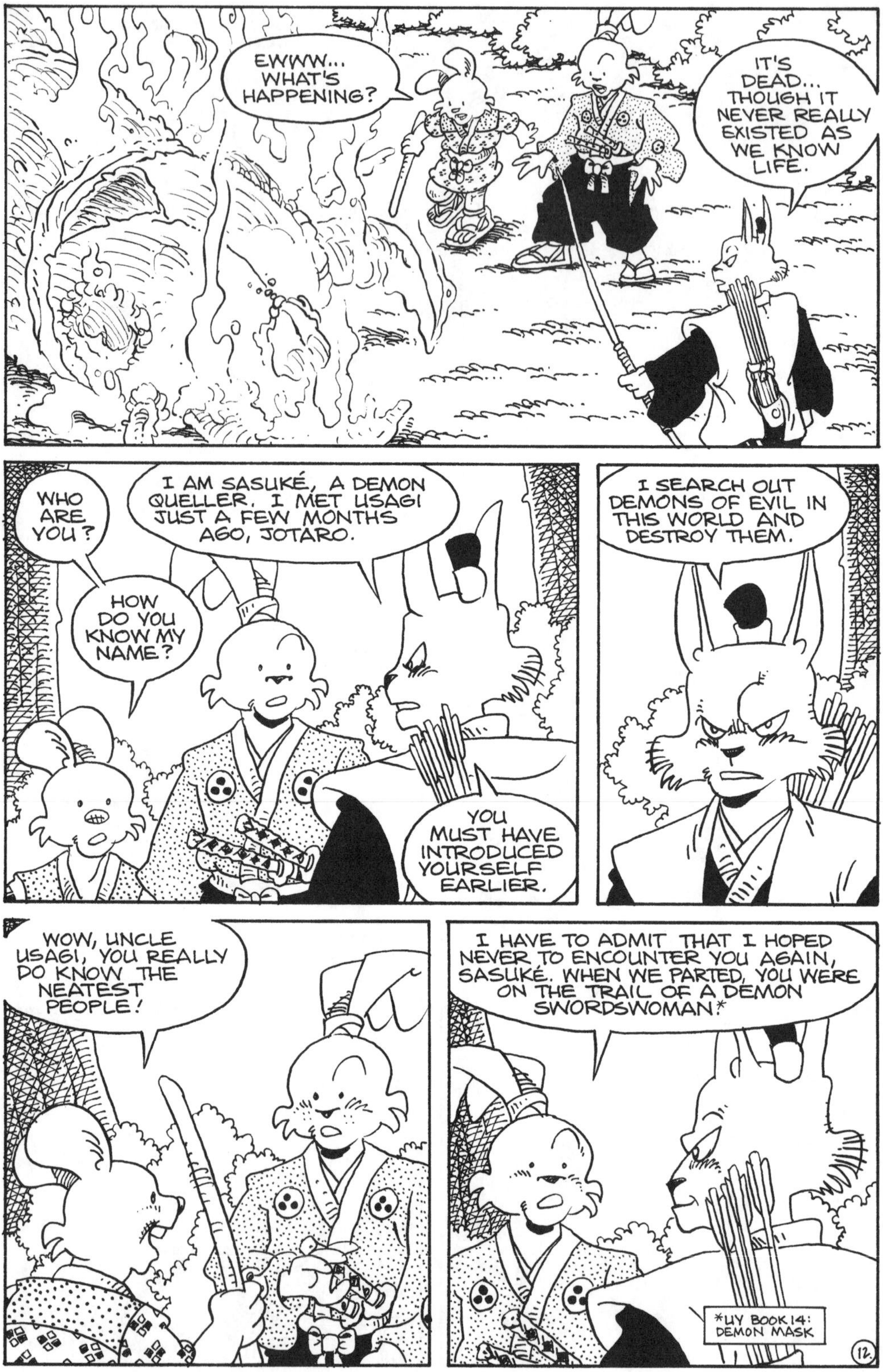
EWWW... WHAT'S HAPPENING?
IT'S DEAD... THOUGH IT NEVER REALLY EXISTED AS WE KNOW LIFE.
WHO ARE YOU?
HOW DO YOU KNOW MY NAME?
I AM SASUKÉ, A DEMON QUELLER. I MET USAGI JUST A FEW MONTHS AGO, JOTARO.
YOU MUST HAVE INTRODUCED YOURSELF EARLIER.
I SEARCH OUT DEMONS OF EVIL IN THIS WORLD AND DESTROY THEM.
WOW, UNCLE USAGI, YOU REALLY DO KNOW THE NEATEST PEOPLE!
I HAVE TO ADMIT THAT I HOPED NEVER TO ENCOUNTER YOU AGAIN, SASUKÉ. WHEN WE PARTED, YOU WERE ON THE TRAIL OF A DEMON SWORDSWOMAN.*
*UY BOOK 14: DEMON MASK
12.

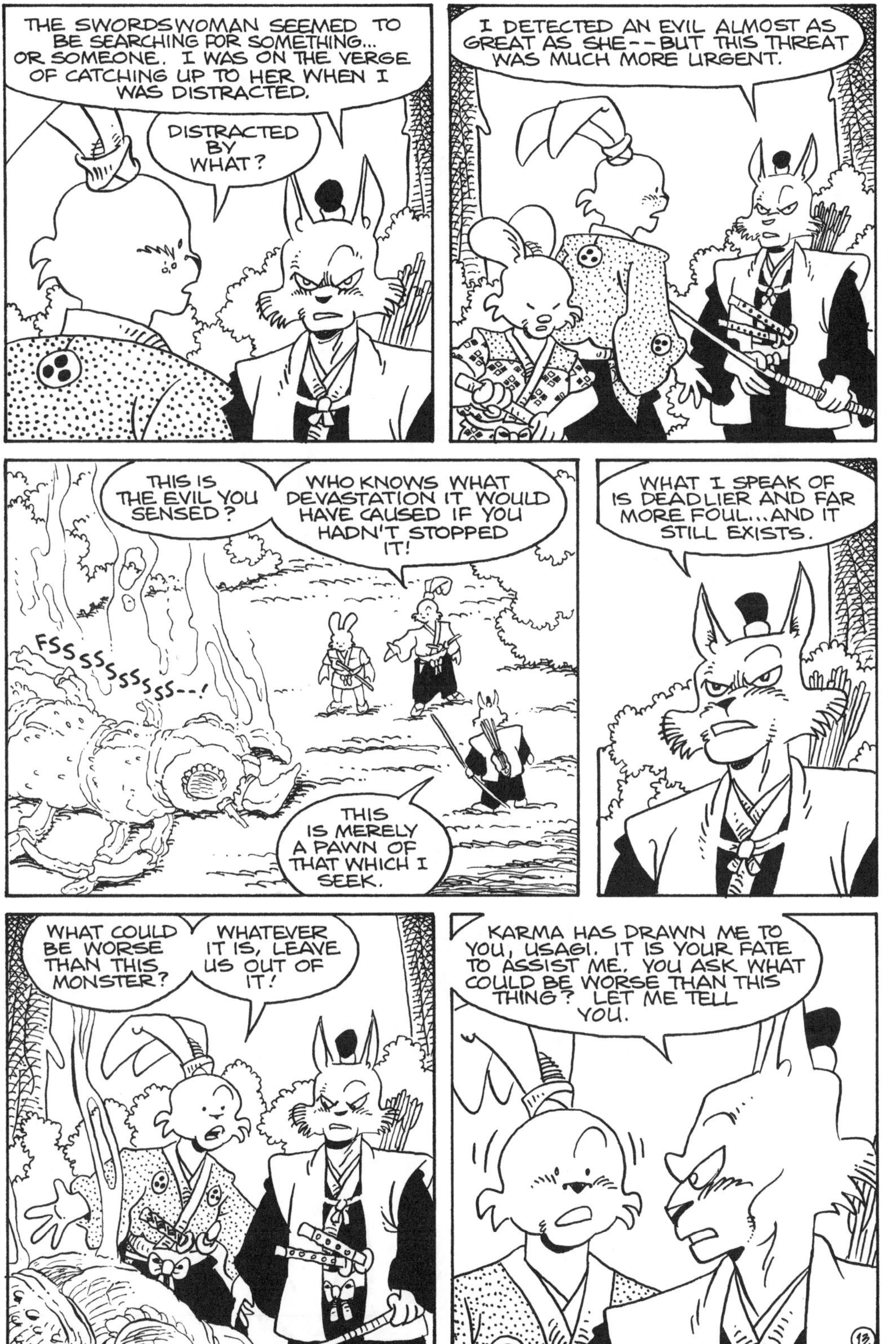
THE SWORDSWOMAN SEEMED TO BE SEARCHING FOR SOMETHING... OR SOMEONE. I WAS ON THE VERGE OF CATCHING UP TO HER WHEN I WAS DISTRACTED.
DISTRACTED BY WHAT?
I DETECTED AN EVIL ALMOST AS GREAT AS SHE--BUT THIS THREAT WAS MUCH MORE URGENT.
THIS IS THE EVIL YOU SENSED?
WHO KNOWS WHAT DEVASTATION IT WOULD HAVE CAUSED IF YOU HADN'T STOPPED IT!
FSSSSSSSSSSS--!
THIS IS MERELY A PAWN OF THAT WHICH I SEEK.
WHAT I SPEAK OF IS DEADLIER AND FAR MORE FOUL...AND IT STILL EXISTS.
WHAT COULD BE WORSE THAN THIS MONSTER?
WHATEVER IT IS, LEAVE US OUT OF IT!
KARMA HAS DRAWN ME TO YOU, USAGI. IT IS YOUR FATE TO ASSIST ME. YOU ASK WHAT COULD BE WORSE THAN THIS THING? LET ME TELL YOU.
13.

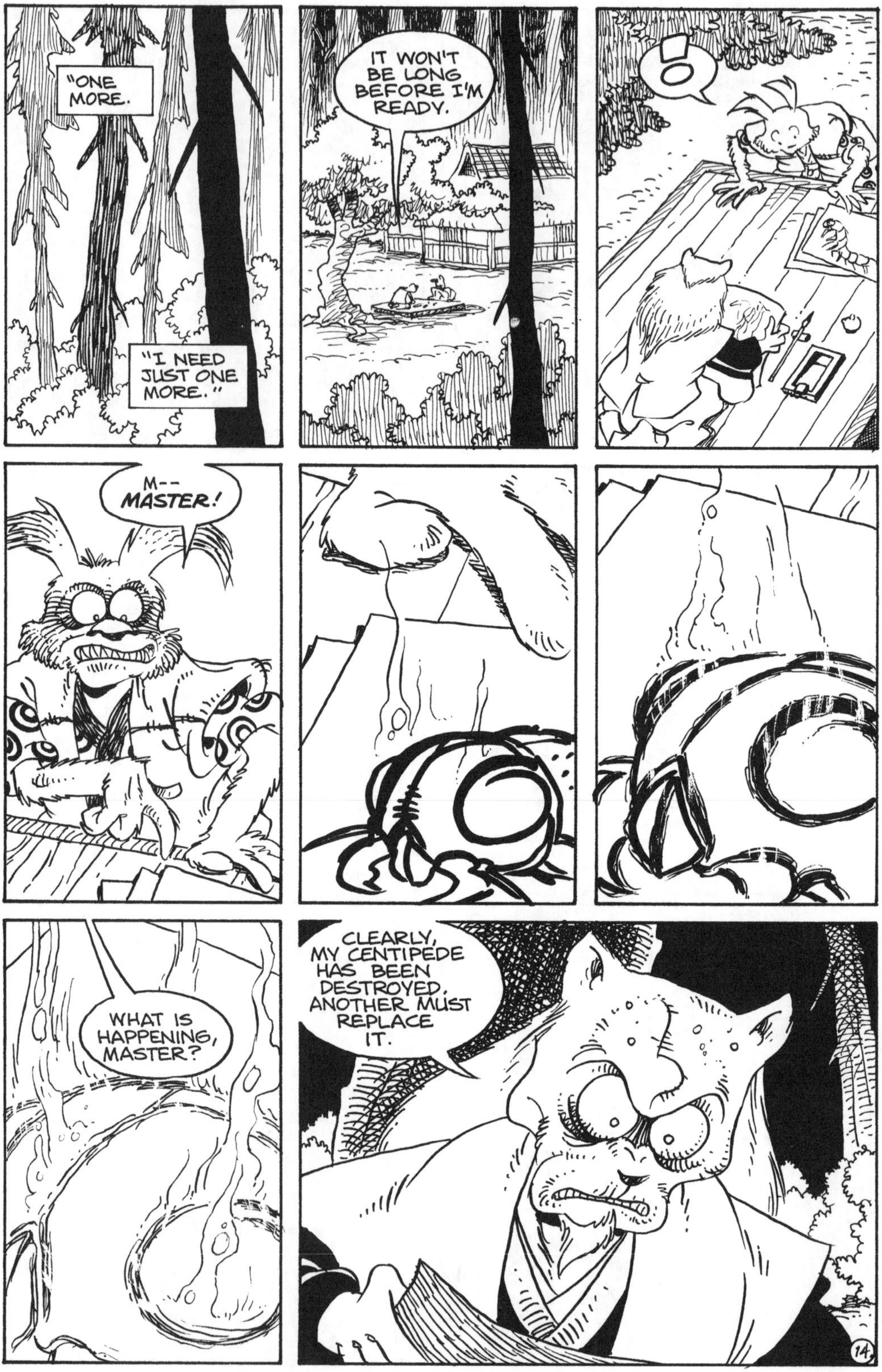
"ONE MORE.
"I NEED JUST ONE MORE."
IT WON'T BE LONG BEFORE I'M READY.
!
M-- MASTER!
WHAT IS HAPPENING, MASTER?
CLEARLY, MY CENTIPEDE HAS BEEN DESTROYED. ANOTHER MUST REPLACE IT.
14

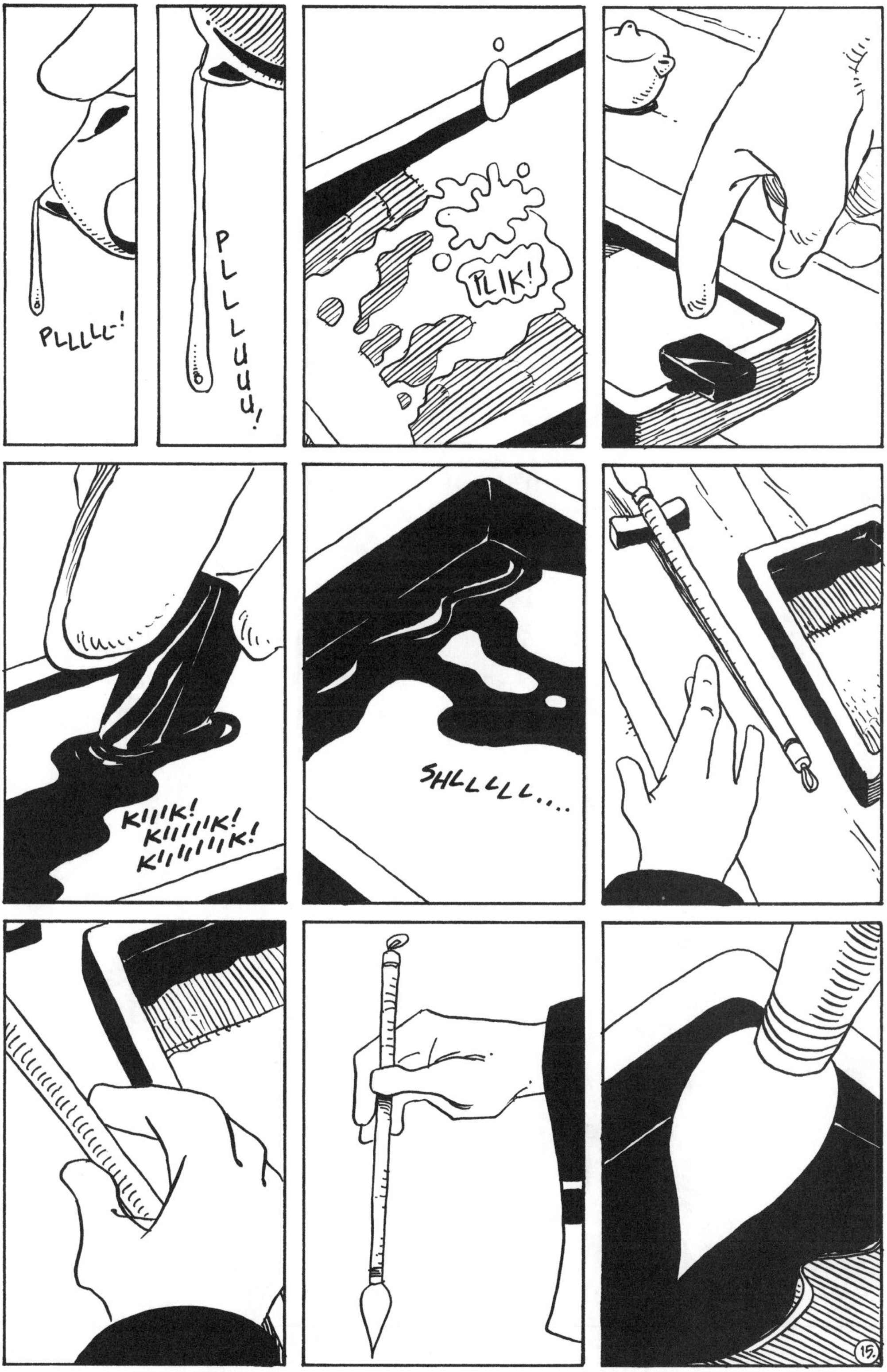
PLLLLL!
PLLLLUUUU!
PLIK!
KIIIK! KIIIIIK! KIIIIIIK!
SHLLLLLL....
15.

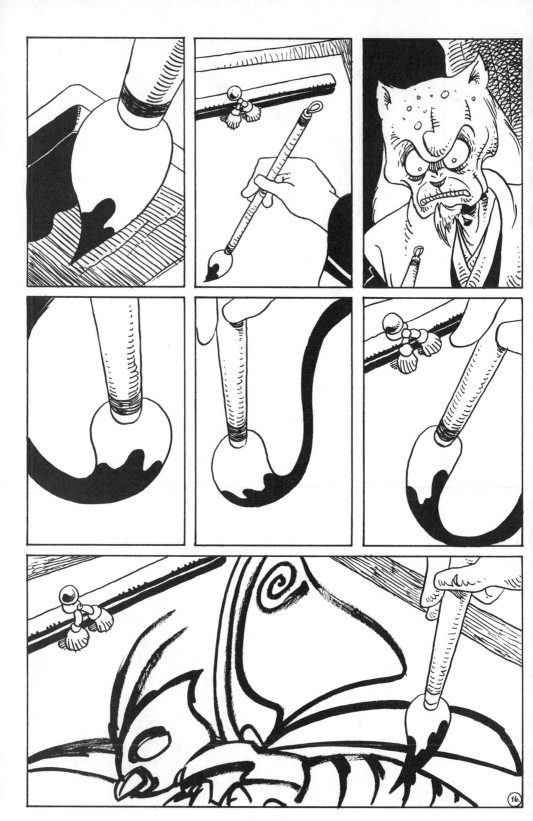

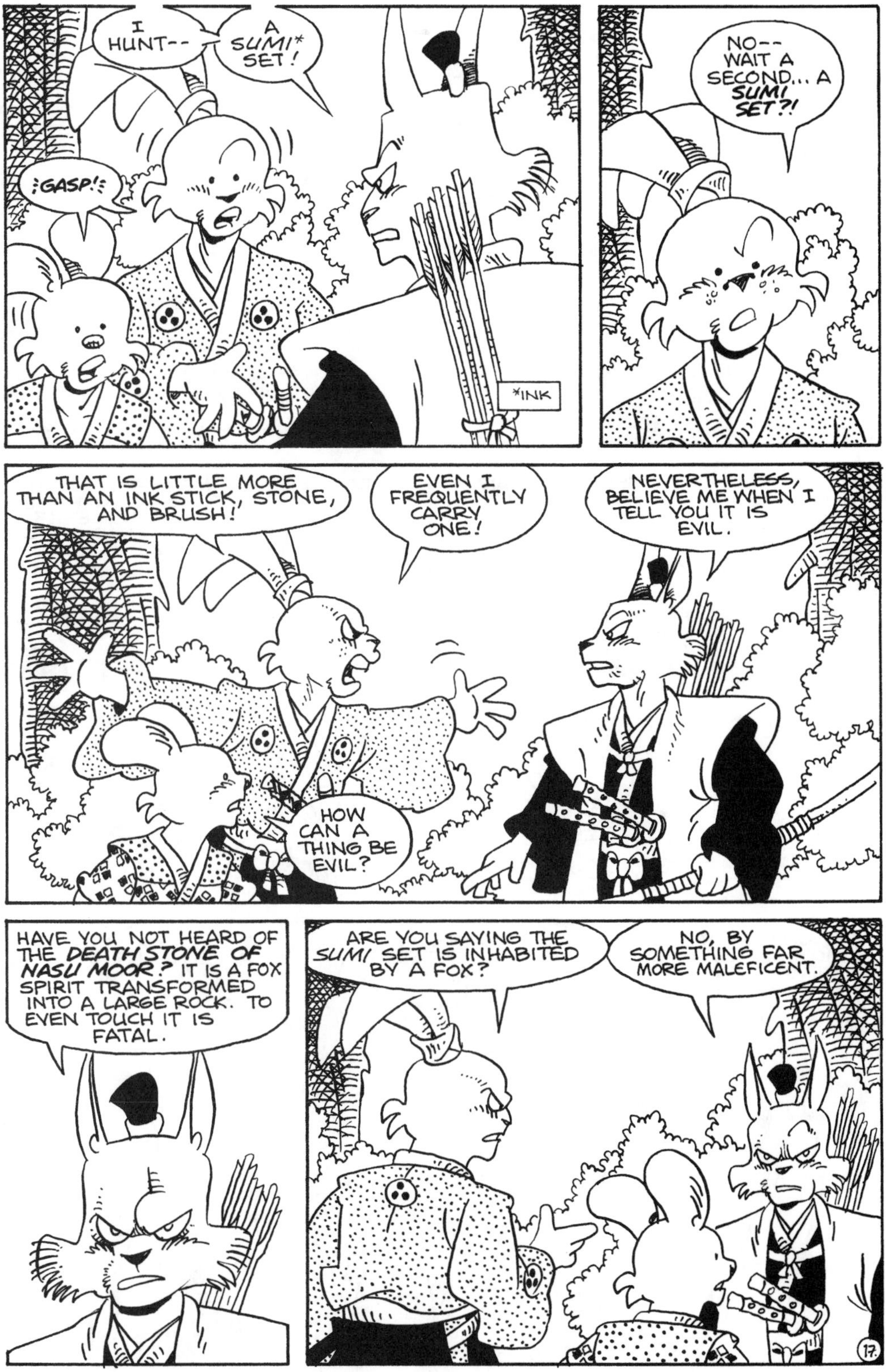
I HUNT--
A SUMI* SET!
:GASP!:
*INK
NO-- WAIT A SECOND... A SUMI SET?!
THAT IS LITTLE MORE THAN AN INK STICK, STONE, AND BRUSH!
EVEN I FREQUENTLY CARRY ONE!
NEVERTHELESS, BELIEVE ME WHEN I TELL YOU IT IS EVIL.
HOW CAN A THING BE EVIL?
HAVE YOU NOT HEARD OF THE DEATH STONE OF NASU MOOR? IT IS A FOX SPIRIT TRANSFORMED INTO A LARGE ROCK. TO EVEN TOUCH IT IS FATAL.
ARE YOU SAYING THE SUMI SET IS INHABITED BY A FOX?
NO, BY SOMETHING FAR MORE MALEFICENT.
17.

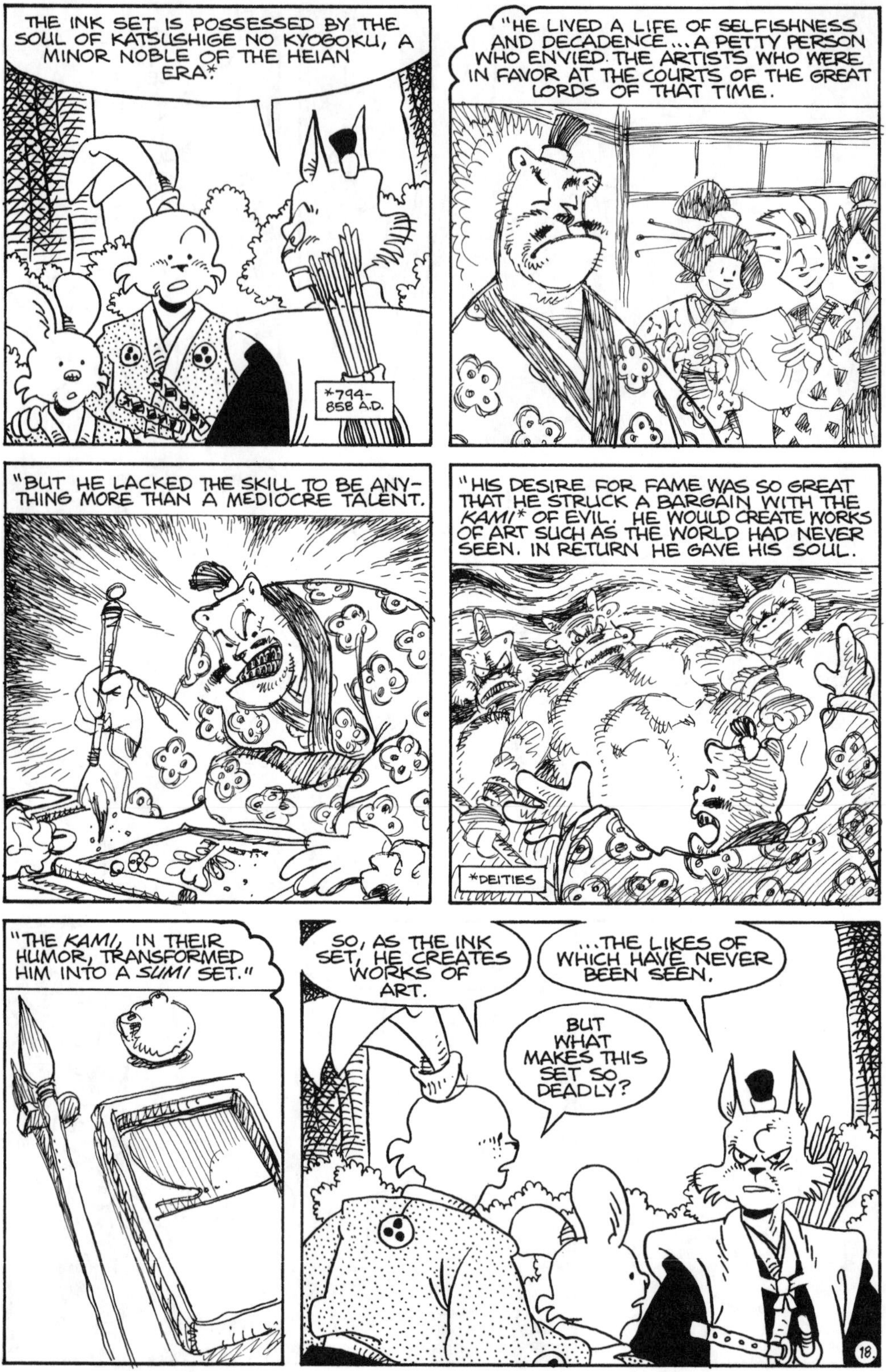
THE INK SET IS POSSESSED BY THE SOUL OF KATSUSHIGE NO KYOGOKU, A MINOR NOBLE OF THE HEIAN ERA*.
*794-858 A.D.
"HE LIVED A LIFE OF SELFISHNESS AND DECADENCE... A PETTY PERSON WHO ENVIED THE ARTISTS WHO WERE IN FAVOR AT THE COURTS OF THE GREAT LORDS OF THAT TIME.
"BUT HE LACKED THE SKILL TO BE ANYTHING MORE THAN A MEDIOCRE TALENT.
"HIS DESIRE FOR FAME WAS SO GREAT THAT HE STRUCK A BARGAIN WITH THE KAMI* OF EVIL. HE WOULD CREATE WORKS OF ART SUCH AS THE WORLD HAD NEVER SEEN. IN RETURN HE GAVE HIS SOUL.
*DEITIES
"THE KAMI, IN THEIR HUMOR, TRANSFORMED HIM INTO A SUMI SET."
SO, AS THE INK SET, HE CREATES WORKS OF ART.
...THE LIKES OF WHICH HAVE NEVER BEEN SEEN.
BUT WHAT MAKES THIS SET SO DEADLY?
18.

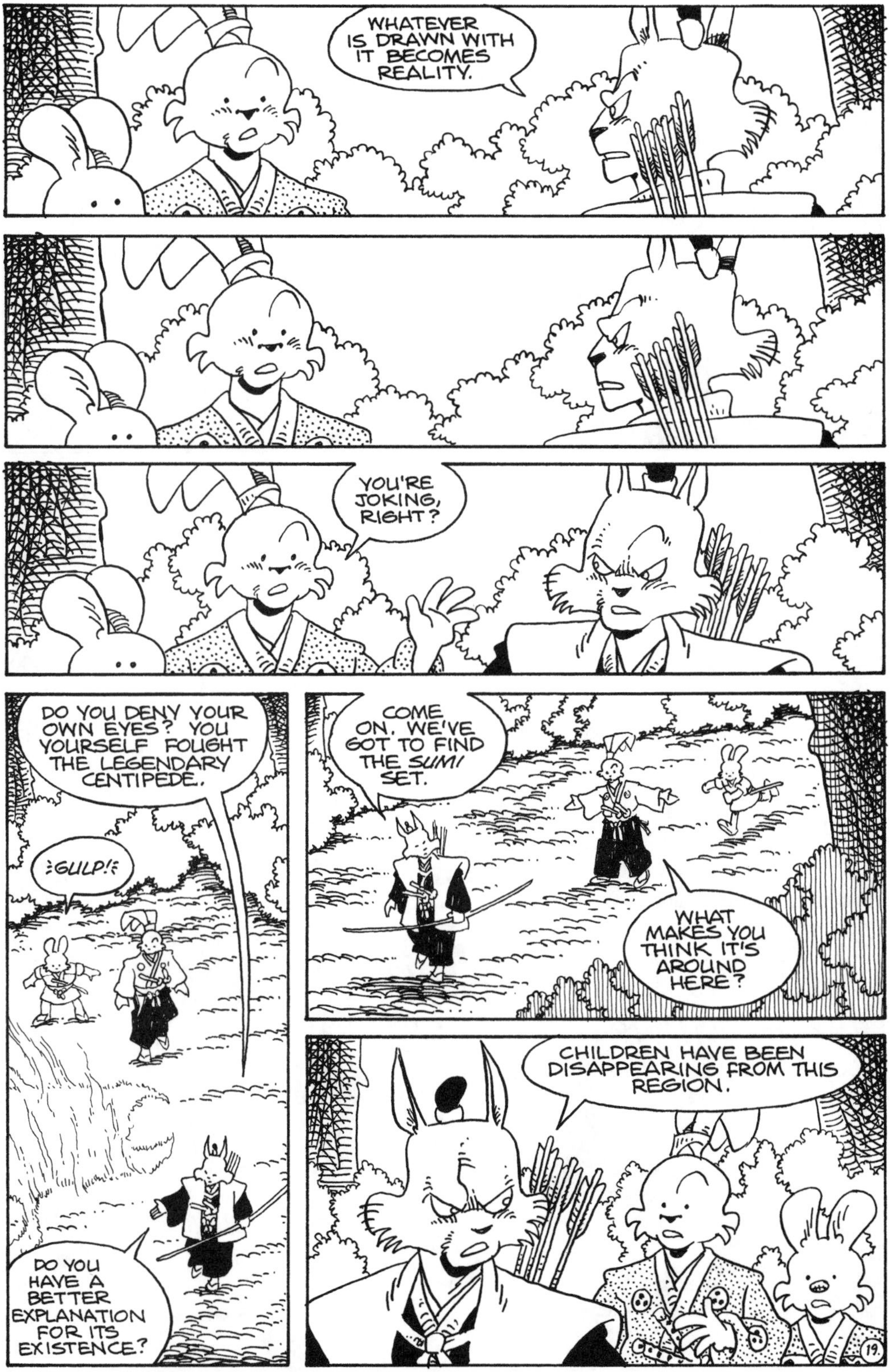
WHATEVER IS DRAWN WITH IT BECOMES REALITY.
YOU'RE JOKING, RIGHT?
DO YOU DENY YOUR OWN EYES? YOU YOURSELF FOUGHT THE LEGENDARY CENTIPEDE.
GULP!
DO YOU HAVE A BETTER EXPLANATION FOR ITS EXISTENCE?
COME ON. WE'VE GOT TO FIND THE *SUMI* SET.
WHAT MAKES YOU THINK IT'S AROUND HERE?
CHILDREN HAVE BEEN DISAPPEARING FROM THIS REGION.
19.

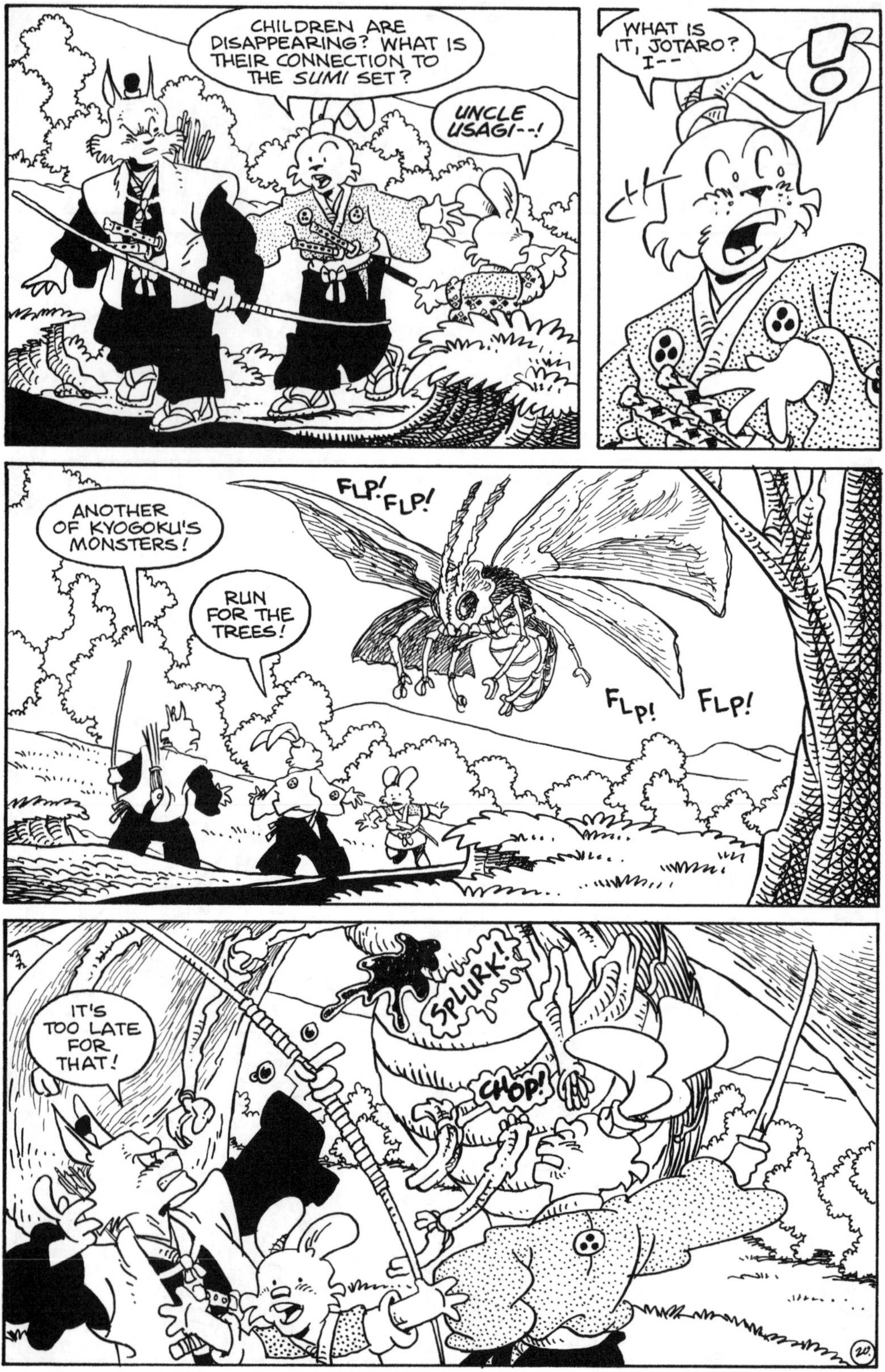
CHILDREN ARE DISAPPEARING? WHAT IS THEIR CONNECTION TO THE SUMI SET?
UNCLE USAGI--!
WHAT IS IT, JOTARO? I--
!
ANOTHER OF KYOGOKU'S MONSTERS!
RUN FOR THE TREES!
FLP! FLP!
FLP! FLP!
IT'S TOO LATE FOR THAT!
SPLURK!
CHOP!
20.

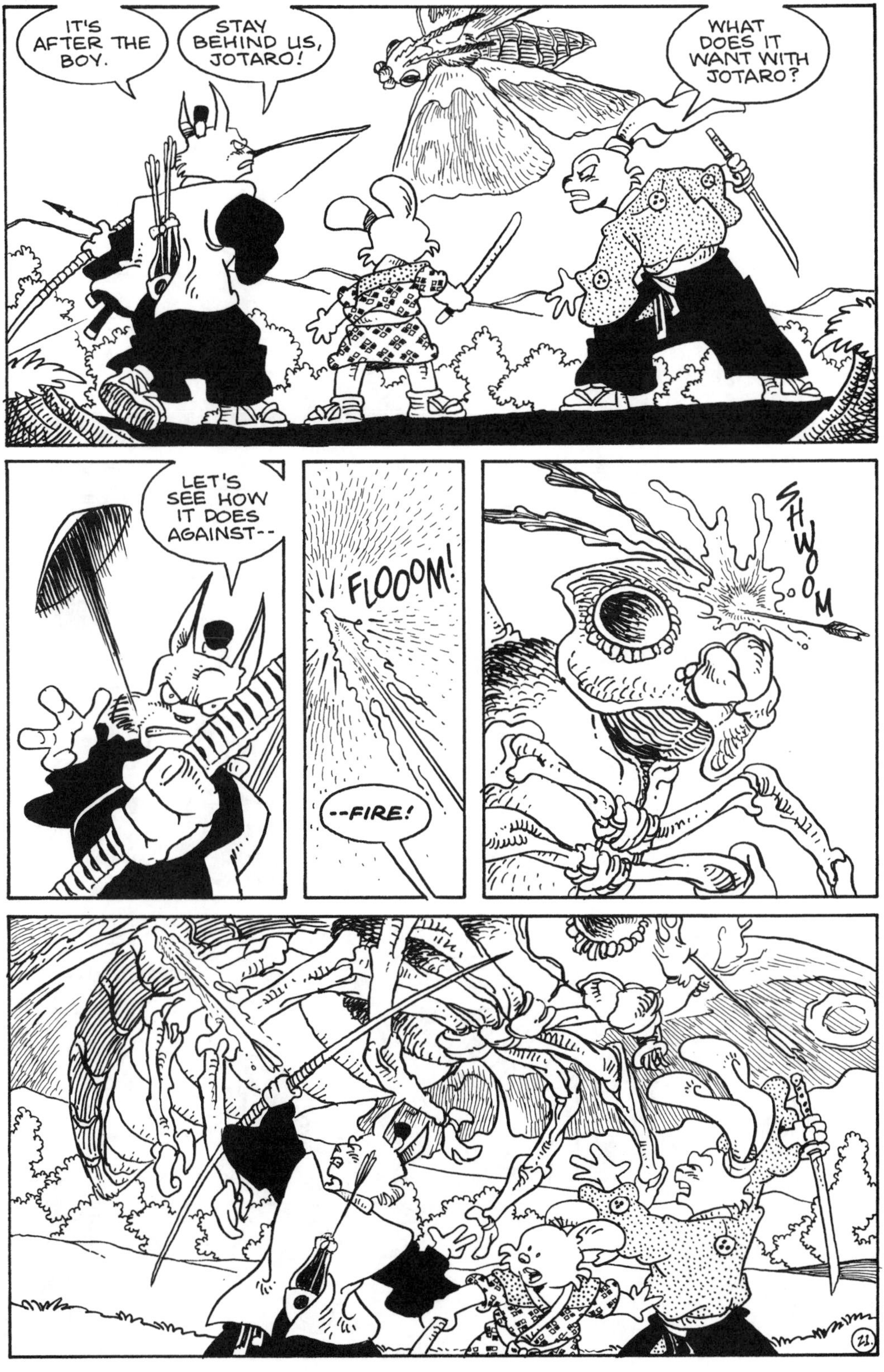
IT'S AFTER THE BOY.
STAY BEHIND US, JOTARO!
WHAT DOES IT WANT WITH JOTARO?
LET'S SEE HOW IT DOES AGAINST--
FLOOOM!
--FIRE!
SHWOOOM
21.

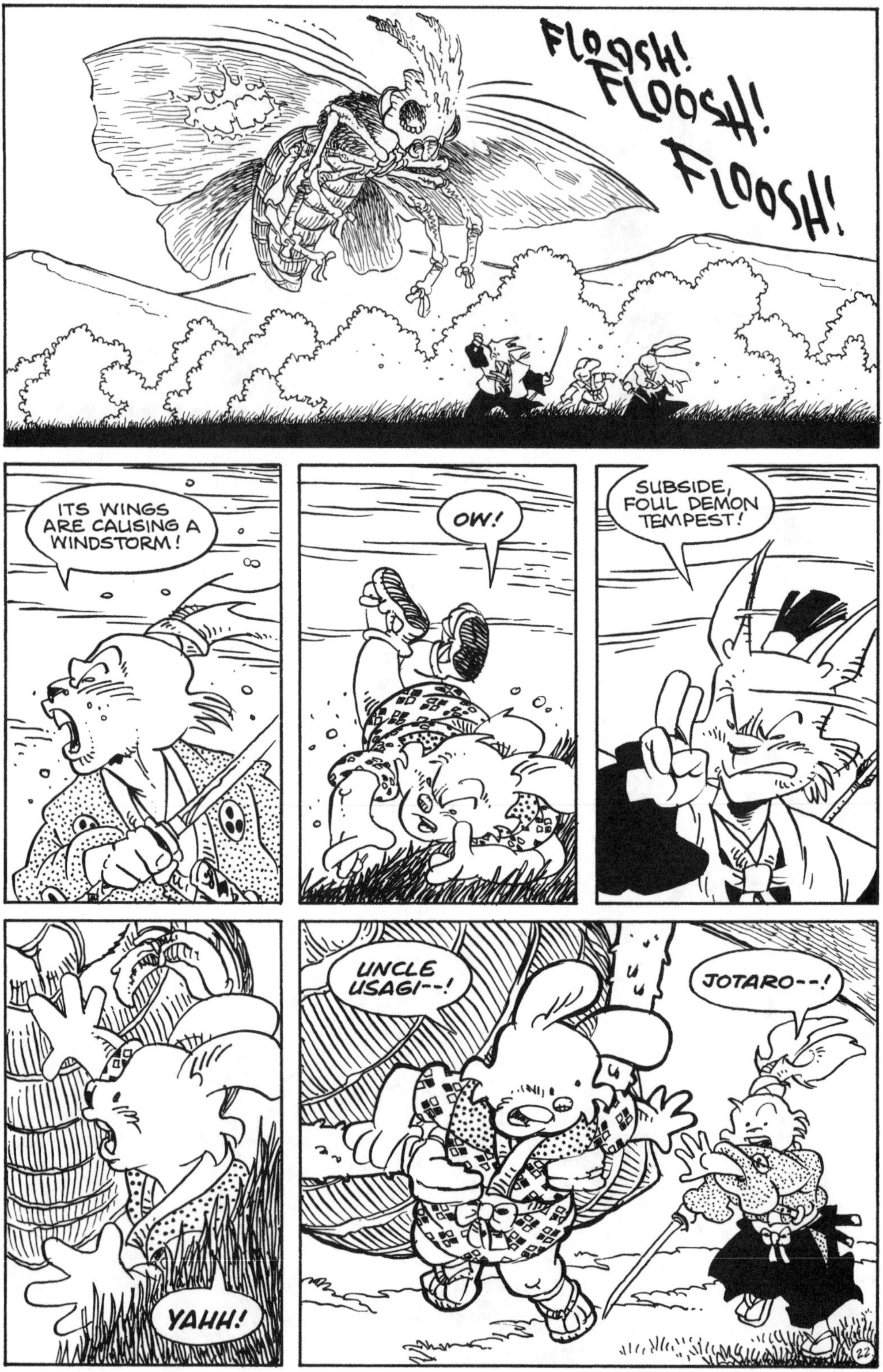
FLOOSH!
FLOOSH!
FLOOSH!
ITS WINGS ARE CAUSING A WINDSTORM!
OW!
SUBSIDE, FOUL DEMON TEMPEST!
YAHH!
UNCLE USAGI--!
JOTARO--!
22

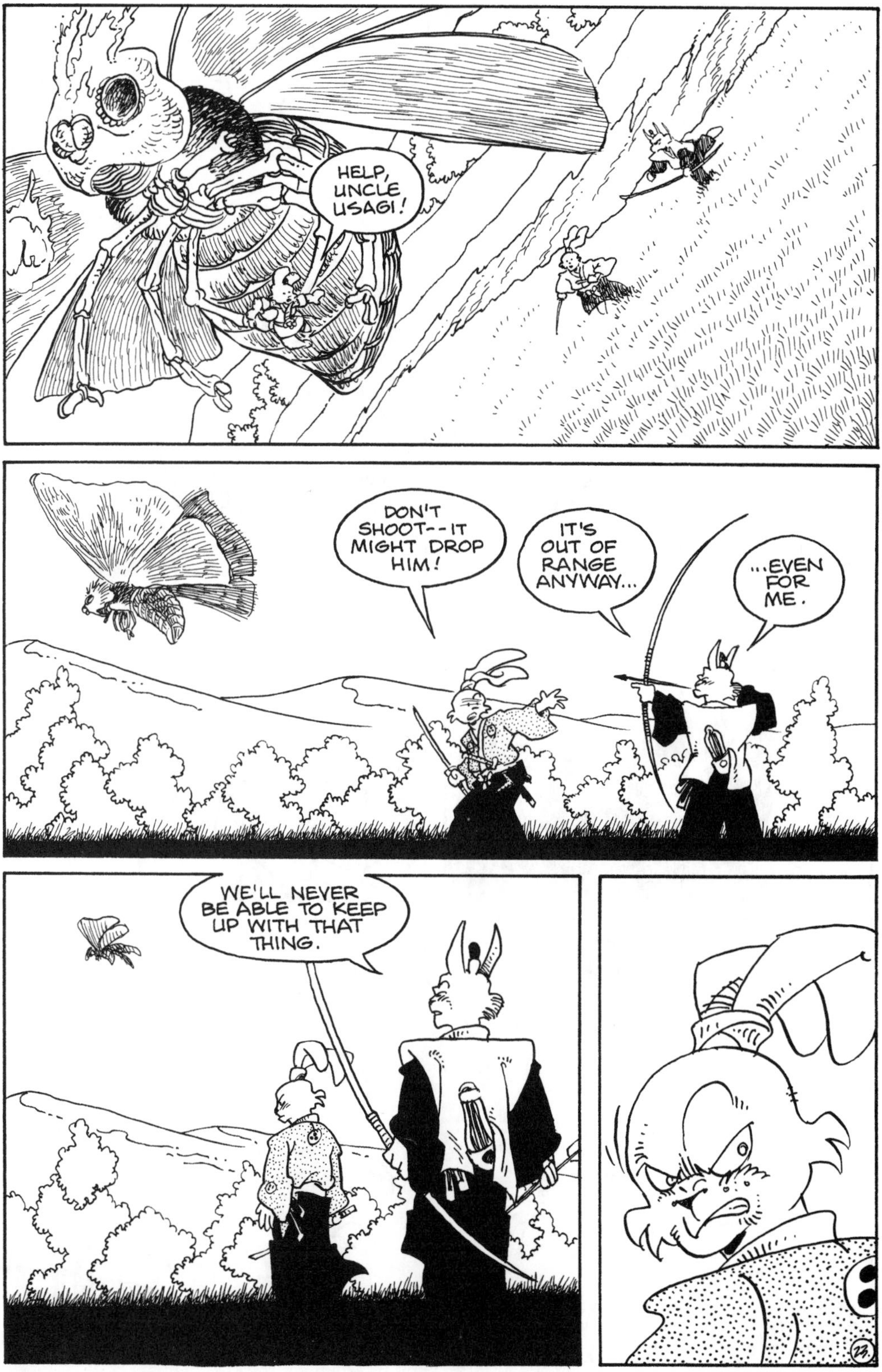
HELP, UNCLE USAGI!
DON'T SHOOT--IT MIGHT DROP HIM!
IT'S OUT OF RANGE ANYWAY...
...EVEN FOR ME.
WE'LL NEVER BE ABLE TO KEEP UP WITH THAT THING.
23.

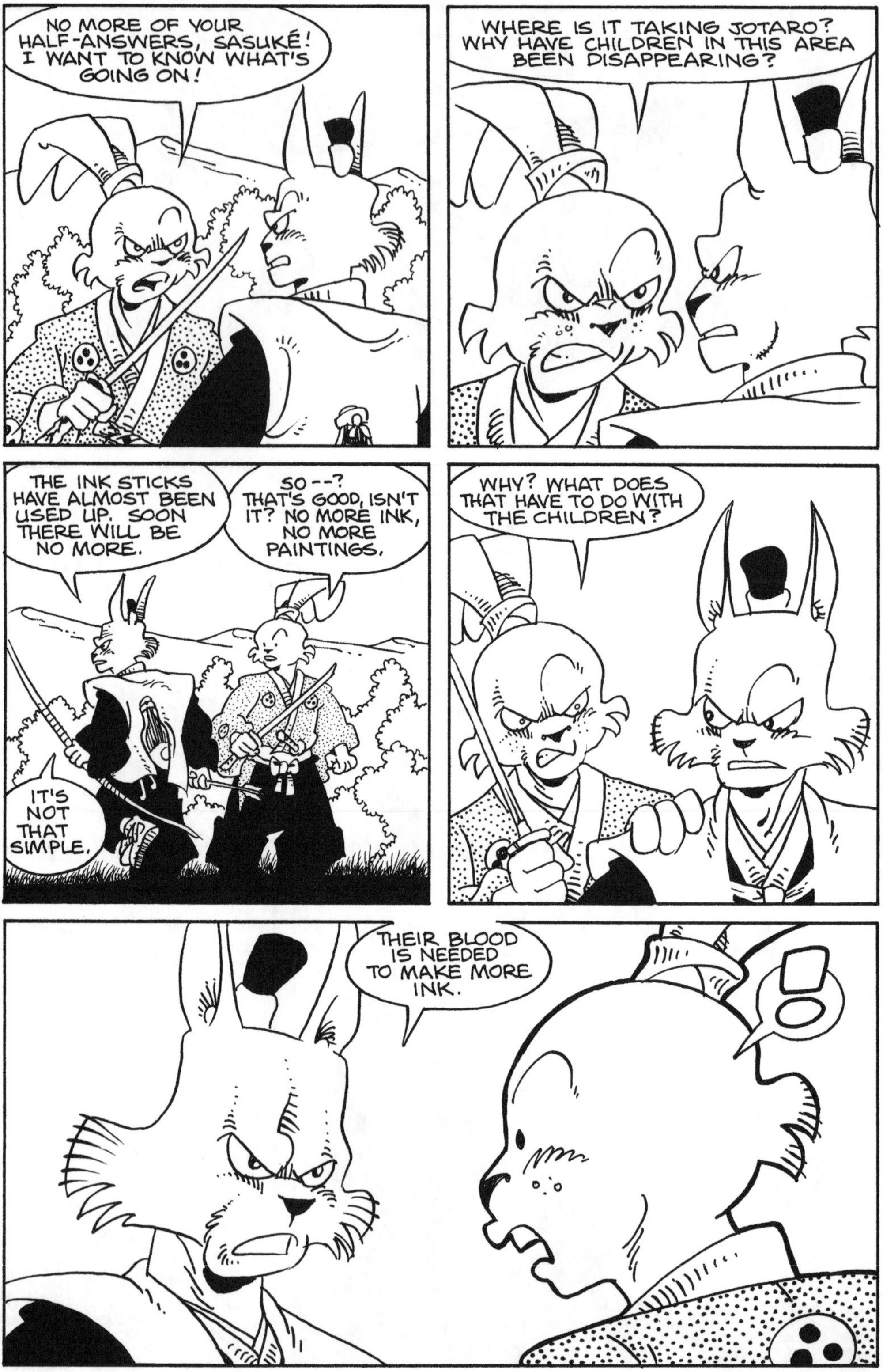
NO MORE OF YOUR HALF-ANSWERS, SASUKÉ! I WANT TO KNOW WHAT'S GOING ON!
WHERE IS IT TAKING JOTARO? WHY HAVE CHILDREN IN THIS AREA BEEN DISAPPEARING?
THE INK STICKS HAVE ALMOST BEEN USED UP. SOON THERE WILL BE NO MORE.
SO--? THAT'S GOOD, ISN'T IT? NO MORE INK, NO MORE PAINTINGS.
IT'S NOT THAT SIMPLE.
WHY? WHAT DOES THAT HAVE TO DO WITH THE CHILDREN?
THEIR BLOOD IS NEEDED TO MAKE MORE INK.
!

END OF PART 1

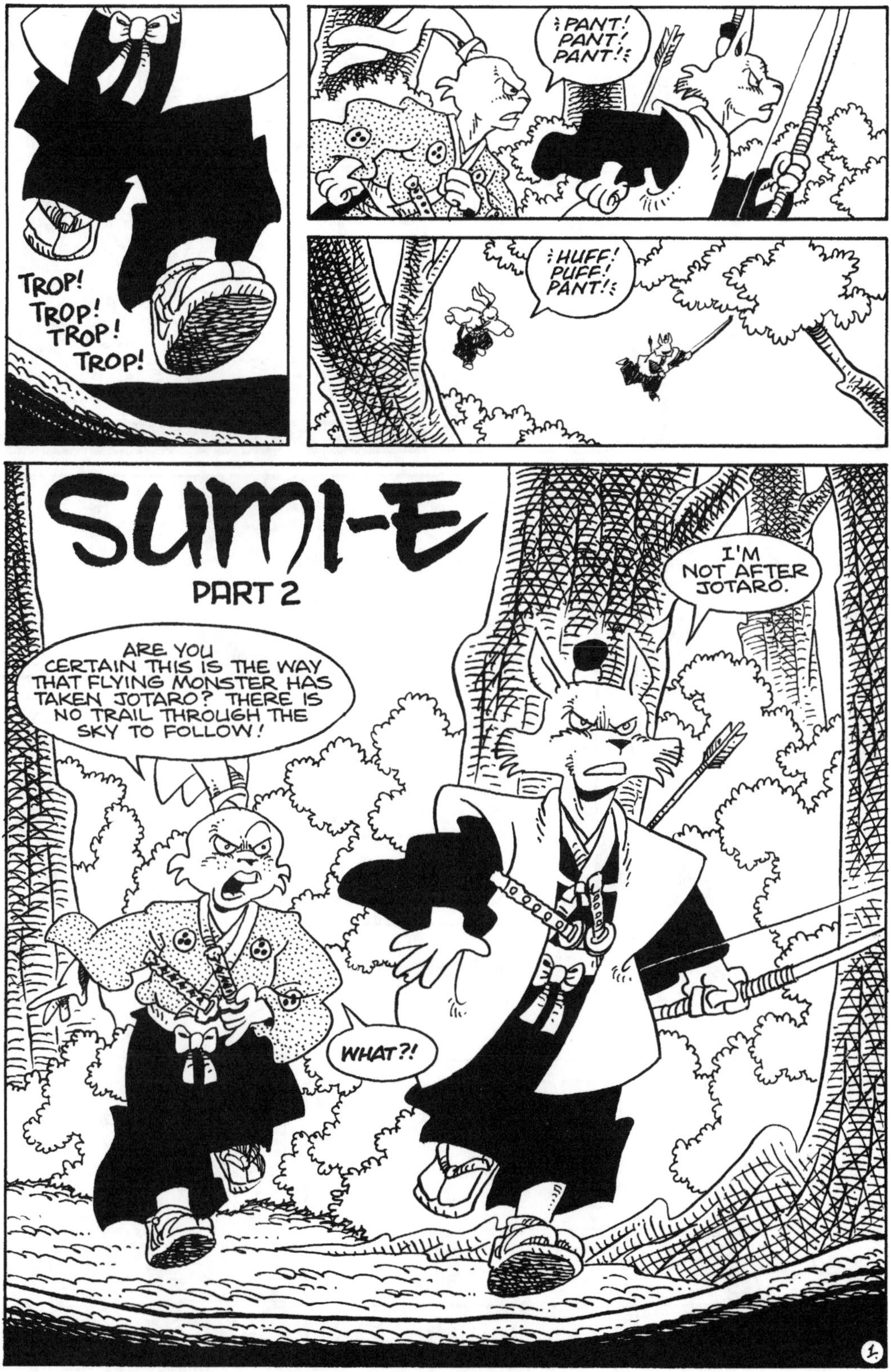
TROP! TROP! TROP! TROP!
PANT! PANT! PANT!
HUFF! PUFF! PANT!
SUMI-E
PART 2
ARE YOU CERTAIN THIS IS THE WAY THAT FLYING MONSTER HAS TAKEN JOTARO? THERE IS NO TRAIL THROUGH THE SKY TO FOLLOW!
I'M NOT AFTER JOTARO.
WHAT?!
1.

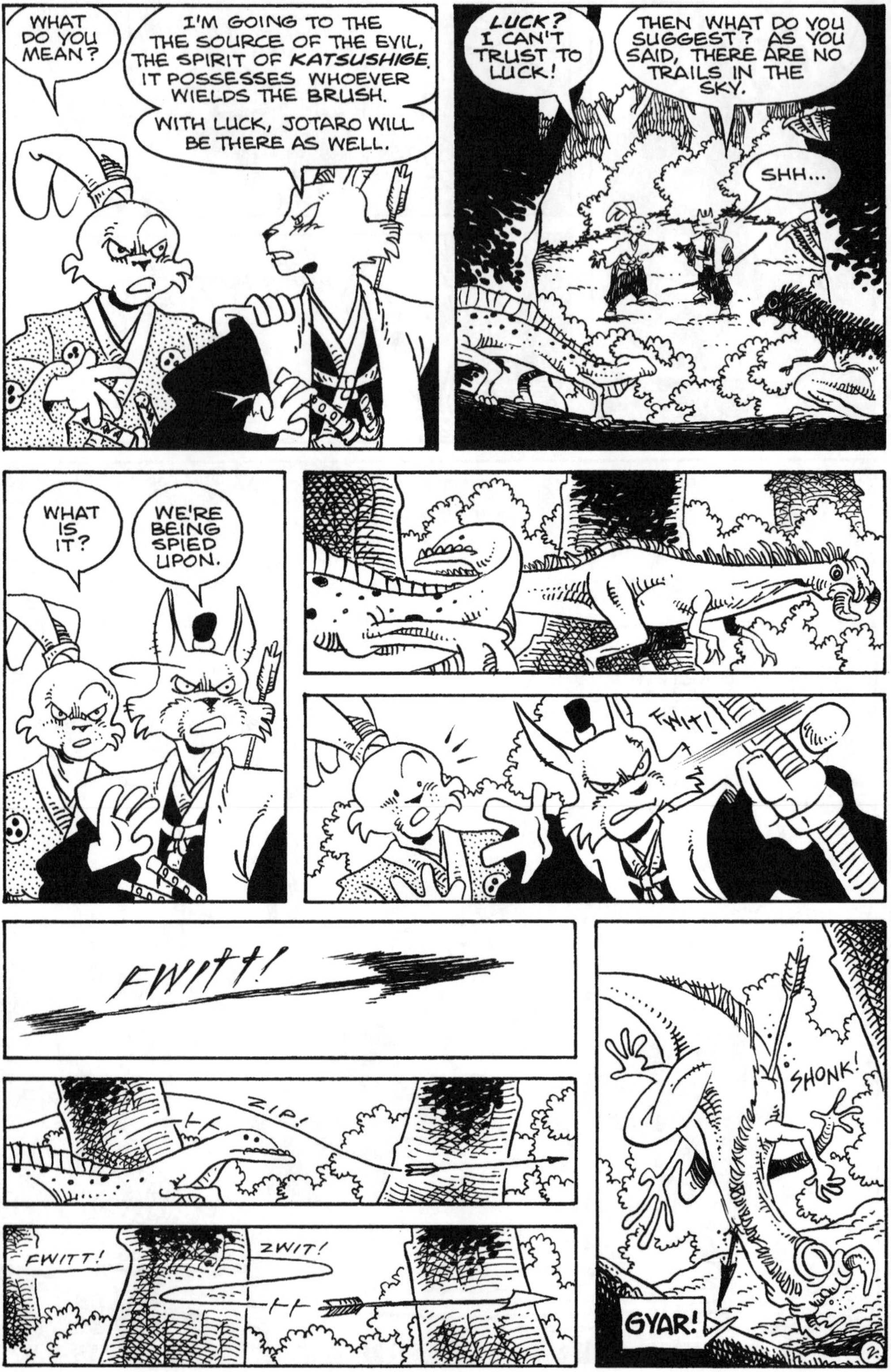

WHAT DO YOU MEAN?
I'M GOING TO THE THE SOURCE OF THE EVIL, THE SPIRIT OF KATSUSHIGE. IT POSSESSES WHOEVER WIELDS THE BRUSH.
WITH LUCK, JOTARO WILL BE THERE AS WELL.
LUCK? I CAN'T TRUST TO LUCK!
THEN WHAT DO YOU SUGGEST? AS YOU SAID, THERE ARE NO TRAILS IN THE SKY.
SHH...
WHAT IS IT?
WE'RE BEING SPIED UPON.
FWIT!
FWITT!
ZIP!
FWITT!
ZWIT!
SHONK!
GYAR!

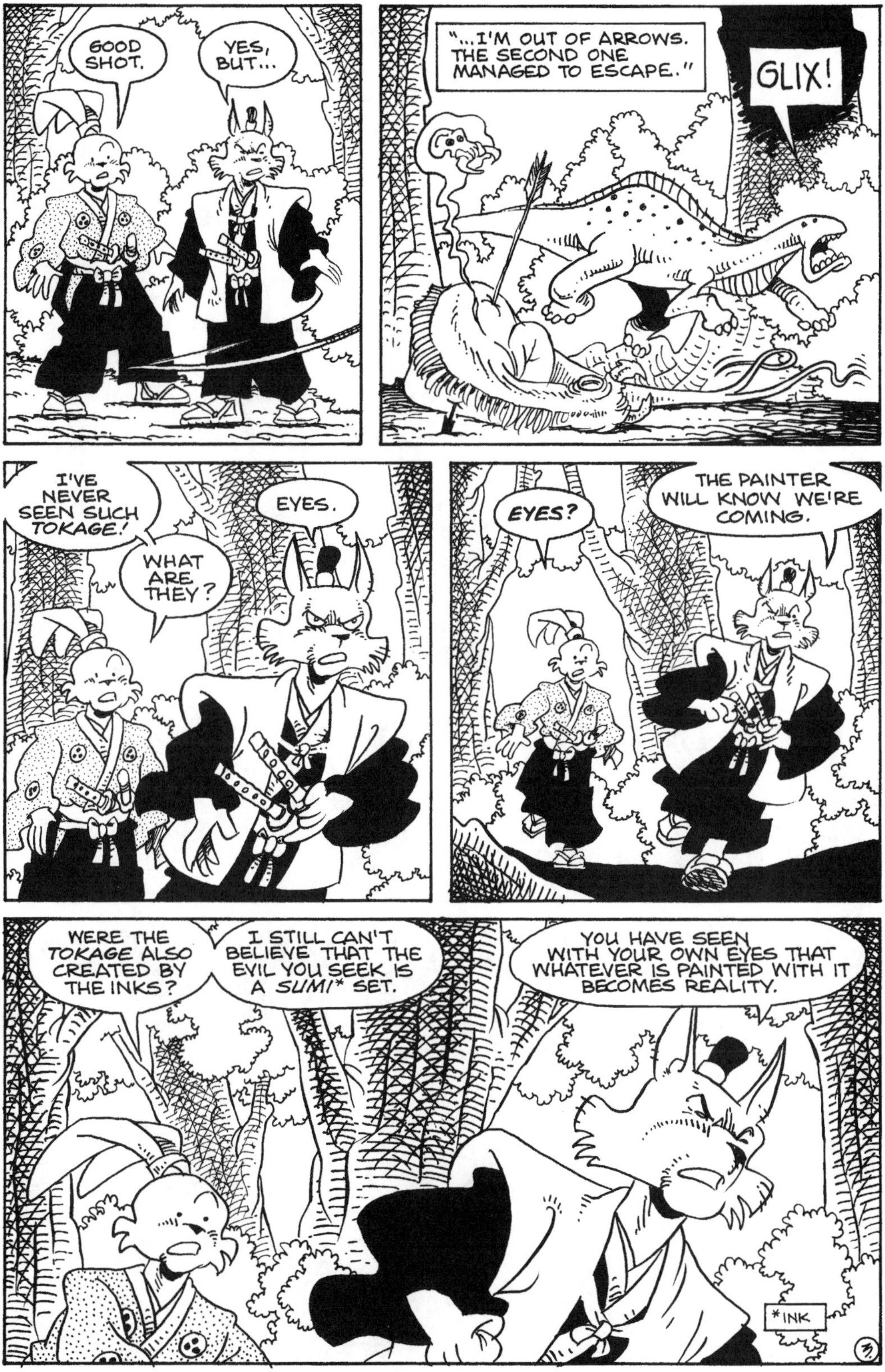
GOOD SHOT.
YES, BUT...
"...I'M OUT OF ARROWS. THE SECOND ONE MANAGED TO ESCAPE."
GLIX!
I'VE NEVER SEEN SUCH TOKAGE!
WHAT ARE THEY?
EYES.
EYES?
THE PAINTER WILL KNOW WE'RE COMING.
WERE THE TOKAGE ALSO CREATED BY THE INKS?
I STILL CAN'T BELIEVE THAT THE EVIL YOU SEEK IS A SUMI* SET.
YOU HAVE SEEN WITH YOUR OWN EYES THAT WHATEVER IS PAINTED WITH IT BECOMES REALITY.
*INK
3

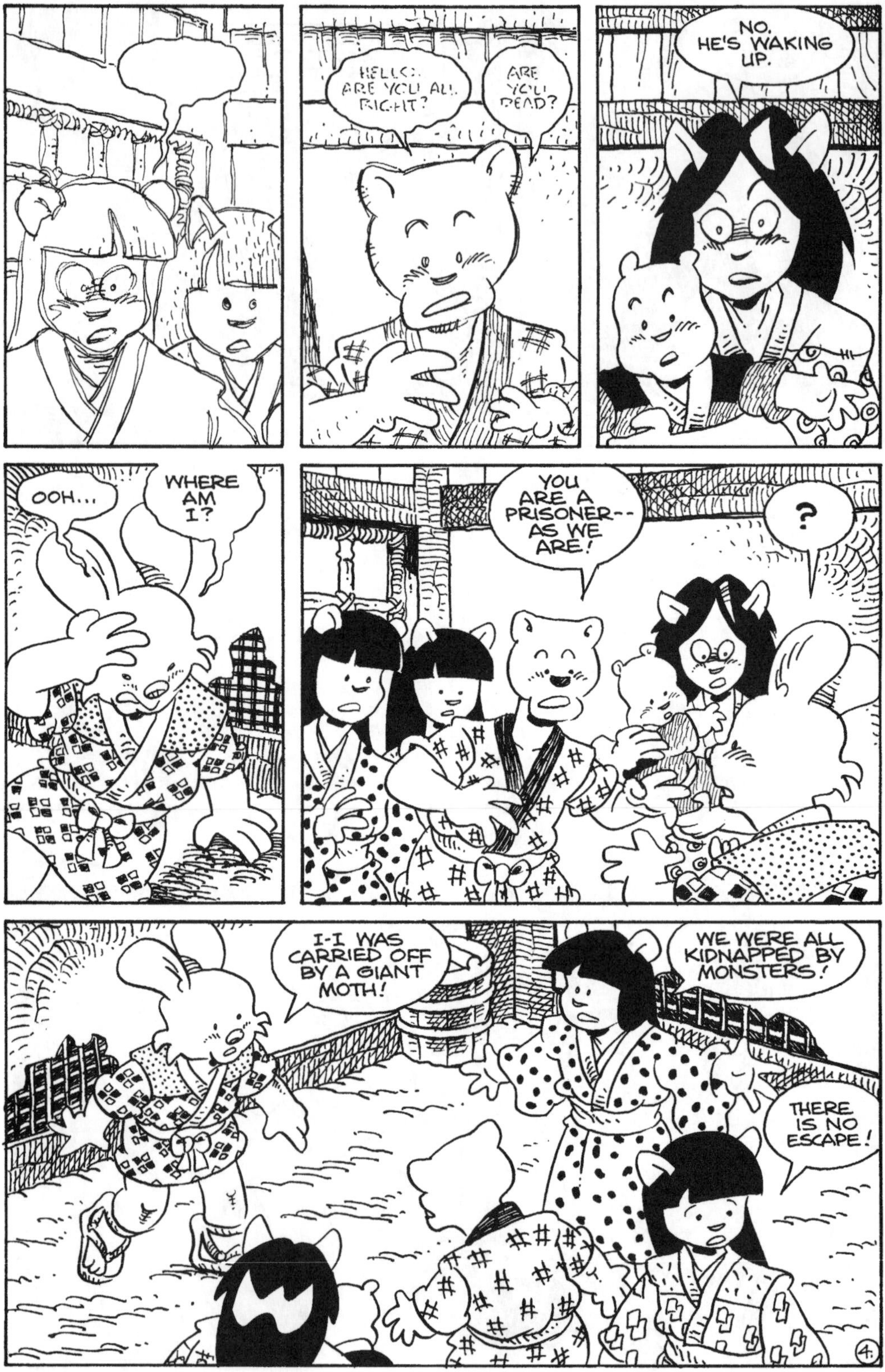
HELLO? ARE YOU ALL RIGHT?
ARE YOU DEAD?
NO. HE'S WAKING UP.
OOH...
WHERE AM I?
YOU ARE A PRISONER-- AS WE ARE!
?
I-I WAS CARRIED OFF BY A GIANT MOTH!
WE WERE ALL KIDNAPPED BY MONSTERS!
THERE IS NO ESCAPE!
4.

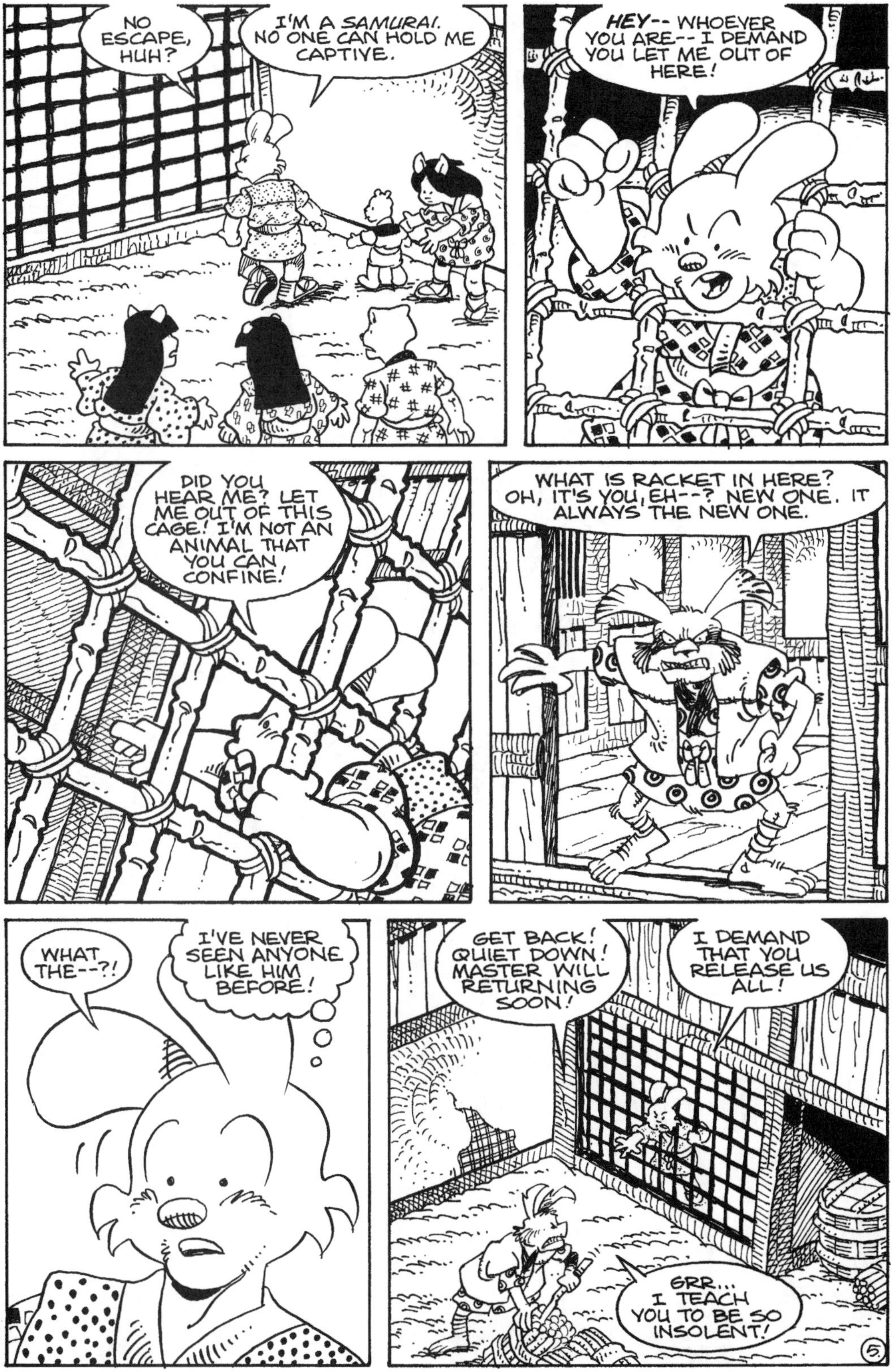
NO ESCAPE, HUH?
I'M A SAMURAI. NO ONE CAN HOLD ME CAPTIVE.
HEY-- WHOEVER YOU ARE-- I DEMAND YOU LET ME OUT OF HERE!
DID YOU HEAR ME? LET ME OUT OF THIS CAGE! I'M NOT AN ANIMAL THAT YOU CAN CONFINE!
WHAT IS RACKET IN HERE? OH, IT'S YOU, EH--? NEW ONE. IT ALWAYS THE NEW ONE.
WHAT THE--?!
I'VE NEVER SEEN ANYONE LIKE HIM BEFORE!
GET BACK! QUIET DOWN! MASTER WILL RETURNING SOON!
I DEMAND THAT YOU RELEASE US ALL!
GRR... I TEACH YOU TO BE SO INSOLENT!
5

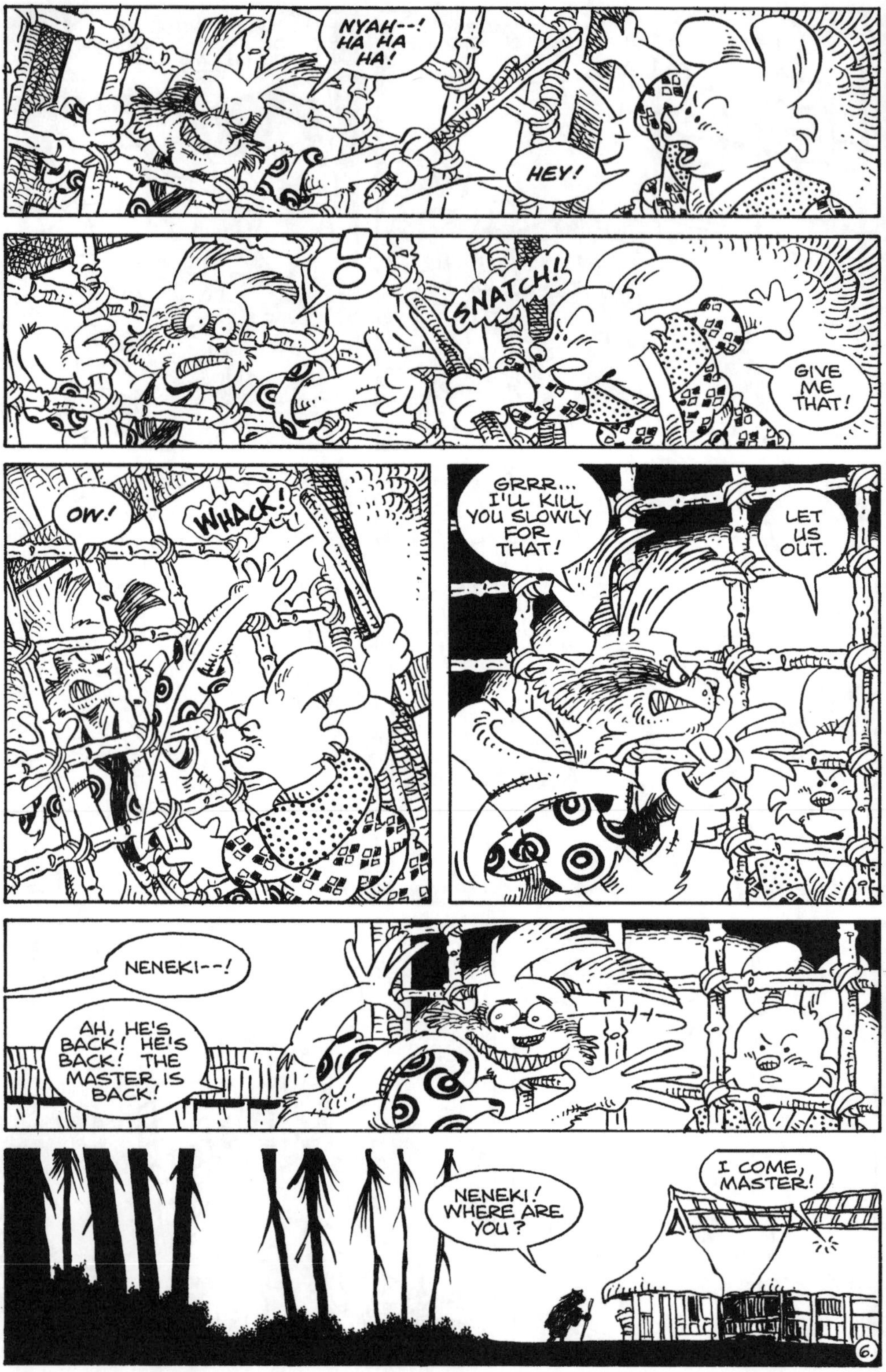
NYAH--! HA HA HA!
HEY!
!
SNATCH!
GIVE ME THAT!
OW!
WHACK!
GRRR... I'LL KILL YOU SLOWLY FOR THAT!
LET US OUT.
NENEKI--!
AH, HE'S BACK! HE'S BACK! THE MASTER IS BACK!
NENEKI! WHERE ARE YOU?
I COME, MASTER!
6.

I COME, MASTER, I COME.

IF YOU'RE THINKING OF ESCAPE, DON'T BOTHER.

BUT IF WE COULD GET OUT OF THIS CAGE, WE COULD ESCAPE THROUGH THAT WINDOW.

DO YOU THINK WE HAVEN'T THOUGHT OF THAT?

WE'VE TRIED EVERYTHING--PUSHING, KICKING, EVEN BITING THE BARS UNTIL OUR GUMS BLEED...

...BUT THEY'RE JUST TOO STRONG.

BESIDES, NENEKI CHECKS UP ON US REGULARLY. WE'D NEED A KNIFE TO CUT THROUGH THOSE TIES BEFORE HE CAME BACK AGAIN.

WELL, I MIGHT HAVE SOMETHING THAT WILL HELP.

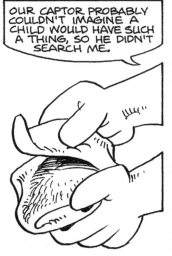

OUR CAPTOR PROBABLY COULDN'T IMAGINE A CHILD WOULD HAVE SUCH A THING, SO HE DIDN'T SEARCH ME.

THIS WAS GIVEN TO ME BY A *NINJA* LADY A COUPLE OF WEEKS AGO.

159

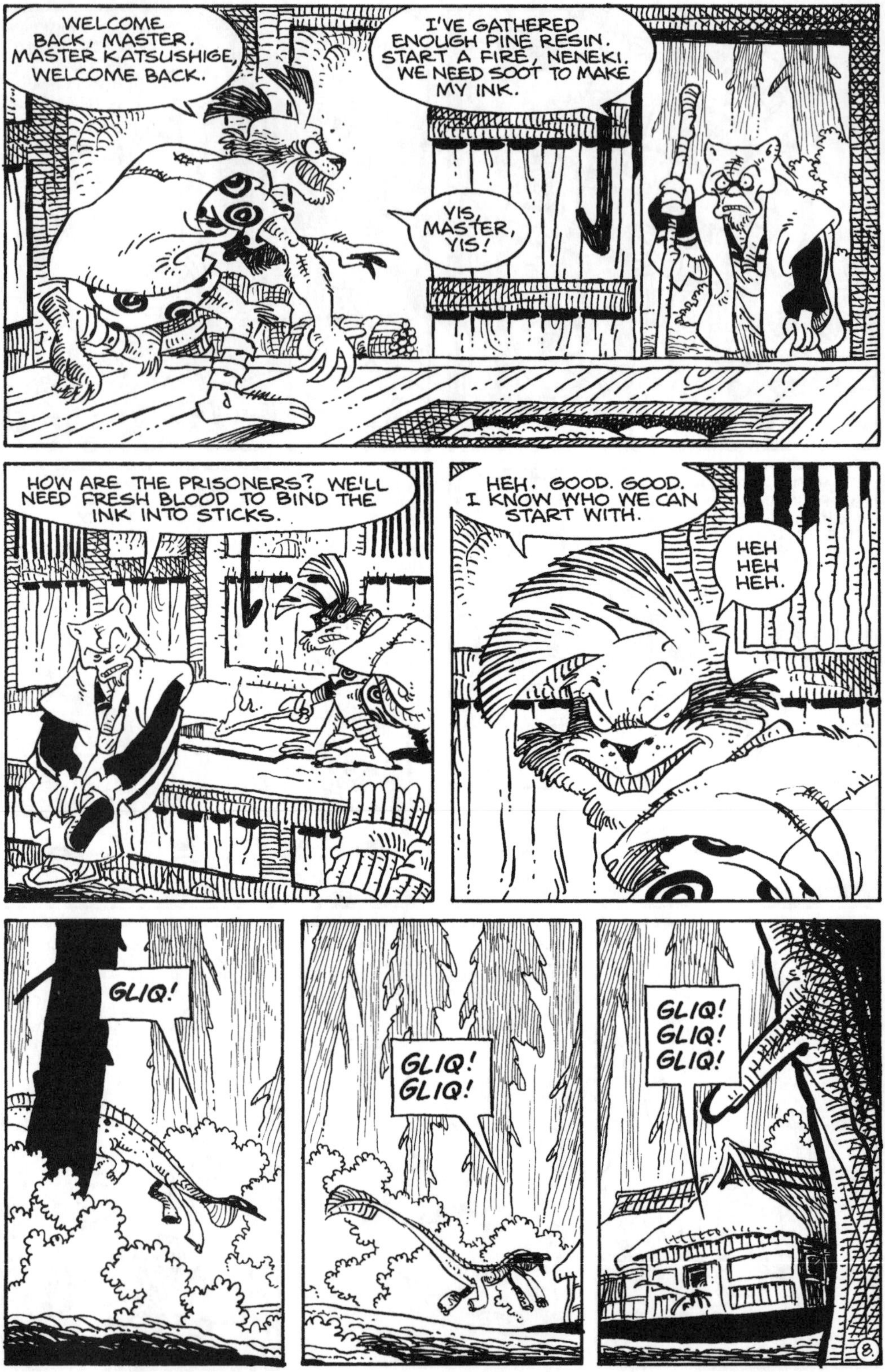
WELCOME BACK, MASTER. MASTER KATSUSHIGE, WELCOME BACK.
I'VE GATHERED ENOUGH PINE RESIN. START A FIRE, NENEKI. WE NEED SOOT TO MAKE MY INK.
YIS, MASTER, YIS!
HOW ARE THE PRISONERS? WE'LL NEED FRESH BLOOD TO BIND THE INK INTO STICKS.
HEH. GOOD. GOOD. I KNOW WHO WE CAN START WITH.
HEH HEH HEH.
GLIQ!
GLIQ! GLIQ!
GLIQ! GLIQ! GLIQ!
8.

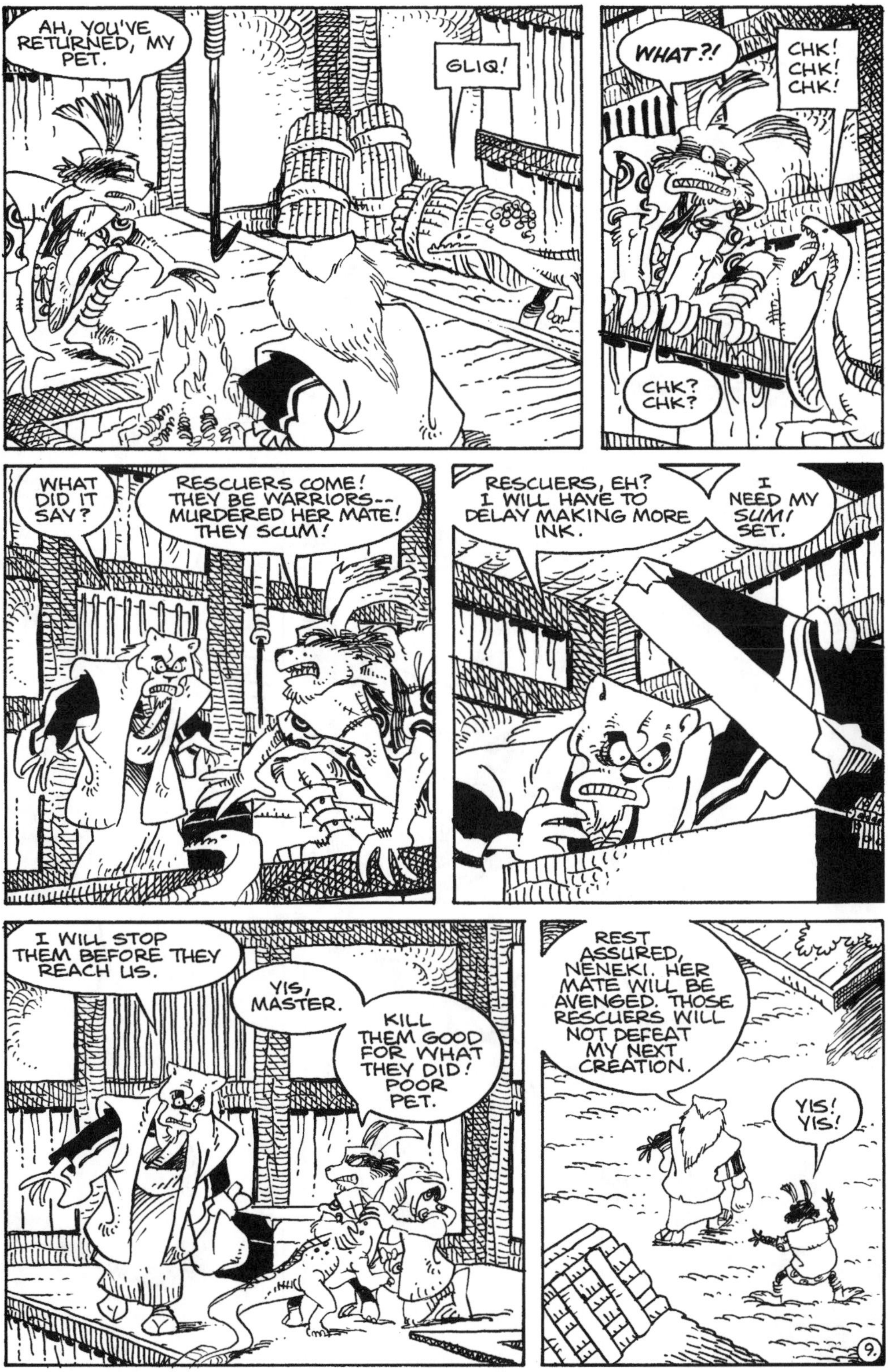
AH, YOU'VE RETURNED, MY PET.
GLIQ!
WHAT?!
CHK! CHK! CHK!
CHK? CHK?
WHAT DID IT SAY?
RESCUERS COME! THEY BE WARRIORS-- MURDERED HER MATE! THEY SCUM!
RESCUERS, EH? I WILL HAVE TO DELAY MAKING MORE INK.
I NEED MY SUMI SET.
I WILL STOP THEM BEFORE THEY REACH US.
YIS, MASTER.
KILL THEM GOOD FOR WHAT THEY DID! POOR PET.
REST ASSURED, NENEKI. HER MATE WILL BE AVENGED. THOSE RESCUERS WILL NOT DEFEAT MY NEXT CREATION.
YIS! YIS!
9.

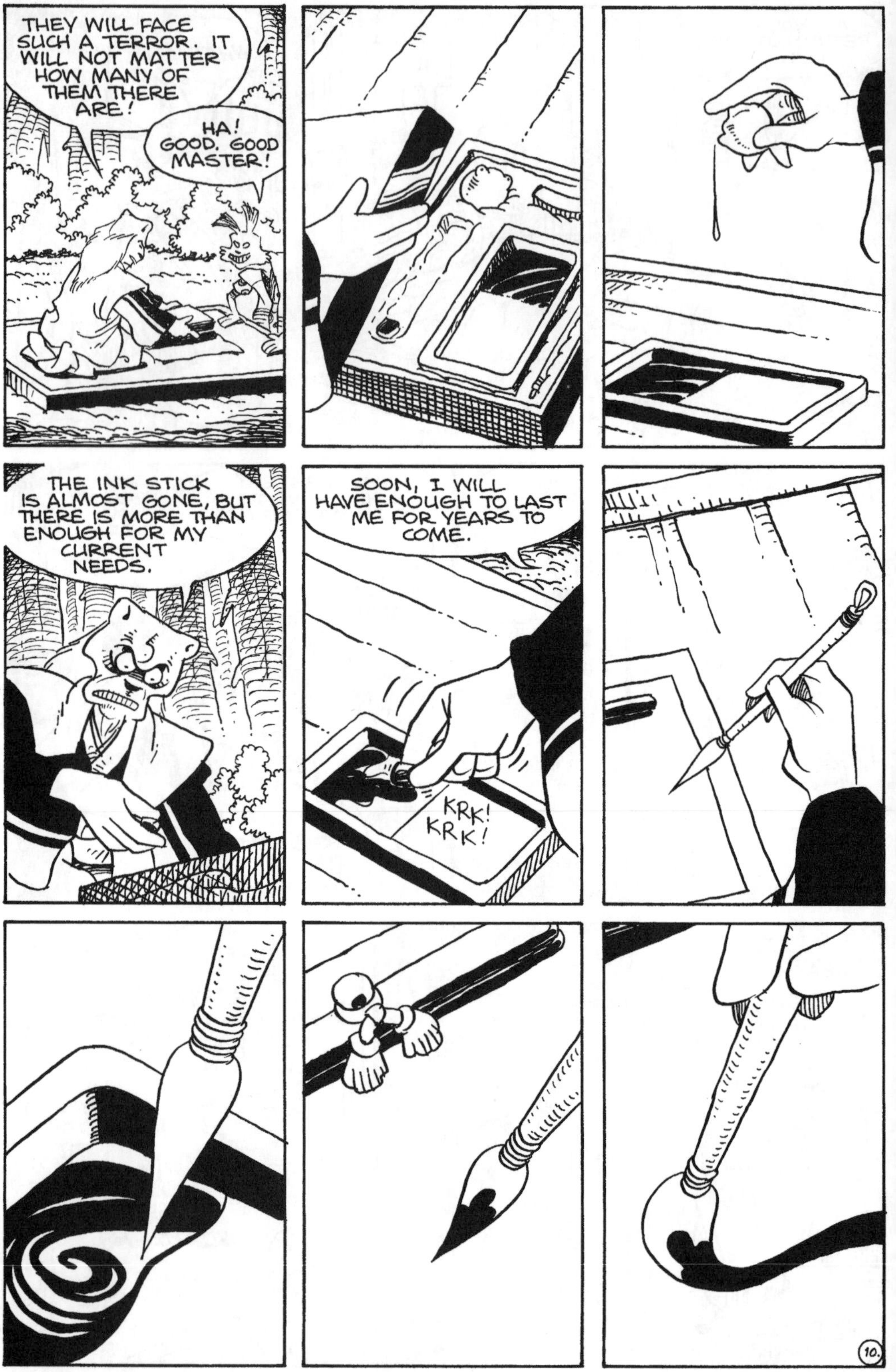
THEY WILL FACE SUCH A TERROR. IT WILL NOT MATTER HOW MANY OF THEM THERE ARE!
HA! GOOD. GOOD MASTER!
THE INK STICK IS ALMOST GONE, BUT THERE IS MORE THAN ENOUGH FOR MY CURRENT NEEDS.
SOON, I WILL HAVE ENOUGH TO LAST ME FOR YEARS TO COME.
KRK! KRK!
10.

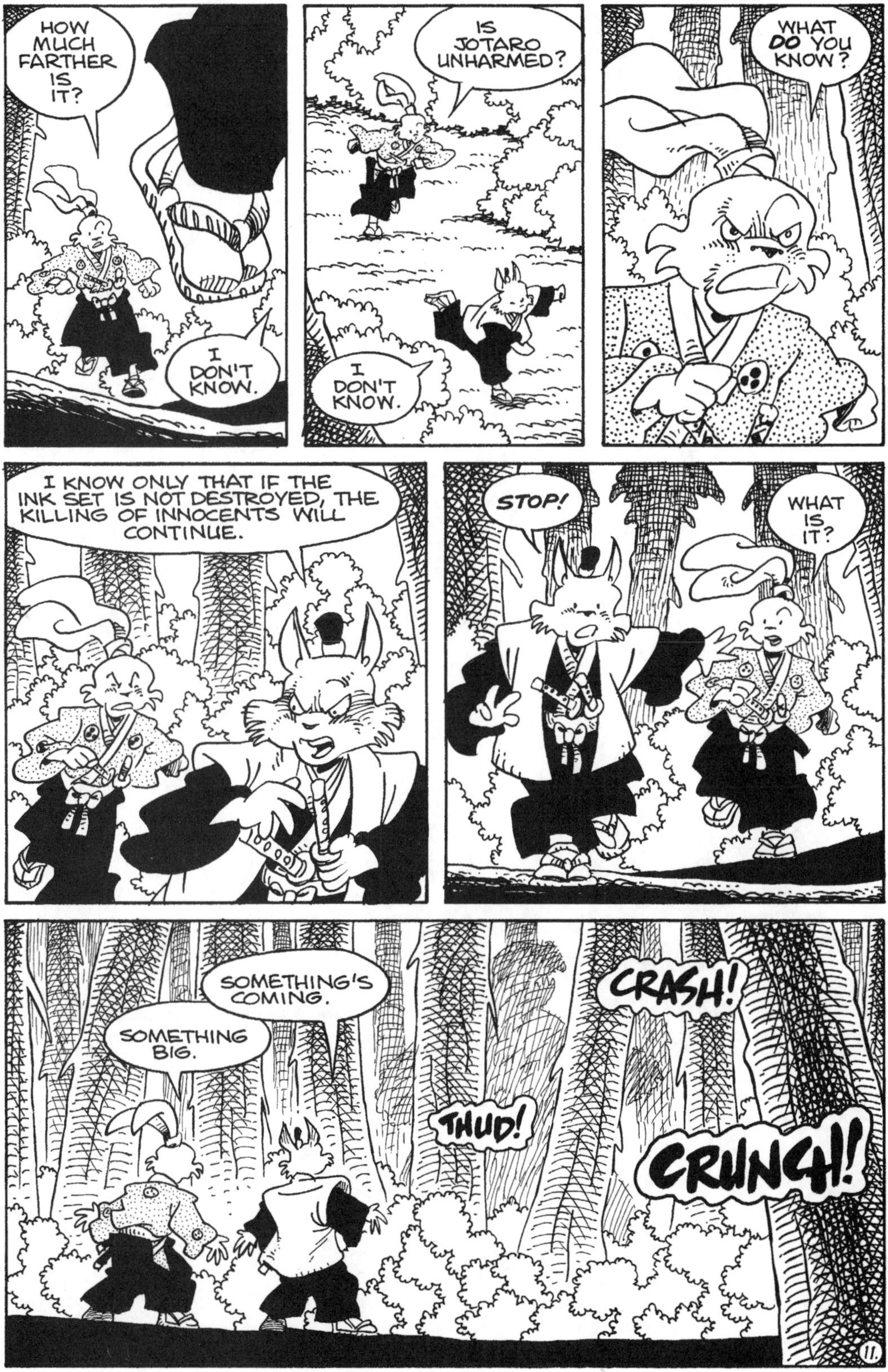
HOW MUCH FARTHER IS IT?
I DON'T KNOW.
IS JOTARO UNHARMED?
I DON'T KNOW.
WHAT DO YOU KNOW?
I KNOW ONLY THAT IF THE INK SET IS NOT DESTROYED, THE KILLING OF INNOCENTS WILL CONTINUE.
STOP!
WHAT IS IT?
SOMETHING'S COMING.
SOMETHING BIG.
CRASH!
THUD!
CRUNCH!
11.

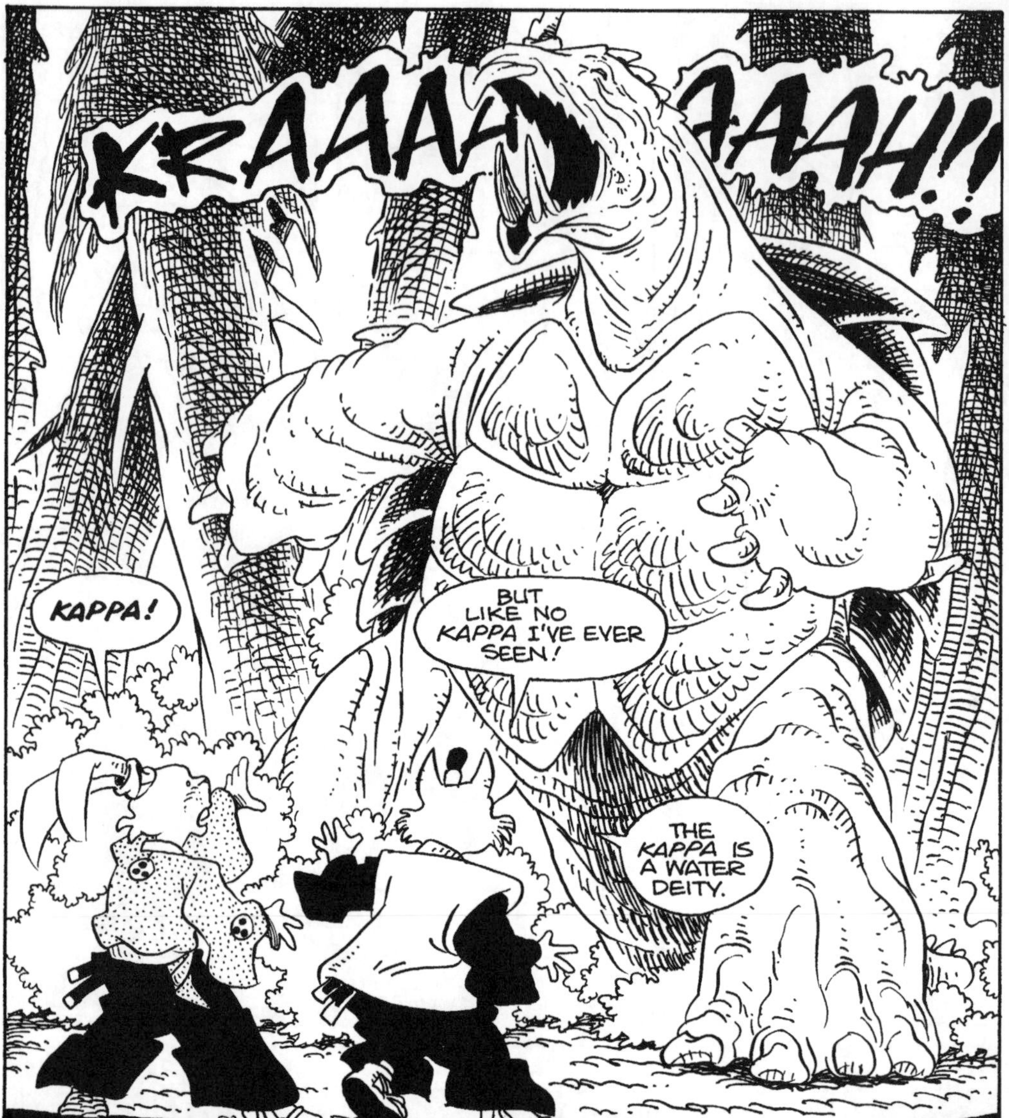
KRAAAAAAAAH!!
KAPPA!
BUT LIKE NO KAPPA I'VE EVER SEEN!
THE KAPPA IS A WATER DEITY.

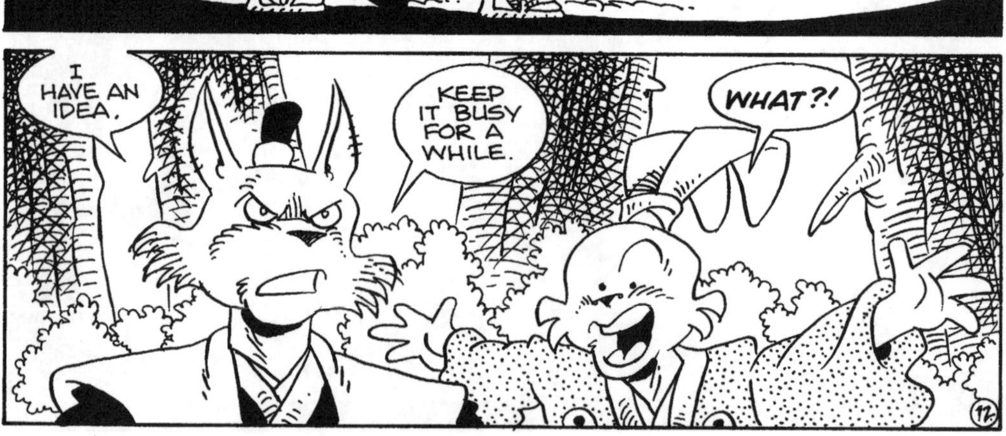
I HAVE AN IDEA.
KEEP IT BUSY FOR A WHILE.
WHAT?!
12

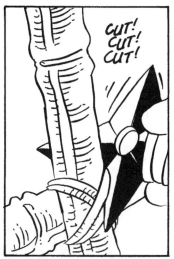

CUT! CUT! CUT!

SNAP!

THERE!

¡UGH!¡ IT'S A TIGHT FIT, BUT WE'LL ALL GET OUT.

HURRY-- BUT QUIETLY.

IT SHOULDN'T TAKE LONG TO CUT THROUGH ONE OF THESE BARS.

HURRY! NENEKI WILL BE BACK SOON!

THE KAPPA-DEMON WILL TAKE CARE OF THOSE MEDDLERS.

START A FIRE TO BURN THE RESIN, AND PREPARE THE PRISONERS.

YIS, MASTER.

IT WILL BE PLEASURE. HEH HEH HEH.

WHERE IS BEAST? SHE WILL HELP ME CONTROL THOSE WHELPS.

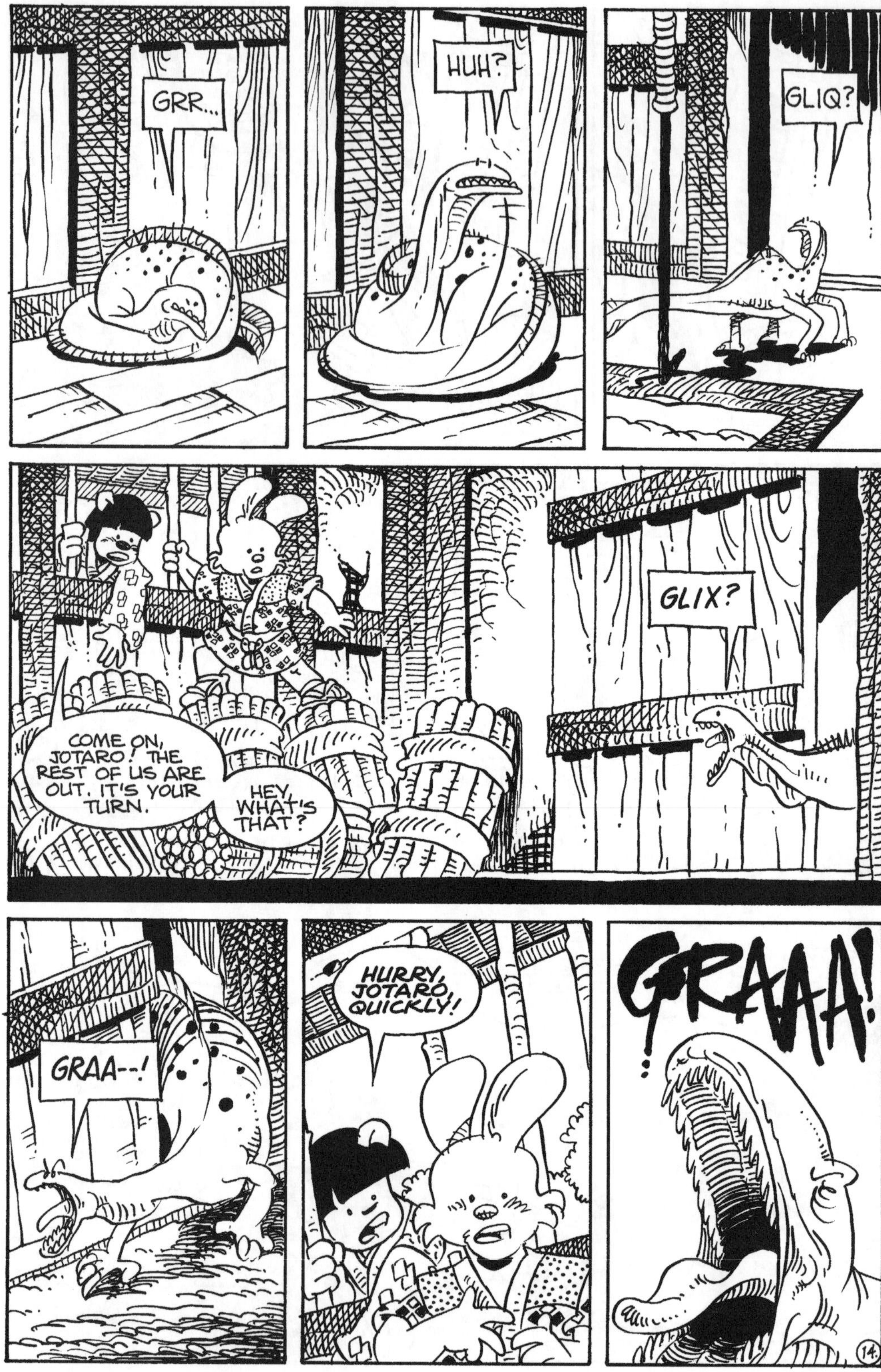
GRR...
HUH?
GLIQ?
COME ON, JOTARO! THE REST OF US ARE OUT. IT'S YOUR TURN.
HEY, WHAT'S THAT?
GLIX?
GRAA--!
HURRY, JOTARO QUICKLY!
GRAAA!
14.

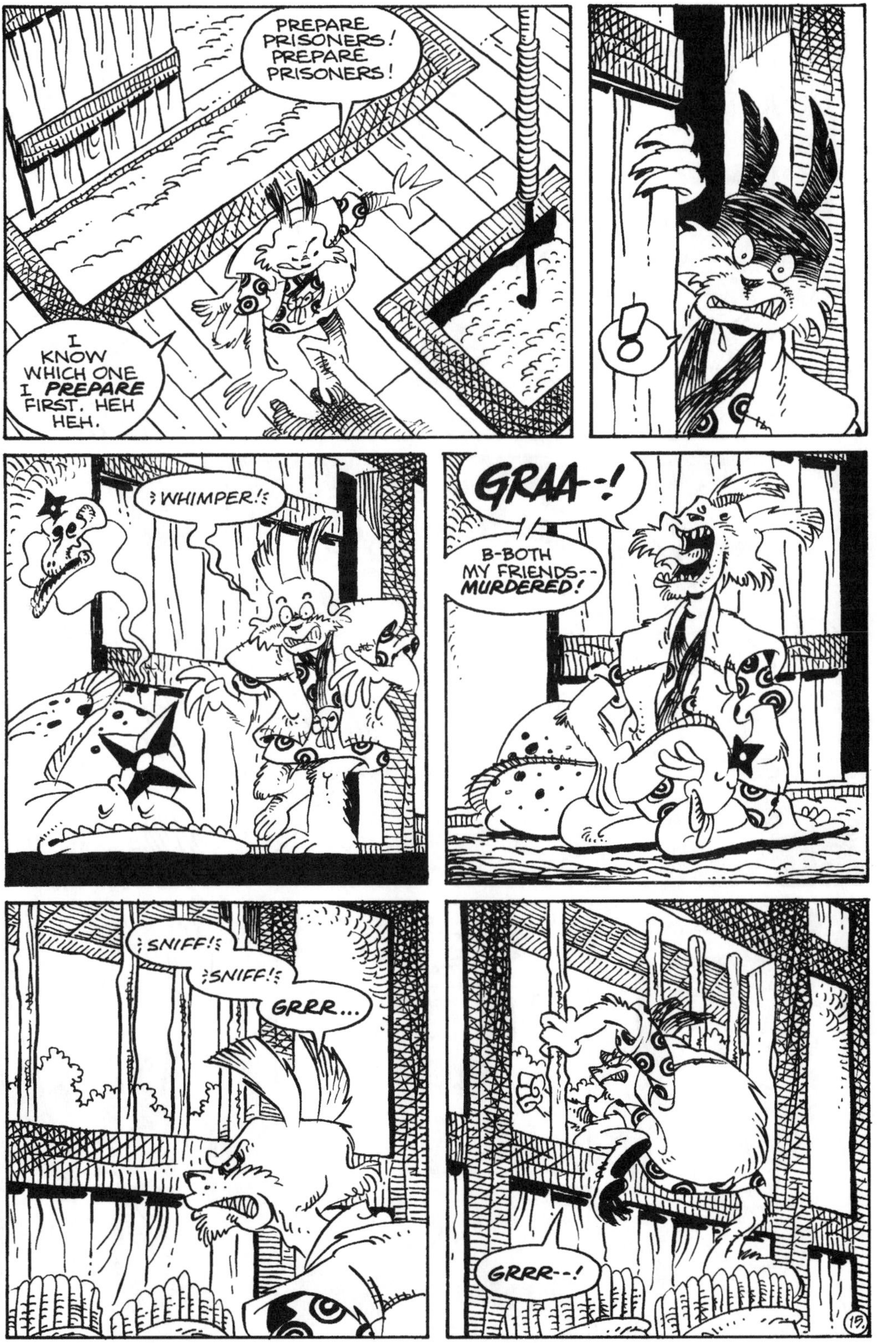
PREPARE PRISONERS! PREPARE PRISONERS!
I KNOW WHICH ONE I PREPARE FIRST. HEH HEH.
!
WHIMPER!
GRAA--!
B-BOTH MY FRIENDS-- MURDERED!
SNIFF!
SNIFF!
GRRR...
GRRR--!
15

HIIIYAHH!
CHIP! CHOP!
CHOP! CHOP!
HURRY, SASUKÉ! WHATEVER YOU'RE GOING TO DO-- DO IT NOW!
HACK! CHOP! CHOP! CHIP! SLICE! HACK!
KRAAH!
.....
UH..., SASUKÉ--?
KRAAAA..!
SASUKÉ!
I'LL NEED A DIVERSION TO SLOW IT DOWN WHILE I PREPARE THE REAL ATTACK.
SASUKÉ!
KIMA
16.

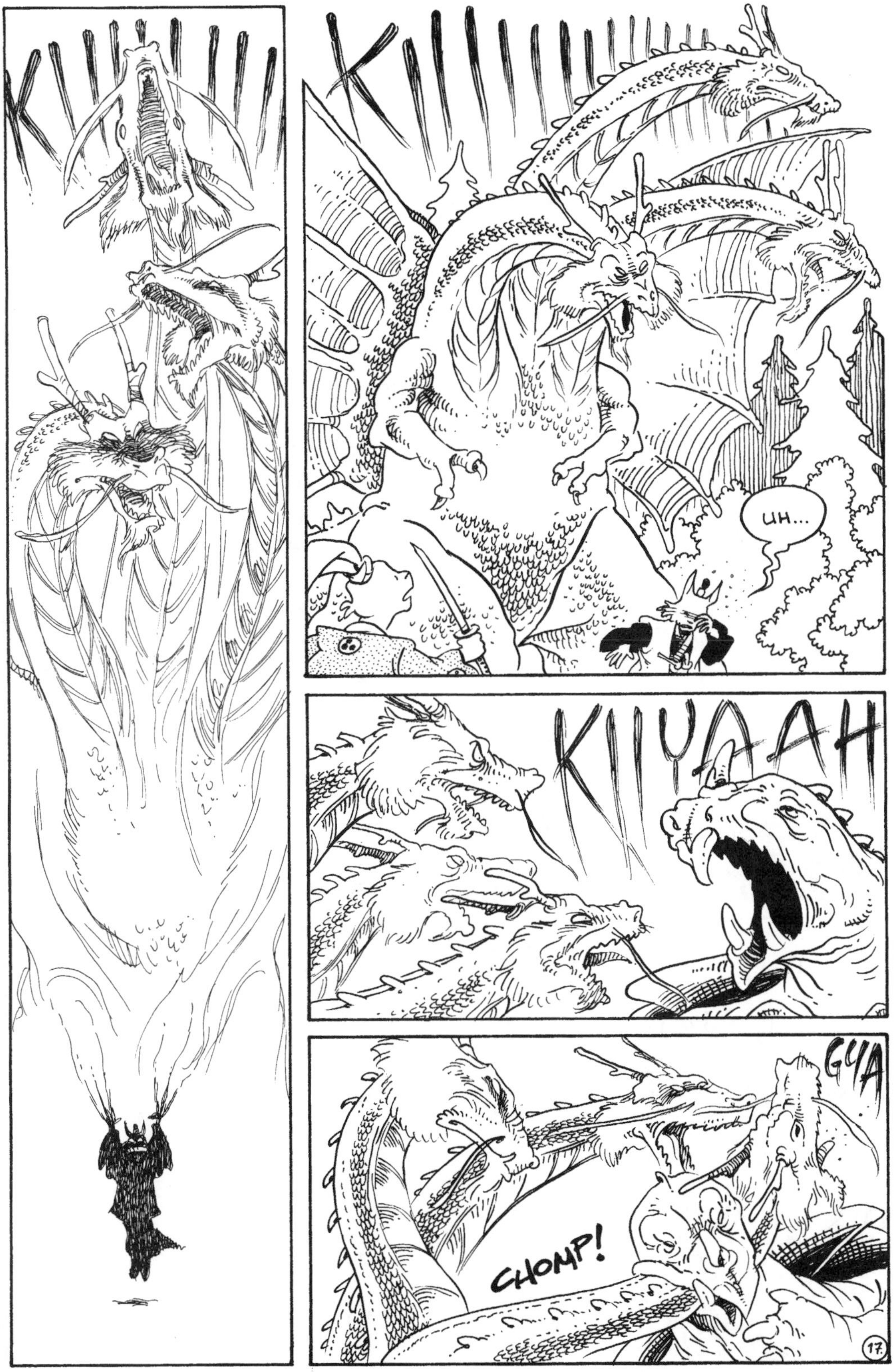
UH...
KIIYAAH
GYA
CHOMP!
17.

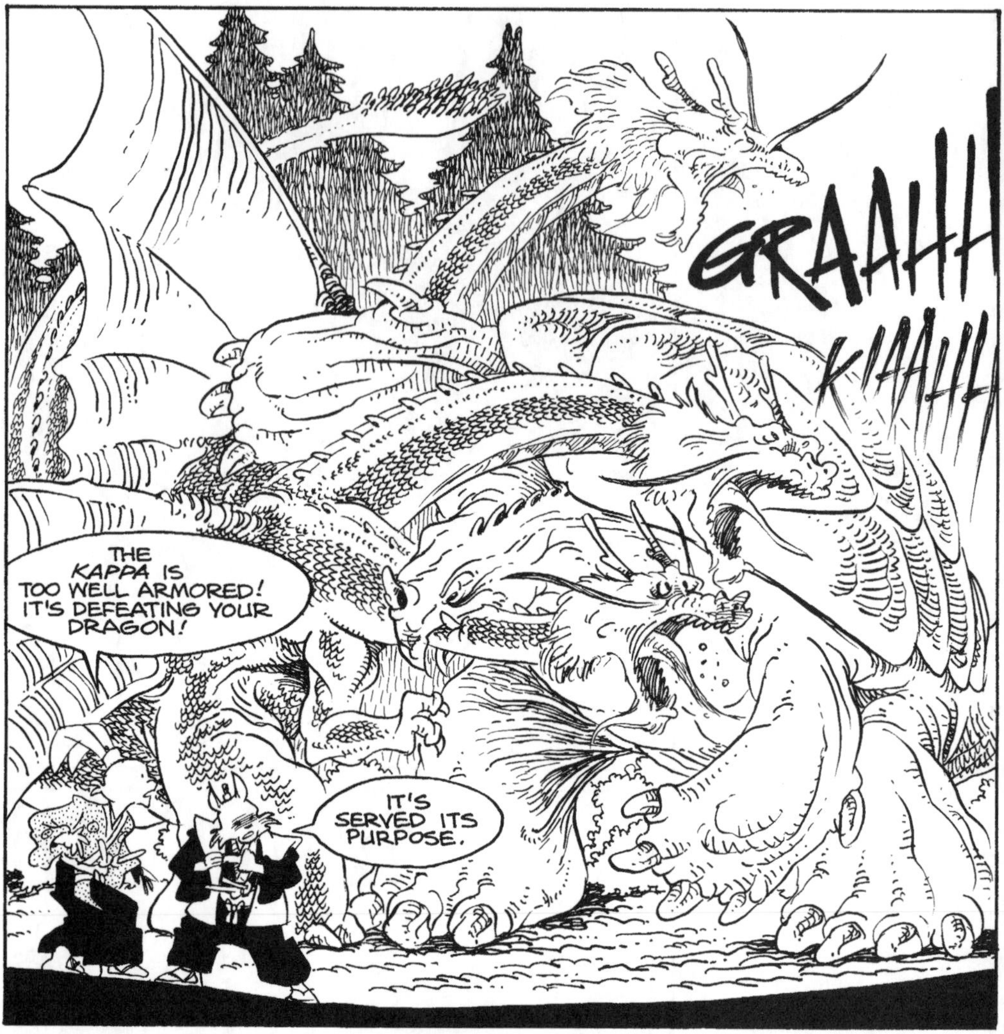
GRAAHH
KIAAHH
THE *KAPPA* IS TOO WELL ARMORED! IT'S DEFEATING YOUR DRAGON!
IT'S SERVED ITS PURPOSE.

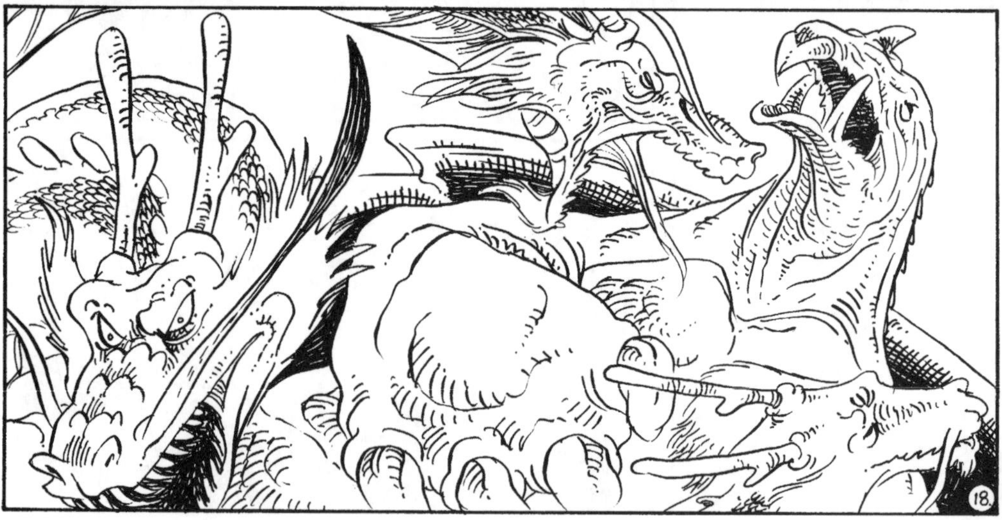
18.

TO COMBAT A WATER DEITY WE NEED ITS OPPOSITE ELEMENT--FIRE.

FIRE IS ITS ENEMY!

FLOOM!

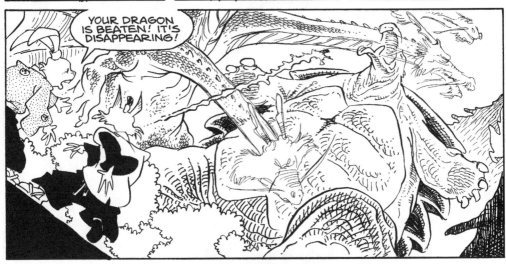

YOUR DRAGON IS BEATEN! IT'S DISAPPEARING!

KRAA

SLAP!

AAAA

AAAA

FLOOM!

19.

171

AAAAAAAAAA

AAAAAAAAAAAA---!

SASUKÉ-- ARE YOU ALL RIGHT?

THE BATTLE WITH THE *KAPPA* HAS DRAINED MUCH OUT OF ME.

YOU LOOK TERRIBLE. YOU SHOULD REST A WHILE.

REST...?

THERE IS NO TIME FOR REST. TOO MUCH IS AT STAKE!

COME ON. IT CAN'T BE VERY FAR NOW.

20.

172

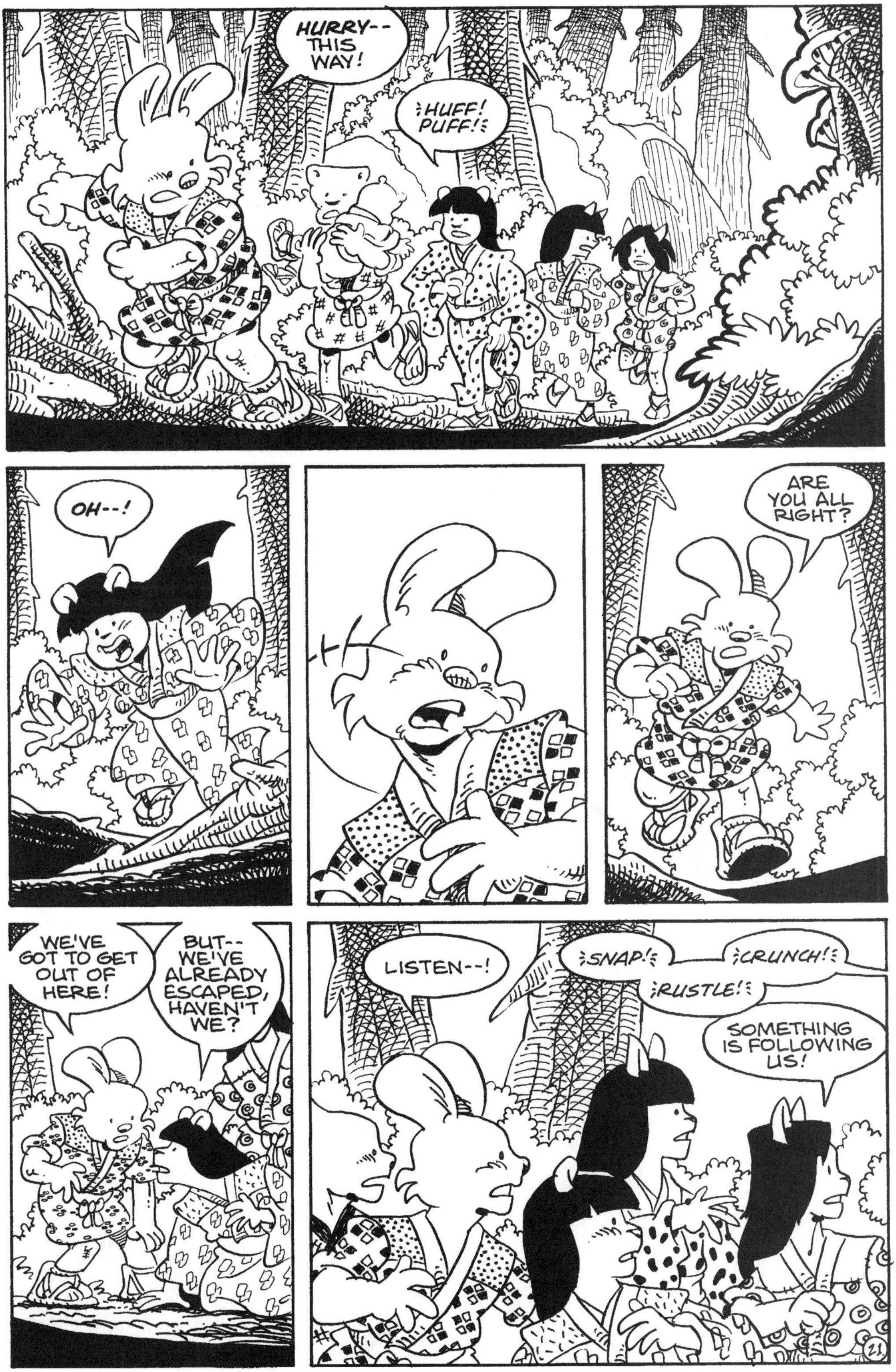
HURRY-- THIS WAY!
HUFF! PUFF!
OH--!
ARE YOU ALL RIGHT?
WE'VE GOT TO GET OUT OF HERE!
BUT-- WE'VE ALREADY ESCAPED, HAVEN'T WE?
LISTEN--!
SNAP!
CRUNCH!
RUSTLE!
SOMETHING IS FOLLOWING US!
21

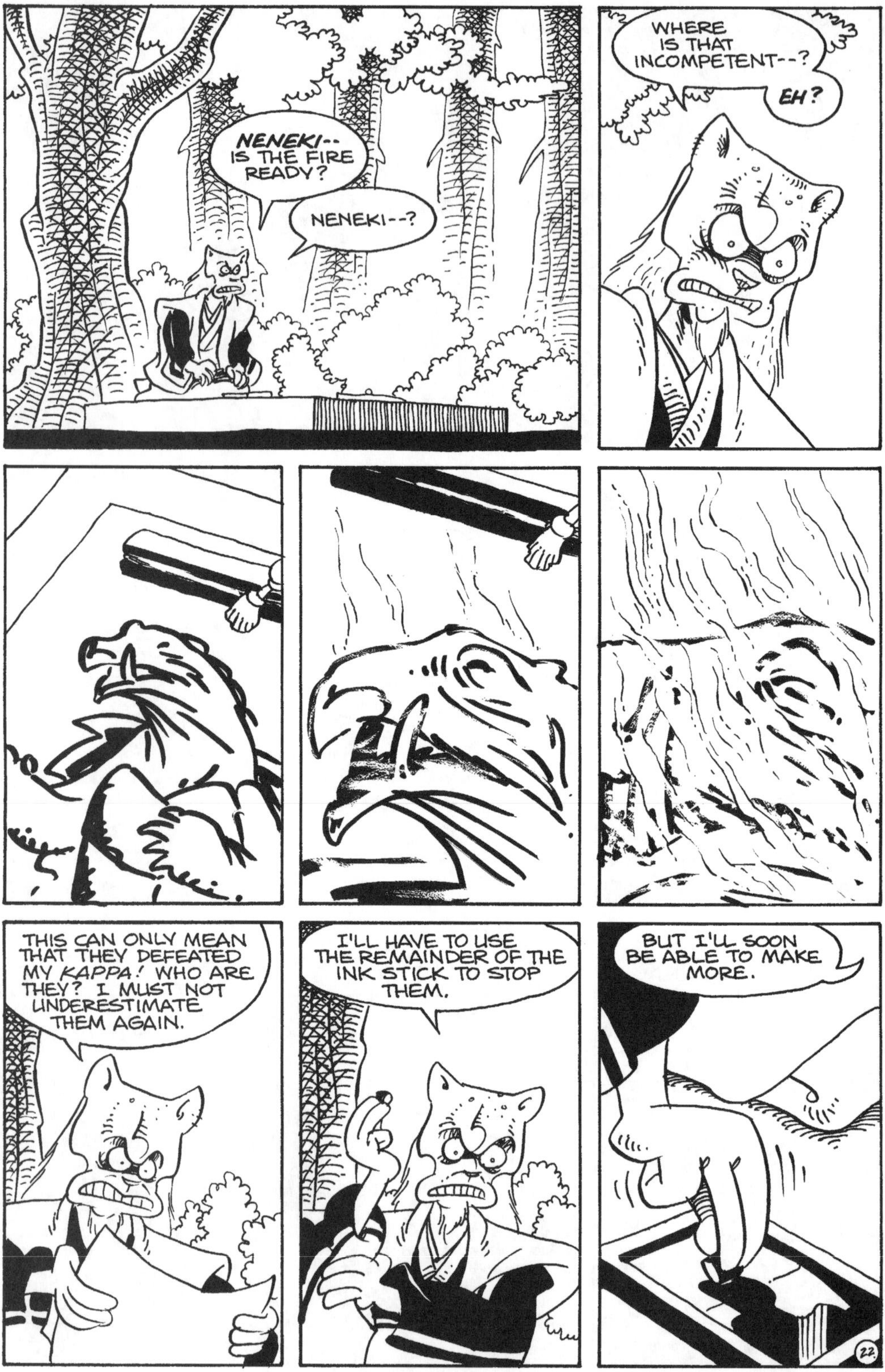
NENEKI-- IS THE FIRE READY?
NENEKI--?
WHERE IS THAT INCOMPETENT--?
EH?
THIS CAN ONLY MEAN THAT THEY DEFEATED MY KAPPA! WHO ARE THEY? I MUST NOT UNDERESTIMATE THEM AGAIN.
I'LL HAVE TO USE THE REMAINDER OF THE INK STICK TO STOP THEM.
BUT I'LL SOON BE ABLE TO MAKE MORE.
22

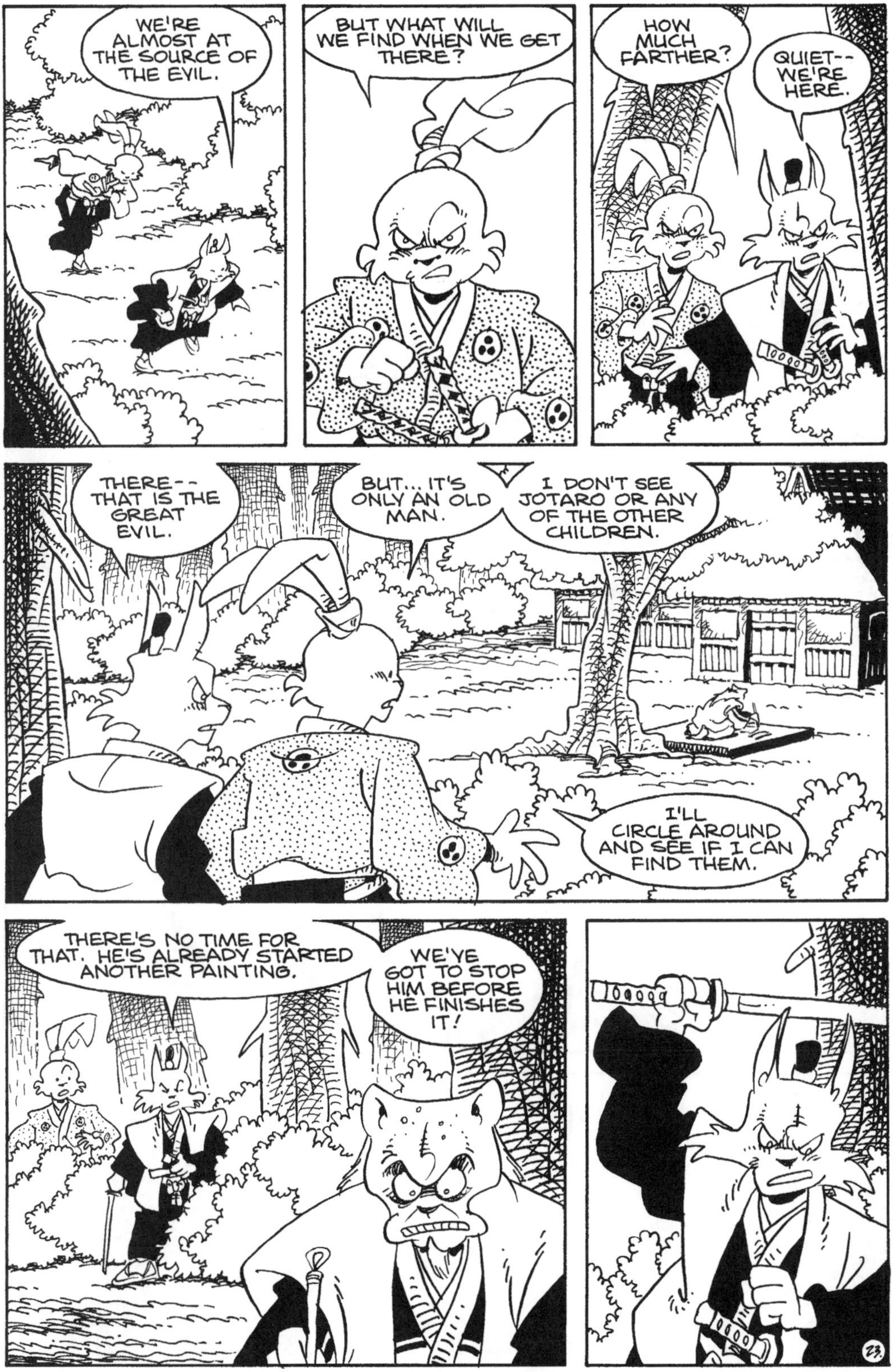
WE'RE ALMOST AT THE SOURCE OF THE EVIL.
BUT WHAT WILL WE FIND WHEN WE GET THERE?
HOW MUCH FARTHER?
QUIET-- WE'RE HERE.
THERE-- THAT IS THE GREAT EVIL.
BUT... IT'S ONLY AN OLD MAN.
I DON'T SEE JOTARO OR ANY OF THE OTHER CHILDREN.
I'LL CIRCLE AROUND AND SEE IF I CAN FIND THEM.
THERE'S NO TIME FOR THAT. HE'S ALREADY STARTED ANOTHER PAINTING.
WE'VE GOT TO STOP HIM BEFORE HE FINISHES IT!
23.

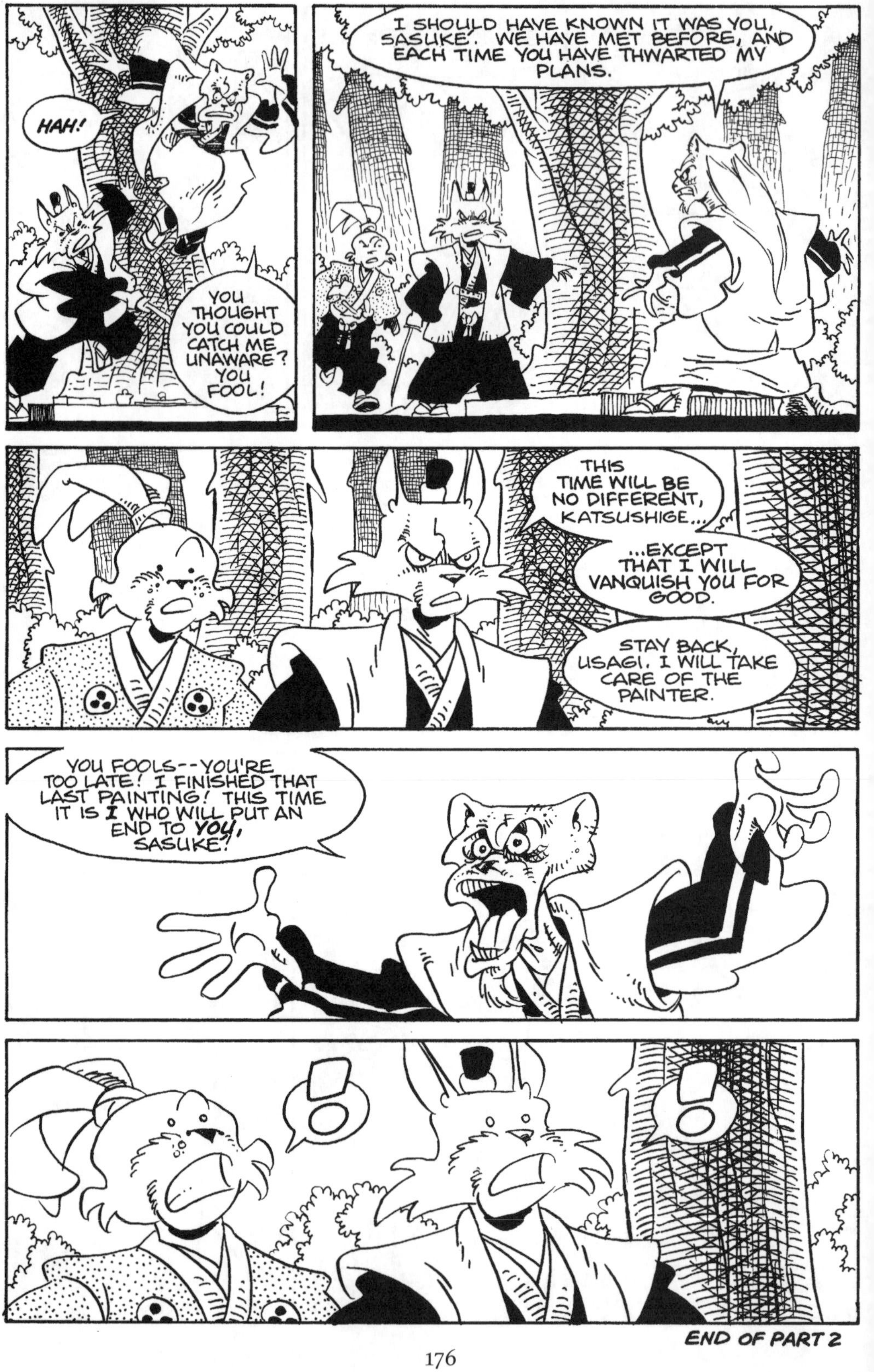
HAH!
YOU THOUGHT YOU COULD CATCH ME UNAWARE? YOU FOOL!
I SHOULD HAVE KNOWN IT WAS YOU, SASUKE. WE HAVE MET BEFORE, AND EACH TIME YOU HAVE THWARTED MY PLANS.
THIS TIME WILL BE NO DIFFERENT, KATSUSHIGE...
...EXCEPT THAT I WILL VANQUISH YOU FOR GOOD.
STAY BACK, USAGI. I WILL TAKE CARE OF THE PAINTER.
YOU FOOLS--YOU'RE TOO LATE! I FINISHED THAT LAST PAINTING! THIS TIME IT IS I WHO WILL PUT AN END TO YOU, SASUKE!
!
!

END OF PART 2

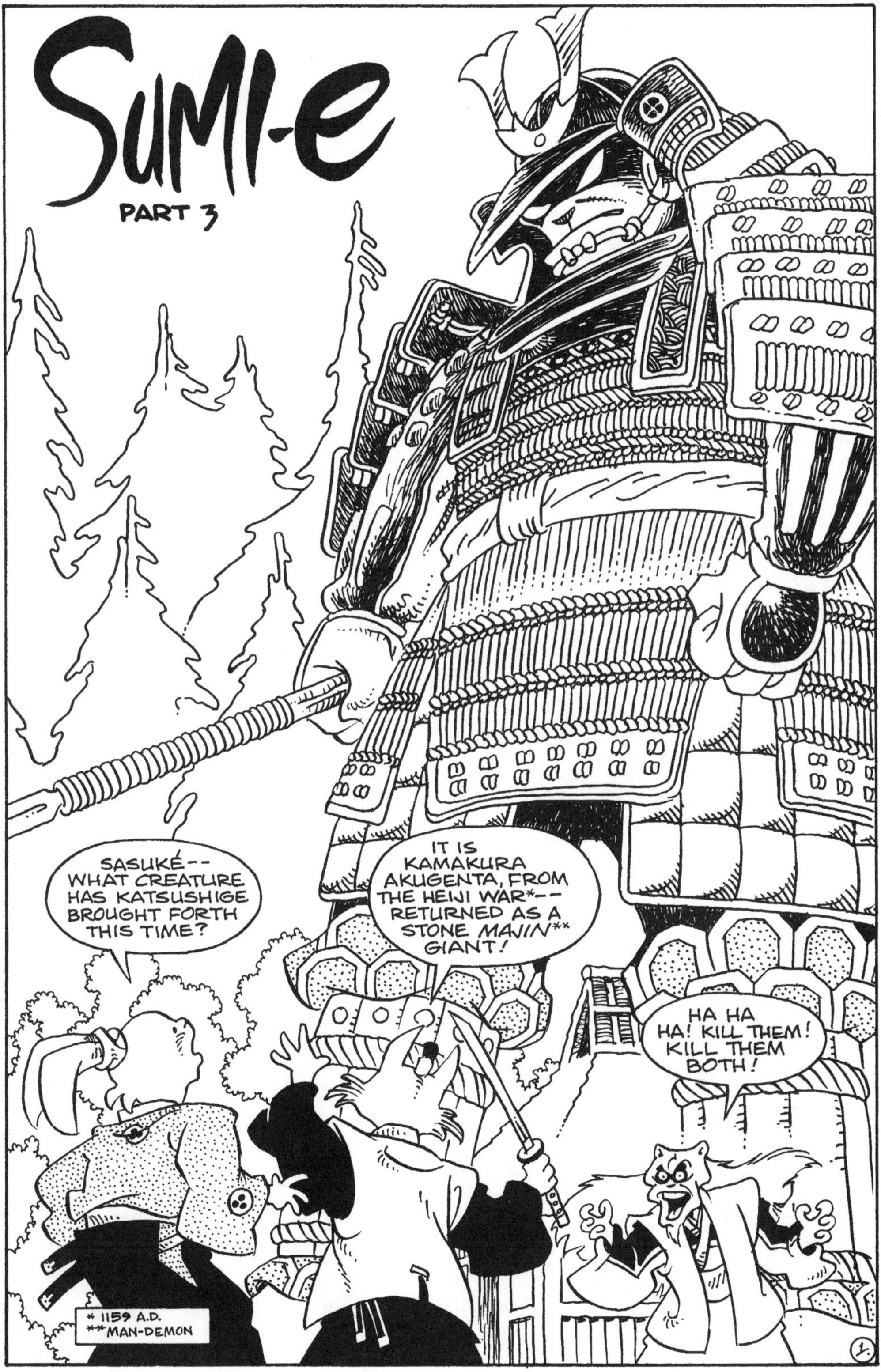
SUMI-E
PART 3
SASUKÉ-- WHAT CREATURE HAS KATSUSHIGE BROUGHT FORTH THIS TIME?
IT IS KAMAKURA AKUGENTA, FROM THE HEIJI WAR*-- RETURNED AS A STONE MAJIN** GIANT!
HA HA HA! KILL THEM! KILL THEM BOTH!
* 1159 A.D.
** MAN-DEMON
1.

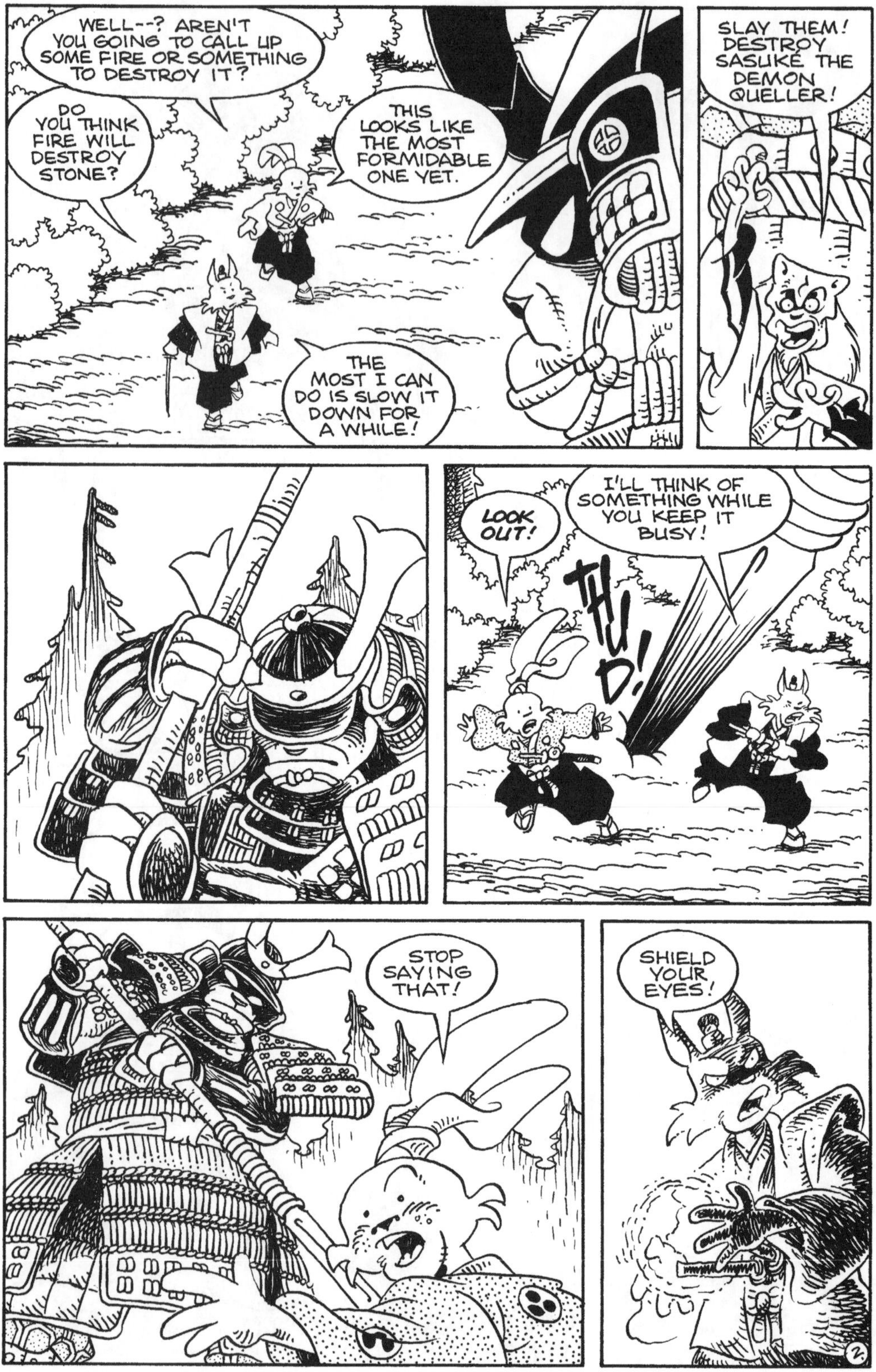
WELL--? AREN'T YOU GOING TO CALL UP SOME FIRE OR SOMETHING TO DESTROY IT?
DO YOU THINK FIRE WILL DESTROY STONE?
THIS LOOKS LIKE THE MOST FORMIDABLE ONE YET.
THE MOST I CAN DO IS SLOW IT DOWN FOR A WHILE!
SLAY THEM! DESTROY SASUKE THE DEMON QUELLER!
LOOK OUT!
I'LL THINK OF SOMETHING WHILE YOU KEEP IT BUSY!
THUD!
STOP SAYING THAT!
SHIELD YOUR EYES!

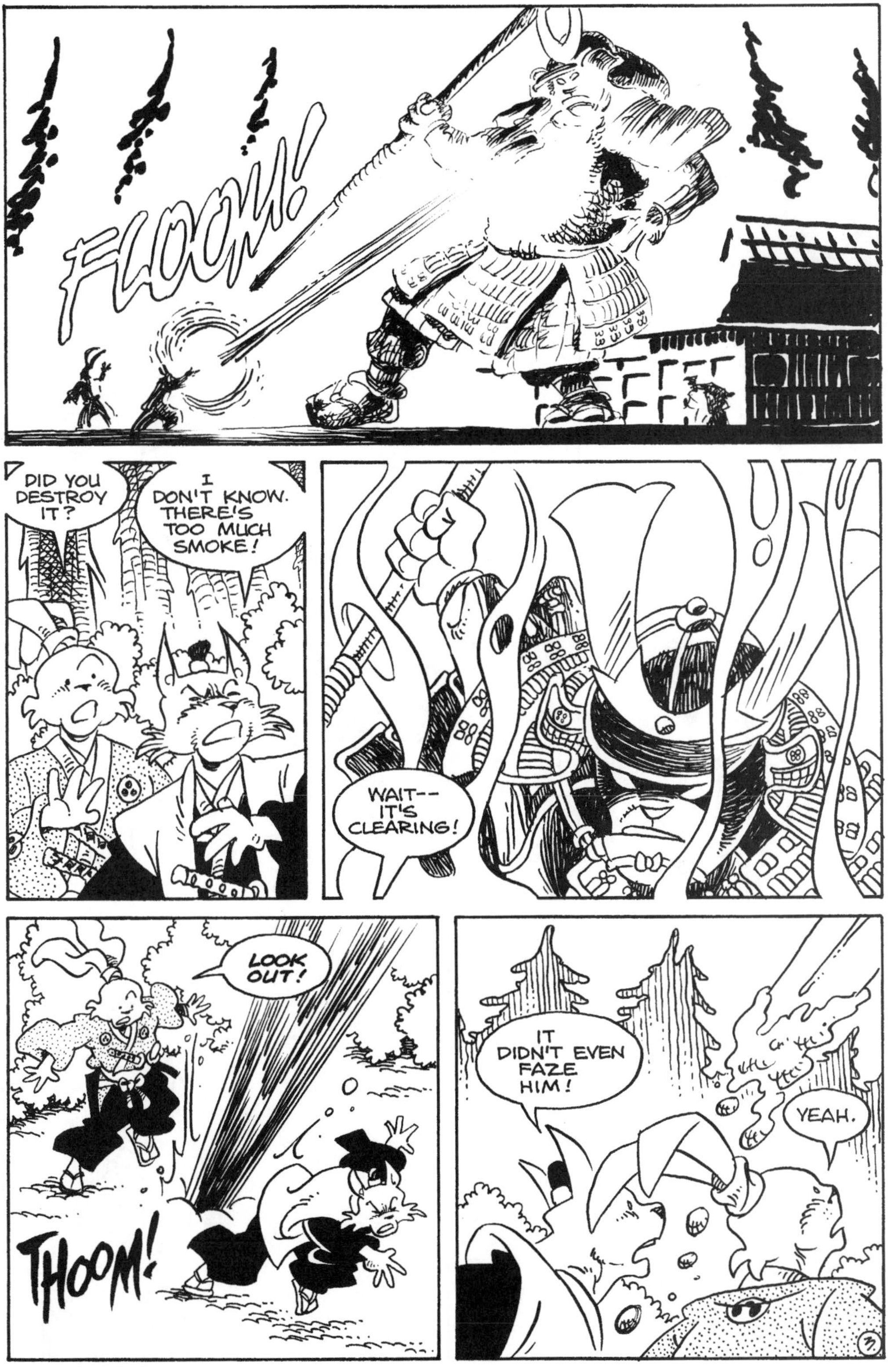
FLOOM!
DID YOU DESTROY IT?
I DON'T KNOW. THERE'S TOO MUCH SMOKE!
WAIT-- IT'S CLEARING!
LOOK OUT!
THOOM!
IT DIDN'T EVEN FAZE HIM!
YEAH.

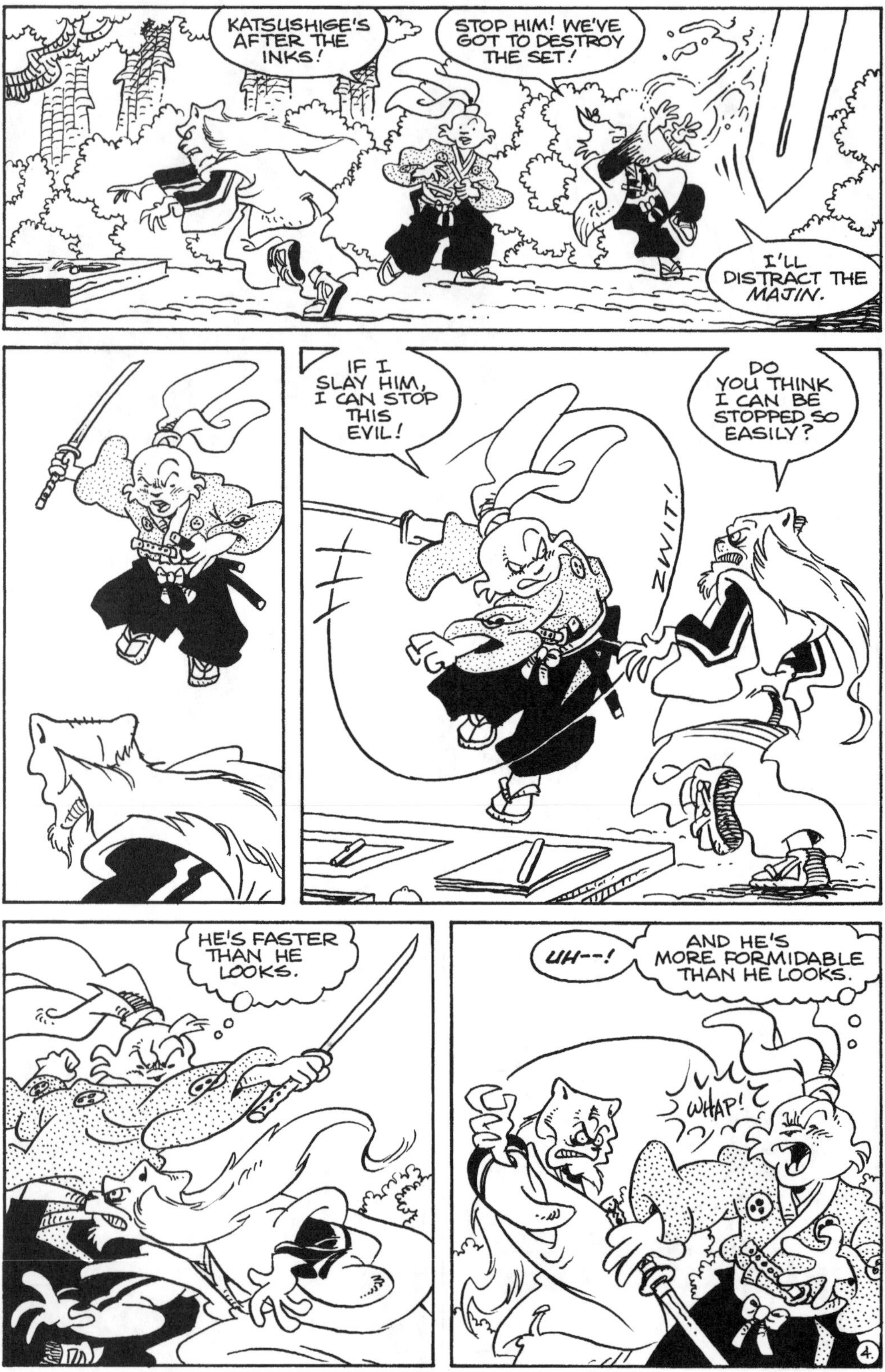
KATSUSHIGE'S AFTER THE INKS!
STOP HIM! WE'VE GOT TO DESTROY THE SET!
I'LL DISTRACT THE *MAJIN*.
IF I SLAY HIM, I CAN STOP THIS EVIL!
DO YOU THINK I CAN BE STOPPED SO EASILY?
ZWIT!
HE'S FASTER THAN HE LOOKS.
UH--!
AND HE'S MORE FORMIDABLE THAN HE LOOKS.
WHAP!
4.

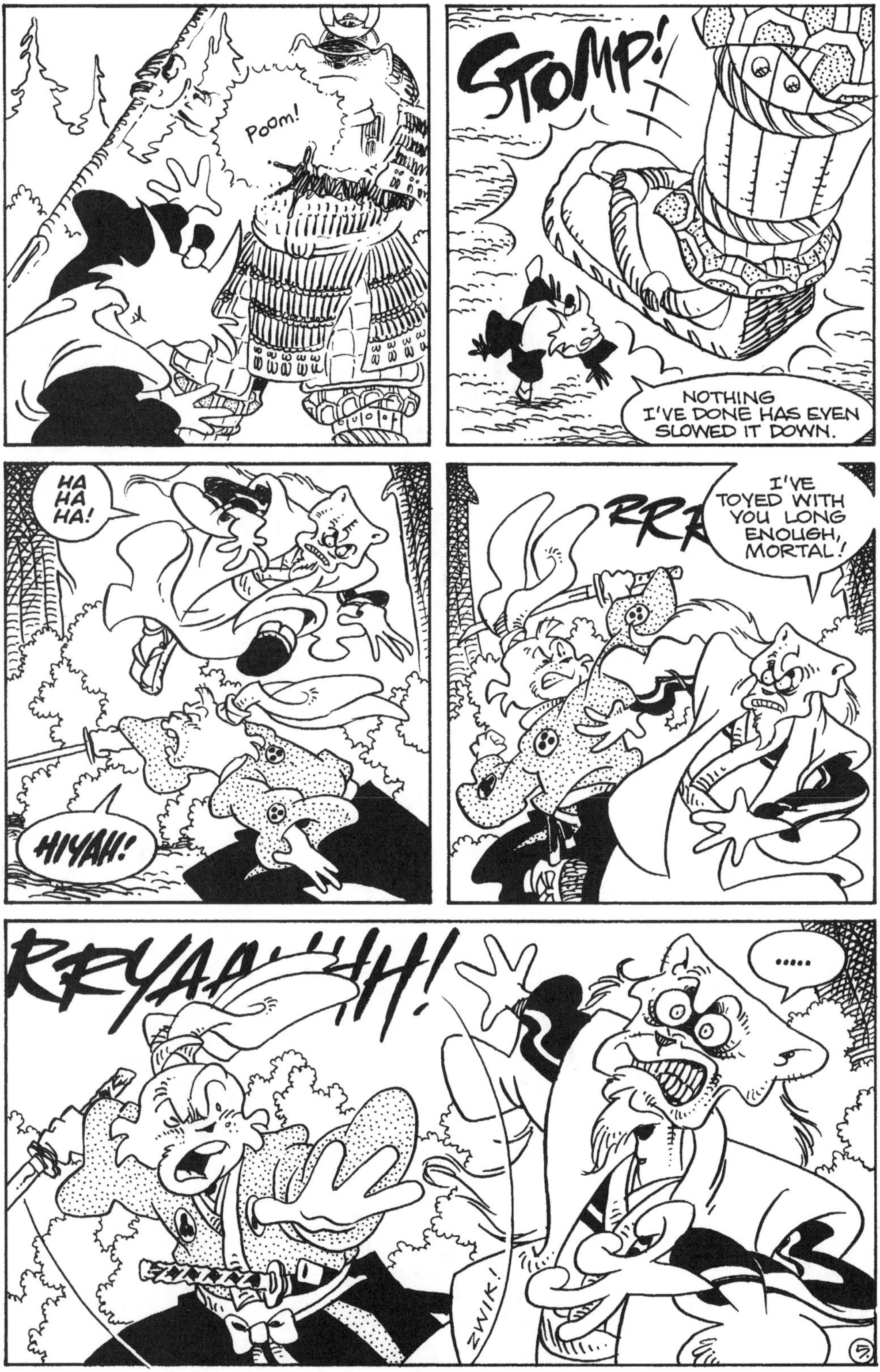

Poom!
STOMP!
NOTHING I'VE DONE HAS EVEN SLOWED IT DOWN.
HA HA HA!
HIYAH!
RRR
I'VE TOYED WITH YOU LONG ENOUGH, MORTAL!
RRYAAHHH!
.....
ZWIK!
5

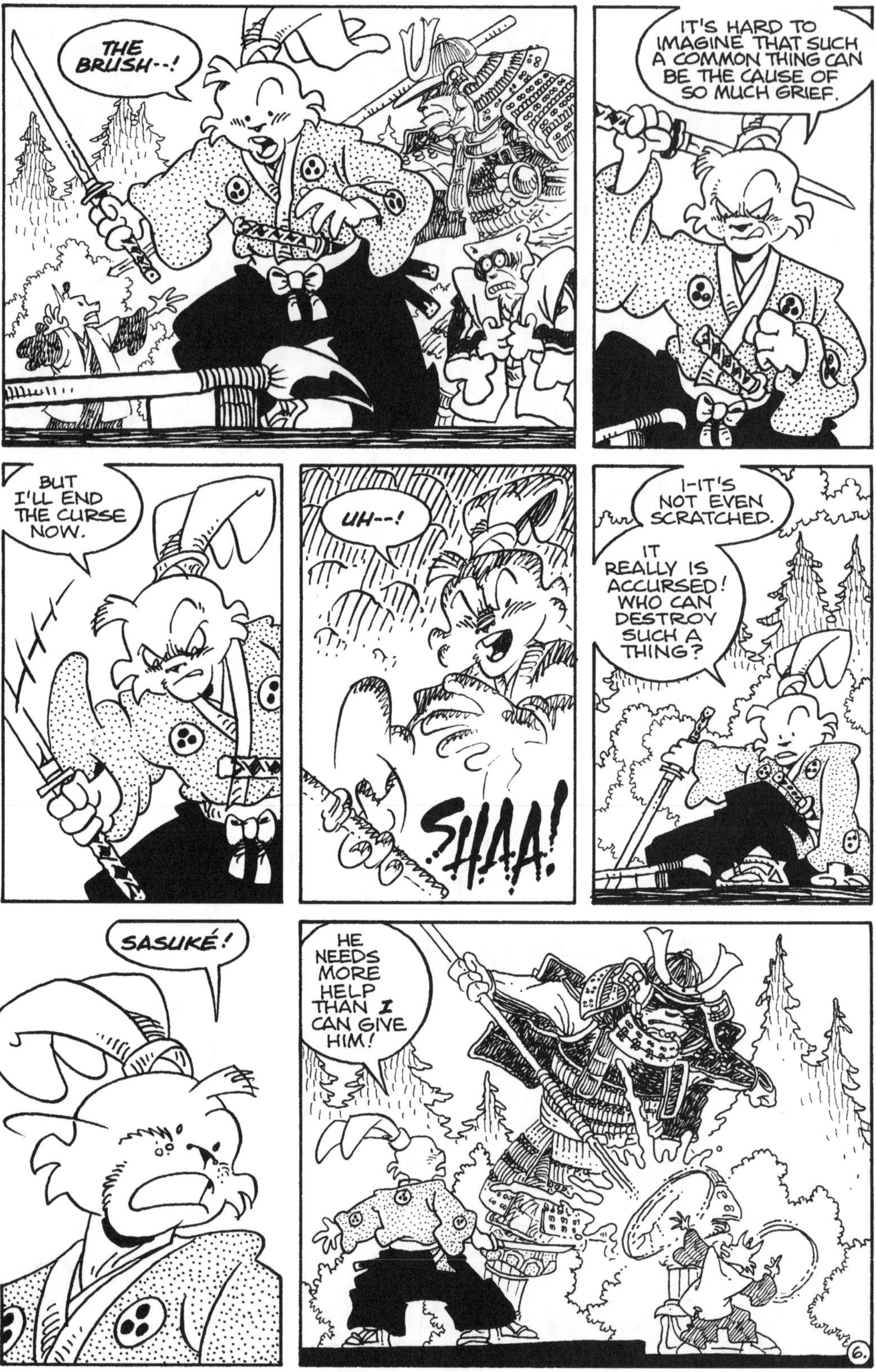
THE BRUSH--!
IT'S HARD TO IMAGINE THAT SUCH A COMMON THING CAN BE THE CAUSE OF SO MUCH GRIEF.
BUT I'LL END THE CURSE NOW.
UH--!
SHAA!
I-IT'S NOT EVEN SCRATCHED.
IT REALLY IS ACCURSED! WHO CAN DESTROY SUCH A THING?
SASUKÉ!
HE NEEDS MORE HELP THAN I CAN GIVE HIM!
6.

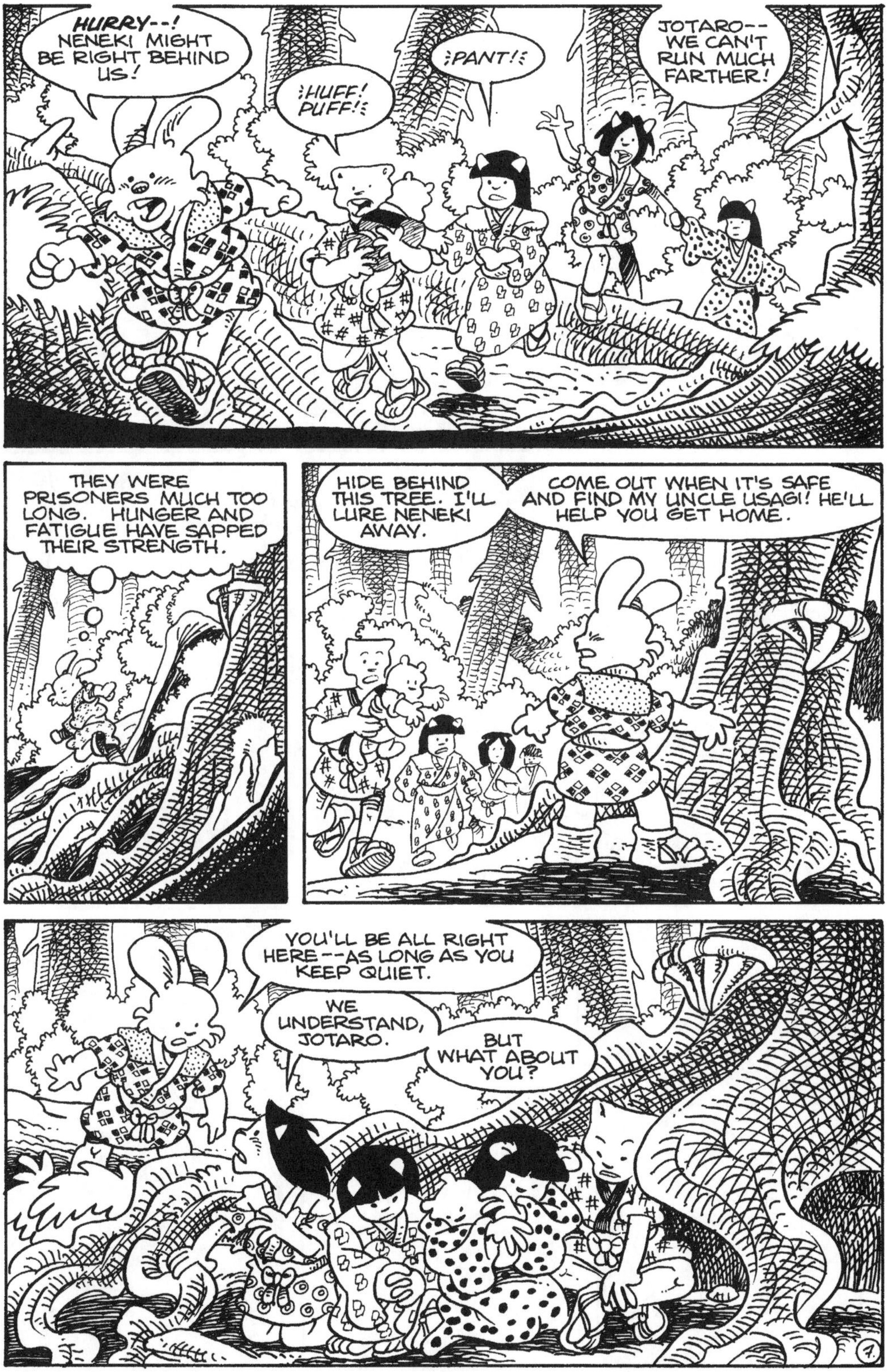
HURRY--! NENEKI MIGHT BE RIGHT BEHIND US!
HUFF! PUFF!
PANT!
JOTARO-- WE CAN'T RUN MUCH FARTHER!
THEY WERE PRISONERS MUCH TOO LONG. HUNGER AND FATIGUE HAVE SAPPED THEIR STRENGTH.
HIDE BEHIND THIS TREE. I'LL LURE NENEKI AWAY.
COME OUT WHEN IT'S SAFE AND FIND MY UNCLE USAGI! HE'LL HELP YOU GET HOME.
YOU'LL BE ALL RIGHT HERE--AS LONG AS YOU KEEP QUIET.
WE UNDERSTAND, JOTARO.
BUT WHAT ABOUT YOU?
7.

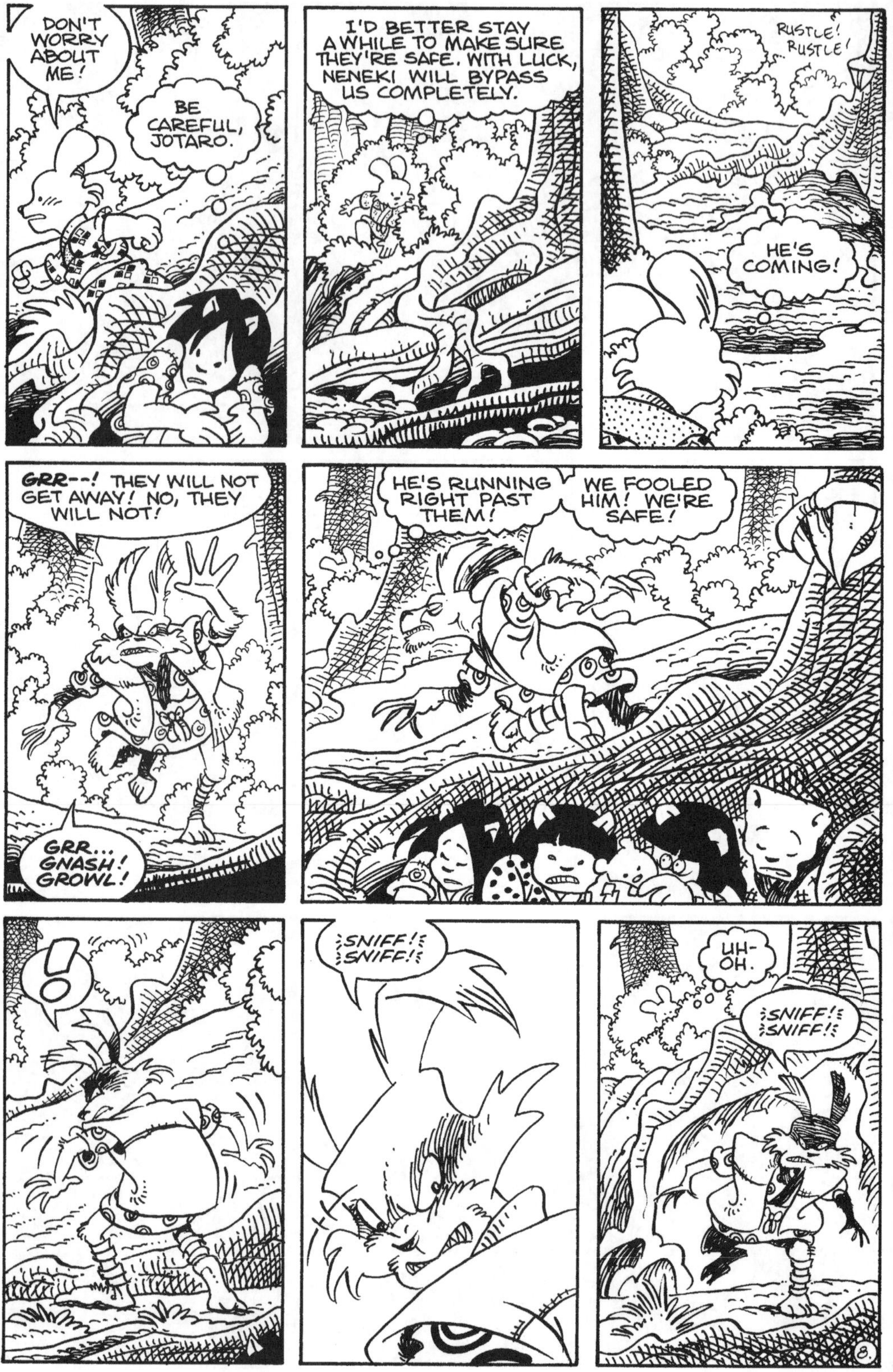

DON'T WORRY ABOUT ME!
BE CAREFUL, JOTARO.
I'D BETTER STAY A WHILE TO MAKE SURE THEY'RE SAFE. WITH LUCK, NENEKI WILL BYPASS US COMPLETELY.
RUSTLE! RUSTLE!
HE'S COMING!
GRR--! THEY WILL NOT GET AWAY! NO, THEY WILL NOT!
GRR... GNASH! GROWL!
HE'S RUNNING RIGHT PAST THEM!
WE FOOLED HIM! WE'RE SAFE!
!
SNIFF! SNIFF!
UH-OH.
SNIFF! SNIFF!
8.

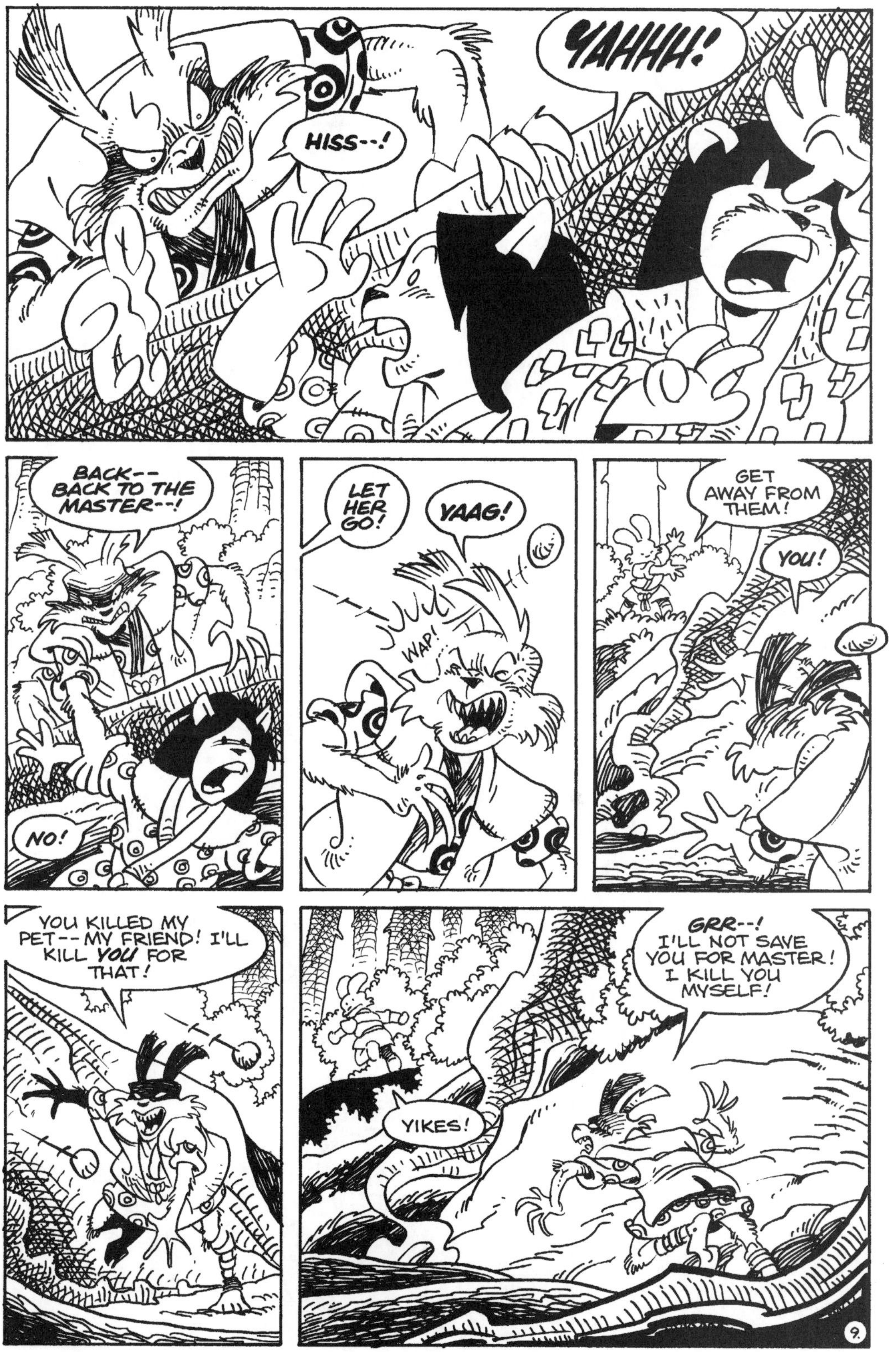

YAHHH!
HISS--!
BACK-- BACK TO THE MASTER--!
NO!
LET HER GO!
YAAG!
WAP!
GET AWAY FROM THEM!
YOU!
YOU KILLED MY PET-- MY FRIEND! I'LL KILL YOU FOR THAT!
GRR--! I'LL NOT SAVE YOU FOR MASTER! I KILL YOU MYSELF!
YIKES!
9.

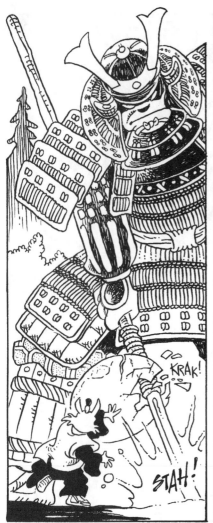

SHOONK!

KRAK!

STAH!

SASUKÉ CAN'T KEEP THIS UP TOO MUCH LONGER. THE GIANT IS TOO POWERFUL.

BUT HOW CAN I HELP HIM AGAINST SUCH A MONSTER?

UNLESS...

THERE'S SOME INK STILL IN THE WELL.

10.

DO I EVEN DARE...?
I HAVE NO CHOICE.
WHAT TO DRAW... WHAT TO DRAW...
A NUE? NO. A TENGU? NO. ONI? NO. ROKUROKUBI? UH-UH. KIRIN? NO...
THIS HAD BETTER WORK.
11.

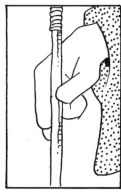

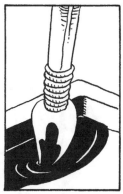

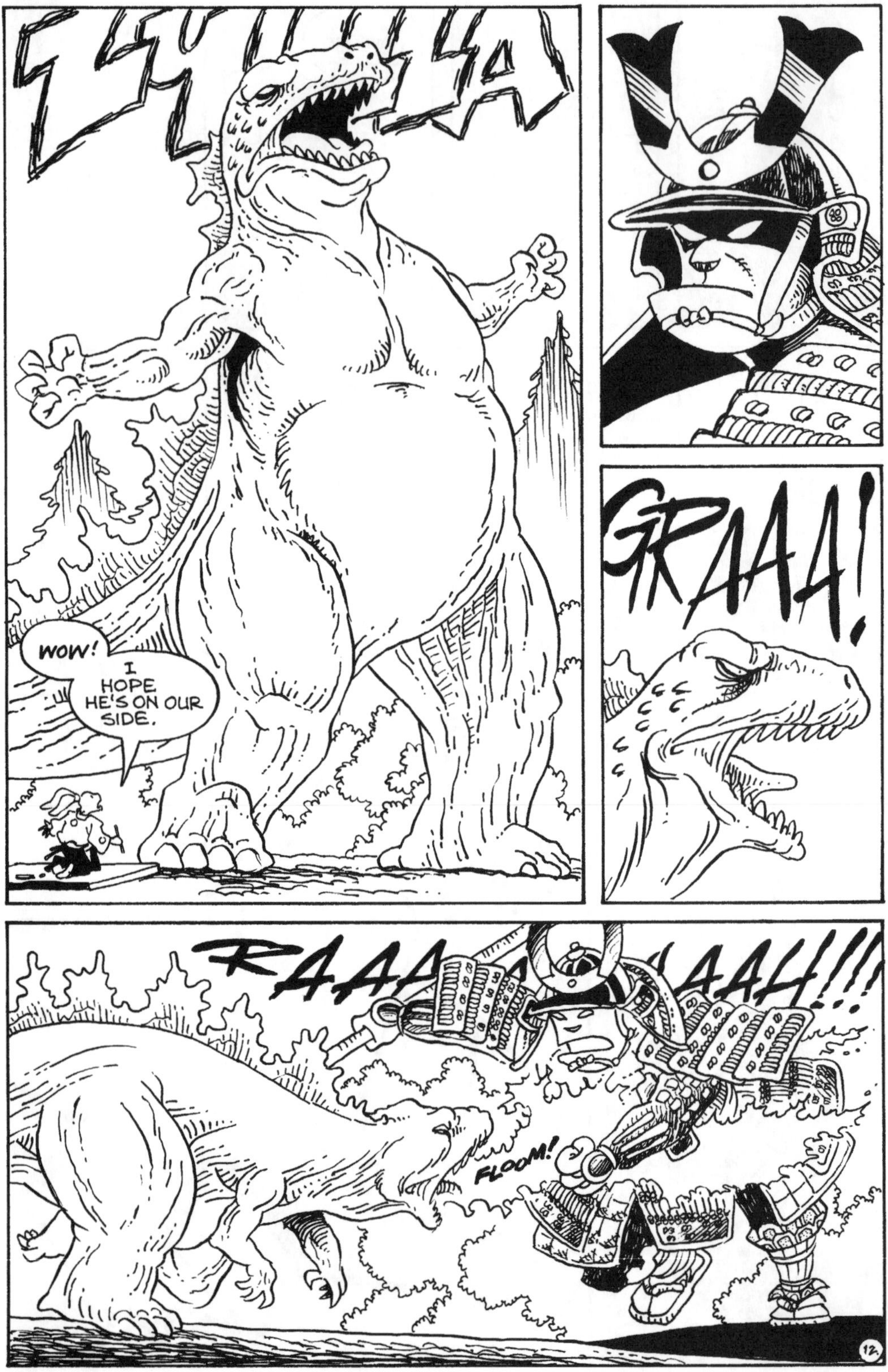
SSQUEEEEEA!
WOW!
I HOPE HE'S ON OUR SIDE.
GRAAA!
RAAAAAAAAAAH!!!
FLOOM!
12

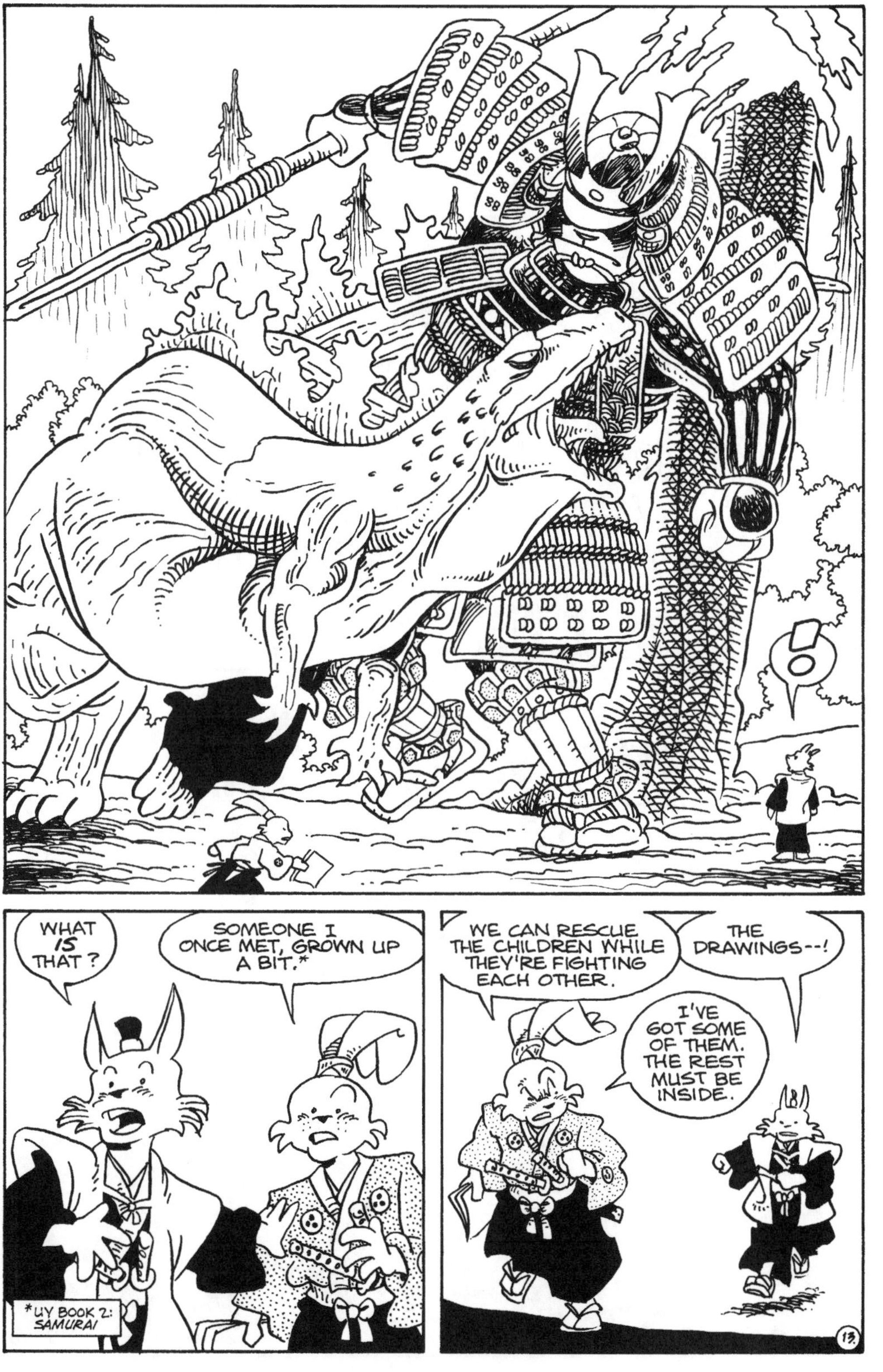
!
WHAT IS THAT?
SOMEONE I ONCE MET, GROWN UP A BIT.*
*UY BOOK 2: SAMURAI
WE CAN RESCUE THE CHILDREN WHILE THEY'RE FIGHTING EACH OTHER.
THE DRAWINGS--!
I'VE GOT SOME OF THEM. THE REST MUST BE INSIDE.
13.

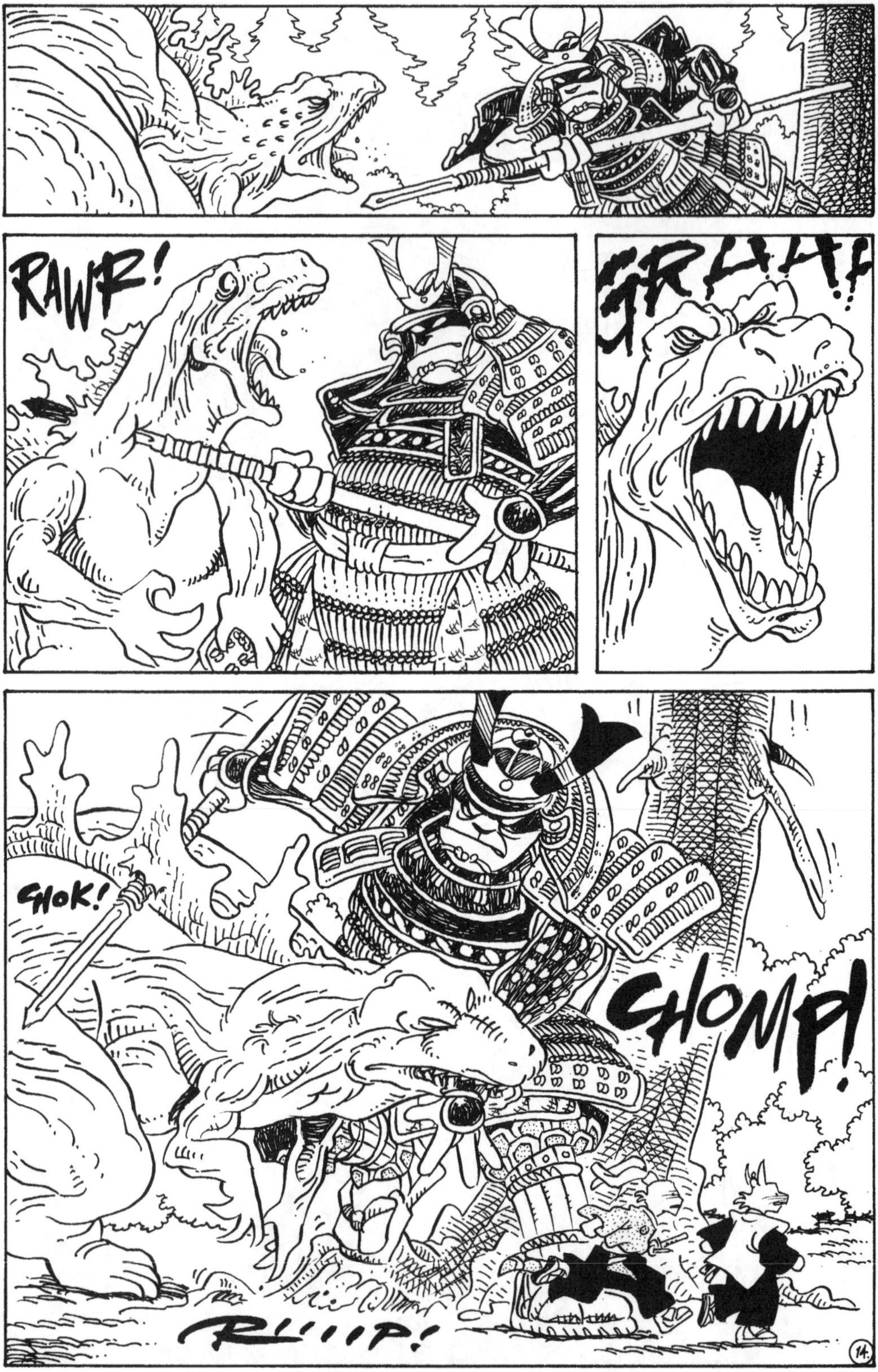
RAWR!
GRAAA!!
CHOK!
CHOMP!
RIIIP!
14.

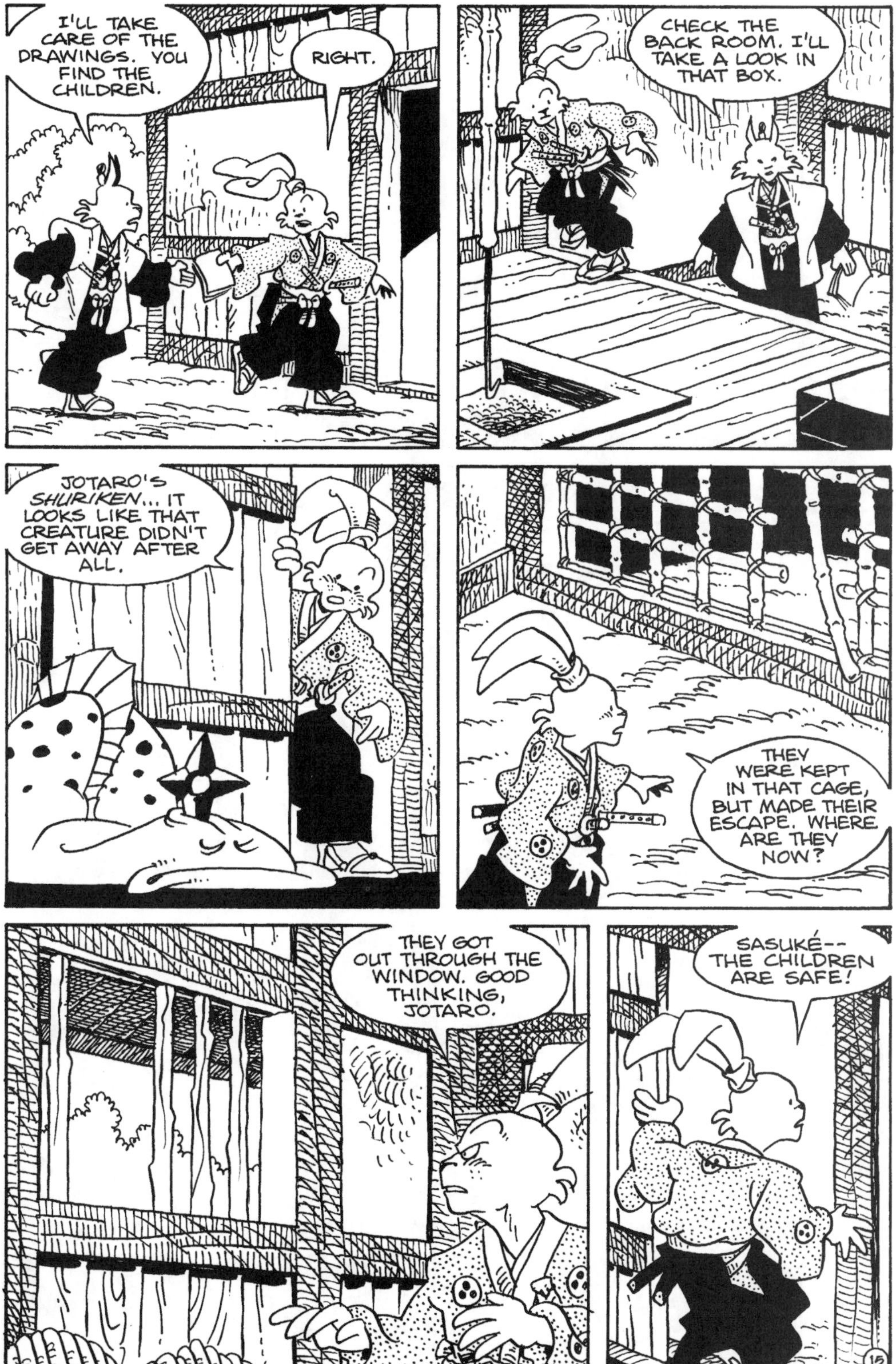
I'LL TAKE CARE OF THE DRAWINGS. YOU FIND THE CHILDREN.
RIGHT.
CHECK THE BACK ROOM. I'LL TAKE A LOOK IN THAT BOX.
JOTARO'S *SHURIKEN*... IT LOOKS LIKE THAT CREATURE DIDN'T GET AWAY AFTER ALL.
THEY WERE KEPT IN THAT CAGE, BUT MADE THEIR ESCAPE. WHERE ARE THEY NOW?
THEY GOT OUT THROUGH THE WINDOW. GOOD THINKING, JOTARO.
SASUKÉ-- THE CHILDREN ARE SAFE!
15

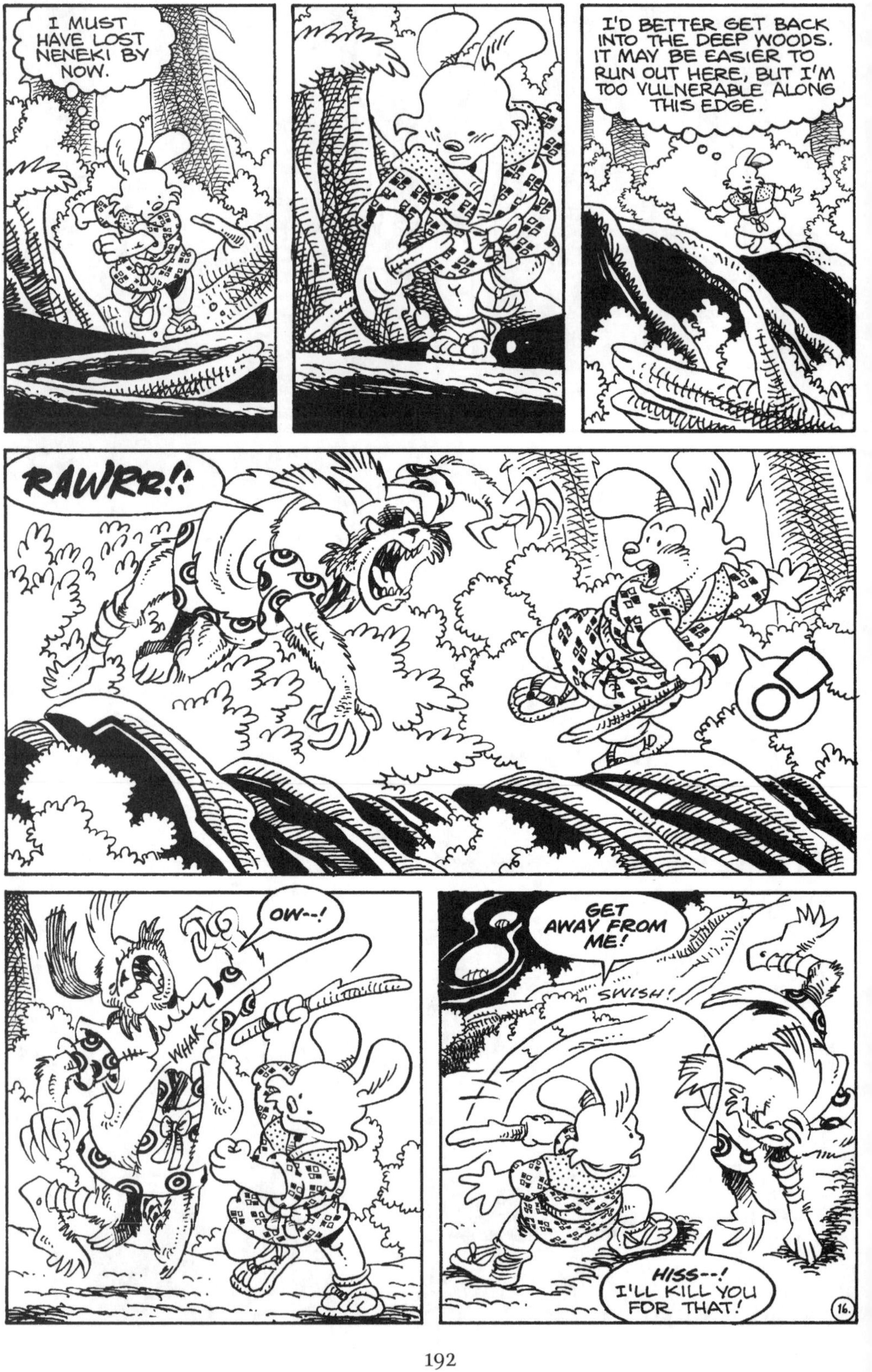
I MUST HAVE LOST NENEKI BY NOW.
I'D BETTER GET BACK INTO THE DEEP WOODS. IT MAY BE EASIER TO RUN OUT HERE, BUT I'M TOO VULNERABLE ALONG THIS EDGE.
RAWRR!!
OW--!
WHAK
GET AWAY FROM ME!
SWISH!
HISS--! I'LL KILL YOU FOR THAT!
16.

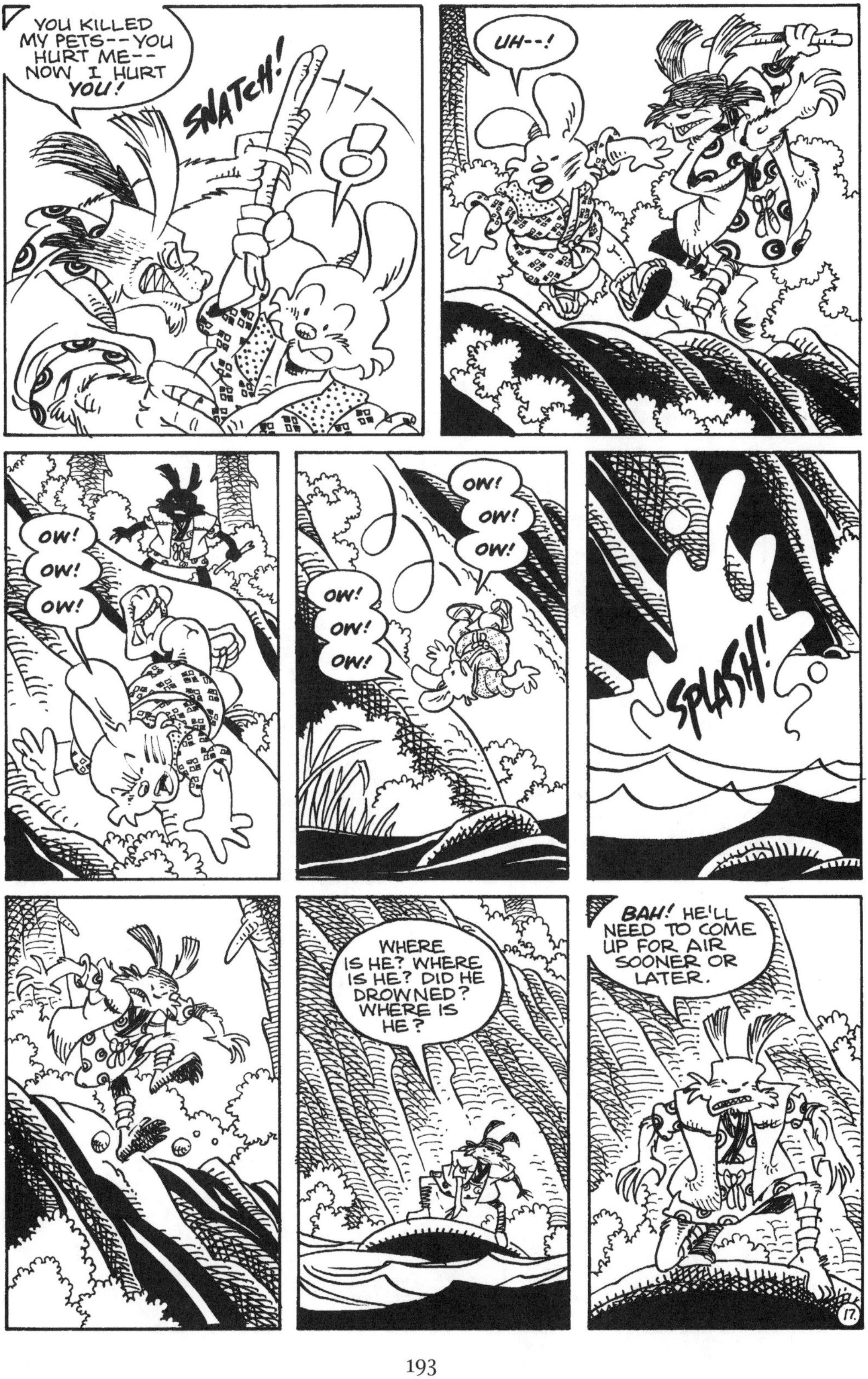
YOU KILLED MY PETS--YOU HURT ME-- NOW I HURT YOU!
SNATCH!
UH--!
OW! OW! OW!
OW! OW! OW!
OW! OW! OW!
SPLASH!
WHERE IS HE? WHERE IS HE? DID HE DROWNED? WHERE IS HE?
BAH! HE'LL NEED TO COME UP FOR AIR SOONER OR LATER.
17.

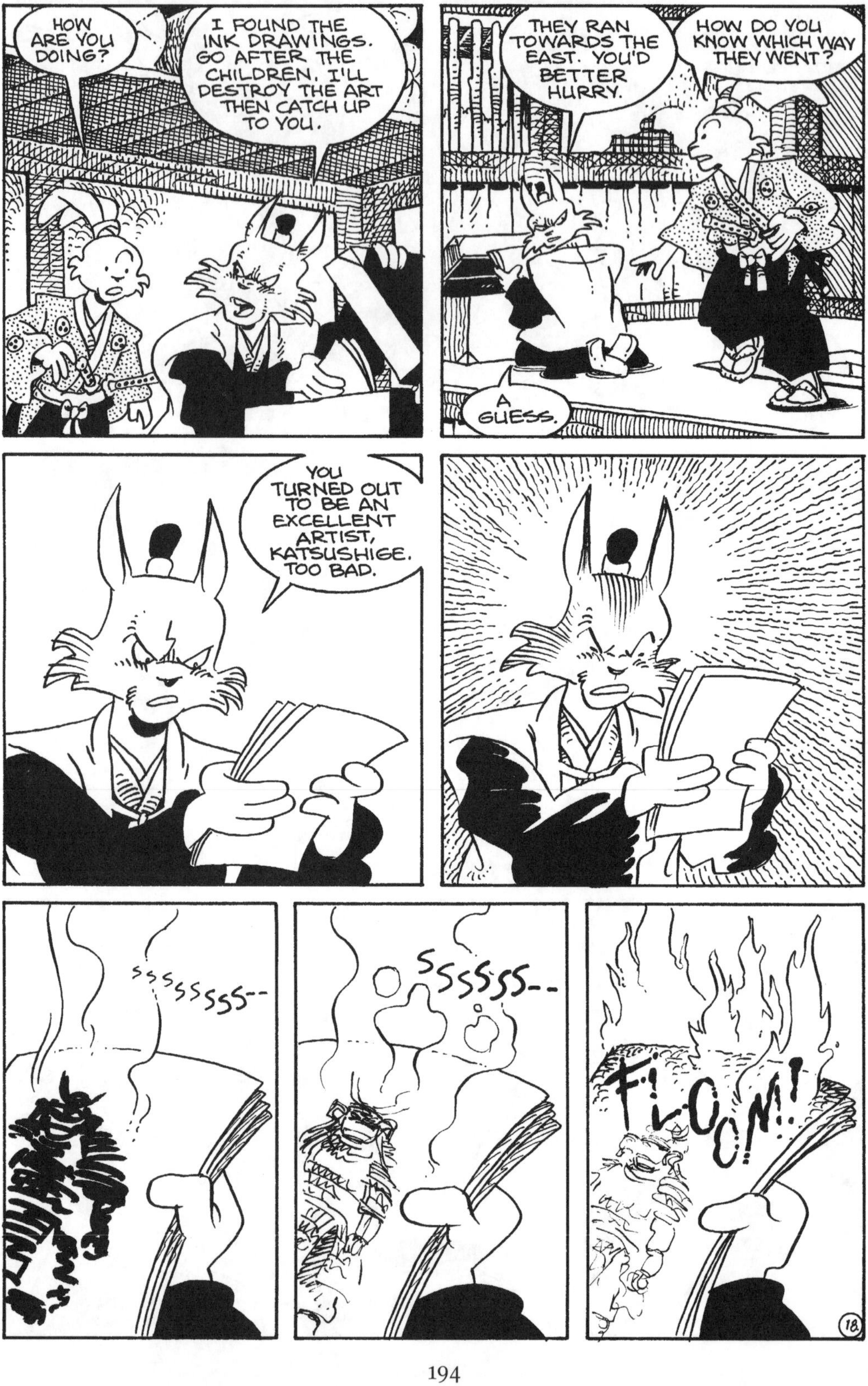
HOW ARE YOU DOING?
I FOUND THE INK DRAWINGS. GO AFTER THE CHILDREN. I'LL DESTROY THE ART THEN CATCH UP TO YOU.
THEY RAN TOWARDS THE EAST. YOU'D BETTER HURRY.
HOW DO YOU KNOW WHICH WAY THEY WENT?
A GUESS.
YOU TURNED OUT TO BE AN EXCELLENT ARTIST, KATSUSHIGE. TOO BAD.
SSSSSSSS--
SSSSSS--
FLOOM!
18

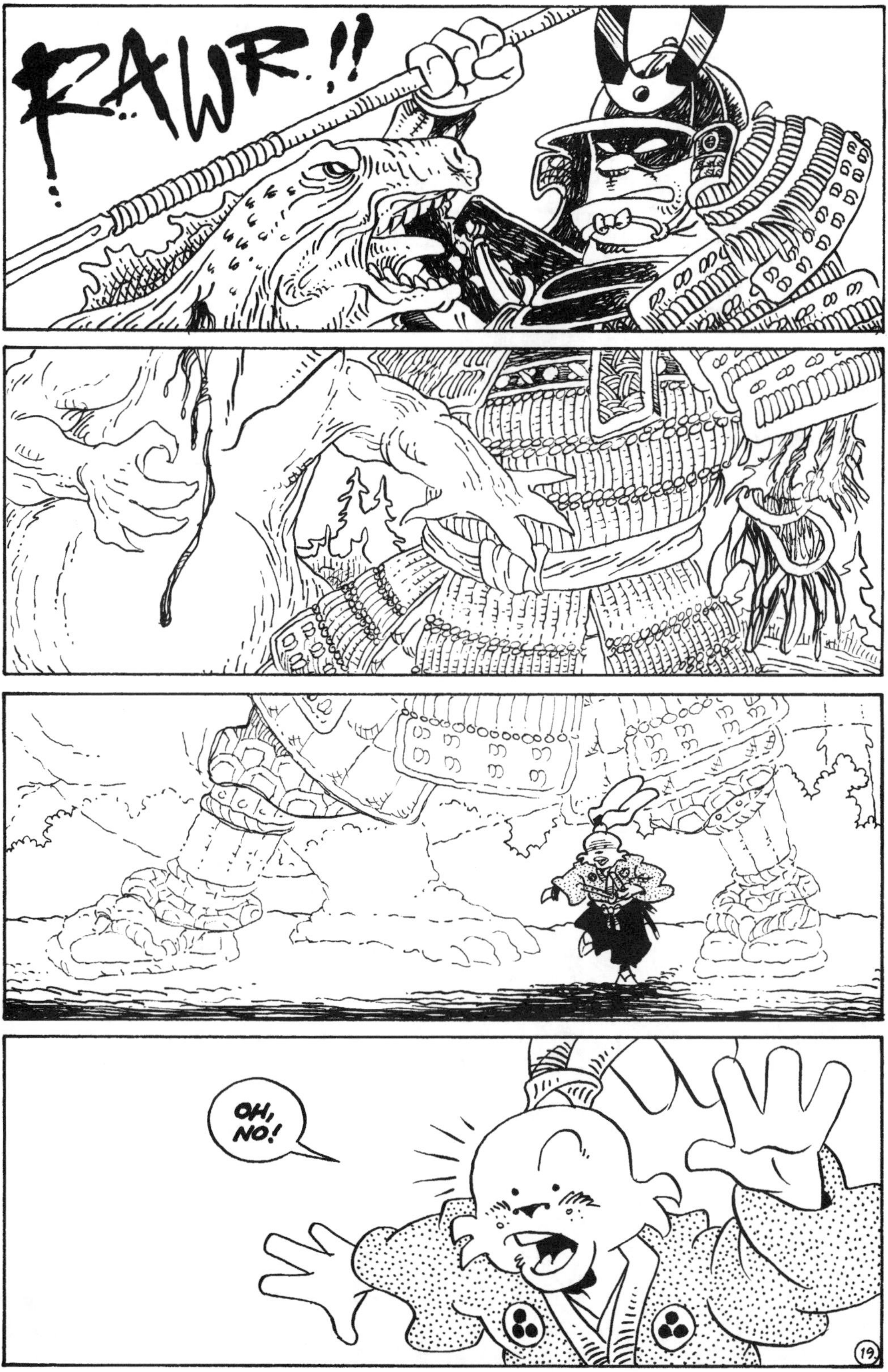
RAWR!!
OH, NO!
19

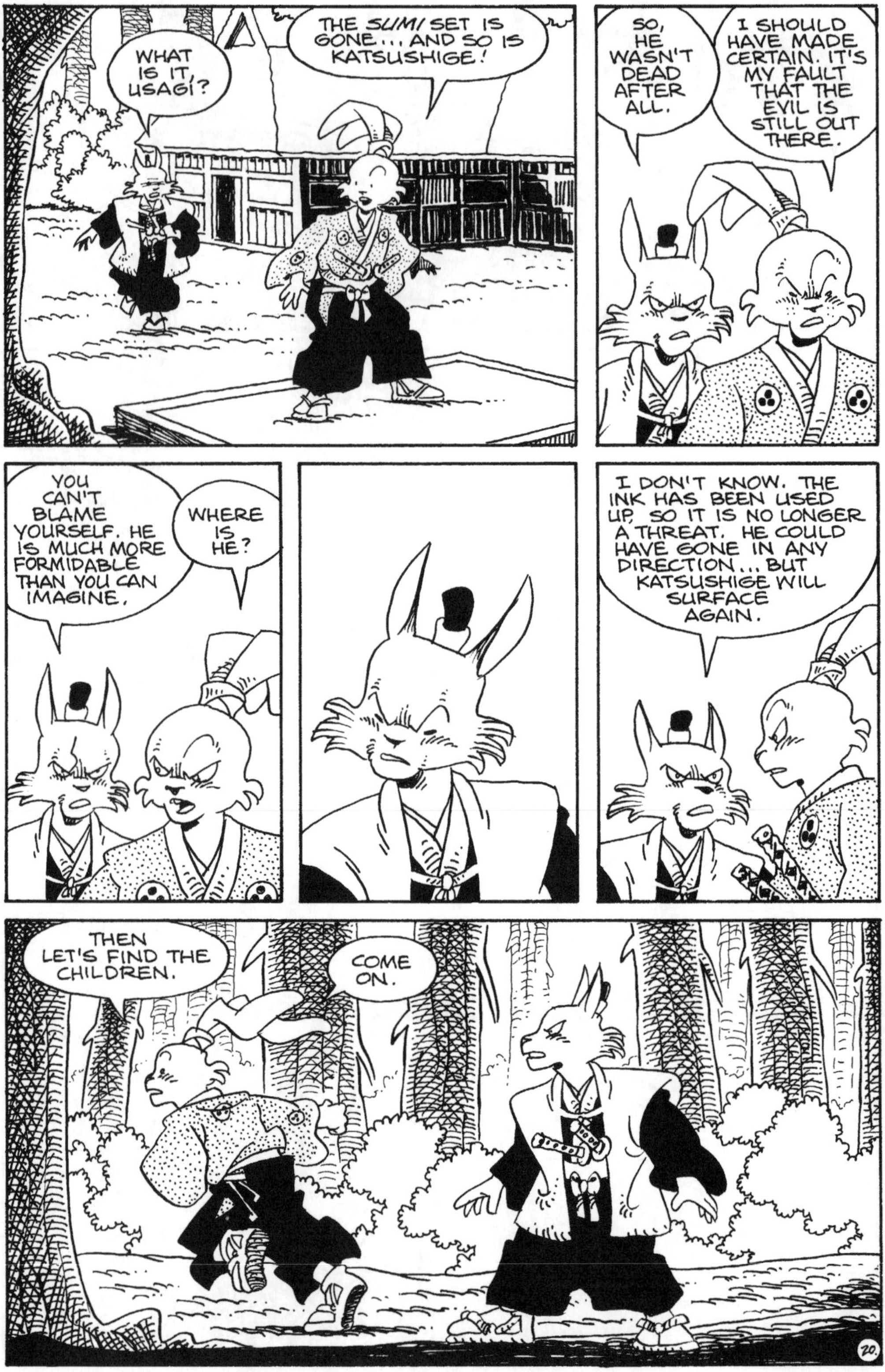
WHAT IS IT, USAGI?
THE SUMI SET IS GONE... AND SO IS KATSUSHIGE!
SO, HE WASN'T DEAD AFTER ALL.
I SHOULD HAVE MADE CERTAIN. IT'S MY FAULT THAT THE EVIL IS STILL OUT THERE.
YOU CAN'T BLAME YOURSELF. HE IS MUCH MORE FORMIDABLE THAN YOU CAN IMAGINE.
WHERE IS HE?
I DON'T KNOW. THE INK HAS BEEN USED UP, SO IT IS NO LONGER A THREAT. HE COULD HAVE GONE IN ANY DIRECTION... BUT KATSUSHIGE WILL SURFACE AGAIN.
THEN LET'S FIND THE CHILDREN.
COME ON.
20.

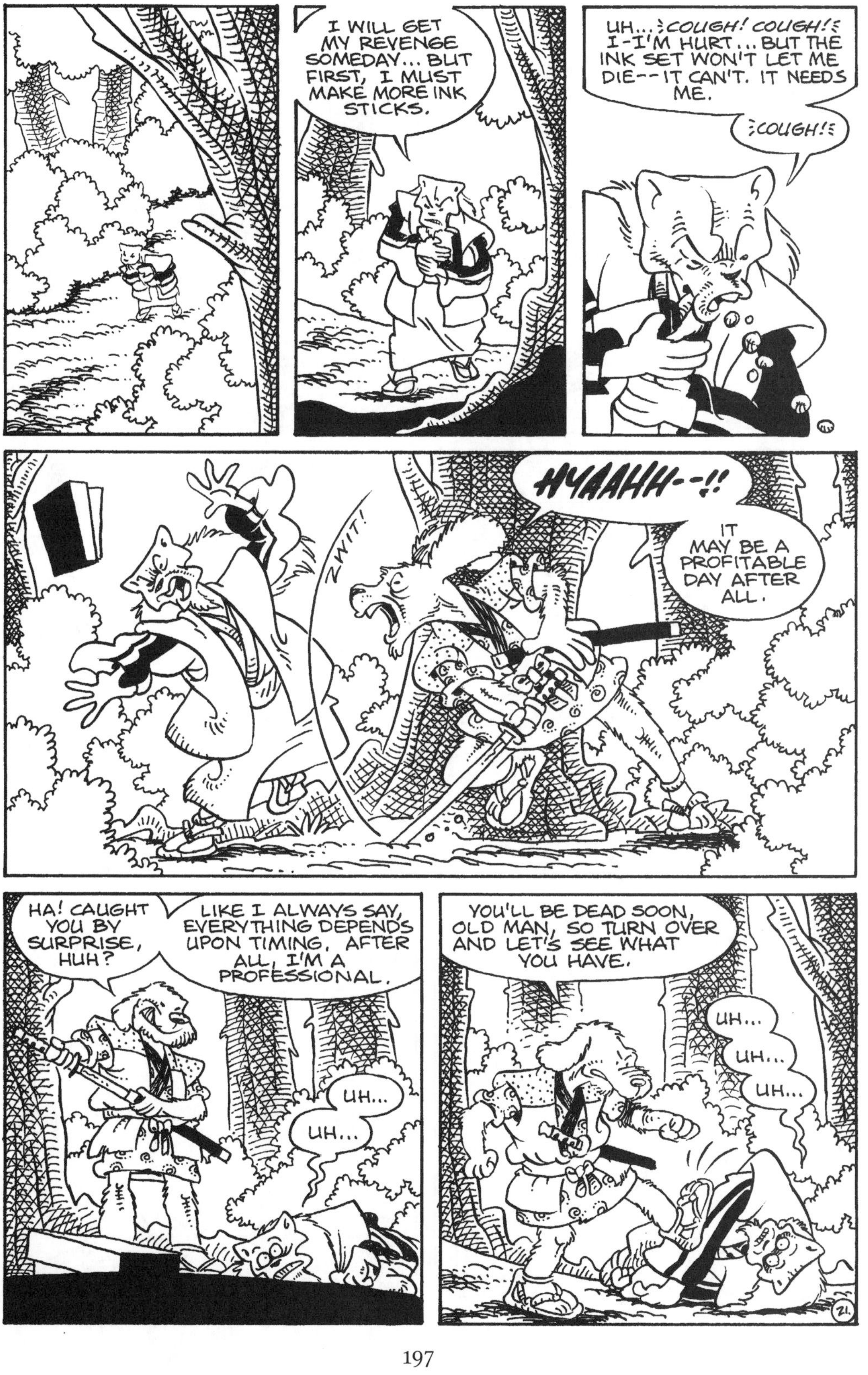
I WILL GET MY REVENGE SOMEDAY... BUT FIRST, I MUST MAKE MORE INK STICKS.
UH... COUGH! COUGH! I-I'M HURT... BUT THE INK SET WON'T LET ME DIE-- IT CAN'T. IT NEEDS ME.
COUGH!
HYAAHH--!!
ZWIT!
IT MAY BE A PROFITABLE DAY AFTER ALL.
HA! CAUGHT YOU BY SURPRISE, HUH?
LIKE I ALWAYS SAY, EVERYTHING DEPENDS UPON TIMING. AFTER ALL, I'M A PROFESSIONAL.
UH...
UH...
YOU'LL BE DEAD SOON, OLD MAN, SO TURN OVER AND LET'S SEE WHAT YOU HAVE.
UH...
UH...
UH...
21.

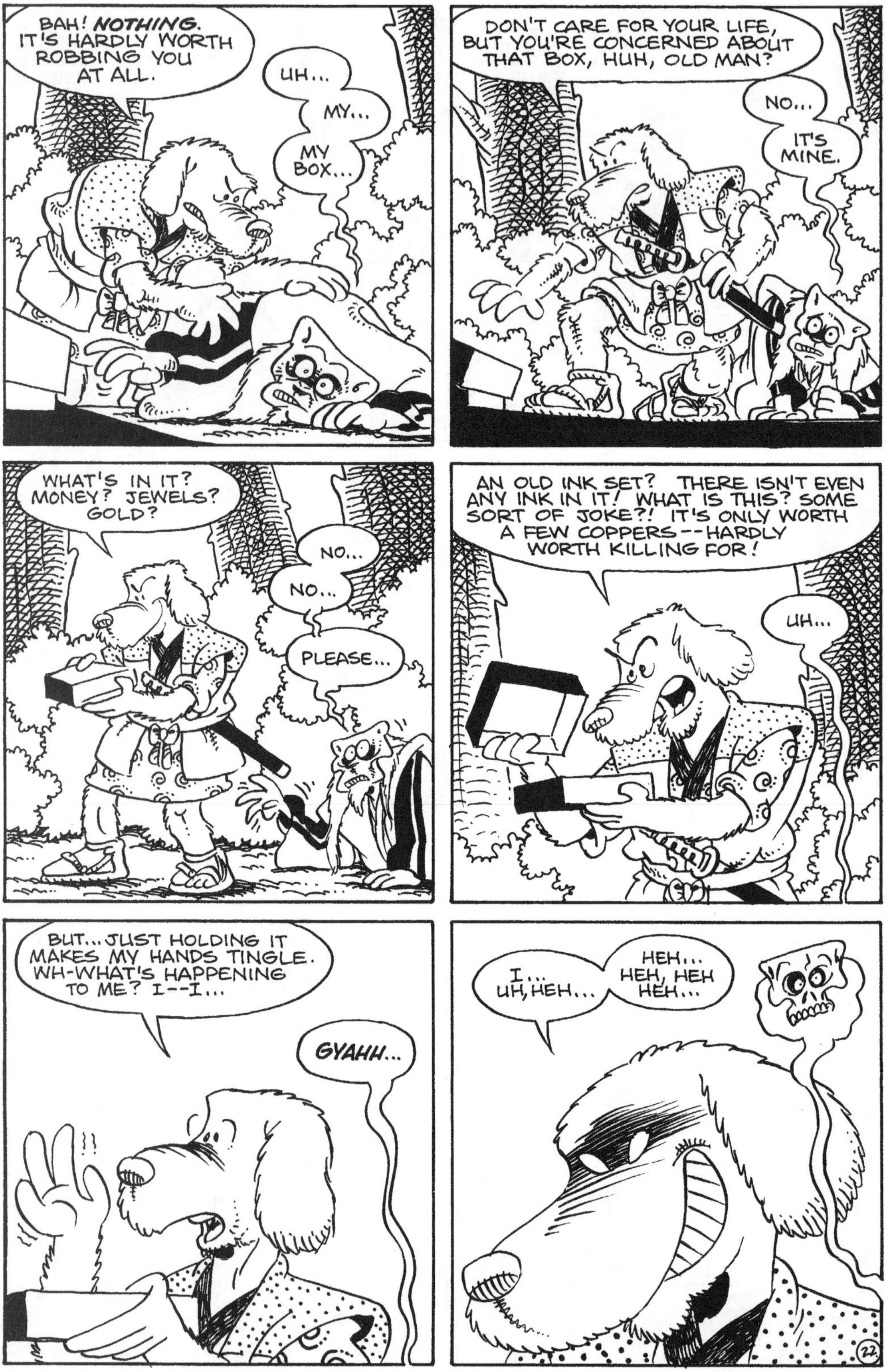
BAH! NOTHING. IT'S HARDLY WORTH ROBBING YOU AT ALL.
UH...
MY...
MY BOX...
DON'T CARE FOR YOUR LIFE, BUT YOU'RE CONCERNED ABOUT THAT BOX, HUH, OLD MAN?
NO...
IT'S MINE.
WHAT'S IN IT? MONEY? JEWELS? GOLD?
NO...
NO...
PLEASE...
AN OLD INK SET? THERE ISN'T EVEN ANY INK IN IT! WHAT IS THIS? SOME SORT OF JOKE?! IT'S ONLY WORTH A FEW COPPERS--HARDLY WORTH KILLING FOR!
UH...
BUT...JUST HOLDING IT MAKES MY HANDS TINGLE. WH-WHAT'S HAPPENING TO ME? I--I...
GYAHH...
I... UH, HEH...
HEH... HEH, HEH HEH...
22

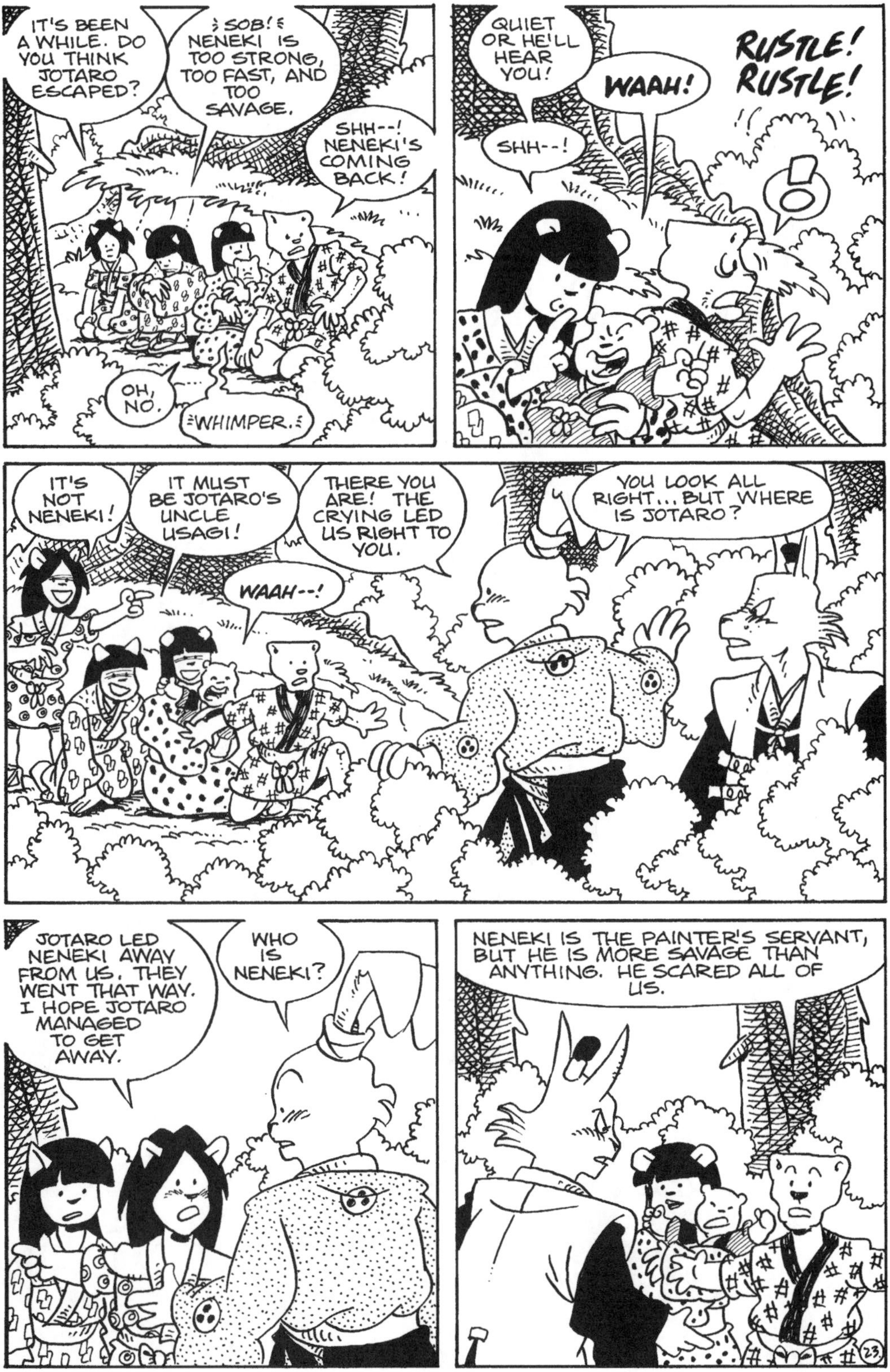
IT'S BEEN A WHILE. DO YOU THINK JOTARO ESCAPED?
SOB! NENEKI IS TOO STRONG, TOO FAST, AND TOO SAVAGE.
SHH--! NENEKI'S COMING BACK!
OH, NO.
WHIMPER.
QUIET OR HE'LL HEAR YOU!
WAAH!
RUSTLE! RUSTLE!
SHH--!
IT'S NOT NENEKI!
IT MUST BE JOTARO'S UNCLE USAGI!
THERE YOU ARE! THE CRYING LED US RIGHT TO YOU.
WAAH--!
YOU LOOK ALL RIGHT... BUT WHERE IS JOTARO?
JOTARO LED NENEKI AWAY FROM US. THEY WENT THAT WAY. I HOPE JOTARO MANAGED TO GET AWAY.
WHO IS NENEKI?
NENEKI IS THE PAINTER'S SERVANT, BUT HE IS MORE SAVAGE THAN ANYTHING. HE SCARED ALL OF US.
23

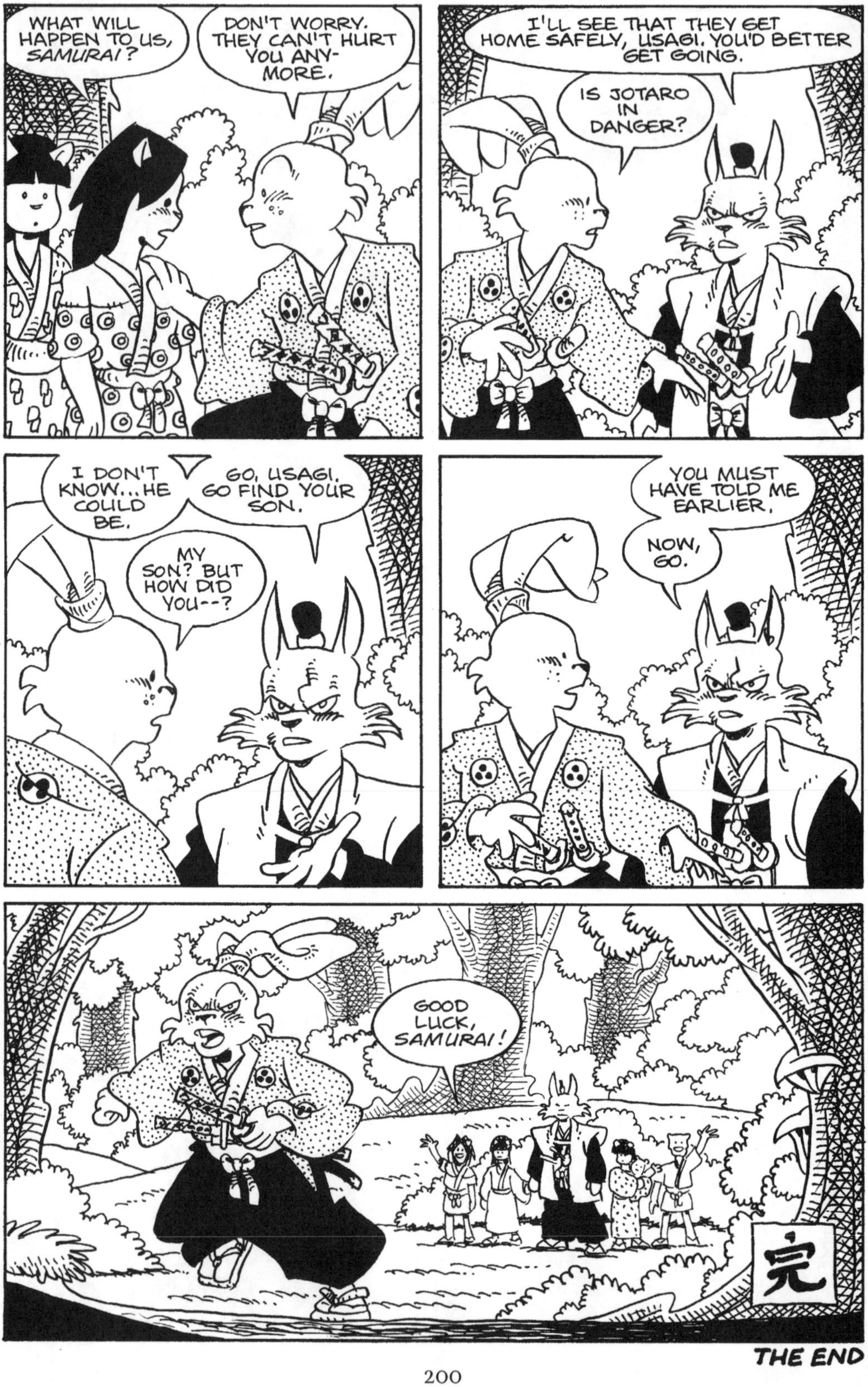
WHAT WILL HAPPEN TO US, SAMURAI?
DON'T WORRY. THEY CAN'T HURT YOU ANY-MORE.
I'LL SEE THAT THEY GET HOME SAFELY, USAGI. YOU'D BETTER GET GOING.
IS JOTARO IN DANGER?
I DON'T KNOW... HE COULD BE.
GO, USAGI. GO FIND YOUR SON.
MY SON? BUT HOW DID YOU--?
YOU MUST HAVE TOLD ME EARLIER.
NOW, GO.
GOOD LUCK, SAMURAI!
完

THE END

Usagi Yojimbo

Story Notes

KOMAINU

The *Komainu* are a pair of stone dogs that face each other at the entrance to a Shinto shrine or the approach to the oratory on the shrine grounds. They are usually carved from stone but are sometimes made of wood or metal. One dog, named *A*, is breathing in with an open mouth, while his companion, *Un*, is breathing out with his mouth closed, suggesting the inhalation and exhalation of heavenly forces and the balance of yin and yang. The phrase, *a-un-no-kokyu*, or "A-Un breathing," describes the relationship of people so close they can communicate without speech. The two protect the shrine against evil spirits with their fierce appearance.

The *Komainu* can be traced to India and that culture's stylized representation of the lion. The Chinese adopted the lion and added attributes of their native tiger as well as the Pekinese dogs that were the pride of the Chinese Imperial family. That passed over to the Korean peninsula and on to Japan, where the lions were transformed into dogs. They are sometimes called *Karashishi* (Chinese lions). Okinawa has a similar creature called *Shissa*.

TAMAGO

Master Zhaozhou (or Joshu in Japanese) was one of the most eminent teachers in the history of Buddhism. He spent much of his life in China searching for spiritual teachers and, at the age of 80, arrived at Beilin Temple, where he lived the rest of his life. Zhaozhou

is noted for his ability to express the enlightened mind in a pithy manner with his teachings of "extraordinary ordinariness." In a typical lesson, a monk newly arrived to the temple asked Zhaozhou to teach him. The Master asked if he had eaten his morning gruel. The student replied that he had. Zhaozhou then said, "Go wash out your bowl."

Zhaozhou died in 897 A.D. at the age of 120. His lessons are included in most Koan anthologies, even today. Beilin Temple is regarded as one of the most sacred sites of Zen Buddhism.

Fukurokuju is one of the *Shichifukujin*, or Seven Gods of Luck. They can be seen in paintings or carved into statues or made into ornaments and toys either singly or in a group. The Buddhist priest Tenkai taught that nobility consists of seven virtues: longevity, fortune, popularity, candor, amiability, dignity, and magnanimity. Fukurokuju represents longevity and also wisdom. He is recognizable by his high-domed head and very short body. He carries a staff on which is tied a *makimono* (scroll) that gives the life limits to all persons. He sometimes has a companion stork, a symbol of long life. In his earthly life, he was a Chinese philosopher and prophet.

Many of the lessons on Zen came from *Zen Speaks: Shouts of Nothingness*, adapted and illustrated by Tsi Chih Chung, translated by Brian Bruya (New York: Doubleday, 1994).

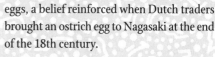
eggs, a belief reinforced when Dutch traders brought an ostrich egg to Nagasaki at the end of the 18th century.

There are two types of *tengu*. The *karasu* (crow) *tengu* are part bird, with long beaks and wings. The *kohana* (long-nose) *tengu* are red, wear cloaks and small black hats, and often take the form of mountain priests called *yamabushi*. They are excellent swordsmen and imparted some of their skill to Japan's greatest hero, Minamoto Yoshitsune. Yoshitsune had been spared by Kiyomori, the rival Taira clan leader, on the condition that he become a priest. He studied the martial arts under Dai Sojobo, the *tengu* of Mt. Kurama. Yoshitsune eventually marched against the Taira clan, destroying them at the Battle of Dannoura in 1185 A.D. (see *UY* Book 12: *Grasscutter*).

The *tengu* came to be regarded as the gods of the forests. If woodcutters refused to make offerings to the *tengu*, they often met with many small accidents. Hunters promised them gifts of food to ensure success. They were also believed to control rain and wind. They were blamed for whirlwinds and mysterious lights in the mountains. In the 19th century, notices were posted along the roads when the *Shogun* traveled, ordering *tengu* and demons to remove themselves elsewhere.

This is a very novice-friendly cartoon book explaining Zen through its teachings. Additional research came from *Quaint Customs and Manners of Japan* by Mock Joya (Tokyo: The Tokyo News Service, Ltd., 1951).

USAGI AND THE TENGU
The *tengu* are minor deities, among the oldest in Japanese mythology. Their origins are a mystery. In Shinto, they could have descended from Susano-o, the brother of Amaterasu the Sun Goddess. They could also have been derived from the Garuda, the Buddhist deities who had wings and the heads of horned birds. Or they might have been imported from Chinese folklore, as they resemble the mountain demons called *t'ien-kou* (celestial dog). Colonies of *tengu* inhabit trees in mountainous areas, particularly pines and cryptomerias, with a king *tengu* in charge. Some legends give them the ability to change themselves into human men or women. They are mischievous in character and enjoy playing tricks, but can be vengeful if one is played on them. *Tengu* are born from giant

References for this story came from: *Japanese Mythology* by Juliet Piggott, 1975, The Hamlyn Publishing Group, Ltd., London, New, York, Sydney, Toronto; *Japanese Ghosts and Demons* by Stephen Addiss, 1985, George Braziller, Inc., New York, in association with the Spencer Museum of Art, University of Kansas; and *Yoshitsune's Thirty-Six Ghosts* by John Stevenson, 1983, John Weatherhill, Inc. of New York and Tokyo and Blue Tiger Books of Hong Kong.

Sumi-E

Sumi-e, the Art of Ink, is comprised of "four treasures": the brush, paper, ink (*sumi*), and ink stone. The arts of calligraphy and ink painting came to Japan from China near the end of the Asuka Period (circa 645 A.D.). Ink painting became an established art form mainly through the works of priests, whose monochrome paintings of nature depicted a world of contemplation and meditation.

Brushes (*fude*) come in various sizes and quality, but the best brushes are made of the straight hairs from the breasts of white sheep.

The paper (*kami*) is thinner and more textured than Western standards. It also has a shine to it, a rough reverse side, and is more absorbent. A paper-weight (*bunchin*) is used to hold the paper stationary. In earlier days, paper was a luxury that few people could afford. The invention of paper is attributed to T'sai Lun, around the year 105 A.D. Chinese paper was generally made from the bark of mulberry trees. Around 600 A.D. paper made its way to Japan by way of Korea, where it was made an art form in itself. (For a quick description of how Japanese paper [*washi*] is made, see *UY* Book 5: *Lone Goat and Kid*.)

Ink sticks come in small bars, often decorated with motifs or gold writing. Rings at the top indicate their degree of blackness, with five being the darkest. Basically, there are four types of ink: black, black with gold leaf, gray, and oiled-gray, which has an outline of oil formed around each stroke. Making the ink can be a laborious effort. It is made of lamp-black, or plant soot, and glue. The soot is collected from an inverted cover over a lower dish filled with burning oils or wood. Glue is culled from the hides and bones of cows and horses. The two are mixed, then left to dry in molds.

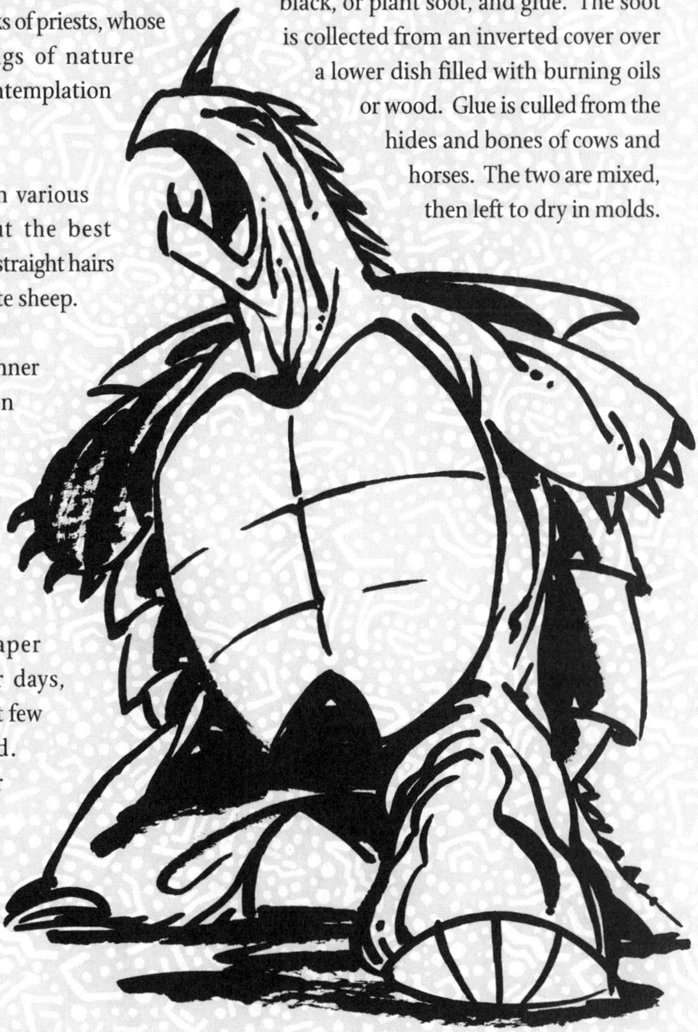

The ink stone (*suzuri*) is a shallow slate dish with a reservoir at one end. The best stones are those that come from the riverbeds near Sendai in Northern Honshu, because of their fine grain and quality.

Fujiwara no Hidesato was a councilor to Emperor Shujaku (reigned 931-46 A.D.). As Hidesato was crossing Seta Bridge near Lake Biwa outside Kyoto, he found his way blocked by a dragon with red eyes and fiery breath. He ignored it and continued on his way, until he heard his name called. He turned to discover that the dragon was, in actuality, Ryujin, the Dragon King, who was on a mission to find a man courageous enough to kill a monstrous centipede that was destroying his kingdom. Hidesato followed Ryujin into the lake and down to the sea. As they were feasting in the Dragon Palace, the centipede attacked. Hidesato, a skilled archer, shot two arrows, but they glanced harmlessly off the monster's body. Remembering that saliva has magical properties, he licked the tip of his next arrow and shot it into the centipede's eye, slaying it. The Dragon King rewarded Hidesato with a bag of rice that never emptied, a never-ending bolt of silk, a large bronze bell, and a cooking pot that heated without fire. Hidesato donated the bell to Mii Temple, from which it was stolen two hundred years later by the warrior priest Benkei.

Soon after abdicating in 1123, Emperor Toba became ill. Abe no Seimei, the court astrologer, determined that the cause was malicious magic. Tamamo no Mae, the Emperor's favorite concubine, was tricked into revealing her true form: a nine-tailed golden fox. Tamamo sprang into the air and flew to Nasu Plain. She was hunted and shot by the famed archer Miura Kuranosuke. Tamamo transformed herself into a rock, which became known as the *sessho seki*, or "death stone." To touch it was fatal; even looking at it was dangerous. A *noh* play describes how, three centuries later, a priest performed religious rites over the stone, whereupon it burst and Tamamo reappeared with a clap of thunder. She then confessed that she had bewitched two other rulers, one in India

and the other in China, before casting her spells on the Japanese emperor.

Research for the first part of "Sumi-E" came primarily from the following books: *Sho: Japanese Calligraphy* by Christopher J. Earnshaw, 1989, Charles E. Tuttle Publishing of Boston, Rutland, VT, and Tokyo; *A Look into Japan* by the Japan Travel Bureau, Inc., 1985; and *Japan Day by Day* by Edward S. Morse, 1990, Cherokee Publishing Co., Atlanta, GA.

The stories of Fujiwara no Hidesato and of the "death stone" were found in *Yoshitsune's Thirty-Six Ghosts* by John Stevenson, 1983, John Weatherhill, Inc. of New York and Tokyo, and Blue Tiger Books of Hong Kong.

Usagi first encountered a *kappa* in a story aptly entitled "Kappa" (*UY Book 2: Samurai*). The *kappa* of folklore resemble monkeys, but with fish scales or a tortoise shell instead of fur. They are greenish in color and as tall as a ten-year-old child. The *kappa* are known to have the ability to heal broken bones, and they can impart this knowledge to humans. They have an indentation on the top of their heads, filled with water. If this water spills out, the *kappa* immediately lose their power and become helpless.

Kappa are vampires and live in rivers, ponds, and other water sources. They are extremely cunning and will entice their victims into the water to be drowned. These creatures have a fondness for cucumbers and can be placated by potential victims writing the names and ages of family members on cucumbers and throwing them into the water where a *kappa* lives. Despite their despicable habits, they are unusually polite and honorable. When meeting a *kappa*, it is advised that you bow, as is the tradition. Many times the *kappa* will return your bow, spilling his water and losing his strength. You can then extract a promise of safety or knowledge, that he is obliged to keep.

Information on the *kappa* was found in *Japanese Mythology* by Juliet Piggott, published in 1969 by The Hamlyn Publishing Group, Ltd., London, New York, Sydney, Toronto.

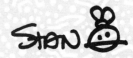

GALLERY

The following pages feature Stan Sakai's cover art from issues sixty-one through sixty-eight of Dark Horse's Usagi Yojimbo Volume Three *series.*

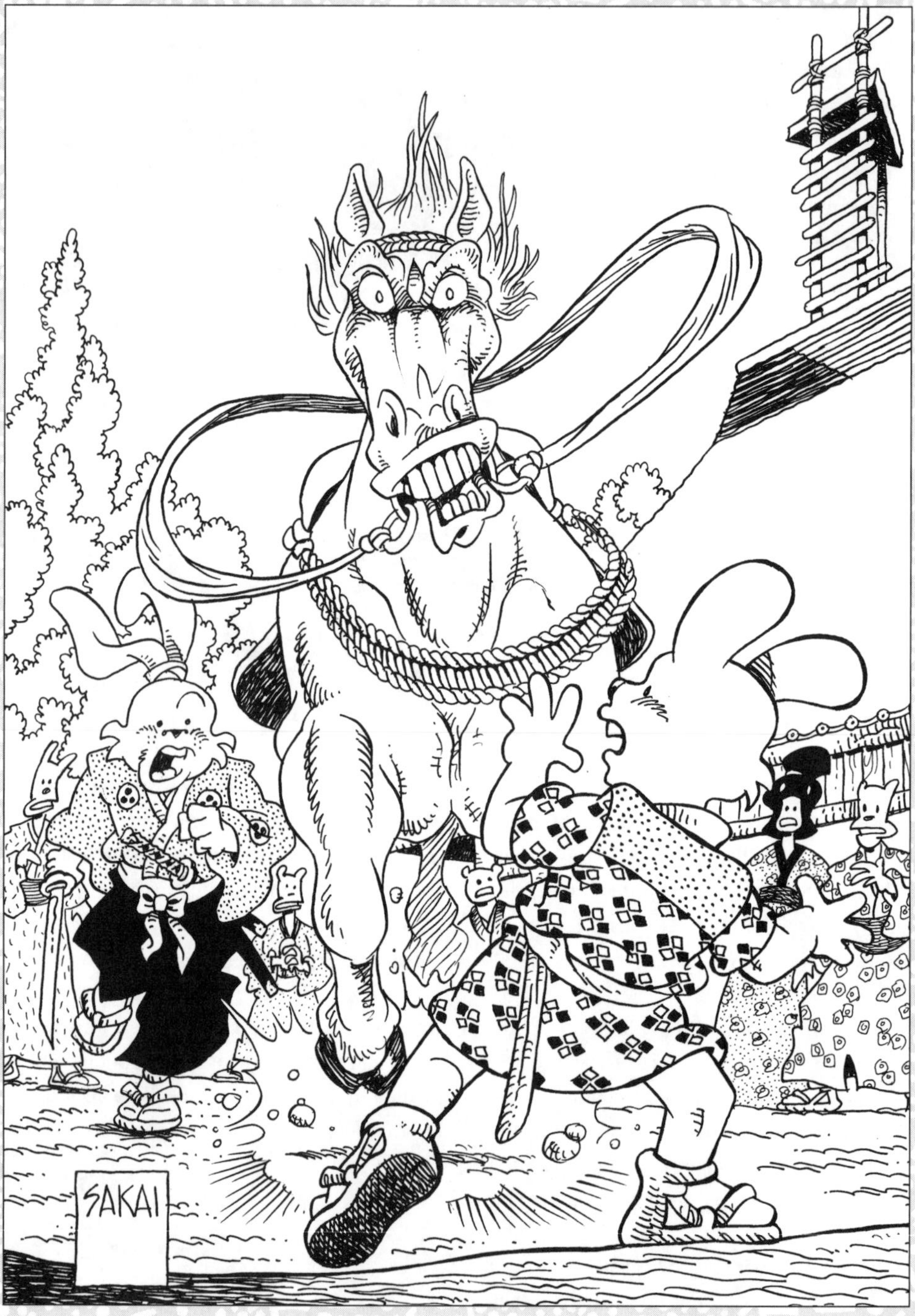
SAKAI

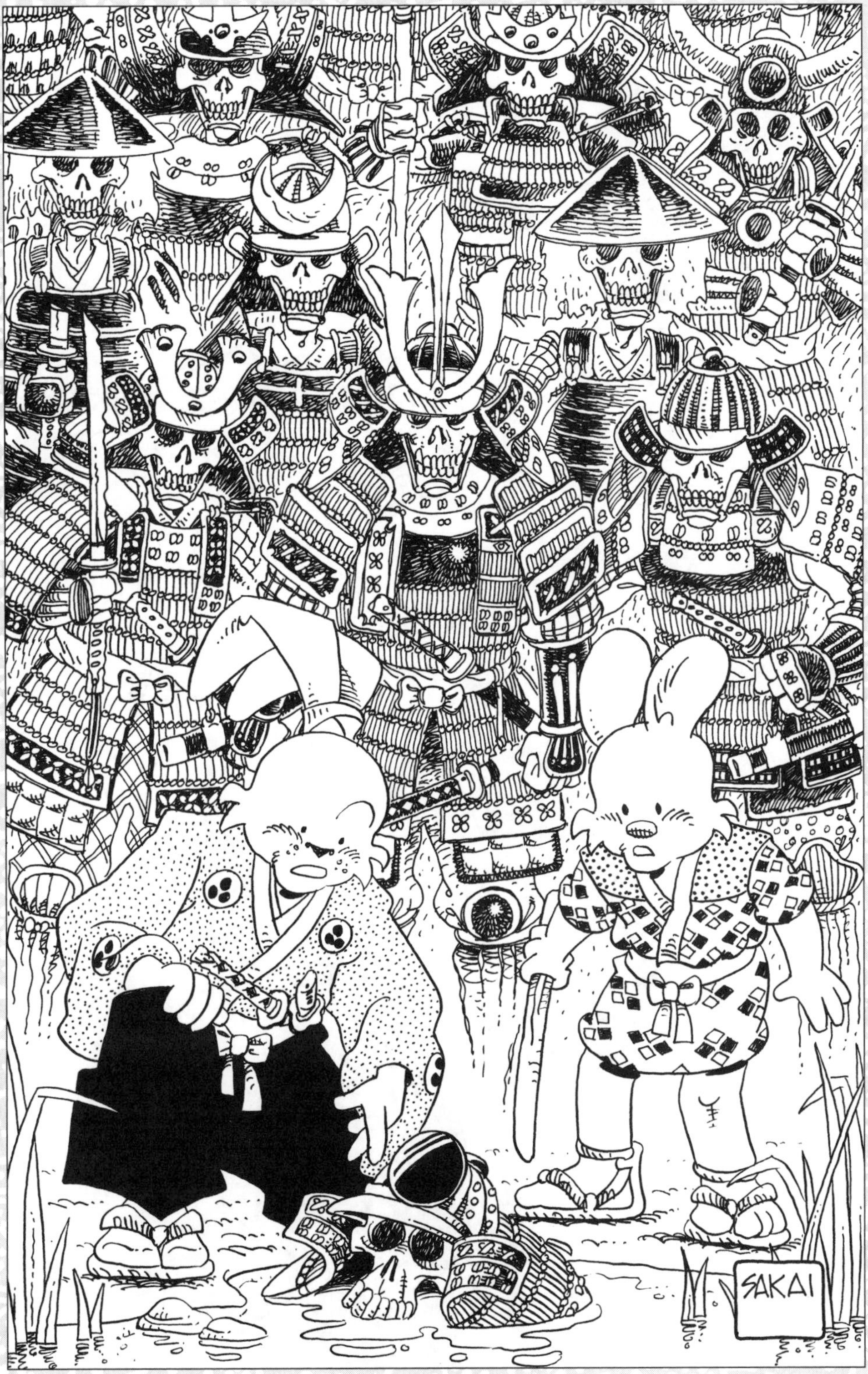
SAKAI

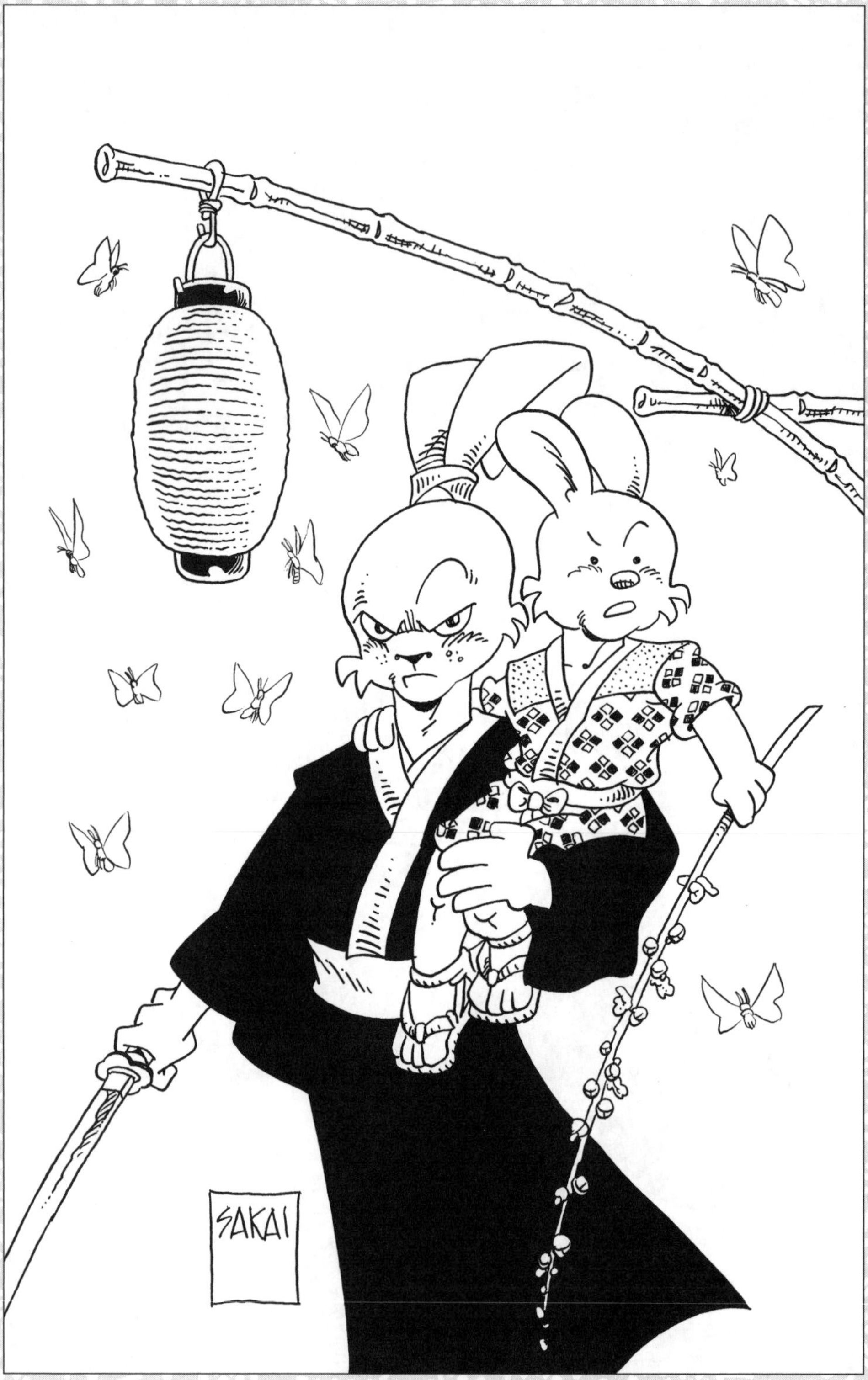
SAKAI

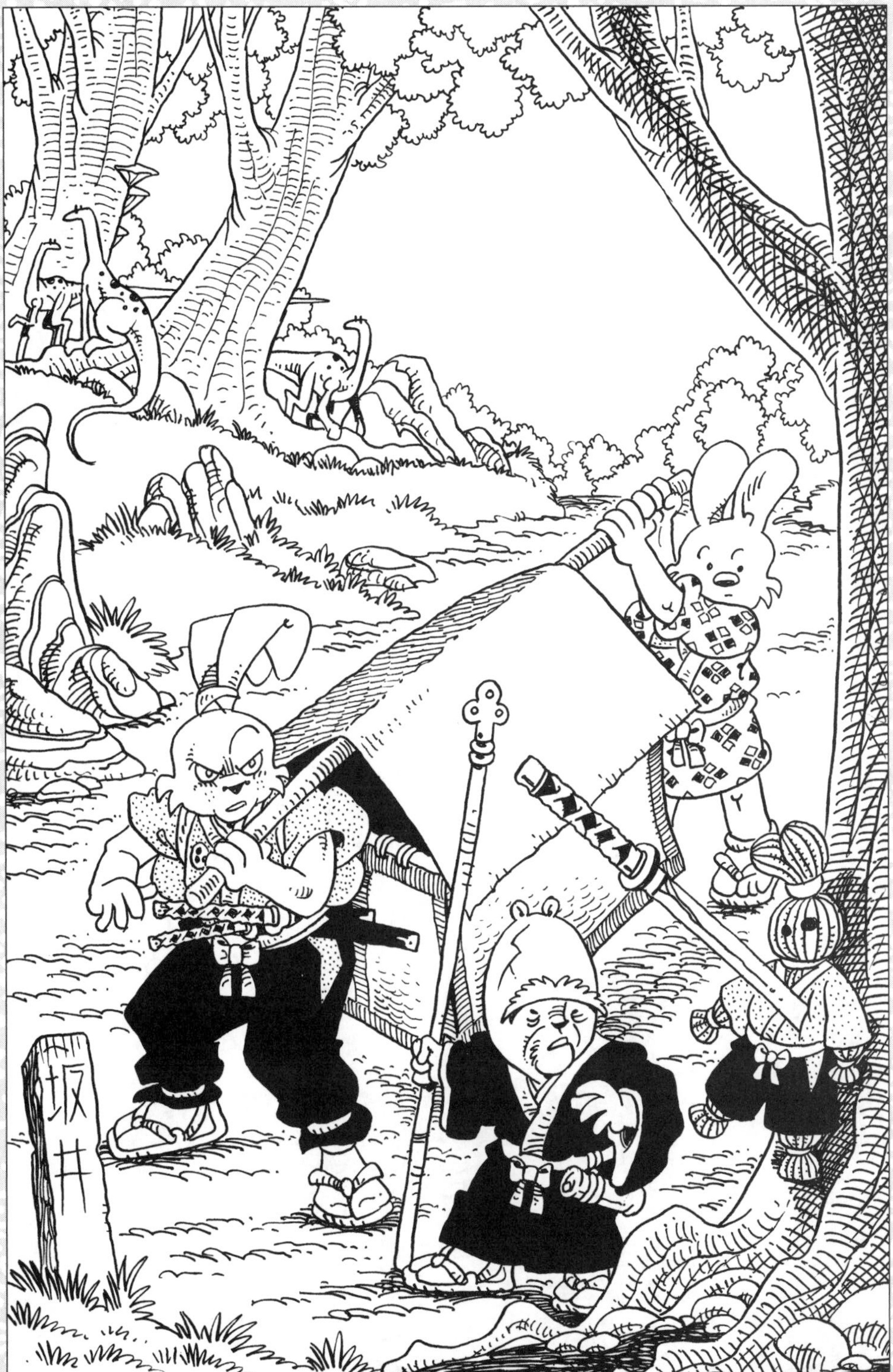
坂井

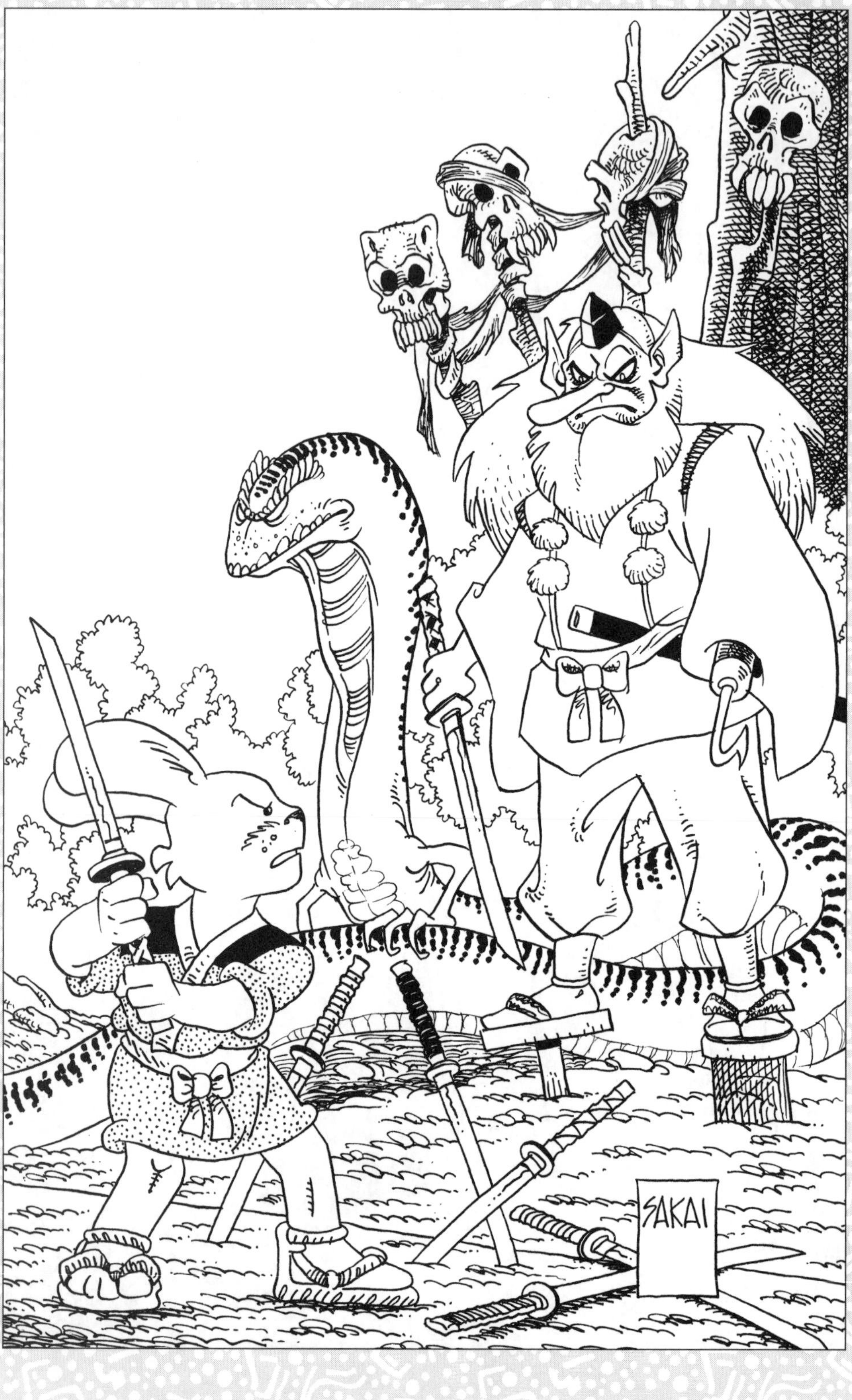
SAKAI

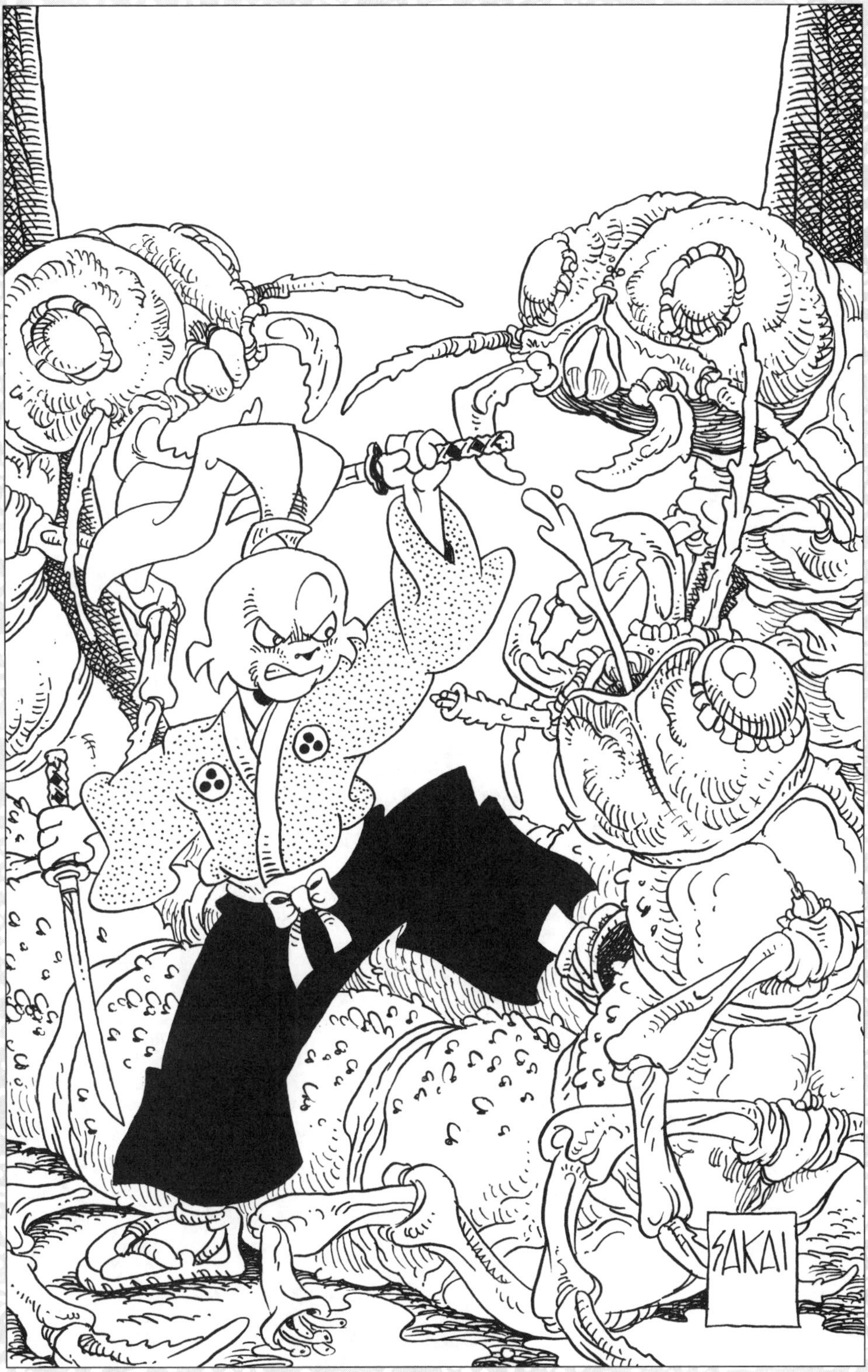
SAKAI

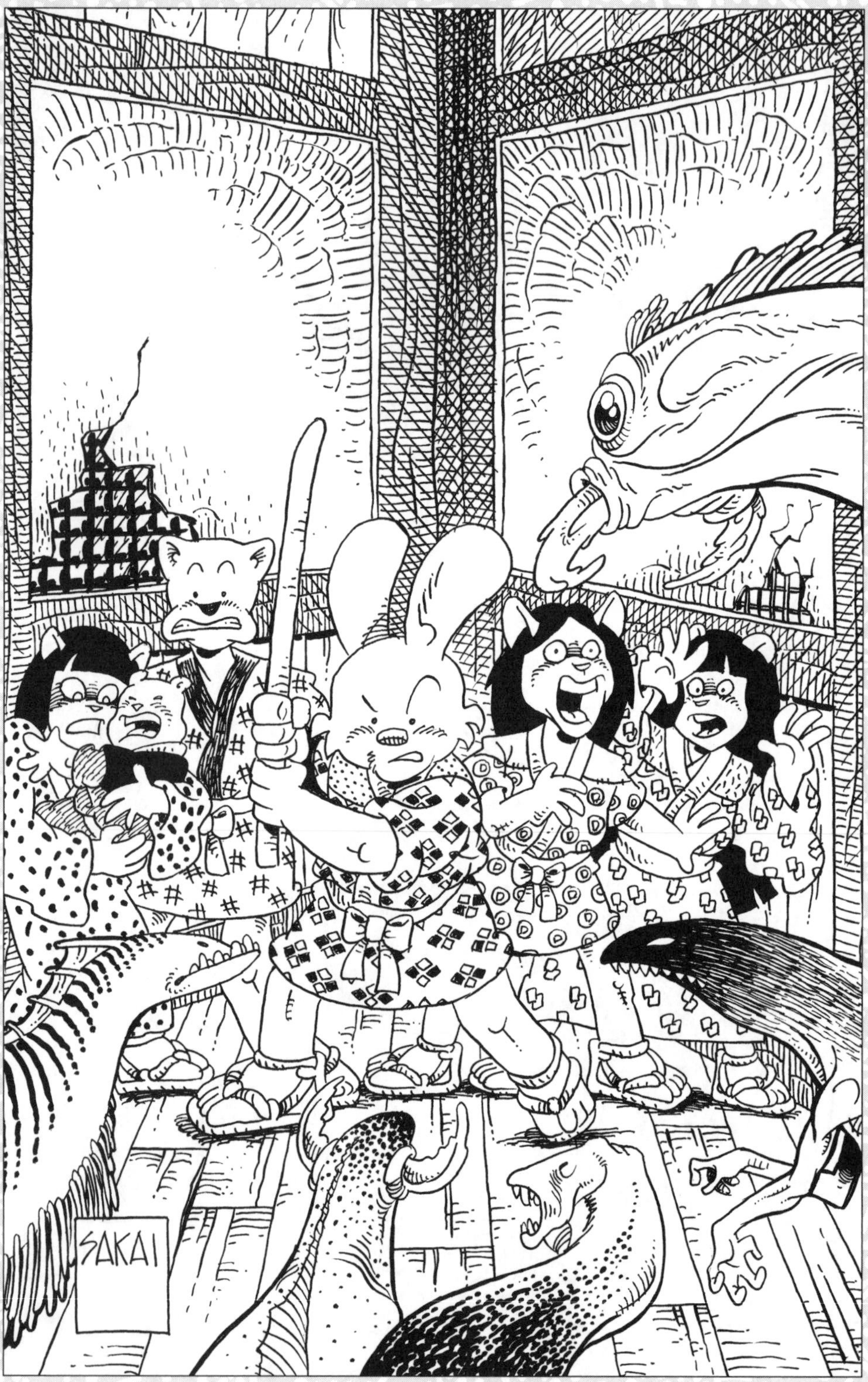
SAKAI

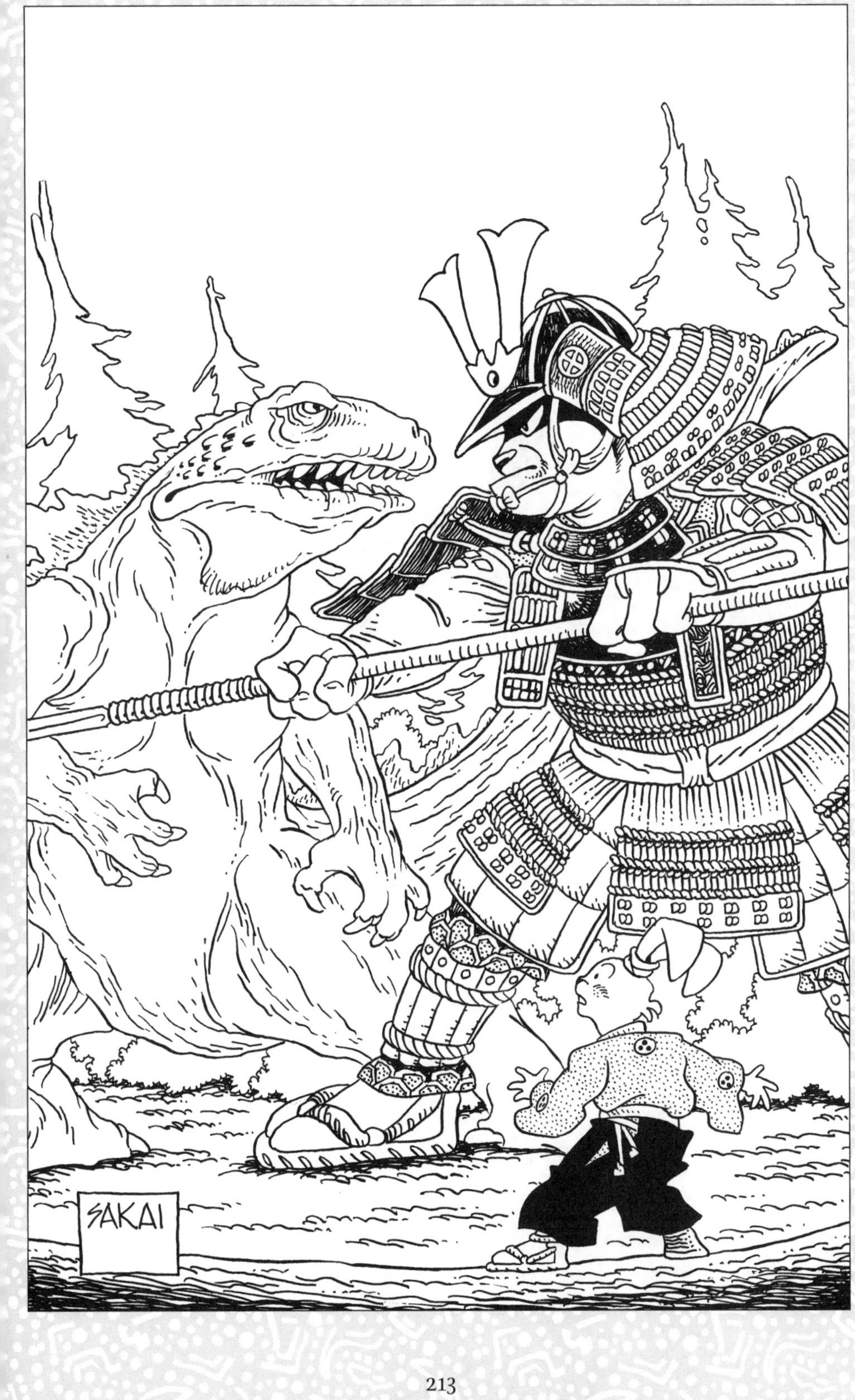
SAKAI

BIOGRAPHY

Stan Sakai

Stan Sakai (at right) with Teenage Mutant Ninja Turtles co-creator Peter Laird, November 2003

STAN SAKAI was born in Kyoto, Japan, grew up in Hawaii, and now lives in California with his wife, Sharon, and children, Hannah and Matthew. He received a Fine Arts degree from the University of Hawaii and furthered his studies at Art Center College of Design in Pasadena, California.

His creation, Usagi Yojimbo, first appeared in comics in 1984. Since then, Usagi has been on television as a guest of the Teenage Mutant Ninja Turtles and has been made into toys, seen on clothing, and featured in a series of trade-paperback collections.

In 1991, Stan created *Space Usagi*, a series about the adventures of a descendant of the original Usagi that dealt with *samurai* in a futuristic setting.

Stan is also an award-winning letterer for his work on Sergio Aragonés' *Groo*, the "Spider-Man" Sunday newspaper strips, and *Usagi Yojimbo*.

Stan is a recipient of a Parents' Choice Award, an Inkpot Award, an American Library Association Award, two Spanish Haxtur Awards, and three Eisner Awards. In 2003 he received the prestigious National Cartoonists Society Comic Book Division Award.

Usagi Yojimbo

Books by Stan Sakai

From Dark Horse Comics
<www.darkhorse.com>

Book 8: Shades of Death
Book 9: Daisho
Book 10: The Brink of Life and Death
Book 11: Seasons
Book 12: Grasscutter
Book 13: Grey Shadows
Book 14: Demon Mask
Book 15: Grasscutter II — Journey to Atsuta Shrine
Book 16: The Shrouded Moon
Book 17: Duel at Kitanoji
Book 18: Travels With Jotaro
Space Usagi

From Fantagraphics Books
<www.fantagraphics.com>

Book 1: The Ronin
Book 2: Samurai
Book 3: The Wanderer's Road
Book 4: The Dragon Bellow Conspiracy
Book 5: Lone Goat and Kid
Book 6: Circles
Book 7: Gen's Story